RISING
from the
ABYSS

*May you create and live
your grandest vision of yourself!*

With love,

Holly Reese

RISING

from the

ABYSS

MY JOURNEY INTO AND OUT OF
CHRONIC ILLNESS

HOLLY REESE, MSOM, L.Ac.

BALBOA.
PRESS

A DIVISION OF HAY HOUSE

Balboa Press books may be ordered through booksellers or by contacting:

Balboa Press
A Division of Hay House
1663 Liberty Drive
Bloomington, IN 47403
www.balboapress.com
1-(877) 407-4847

Because of the dynamic nature of the Internet, any web addresses or links contained in this book may have changed since publication and may no longer be valid. The views expressed in this work are solely those of the author and do not necessarily reflect the views of the publisher, and the publisher hereby disclaims any responsibility for them.

The author of this book does not dispense medical advice or prescribe the use of any technique as a form of treatment for physical, emotional, or medical problems without the advice of a physician, either directly or indirectly. The intent of the author is only to offer information of a general nature to help you in your quest for emotional and spiritual well-being. In the event you use any of the information in this book for yourself, which is your constitutional right, the author and the publisher assume no responsibility for your actions.

Certain stock imagery © Thinkstock.
Any people depicted in stock imagery provided by Thinkstock are models, and such images are being used for illustrative purposes only.

ISBN: 978-1-4525-6402-9 (e)
ISBN: 978-1-4525-6401-2 (sc)
ISBN: 978-1-4525-6403-6 (hc)

Library of Congress Control Number: 2012922175

Printed in the United States of America

Balboa Press rev. date: 12/11/2012

For Mom and Dad,
two rare souls who embodied unconditional love:
it was a priceless gift to be your daughter.
To Jay, my beloved brother: you're simply the best.
And to my loving family and friends, still on this earth or not:
I have been blessed to have you in my life.

You cannot be given a life by someone else.
Of all the people you will know in a lifetime,
you are the only one you will never leave nor lose.
To the question of your life, you are the only answer.
To the problems of your life, you are the only solution.
—Jo Coudert

CONTENTS

PREFACE

It's an enlightening exercise to write about one's own life: to look back at who you were as a child, how you evolved over the years, and who you are now. In all honesty, I can say that I surprised myself.

I grew up in the small town of Lansdale, Pennsylvania, and was raised in a home environment that accepted a physician's opinion as gospel. One of my parents' closest friends was a doctor, and he would make house calls, dispensing whatever medications were deemed necessary at the merest suggestion of a cold, flu, ache, or pain. Drugs were good, along with all the latest and greatest technology of the medical world. I held onto that belief well into my early thirties.

As a teenager, I was a nerd and an avid Trekkie. I absolutely worshiped Mr. Spock, with his logical brilliance and scientific acumen. I was driven to understand how things worked and fell madly in love with the concept of computers and their apparently unlimited potential. It was one of the driving forces for my decision to pursue an electrical engineering degree at MIT. The die had been cast for my life. Or had it?

After graduation, my life should have been complete. I landed a lucrative programming job, purchased a cute home, and maintained a busy social calendar. What more did I need? Apparently, quite a bit. This led me to explore an entirely different side of myself—one that up until then I had neglected—my spirituality. But then the unexpected happened …

In 2002, my life ground to an abrupt halt with a debilitating illness. I was diagnosed with a rare autoimmune disease called mixed connective tissue disorder. I was told by Western medical experts to expect nothing more than a continuous looping from bad days to worse days for the rest of my life. I was offered no hope for a cure—only an ever-lengthening list of medications to manage my symptoms. I traveled down that path for a time until I could go no farther. And then, I chose another way. This book contains my story.

—Holly Reese, MSOM, L.Ac.

ACKNOWLEDGMENTS

This book would not have been possible without the help and support of some amazing people. First and foremost, I would like to thank Majken Talbot. Without your genius and artistry, this book would still be a mountain of raw material. You are an angel in human form. You have been my dearest friend, my inspirational muse, my brilliantly gifted editor, and have held high the continuous flame of belief in me and my mission.

Next, I would like to thank Bruce Gelfand, a truly gifted writer and teacher. You were my first writing coach and source of inspiration. Without you, my story would still be floating chaotically about in the farthest recesses of my mind.

I also want to thank my entire family, but most especially my brother James, my Aunt Dot, and my cousin Beverly. And what would I have done without my friends? I can't imagine, and so thank you to Keshama and your entire amazing family, Kae, Christina, Maria, Kara, Jasmine, Alison, Anne (from Wun Hop Kuen Do), Kellie, and Karen. And you, Sigung Doug Jones, my martial arts teacher, mentor, and dear friend—you helped me reconnect to my qi.

I would also like to acknowledge all the healers who appeared in my life to help me on my journey to wellness, including Jimmie Chan, Laura Stropes, and most especially Dr. Mercola, without whom I wouldn't have my "juice of life." There are so many, and my heart overflows with gratitude and love to you all, forever.

In addition, I would like to thank my spiritual teachers. First and foremost, my heartfelt gratitude goes to Doreen Virtue, PhD. You are an exceptional teacher, healer, and visionary as well as a compassionate and giving person who touched my soul and set me on my path. You continue to blaze a much needed trail for other Lightworkers to follow, and you *inspire* me. And also, my gratitude for my other spiritual teachers: Louise Hay, Sonia Choquette, Eckhart Tolle, Alice Hyatt, Neale Donald Walsch, and Jerry and Esther Hicks, to name but a few...

I hope to pass on what I have learned so that it may help others on their own unique journeys through life.

CHAPTER ONE

DAY OF DECISION—THE LAST STRAW

Life and death are balanced on a razor's edge.
–Homer, *Iliad*

Day after agonizing day, there is no let up, no respite. Every day is a battle, and every night is a massacre. My enemies surround me, circling in for the slow kill. The fibromyalgia causes my muscles to burn unceasingly, as if I'm suspended in a vat of acid. The chronic fatigue drains my life essence. I have barely enough energy to speak in a whisper.

The scleroderma has contracted and hardened the connective tissue around the muscles in my body. I feel as if I'm encased in an unyielding suit of armor. It's difficult to breathe, let alone move. I can no longer swallow or digest solid food. For weeks, I have existed solely on cans of Ensure, a liquid meal-replacement formula. My muscles are atrophied, and every time I look in the mirror, I see an emaciated skeleton. I scare myself. It's hard to believe that two years have passed since my life came to a screeching halt with a rare auto-immune illness known as mixed connective tissue disorder (MCTD).

Another aspect of my illness involves Raynaud's disease, which is a loss of circulation in the extremities. I need to keep my body warm to hot all the time. If I don't, my circulation quite literally stops, and my hands and feet turn purple. The previous house I lived in was poorly insulated and cold all the time. When I started turning up the heat to keep my circulation going, my roommate, Brenda, complained bitterly. I wound up spending most of my days and nights with my hands and feet stuffed under a heating pad. The constant fear of losing my fingers and toes made my living situation untenable. When I mentioned this to my good friend Sofia, she graciously offered to rent her extra basement bedroom to me. I jumped at the chance.

I appreciated that Sofia's house was located in a quiet neighborhood of Oakland, California. However, the best part of renting a room from her was that it came with a bonus: its own wall heater. Since the heat didn't make it upstairs, she let me keep my basement wall heater blasting on high, 24/7. At least, I was no longer in danger of losing any digits.

Shortly after I moved into Sofia's house, my beloved Rottweiler Shika passed away unexpectedly. Her death was the last straw; my inner resolve to fight weakened, and on the night of Saturday, July 17, 2004, it crumbled completely.

Months of unabated torment have taken their toll. I'm exhausted and can't remember the last time I've slept longer than ten or fifteen minutes at a stretch. Sofia's currently in Australia visiting her parents, and I'm alone in the house. I can barely support myself as I crawl onto my futon bed, dreading the coming night of misery. One last strand of innate stubbornness prompts me to try to sleep. I cautiously prop myself upright with many pillows to minimize the acid regurgitation. It's difficult to relax. My muscles are severely atrophied, and because my arms are supported only by my tendons and ligaments, my shoulders ache horribly. Despite the torture, I resolve to try to sleep. The lead weights that are my eyelids slide closed.

As I'm drifting off, my whole body jerks involuntarily. My cell phone is next to my pillow, and the movement sends it sliding down to my side, where it bumps into my hand. The resulting explosion of pain nearly sends me into orbit. I roll onto my left side and cradle my throbbing hand. This is a mistake. My arm gets caught in the sheet and twisted, creating a new wave of agony blasting its way through my right shoulder—the same one that was injured when I was in the police academy more than two years ago. I roll back to the right, but somehow the sheet wraps tighter around my arm. I push up on my left hand, but my wrist is so inflamed that it won't bend or support my weight. My wrist collapses, and I remain twisted and tangled in the unrelenting grip of my own sadistic sheet. I wonder what the headlines might say when my body is discovered: "Martial arts expert brutally defeated in epic battle with homicidal bed sheet!"

I struggle wildly at first, to no avail. I'm angry and frustrated, but clearly, I need to change my tactics. It takes an extreme act of will to stop fighting and lie still. Concentrating on my arm, I can feel some play in the sheet. This gives me an idea. I shift my body in the tiniest of increments and

I'm able to move, perhaps a few millimeters. I try it again. Again success! Imaginary trumpets sound to celebrate my minute triumph! Heartened by progress, I keep going, millimeter by millimeter, until eventually, I'm finally free and positioned back at square one. However, my freedom comes with a price. Incalculable fatigue overwhelms my body and mind. I'm desperate to sleep but wary and suspicious of my next attempt. The exhaustion slowly wins, and my consciousness fades.

A few hours later, my mind becomes aware of something dreadfully wrong. I'm not sure at first, but eventually, I determine that the machete slicing up my abdomen must be real. It feels as if my insides are going to explode at any moment. My digestive system has been failing, backing up with undigested food, so it often cramps horribly. I don't even have the strength to yell and tell it to stop. I clench a pillow against my stomach and hang on. The breath is sucked out of me as I'm stabbed over and over. The torment continues without pause for what seems like hours. I desperately need a distraction, something to take my mind off my suffering. It's impossible to move, but my position allows me to look out the window.

I've grown quite attached to my one window. It's the second-best feature of my room. The wall heater, of course, is the first. My unadorned, single-hung window is an indispensable lifeline that feeds me light and sound: my only connection to the world outside. Every morning it directs the warm sunlight into my room, and through it I can hear birds chirping and other sounds of life. At night I can use it to study the night sky. Tonight is a clear night and filled with countless twinkling stars. After a time, I notice that the stars are flickering in a pattern. I'm even more fascinated when I realize that the stars are pulsating with the same rhythm as my own throbbing limbs. It's a mesmerizing concert of light being conducted by the pain in my body. The hours pass. I'm almost disappointed when my private concert comes to an end as the stars fade and the sky begins to brighten. My position hasn't changed all night, but I think the misery has lessened. Wanting to take advantage of this opportunity, I tentatively relax my contracted body.

Instantly, it all comes flooding back. The intensity is almost beyond my ability to comprehend. A haze of red obstructs my vision, and a small moan escapes my lips. If asked to describe it, I would say that every cell in my body is being continuously struck by tiny gremlins wielding baseball bats. I can't move. Movement only brings more baseball bats. Blinking is excruciating. Time slows to a crawl. I fight to hang on from one miserable moment to the next. Each second that passes is an eternity of hell. I cannot feel the tears rolling down my numb cheeks, but I know they are there when they touch my neck. I feel so helpless. This is not at all how I envisioned my life would turn out.

Ever since I was a little girl, I had always thought I had something important to do with my life. I had imagined I would grow up to be a renowned doctor, a visionary teacher, or a famous scientist. I would do important work that would help better the lives of many people, especially women. So much for the big destiny I had envisioned for my life! If I remain as I am, immersed in this tar pit and incapable of even helping myself, then I'm useless and my life is over. Why do I keep trying? Something inside of me snaps. Merely existing is not enough—not for me. I won't continue my life on earth in this way. No more! Besides, if I no longer existed, who would care? I feel a pang of guilt for my selfish thoughts as my brother and father come to mind.

My brother James, or Jay (the name I use most often), is one of the sweetest guys I've ever known. We're only four months apart in age, which is possible since I'm adopted. I've always adored him, and we've been close our entire lives. Whether we live near each other or not, I know I can count on my brother. He'll be there for me. Mom and Dad taught us that family ties are the ones that can't be broken. When I told him I was moving into Sofia's house, he offered to have me come down to live with his family in Southern California. I was touched and grateful for his offer, but my home is here in the San Francisco Bay Area. I don't want to live anywhere else. Leaving would have meant a huge disruption. These last several years my life has been filled with the agony of loss; I just couldn't handle any more.

Dad lives in upstate Pennsylvania on his mountain property, north of the Poconos. He moved there after Mom passed away in 1999. She had been the glue that held our large extended family together. Her death had drawn Jay, Dad, and me even closer together. We depended upon each other for support. I love Dad, and it hurts me to think about how much he would suffer if I were gone. With a bad heart and lungs, Dad's health is not great either. In the not-too-distant future, he's going to be the one needing help from Jay and me.

My thoughts continue to churn on about the ramifications of me no longer breathing. If I was gone, the world would continue just fine without me. I'm a single woman without any dependents. I'm not working or doing anything of value. Come to think of it, right now I'm more valuable dead than alive. I would save the American taxpayer a bundle of money in disability payments and medical costs. It might total well into the millions! And with me gone, Sofia could get more rent for her basement apartment. I'm sure of it. A few friends would mourn my passing, but it's not like I've seen any of them recently. Their lives already flow along nicely without me in the picture. But I cringe when I think about my brother; Jay would be devastated. Although, he has a loving wife and three wonderful children; he has everything to live for. He would be okay. Oh, but Dad was another matter. Dad still needed me. How could I let him down now?

All thoughts flee my mind as my cells erupt in flames. I need it to stop! I grip my pillow tighter and try to ride it out. Aside from Jay and Dad, there are a few family members and friends who will miss me, but with time, everyone will get over it. I only know that I can't live this way. I'm tired of fighting, of discovering a new way to experience pain with each new day. No one deserves enduring this kind of suffering day in and day out. I'm done! Now what?

My gaze slowly gravitates to the bookcase against the far wall. I know that a bag is buried behind and under a pile of books on the bottom shelf. In that bag, a small case holds a solution—my Glock 9mm handgun and a box of bullets.

All I need to do is get to my bookshelf. I focus on lifting my arm, but it weighs a thousand pounds. I redouble my efforts, and my right hand shifts a few inches. The muscles in my arm contract and tighten, refusing to move any farther. I can't breathe as my attackers have upgraded to sledgehammers. But I'm not ready to quit. This time I try to move my head. With every ounce of desire and willpower I can muster, I pour everything into raising my head. All I accomplish is contracting my neck muscles so tightly it seems that maybe I'll be able to snap my own neck. I stop immediately. If my neck breaks and then I'm only paralyzed, my fate will be worse than it already is. I try to move my leg. My muscles scream and burn and refuse to move. For the moment, I'm held motionless in a vise and unable to force my body to work.

Ten damn feet! That's my entire travel itinerary, but then my destination might as well be the moon. To be so tantalizingly close to my goal—yet unable to reach it—is frustrating beyond belief. I need to see it once more; maybe I'll find the strength to go the distance. I take a few ginger breaths in preparation, hoping that I don't piss off the gremlins.

Centimeter by centimeter, I turn my head to the side. By the time my gaze finally rests on the bookshelf against the far wall, I'm sure I've sprouted gray hair. Again and again, I try to move. Each attempt ends in failure, and the little gremlins are now crashing Mack trucks into my cells. I have no choice but to surrender to the moment and let go. Maybe my heart will stop and my suffering will end?

Helpless, I'm floating into all the pain. Everywhere I go, it's there. There is no escape. I have no strength, no will, and no ability to control what is happening. My breathing is slowing down, and my awareness is magnified. I'm every sensation, everywhere in my body, all at the same time. And yet, I'm also a floating third-party observer of events. This is strange. Maybe I'm dying.

CHAPTER TWO
MY FIRST PATIENT

Every action in our lives touches on some
chord that will vibrate in eternity.
–Edwin Hubbell Chapin

It was hot, but the humidity was bearable—not the kind that causes you to sweat just from thinking about being outside. The distinctive buzzing of cicadas, which saturated the air, heralded yet another glorious summer day in my rural hometown of Lansdale, Pennsylvania. At the age of eleven, I was a full-blown tomboy—a female Huck Finn—with shoulder-length blonde hair, blue eyes, and a tough, wiry frame. After breakfast, I rushed outside and sprinted toward the dirt trail leading through the dense forest behind my house. I didn't stop until I reached the familiar maple tree that signaled the edge of the woods. I casually leaned back against it. From there, I surveyed the brush-covered meadow before me.

My favorite place to play was immense, easily larger than four football fields put together. I stood poised between two different worlds. One was the cool, musky forest filled with ferns and illuminated by filtered sunlight, where I played with all manner of wood nymphs and tree spirits. The other world contained the sun-drenched fields covered with tall weeds and thick brush that all smelled like a sweet salad to me. Bridging these two worlds was the noise of my favorite insect, the cicada—the transparent-winged creature that lived in both. The mating call of the males was a high-frequency sound that rose and softened in a rhythmic hum—a primal *om*. I expected it to be there. Whenever I heard them, without ever knowing why, I felt invincible.

Eyes closed, I took a deep breath and inhaled the combined smells of the woods mixed in with the field. The heady aroma soothed and centered me in preparation for my favorite game. I loved pretending that I was a cyborg, just like Steve Austin in the *Six Million Dollar Man* TV series. It was time. My eyelids snapped open, and my bionic eyes scanned the field for my next mission objective. They came to rest on a huge old oak all the way on the opposite side of the field. My favorite climbing tree brought a smile to my lips. I squatted down in a runner's starting position and prepared to activate my enhanced legs. With a quick burst of power, I was off and running like the wind, easily swatting aside the waist-high weeds and dodging thick bushes that loomed in my path. How glorious it was to feel the adrenaline surging through me, my muscles pumping, and my bionic legs moving as fast as they could. Life was simple and good.

Halfway across the field, I spotted a flash of movement near my tree and immediately slid into cover behind a thick rhododendron bush. Peering carefully through the branches, I could make out four boys crawling around on the ground. They piqued my curiosity. My new mission became to spy on these intruders without getting caught. I stealthily worked my way across the field, sprinting from bush to bush in short bursts of speed, while staying out of their line of sight. About sixty paces from my old oak tree, I stopped to note their movements. They were collecting small rocks and tossing them onto a growing pile. I wondered what the heck they were doing. Ever so slowly, I quietly snuck closer. Eventually, I stopped behind a forsythia bush about twenty feet away.

I recognized Bradley as soon as I saw the military-style blond hair and stocky, junior football player's body. He was the leader of the pack and a notorious neighborhood bully. Just last week, Bradley and his goon squad had tied up Skinny Zack, my neighbor from down the street, and left him hanging upside down from a tree. The neighborhood kids often teased Zack simply because he happened to be shy and scrawny. Bullies just plain infuriated me. Knowing Bradley, I had to find out exactly what mischief he was up to.

I recognized the other three boys hovering around him as the rest of his gang. Tommy and John were often mistaken for brothers with their similar lanky frames and dark, curly hair. Scottie was the smallest boy, bringing up the rear as usual. There was no way to miss that head of unruly, bright red hair. They were all my age except for Scottie, who was a year younger.

A flash of light caught my eye, and I saw that they'd set soda cans onto the branches of a thick bush on the opposite side of my oak tree. I watched Bradley pick up some stones and then load and aim his slingshot at the cans. It looked like they were having a competition. Curious to find out who was the best shot, I hunkered down and made myself comfortable behind my bush. Surprisingly, the winner turned out to be Scottie. That made me grin because it probably annoyed the heck out of Bradley.

After a while, they took a break from their target practice. I was about to crawl away and play on the other side of the field when, suddenly, Bradley motioned for his buddies to get down on the ground. He put his fingers to his lips for silence as he stared straight up into my oak tree. When I followed his gaze, my heart started pounding. A bright orange robin was perched on a branch about halfway up the tree. Bradley quickly loaded his slingshot and took aim at the defenseless bird. Without a moment's hesitation, I sprang up onto my bionic legs and raced as fast as I could straight at Bradley.

It only took me a few seconds to reach him, but he fired just before I launched into a flying tackle and slammed into him as hard as I could. It was satisfying to hear the rush of air from his lungs as he hit the ground and had the wind knocked out of him. My heart was in my throat when I spotted the robin, motionless on the ground. I jumped up and quickly placed myself between the boys and the fallen bird. They'd have to get past me to get to it.

Fortunately, Bradley was still on the ground, moaning and cradling his left arm, so I focused on the backup leader, Tommy. "If any of you bullies go near that bird, I will beat you black and blue. Don't think I can't!" I stepped toward Tommy with my fists clenched. It pleased me to see him quickly back up. They knew I was strong since they had all played "King of the Hill" with me; I never lost. "Get out of here—and take Bradley with you. Why don't you go target practice on one another? That would be better than picking on a defenseless bird!"

My guard was up as Bradley slowly rose to his feet. "You just watch your back, Little Miss Tomboy. Why don't you go put on a dress and act like a girl, like you're supposed to do," he said, targeting a look of pure hatred at me.

That got me even more riled up. I had never put up with anyone telling me that I had to act a certain way or that I couldn't do anything simply because I was a girl. It only served to harden my resolve to protect the robin. I crossed my arms, slowly and deliberately, and glared at the boys. With Bradley injured, they had no stomach for a battle with me. I remained where I was and watched while they turned and walked away.

As soon as I felt safe, I slowly knelt down beside the bird. He wasn't moving, and I was afraid he was dead. When I leaned closer to examine him, I could see his chest was rising and falling. He was breathing! Relief flooded through me. It wasn't too late to try to help him! The robin was clearly stunned, and maybe a wing was broken, but at least he had a chance. I took off my sweatshirt and gently placed him onto it. My only thought was to get the injured bird back home, where I could help and protect him until he recovered.

Walking as quickly and as smoothly as I could, I headed back across the field and through the woods to my house. Once inside, my trajectory was straight up the stairs into my bedroom, where I laid my precious bundle onto the bed. My heart was in my throat as I raced back downstairs into our basement. I grabbed one of the many cardboard boxes and rushed back to my room. I was careful to move slowly once I was inside. I arranged an old soft towel into a nest in the box and gently moved the robin onto it. He still wasn't moving, and his eyes were closed, but as long as I could see him breathing, I still had hope. I settled down next to my precious little patient. Sitting on the floor with my back against the wall, I thought about what else I could do for him. He was an unusually large robin with bright orange chest feathers that seemed to glow from within. Without a doubt, this was a special creature.

I leaned over the box. "I'm going to do everything I can to help you. I promise," I whispered. And then, as if in response to my promise, my entire body started to tingle. It felt as if an intense energy was pouring into me from everywhere, charging every cell in my body. I radiated power and suddenly knew what I had to do. Without conscious thought, my hands moved with a mind of their own. I reached into the box and placed them carefully around the injured creature. There was an electrical connection between us, and I instinctively directed the energy that was pouring into me to flow out of my hands and into my patient. My thoughts were focused on an image of the robin flying happily in the sky. My heart was vibrating with a love for this beautiful spirit, motionless in the box in front of me. I was content to stay there as long as it took.

After I had been performing my healing ritual for more than an hour, the robin opened its eyes. My heart skipped a beat, and I tried not to make any sudden moves, for fear that I might startle him into a heart attack. I stared into the beautiful bird's eye that was staring back at me and sensed an immediate connection. I felt an instinctive protectiveness and mentally projected that I was a friend. He seemed to understand that I meant him no harm and didn't struggle. Instead, he closed his eyes and went back to sleep. I was awed by the bond I had formed with this amazing little life. I felt so peaceful and wonderful.

Wanting to keep a close eye on my guest, I lounged around in my room, mostly reading, for the rest of the day. The robin remained asleep. I didn't want to go downstairs when Mom hollered from the kitchen that dinner was ready. I was afraid he might need me, but if I didn't go down to eat I'd have both Mom and Dad wondering what was going on. I didn't want anyone to know about my little patient. If Dad found out, he would just want to put it out of its misery. Mom would let me help him but not inside the house. And if anyone saw me doing my healing ritual, they would think I was nuts. Since I didn't want to deal with any of that, I showed up at the dinner table and tried to eat normally without squirming.

The second my plate was empty, I looked over at Mom. "That was a great dinner. Thanks." I smiled appreciatively. "I'm in the middle of a good sci-fi novel. Do you mind if I get back to it?" It was helpful that I was a huge bookworm. It provided me with a believable reason to escape back to my room.

"You're welcome, honey. I'm glad you enjoyed it." She beamed at the compliment. "Just clear your plate first, before you disappear," she added. I immediately grabbed my plate and washed it off before putting it in the dishwasher.

"Thanks, Mom," I said, bounding up the stairs. When I got to my door, I opened it slowly and peered cautiously into the room. All appeared calm as I tiptoed over to the box. My little robin was so cute I could hardly stand it. He was still wrapped in the towel, but he was holding his head up and looking curiously around my room. He cocked his adorable little head to the side and focused an eye on me. I was certain that he understood I was helping him.

Moving as slow as molasses, I sat down beside him. He didn't try to move, but he never took his eye off me. He remained still, even when I carefully reached into the box to unwrap the towel from around him. I suspected that he was more seriously injured than I had first thought. I simply had no way of knowing. My heart went out to him. It occurred to me that staying hydrated was important when injured, so I put some water in a small bowl in his box and settled down beside him once more. I loved how he watched me the whole time and didn't seem afraid. We had a connection, my little robin and I. As I sat next to him, keeping my vigil, I imagined him flying high above the trees, happy and in perfect health.

After several hours, I felt myself getting too sleepy to stay awake any longer. I changed into my pajamas as quietly as I could, grabbed a pillow from my bed, and stretched out next to the box. I wanted to stay close, in case he needed me in the middle of the night. Enough moonlight was shining through my window that I could make out the light blue color of the ceiling. I imagined that it was the sky. As I slowly drifted off to sleep, I pictured a small bird with bright orange chest feathers flying happily all around.

When I did wake up, it was because something startled me. I turned my head toward the commotion and saw the robin fluttering around in his box. I was ecstatic! It must mean that he was going to live! Oh, but now what? I had to get him outside before he started flying around my room. He might injure himself all over again. There would be no way to hide him then—and Mom and Dad would be upset with me for keeping a bird in the house.

I crept quietly over to the window and slid it up as far as it would go. When I tried to push the screen up, it got stuck. I hit it hard with my palm. Fortunately, that got it moving, and then it slid smoothly up to its highest position. The robin was hopping curiously around in his box but hadn't gotten out yet. I worked my way back to him with agonizing slowness. All the while, I fervently hoped he would stay put long enough for me to release him. It was a miracle that he didn't move when I picked up the box and held it up level with the windowsill.

Mesmerized, I held my breath as he nonchalantly hopped up on the side of the box and then onto the windowsill. He wasn't panicked at all and seemed to know what to do. It was then that my adorable patient cocked an eye at me and chirped. It was like a National Geographic nature film. I was stunned and so touched. Was he saying thank you? My heart melted again as he hopped to the edge of the windowsill, chirped once more, and launched himself into the air. I anxiously craned my neck to track his progress, desperately hoping that he would be able to stay aloft. He circled our yard once and took off straight into the sun. It was glorious! I was still staring out the window when I heard Mom calling from downstairs asking what I wanted for breakfast.

CHAPTER THREE

DAY OF DECISION II—THE GUN

Name me no names for my disease, with uninforming breath;
I tell you I am none of these, but homesick unto death...
—Witter Bynner, *Hills of Home*

The gradual brightening of my room is in stark contrast to the intolerable pain coursing through me. It's going to be a sunny summer day in Oakland. I hear the chirping of the family of birds that lives in the tree outside my window. What I wouldn't give to be one right now, carefree and soaring through the skies with complete freedom. My only worry would be finding my next worm or bug to eat. Instead, for me, another day of despair begins. My Glock 9mm semiautomatic remains the solution to my misery. It rests a mere ten feet away, calling to me with an easy way out. I can see its case across the room on the bottom shelf of my bookcase. But every time I try to get off the bed, I'm paralyzed by the pain. Is it really the pain that's stopping me? Or is it something else? Because if I'm going to end my life, what does additional pain matter? It would only be temporary. Could I not bear a few minutes more of agony in exchange for an eternity of peace?

My bed is a simple futon mattress on top of a low, wooden frame—a mere twelve inches above the floor. I'm close to the edge of it; if I rolled even partway over the side, gravity would do the rest and get me to the floor. *All right, now I have a plan.* I relax my right shoulder, allowing my body to sink toward it. It's difficult to ignore the searing agony that screams out to make me stop. I tell myself it's only temporary, only temporary. Over and over, I repeat my new mantra. It seems to work.

My left side is now slightly past my center, poised over the edge of the bed. With no small amount of trepidation, I realize I'm past the point of no return. I can't stop myself from falling even if I want to. Twelve inches is an awfully long way to drop. My body slips toward the floor in slow motion. I can only hope that I don't break anything. I close my eyes and brace for impact. When my legs hit the floor with a thud, I let out a tiny scream. But then, oddly, nothing else happens.

I crack one eye open to survey the scene and discover that the sheet is still wrapped around me. My upper body is dangling a few inches above the carpet. This is a curious development. After a few feeble attempts to dislodge myself, I lose the will to do anything more. I'm not sure how long I remain suspended in the air. I only know that I can still hear the sound of the birds chirping outside my window. Just when I've resigned myself to remaining where I am for the rest of my short time left on this planet, the weight of my body manages to pull the sheet loose. I'm deposited gently onto the carpet. At first I'm hesitant to breathe, but when nothing more happens, I snicker and stick my tongue out in defiance. A useless gesture, but it feels good nonetheless.

I've only fallen twelve inches, but my environment down here seems dramatically different. For one thing, it's much cooler lying on the floor than I would have expected. Of course, that might have something to do with the rug being on top of a cement slab. However, it hasn't escaped my keen sense of awareness that I've been presented with a fresh opportunity for progress. Sliding off the bed has left me positioned on my side. If I can repeat the same shoulder maneuver that got me started, I might manage another revolution toward the bookshelves.

Before I can talk myself out of it, I tilt my right shoulder and allow myself to fall back. As it smacks the ground, I'm sure it's been ripped out of the socket. The pain itself seems to push me along until I'm past my back and onto my stomach. My nose has wound up practically embedded in the carpet, and the damp musty smell is a bit overpowering. I'm not at all sure how my arms have landed where they are with palms down and conveniently positioned on either side of my head. Regardless, now it's time to pay the piper. My tiny gremlin friends gleefully return with their baseball bats to pound my body. Just in case I've forgotten what *real* pain feels like.

I don't even try to hold back the sobs. I can't feel the tears on my nerve-damaged cheeks, but I know they're falling because the rug is getting wet underneath my ear. It's strange to feel my ear but not my cheek. It's time to take stock of my circumstances once again. From my current position, I can see between the books on the bottom shelf of the bookcase. My body shudders involuntarily when I glimpse part of the case that holds my gun. At long last, I'm making progress. Suddenly my goal seems possible. What bit of leverage can I use to move closer now? It's hard to think through the flames that are burning the muscles off of my bones, but somehow I've got to reason it out. The strongest part of me has always been my legs, and they are advantageously positioned to help me. I'm not wearing any socks, and I can still move my toes. My left leg is partially bent. If I can dig into the carpet with my toes and push, maybe I can straighten my leg and propel myself forward. It turns out that my hands can be used as a kind of rudder to help me steer, and if I keep screaming, my legs and toes will continue pushing.

My hand bumps into something hard and cold. It takes me several minutes to recover from the shock of renewed pain to realize that I'm touching the bottom shelf of the bookcase. Can this be real? Am I finally going to be able to put an end to my suffering? It takes a superhuman effort to raise my left hand and move it to rest on the gun case. The fact that scleroderma has frozen my fingers into a half-open position comes in handy since it allows me to hook them over the edge of the case. With a yank that sends me into orbit and nearly rips my shoulder out of the socket, the gun case is pulled off the shelf and onto the floor. A few books land on me for good measure, I'm sure. But what can stop me now? I've made it to my gun. My fingers don't even have to bend to dial the combination lock that opens the case. It seems too good to be true that I've made it this far. I can feel the weight of the gun as I flip it out of the case and onto the carpet. Ironically, it lands with the muzzle pointing directly at my face. Perfect! I don't even have to aim it. And best of all, the safety on a Glock is actually *on* the trigger itself. Squeezing the trigger releases it. I position my hand with my thumb on top of the trigger, ready to pull it.

Now that I'm here, having surmounted impossible obstacles, is there anything I'm missing? Do I need to consider anything more? Oddly, I'm feeling a new, different kind of pain. I thought I had experienced every kind of suffering the human body could endure, so what is this? I'm compelled to explore it a moment. It's an intense pressure that's centered in my heart. Maybe it's a heart attack, and I won't have to squeeze the trigger after all. The pressure is building rapidly, and I'm having trouble breathing. This is wrong. Everything is wrong! I hear someone screaming and realize it's me, and then the world goes black.

My eyes gradually open, and I find myself staring at my ceiling. Where am I? What happened? It's hard to think. My brain is fuzzy, and I can't focus my thoughts. Eventually, I recognize a particular crack in the ceiling that I've grown accustomed to seeing from my bed. When I tilt my head to the side, I can see my bookshelves across the room. The bottom shelf looks undisturbed with the books all in place. I can easily make out the gun case right where it's always been. Obviously, I'm not dead yet. My heart is beating, and my gremlin companions are still making their presence known. I realize that I never even made it off of my bed. It was all just a dream.

What isn't a dream is the flare-up of searing agony in my hands when I clench them in frustration. I regret how often I took my hands for granted instead of appreciating them as the miracles of motion and dexterity that they truly were. I struggle to raise my swollen right hand high enough so that I can see it and sigh in despair over what it can no longer do. With this hand, I had been able to manipulate fine needles inserted into my acupuncture patients or break boards cleanly in half with lightning speed and power.

CHAPTER FOUR
BLACK BELT

So many of our dreams at first seem impossible,
then they seem improbable, and then, when we
summon the will, they soon become inevitable.
—Christopher Reeve

It was a scorching, humid Saturday in July, and I was grateful that the martial arts studio had air-conditioning. The training room was packed with students who weren't testing for promotion but were there just to support us. The test had been grueling so far, and sweat was pouring down my back, despite the air-conditioning. At fifteen, I was the youngest of the five black belt contestants, but that didn't deter me at all. Instead, it motivated me. I had been training for this day since I was twelve.

A table for the panel of five judges was set up in the front of the room—none of the stern, older Korean men had a trace of a smile. Master Park, my instructor, directed me to break a board with one hand while holding it with the other. That was a difficult technique to perform. It required speed, precision, and perfect timing; my power needed to be channeled, at just the right moment, through the breaking hand and into the board. At the same time, the hand holding the board needed to remain absolutely still. I stood at attention in front of the judges' panel while Steve, who had jumped up the fastest to help out, brought over a stack of boards and set them at my feet.

I took my time in selecting a flat board with no knots, all the while focusing on my breath. Air filled my lungs, instantly translating into energy, which I guided down into my center of power just below my navel. I shifted my feet into a low, wide forward stance that provided me with a strong, stable foundation. As I positioned my striking hand over the board, my preparations were interrupted by Master Young, the head judge.

"Hold," he ordered, raising his hand to get my attention. I froze in place at his command and waited. He turned his regal head toward my instructor. "Master Park, pick out a second board and give it to your student. I want her to break two at a time." There was a murmur of voices heard around the room. Master Park grunted and shook his head at the crowd. They immediately fell silent again. Then he picked up a fresh board from the top of the stack and handed it to me.

My stomach was doing flip flops. Breaking two boards that I held myself was orders of magnitude more difficult than one. Each board was an inch thick, and it took me several moments to lock the fingers of my left hand around them tightly enough to hold them steady. I dug my toes into the carpet and sunk even lower into my stance. Once again, I positioned my right hand over the boards. I closed my eyes for a moment and imagined raising my hand and striking down with the speed of light toward the boards. When my hand made contact, they blew apart as if they were made of Styrofoam. My eyes snapped open. I was ready.

My breathing had slowed way down, and I could feel the power running from my center into my right hand. In slow motion, I lifted my right hand up by my ear and slowly traced the path it would take to break the boards, until it was touching them. Raising my hand the final time, I let out a yell, and it exploded into motion. At precisely the right moment, I snapped my wrist and directed my power through and beyond my target. As in my visualization, the boards split cleanly and crashed to the floor in the most satisfying manner. Without pause, I jumped to attention and bowed to the judges. Master Young acknowledged me with a brief nod and motioned for the next candidate to take my place.

I was grateful for the chance to rest and drink some water. It was hard to believe that I was actually in the middle of my black belt test. So far, it felt like one to rival some of the arduous trials of Kwai Chang Caine in *Kung Fu,* the hit TV series. I took great comfort knowing that my hero had somehow always managed to take care of the bad guys. As a kid, I had frequently been glued to the tube and mesmerized by Kwai Chang's amazing physical skills of strength, speed, and agility. It had fascinated me that, through his martial arts training, he was able to perform seemingly impossible mental and physical feats. I had admired his perpetual calm and serene nature along with his desire to do good deeds. Wherever he had traveled, he rescued people in trouble. I had wanted to be just like him.

When I was eleven, I had asked my parents if I could study martial arts. At first they had said no, but eventually they had agreed—on two conditions. The first was that I had to pay for all my classes and equipment. And the second was that I needed to put together the money for an *entire* year of classes before I could even start. I had known that they didn't think I could do it. In defiance, I had taken on every odd job I could find. By the end of the summer of my twelfth birthday, I had earned enough money to join. From my very first class, I had fallen head over heels in love with martial arts. I had thrived on everything about it: the intensity of the physical training; always pushing oneself to do more; and a philosophy that promoted honor, integrity, humility, and respect. In order to reach my black belt test, I had trained six days a week for three years, living and breathing only martial arts.

"Put your sparring gear on and loosen up!" Master Park barked, snapping me out of my reverie. I jogged over to the wall where I had left my equipment. It didn't take me long to don my elbow pads and shin guards. I hopped in place to warm up, which also helped to quiet the butterflies in my stomach. Our opponents were selected from the brown and black belt students who weren't testing. My first opponent was an unfamiliar brown belt from another school. He was lean, maybe eighteen or nineteen years old, and taller than me with fiery red hair. Judging from the determined look in his eyes, I knew I would receive no quarter from him.

Master Park stepped onto the floor to referee the fight. I didn't dare look at him for fear I'd lose my focus. I faced my adversary with my hands raised in front of me in a classic openhanded guard position. The brown belt mirrored my stance and watched me with steely eyes. Mine were locked onto my opponent's torso, ready to spot the slightest movement. Master Park raised his hand high and then brought it down quickly. "Begin!" he commanded.

My adrenalin soared as we began circling one another, sizing each other up. The brown belt launched the first salvo with a rapid series of kicks. I met each one with a solid arm block but didn't retaliate right away. I wanted to learn his style. When it felt right, I launched an attack of my own, using some of my favorite combinations. I let loose with a double right front roundhouse kick. His front guard was pulled low on the first kick, which enabled me to tap his head with the second. Immediately spinning in the opposite direction, I caught him in the midsection with a right back kick as he was trying to get away. My opponent simply smiled and responded with a blistering assault, tagging me with a lightning fast roundhouse kick to the side. Our fight continued to heat up with each of us scoring several well-executed hits. We were evenly matched, and I used it to run through all my favorite sparring combinations.

Suddenly, I heard Master Park yell, "Halt!" We dropped our guard and then bowed to each other. Master Park waved us off the floor. Satisfied with my first fight, I welcomed the chance to rest while the other students took their turn sparring. I visualized my heartbeat slowing down, and that energy was pouring into me, recharging my bionic limbs for the next fight. I didn't have long to wait before I was called back on the floor with a new sparring partner.

This time, I was paired with a black belt, older than the last, but shorter and stocky with a shaved head. I heard Master Park's command to begin, and we moved cautiously around each other. My new opponent put a lot of power into his techniques, and I had to block hard to stop them. Bruises were forming on my forearms and shins, but I fought well, giving as much as I was getting. It wasn't long before I was off the floor, waiting my turn again. All of us who were testing rotated once through the pool of five opponents. Then the judges decided to make it a little more interesting.

We were told to spar two opponents at a time. I felt my adrenalin level surging to a new high. Again, I was called up first and this time, paired against my two original opponents. I began the match by aggressively going on the offense. Unwilling to let him build any momentum, I targeted the stocky black belt. My attack sent him backing up into the brown belt. The next instant, I followed up with a jumping front kick. They both stumbled but quickly recovered. The black belt looked annoyed and caught his teammate's eye. They nodded to each other, wordlessly agreeing upon a plan of attack. My opponents separated and moved to stand on opposite sides of me. I charged after the black belt, not wanting to give them time to coordinate. I fired off a side kick to his midsection, and immediately spun around to block the attack I knew was coming from behind. The brown belt smiled at me when I managed to block his front kick and spin out from between them. My strategy was to avoid the worst of their blows and keep them entangled as much as possible. It was exhausting, and my energy level was dropping rapidly. Soon my arms and legs felt like lead weights, and my techniques were losing power. I circled around the floor, entirely on the defensive, trying to keep them both to one side. I wasn't sure how much longer I could keep my arms up to block. At long last, Master Park ended the fight. It was all I could do to remain upright.

While the other candidates were sparring, I gratefully gulped down water and concentrated on restoring my energy. I closed my eyes and practiced the centering and reenergizing technique that Master Park had taught me. It involved drawing energy from the earth and channeling it into my center of power to enhance my own personal qi, or life force energy. My breathing was slowing down, and I felt a calm strength flowing into me.

The judges wanted my final breaking technique to be the jumping flying side kick, but with a twist. They also wanted me to jump over five students on my way to the board. I swallowed hard. That maneuver would be a personal best. I'd only ever attempted jumping over three people. I was so close to the end, if only I could just reach inside myself for a little more. I told myself: "I can do this. I'm Kwai Chang Caine and the *Six Million Dollar Man* rolled into one."

I continued drawing earth energy into myself, while five volunteers lined up next to each other. I completed my preparations as they bent over until their upper torsos were parallel to the ground. Fortunately, the judges allowed me to take a running start from the other side of the room. My eyes saw only the board and the exact spot I wanted to hit. Nothing else existed. When I was ready, I sprinted hard and fast, and then suddenly I was in the air, flying over my classmates. There was a satisfying crack as my foot sliced cleanly through my target. My feet landed solidly on the floor.

When I turned to bow to the judges, I let a slight smile slip before I caught myself. During testing it was considered bad form for the participants to openly display emotions, especially prideful ones. So it surprised me to see a couple of slight head bows acknowledging my kick. The cheering from around the room was almost deafening.

I was required to stand during the others' breaking techniques, but strangely, I wasn't tired any longer. Unfortunately, two of the students were unable to make all of their breaks. They were miserable, and I felt bad for them. Finally, the judges were done with us and signaled that our testing was complete. Master Park had us remain standing at attention while they conferred with each other. An eternity passed before the panel ended their discussion, and then they all stood up, facing us.

"Two of you have passed, and three have not," Master Young announced. "Those students who have not passed will be allowed to retake their black test in six months." My knees weakened; if I didn't pass, how could I possibly go through this again? "Now, I would like to congratulate and commend the following two students who have earned their black belts with a unanimous vote of this panel," he continued, his voice booming into the completely silent studio. "Juh Young and Holly

Reese, your performance today was outstanding. Please step forward and remove your brown belts." Master Young waved at us to approach the judges' table.

My head spun in disbelief. Had I really done it? The moment was surreal. Master Park stepped in front of me, holding a black belt, and personally tied it around my waist. A rare smile appeared briefly on his stern face, or did I imagine it? As one, Juh Young and I bowed to the judges, and they returned it. As soon as we were dismissed, the room broke into pandemonium. My classmates crowded around me, smacking me on the back with congratulations.

I caught sight of my parents wading through the crowd to reach me. Mom was dabbing the sweat off of her neck with a tissue. Dad was wearing dirty jeans and must have come straight from work. When they reached me, Dad had a huge grin and proudly thumped me on the back.

"Move over, Jimmy. Give me a turn," Mom said as she slipped under Dad's arm and wrapped hers around me in a great big hug. My nose immediately detected the familiar scent of gardenias. I breathed deeply of Mom. This day couldn't get any better. "We're so proud of you, honey!" She squeezed me hard again. It was, without a doubt, one of the proudest moments of my young life.

So much of my life over the previous three years had been spent training for that one moment. It was hard to believe that I was finally a black belt. I had run through the gauntlet and come out the other side. Little did I know then that I would need all my strength and skills as a martial artist to surmount the greatest challenge of my adult life. My real training was yet to begin.

CHAPTER FIVE
DAY OF DECISION—HOPE RETURNS

There is no medicine like hope, no incentive so great, and no tonic so powerful as expectation of something better tomorrow.
–Orison Swett Marden

The exhaustion sinks deep into my core, preceding the tidal wave of despair that swallows everything in its path. I've got to stop this plunge into the abyss, or I'll never make it off my damn bed. But how? Aside from Mom's death, last night was the worst night of my life. Everything in my world is suffering. Even the sound of my own breathing is bothering me. It's raspy and interspersed with annoyingly loud moans that hurt my sensitive ears. Then it occurs to me. My breathing is one thing that I still have control over. I slow it down instinctively, and then I lengthen my diaphragm to draw my breaths ever deeper. It's a familiar habit and a useful technique I learned in my many years of martial arts training.

My attention remains on my breath. Eventually, I'm able to lead it all the way down to my navel—something I haven't done since before I became ill. Gradually, my breathing becomes quieter, and it brings me comfort to succeed at this small thing. I realize that I haven't truly meditated since before the police academy. It used to be an almost daily habit. I've strayed too long from my spiritual rituals, the source of my strength and vitality.

Over the years, various meditation classes had gradually introduced me to many methods for connecting to my inner wisdom and messages of guidance. My early sessions had begun with deep abdominal breathing. I had then moved into a meditative state, which allowed me to build up my reserves of qi. Whenever I had connected with my center of power, located just below my navel, I had felt protected by a cloak of invincibility. Over time, this sensation had transformed itself into a separate entity: a guardian that had appeared every time I initiated my deep breathing. Eventually, it

23

had developed distinctive male characteristics, and I had identified with him as a benevolent spirit-guide.

Without consciously directing my thoughts, a tiny symbolic replica of me appears in my mind's eye. It's a technique I've used often in the past to check in on myself both physically and energetically. It still shocks me to see myself so frail and weak. My aura glows only dimly. The longer I study myself, the more I see. All around me is a violent storm with red lightning bolts striking the ground. I'm compelled to quiet the storm, but I don't know how. My mind is a blank slate and open to whatever comes. A sturdy oak door materializes next to me, and when I turn toward it, it opens. I can't see anything on the other side. The doorway frames only darkness. My solitary thought is that the grass *has* to be greener on the other side. Without waiting a moment longer, I step past the thick oak door, and it shuts immediately behind me.

The silence that envelops me is a blessed relief to my entire being. I rotate my body slowly clockwise; it is pitch black for the entire circle. Now unmoving, I detect an area of slight warmth in front of me and know there is something else here with me, a presence. I'm not afraid. In fact, I'm drawn toward it. The air becomes fragrant, sweet like honeysuckle. It's enticing me closer. After a few more steps, the sense of welcome coalesces into the familiar form of my first guardian spirit-guide. It's as if I'm seeing an old friend for the first time in a long time. The nearer I get to him, the stronger our connection becomes. This time it's greater than in any previous meditation. His presence soothes my anguished soul. Why have I waited so long to do this?

It doesn't matter now. I'm grateful that my protector has returned in my darkest hour. (Now don't laugh—or better yet, do laugh—because what follows may sound funny and quite inexplicable, but it's what I experienced.) He looks just as I last remember seeing him: as a bigger, stockier version of James Dean. As usual, he's dressed in a black leather motorcycle jacket, denim jeans, and boots. I don't know his name. He's never spoken to me directly and has only communicated to me through emotions. I fondly refer to him as J.D. He moves behind me with his hand resting protectively on my right shoulder. It's his familiar way of greeting me from past meditative exercises, and it's instantly reassuring.

It seems that I can also detect another presence, but this one is unfamiliar. It appears to have an energy that's lighter than J.D.'s, but it doesn't have a human form, just a shape. I study it. After a while, it begins to resemble a glowing emerald-green rugby ball—an appropriate choice of form for a die-hard rugby player such as myself. The familiar shape connects me to it, and I feel a deep caring and concern for my well-being emanating from it.

Please help me; I'm so lost, I pray internally. *If my heart is to keep beating, I can't take another step alone. There is no reason to continue living in this hell.* My despair continues to pour out.

"Help me, damn it, or let me go!" I can't refrain from yelling my final ultimatum out loud.

My guides move closer to me, and I'm wrapped in a warm blanket of compassion and peace. It's the best I've felt in years. I'm surprised when I receive a response. J.D. speaks first. Although, it's not exactly using words, my mind translates the communication. *We can help, and we're happy that you asked.*

Well, I'm all ears, and apparently I'm not going anywhere at the moment, so how can you help me? I'm a little shocked at my own flippant response.

Thankfully, J.D. is unperturbed. *Your being is flooded with the perception of suffering and pain. It has become your entire existence. First, we would like to help you change your thinking about your current experience. Change your thinking about it, and your experience will change.*

I've heard that before; it sounds good in theory, I reply dubiously. This is the first time I'm speaking directly with my guide, and I've got an attitude. What's wrong with me?

The rugby ball spirit-guide glows brighter. At the same time, I hear words spoken in a clear baritone resounding in my head. *Then let's make it a reality for you. What have you got to lose?*

At this point, I have nothing to lose but time. An ironic smile touches my lips. Well, now I know that my rugby ball guide is also male; I decide to name him R.B. I wonder how they're going to help me. Right now I'm content to stay in this dark room within my mind. The blackness is so complete that I can't see my hand—even when I raise it up right in front of my face. The darkness has an almost palpable quality to it. Normally, this might make me anxious, but instead it feels soothing.

I'm aware of J.D. moving to stand in front of me. A thin layer of white light surrounds his body and enables me to see him perfectly. He really does look like James Dean and exudes confidence and strength. He looks directly into my eyes and grins. I know he's aware of my thoughts. Of course he is; he's in my head. I'm grateful when he takes up his familiar position behind me, and I feel his hand resting on my shoulder once again.

We know that deep down you know anything is possible. His touch and soft words send a feeling of warmth and comfort that eases my aching heart. *Even now there is a glimmer of hope fighting its way back to the edge of your awareness. Let it in, and let's begin.* I do sense it—a tiny, flash of hope—but it disappears as quickly as it arrives.

R.B. hovers in front of me. The intensity of his emerald aura increases until I'm forced to shield my eyes with my hand. *I get it; you want my full intention.* I'm momentarily blinded, but R.B.'s light immediately softens to a pleasant level.

First, we want you to hear this, and this is big, really big—huge as a matter of fact. Okay, it's really important.

J.D's voice echoes inside my head. I'm caught off guard by the clarity and the obvious humor in his message. There's a distinct sensation of their amusement flowing through me. I can't suppress the chuckle that escapes my lips. This is all so odd; maybe I've lost what little I had left of my mind. I'm not sure of anything, except that I really do want to hear what they have to say.

You can no longer dwell on the pain and suffering that you think you are currently experiencing. Right now your mind's eye sees only pain, in all its myriad forms. The universe has responded in kind, and pain is what you've been receiving. By focusing so completely on it, you've magnified it to such a degree that you've created this unbearable state of being, J.D. explains.

I didn't want this, shouldn't the universe know that? I'm indignant.

We know you understand the power of thought-form-energy. It's absolutely necessary to visualize the perfect health and wellness that you intend to create. Somewhere along your journey, you lost your way—and you've forgotten this. Thoughts of wellness and perfect health have changed into those of pain. In fact, your mind is consumed with every aspect of it, leaving no room for anything else. R.B. pulses brightly at me, gently scolding. His words resonate as truth in my heart.

I know. I'm misery incarnate. But how do I change what I'm thinking? It's all consuming.

The easiest way is to start with something small. R.B. moves closer until his emerald aura surrounds me. *Let's begin our work with your hands,* he suggests.

If you can help me with my hands, it would truly be a miracle, I reply. They're inflamed and ache incessantly. I'm barely able use them to do anything. I can't bear to hope.

In order to begin, open your physical eyes and look at your hands, R.B. urges.

I'm reluctant to leave the peace and quiet of the haven I've created, but if I can retrain myself, I want to try. As soon as I make the decision, the door to the room in my mind opens, and light streams inside. The mental image of me loses cohesion, and I'm aware of the weight of my physical eyelids. It takes a superhuman effort to open them. At first, I don't feel anything, but I grimace as soon as my attention shifts to my hands. They're throbbing, aching, and burning all at the same time. My jaw clenches tightly, and I can't suppress tiny groans from mingling with every breath.

My physical eyes are open, and once again I'm staring at the ceiling; at the same time, I can still see my guides inside the sanctuary within my mind. It's a wild kind of double vision, but somehow it's not difficult for me to maintain. In fact, it feels almost natural. J.D. is there, and I feel him sending me strength.

Okay. Begin to narrow your world and place all of your attention on just one hand, he instructs.

I drag my right hand onto my stomach so that it enters my field of vision. It takes a good long while for me to be able to filter out the sensory input from the rest of my body. I'm conscious of my entire hand as an open wound. *It feels as if the throbbing pain in my hand matches the beat of my heart,* I report.

Just let that thought go, and let's restrict your focus even more, J.D. whispers gently. *Become your right hand; sink into it and notice all of the sensations.*

My hand burns red with fire! I retreat quickly from the external world and reappear as the mental image of myself within my sanctuary. *It's too intense.* I cringe.

This time R.B. takes over. He shrinks until he is sitting on top of the mental image of my hand. *Don't try to fight or change anything. Just move your awareness down inside your hand. Be mindful of your surroundings, and keep breathing,* he encourages.

Once more I open my physical eyes and, instantly, I'm pummeled with unpleasant sensations. It's a struggle to maintain my objective and continue breathing, but that serves only to make me more determined. I cautiously will myself to move inside of my right hand.

Good. Now, what does it look like to you? R.B.'s soothing voice grounds me, and the question helps me shift into the role of observer.

I'm standing in a cave. It's dark, but the walls are red and on fire. It's hot, I reply tensely. It's hard to stay put and keep my emotions under wraps.

You're looking inside a single cell in your hand. Pull back a bit and try to perceive a larger group of cells. Then tell us what you see. R.B.'s voice is my anchor.

My viewpoint changes as I follow R.B.'s instructions. *I'm looking at a group of angry red balls, all jammed together with some in flames. Most of them are red and fat. They're trying to move away from each other, but they can't. There's no room. What a mess!* I exclaim, distressed by the chaos.

Try not to judge—just witness what happens. It's J.D.'s turn to advise me. *What is the emotion coming from your cells?*

Anger. Wow—they're all so angry! There's no hesitation in my answer.

I'm clearly aware of R.B. vibrating on top of my mental hand. *Anger is the emotion stored in those cells. It's what you've been sending to them as you're constantly engaged in a battle against anything that hurts. Right now your cells are fighting against everything, including themselves, and you've been pouring more and more anger into them,* he explains carefully.

But anger can be a form of strength, I reply defensively as I shift back to looking at my distraught cells.

These cells are you, the dense physical part of you. Try to consider your body, consisting of trillions of cells, as one big family. J.D. radiates waves of serenity.

My family, as you call it, has been attacking me. I remain defiant.

J.D. puts a hand on each of my mental shoulders, and it's such a comforting gesture that my defensiveness quickly fades. *Your family is in need of your love and support. Their greatest desire and yours is to be perfectly healthy. This is also your natural state of being. Your cells, you, your family feel angry, in pain, and alone. What we want you to do is send love into your cells, send love to your family. You need each other,* he replies.

How do I do that? I ask. My heart aches with a yearning to believe and be whole again.

R.B.'s shape transforms into the blurry image of a full-size human form. He's standing in front of me but remains the same breathtaking shade of emerald green. *It's simple,* he responds confidently. *Imagine how nice it feels when someone radiates love to you. Fill your mind and spirit with how wonderful that feels. Then project that same love into the cells in your hand. Love each and every one of them.* His words are a song that touches my soul.

I'm aware of a pink light flowing from R.B.'s heart chakra into my own. I take a few moments and draw upon the love I feel for Mom, Dad, Jay, Shika, and my friends. As I think about them, the pleasant warmth in my chest becomes a fuzzy pink ball of love. It expands until it overflows my heart. Confidence seeps into my being. Returning to my hand, I know the angry red balls are my family; they are me, and they need me. I *am* needed. That knowledge encourages me. I imagine a stream of pink love energy riding on a wave of cooling and calming blue light that pours over and around my cells, my family. One by one, I put out the fires with the blue energy and comfort and love my cells with the pink. It's fascinating to watch as they go from fiery red to pink, while shrinking. Eventually, they have more room to move and swim calmly around in the blue light. Moving through the tissues of my hand, I'm drawn to wherever there are angry red cells. I shower them with healing, drawing upon an infinite source, the love of my family. There's no sense of the passage of time, but at some point, all of the cells in my hand are vibrating a happy pink.

My guides step back into my awareness. *You've done well. We want you to pull yourself back out of your hand.* J.D.'s soft voice evinces a hint of pride.

I'm reluctant to leave the happy family of cells in my hand. Not surprisingly, when I'm back in my entire body, my senses are again assailed with excruciating pain. I'm losing myself. Suddenly R.B. flashes a blinding light within my entire mind. It drags me out of my physical body and sends me back into my mental sanctuary.

Be careful to stay out of your entire body. Concentrate solely on your hand and monitor the results without delving back inside of it either, J.D. says softly.

It takes me several minutes to work up my nerve to try again. With great trepidation, I send my thoughts back outside. Gratefully, I can feel my guides sending me strength to help me filter out everything except the sensations of my right hand. I see my physical hand resting on my stomach and carefully wiggle my fingers.

What is this? Something must be wrong. I can't feel anything, I exclaim with astonishment.

That's right. Do you remember what it's like not to feel pain? J.D. laughs.

I try to reign in the surge of hope that pours through me. Is my right hand really free of its relentless burden? I turn my attention over to my left hand. My mind explodes with the familiar thunder and lightning. Back to my right hand. I physically gasp in amazement. I feel nothing. My right hand isn't pounding, flaming, or blazing. It feels what? Amazing, it feels peaceful.

Try moving your hand, J.D. suggests.

It's stiff and awkward, but I can move it without causing a burst of torment. The relief is overwhelming, and once more I feel tears on my neck. But for the first time in a long time, they're tears of joy. *Thank you is utterly inadequate,* I reply.

You're welcome. You're doing well, J.D. responds. *We want you to continue this process of sending love to the rest of your body, your family. You have all the time you need. Just remember to concentrate on smaller areas at any one time.* I sense an outpouring of love from both of my guides. It fills my heart. *We're here to support you through this. You're not alone,* they add ardently.

I'm unable to tear my eyes away from my hand. I revel in the blissful cessation of hostilities. When I flex my fingers tentatively and see them contract with no repercussions, I'm positively euphoric. Somewhere inside of me, a tiny spark of hope glows brighter.

CHAPTER SIX
CHOOSING LIFE

*What you need to know about the past is that no matter
what has happened, it has all worked together to bring
you to this very moment. And this is the moment you
can choose to make everything new. Right now.*
–Unknown Author

The early morning sunlight streams through my bedroom window. I've just spent several hours sending healing love energy into my hand at the direction of my spirit-guides: J.D. and R.B. I'm lying on my bed, staring in awe at my right hand. It no longer hurts. Either this is a miracle—or I'm dreaming and about to wake up into the nightmare of my life. R.B., who has remained present in my mind's eye, quickly turns his most vibrant shade of emerald green yet and stops my negative thoughts dead in their tracks.

I close my physical eyes and concentrate on what my guide is telling me.

Imagine each part of yourself as well and whole, perfect, and complete in every way. Gently continue on with your healing session, sending love to the rest of your cells, your family. Raise your vibration into wellness. As R.B. finishes, J.D. squeezes both of my mental shoulders with his hands, and I resonate with confidence.

Following the recommendation of my guides, my first stop is my left hand. There's nothing in my world except my left hand. I stand quietly among all the angry, red, and flaming cells. Reaching out to them and to me, once again, I radiate pink love riding on a wave of cooling blue. I recognize that I'm tapping into an infinite source of healing. It flows effortlessly until all the cells in my hand are a happy pink. They swim calmly around in their new blue environment, relaxed and loved, my family, myself.

When I adjust my attention to reside outside of my hand, the lack of pain takes my breath away. I'm aware of the encouragement and strength that's flowing into my heart chakra from my spirit-guides. Not wanting to disrupt my momentum, I determinedly move on to my forearms. This is followed by my upper arms. My excitement builds with each success. My healing progresses from one body part to the next. Time is not a consideration, and this healing will take as long as it takes. I open my eyes when I'm finished. A small part of my mind registers that daylight is waning, but the rest of me simply wants to experience and enjoy my new self.

What a wonderful thing it is to be lying on my bed, drinking in the sensations. It's delicious and exquisite. For in this moment, my pain is gone. I'm aware of every cell in my body and luxuriate in the rediscovered softness of my mattress. This is heaven, and I'm floating on clouds. *If I can create this miracle respite from pain, I can become well and healthy again. It really is possible.* I shake with the grandness of my epiphany.

In my mind, J.D. wraps his arms around me and hugs me gently. *Yes, you can. Believe it and do it. Use us and connect with us, your guides,* he urges. *You are opening to receiving help and guidance. And receive it you will. It will come to you in myriad ways: from friends, family, music, books, strangers, nature, from everywhere.*

I get it. This is like a treasure hunt with clues to help me follow the path of wellness. I'm feeling high with thoughts of new possibilities. *But how will I know what the right thing is for me to do?* I ask.

Your heart chakra will resonate with your truth, and you will know, R.B. answers.

Doubt returns. Maybe all of this is simply a delirious dream, and nothing has changed. Right now, I could get to my gun and be done with it all.

You are needed, here—now. There's much for you to learn and to heal and just as much for you to teach others. Don't leave! It is not your time! The roar comes from both of them in unison.

I rub my temples. *All right, already. I hear you. Just tune it down a notch,* I reply. My head is pounding from their message. So this *is* my reality. What if I really can heal myself, but instead I leave now? Then this body I'm in now, and this unique life, will end. What is the harm in trying? I have everything to gain. To become well and teach others—that's worth hanging around a little longer. Serenity flows through me.

You have much to share with others, and you can create whatever state of health and wellness you desire. You asked for help, and we would like you to call on us

32

and allow us to love and support you in your process, my dynamic duo speak as a chorus together inside my mind.

Okay, I'm in. And now that I have you here, what is my next step? I'm curious.

You need to supply your physical body with as much nutrition as you can; it's severely depleted, R.B. says. *If you don't act, there will be nothing you can do to stop yourself from leaving. And it will happen in the near future. You need liquid nutrition since you can't digest solid food. This must be your sole focus right now. Get yourself upstairs and have a protein shake. By the time you finish it, you will know your next step. We are with you.*

I don't move for a few minutes. I'm in a state of bliss, drinking in the pleasure of experiencing my body without pain. I'm relaxed and peaceful. I'm also aware that my spirit-guides are firmly nudging me to move. Slowly, I roll onto my right side. Amazingly, I'm okay. The club-wielding gremlins are surprisingly quiescent. I cautiously push myself to a sitting position. I'm sore, but my muscles considerately allow me to move. Tears of gratitude flow. Something hard underneath my hand catches my attention. It's my cell phone. I feel an urge to put it in the pocket of my shorts before I slide off the bed. From there, it's a slow but steady crawl to the desk chair. I use it to pull myself upright. The room spins, and I hang on. It's been several days since I've had anything to eat, and a sense of urgency looms in my mind.

Take your time. Be gentle with yourself, J.D. whispers softly.

The flow of support from my guides strengthens me. My feet move, one shambling step at a time, toward the spiral stairway. Another wave of dizziness passes over me, and I reach out for something to grab. My hand latches onto the bookshelf, and I manage not to fall over. I'm breathing hard from the effort of making it this far. A shudder of fear runs through me as it dawns on me where I am. I can see the small blue sports bag that holds my gun case on the bottom shelf. A few short hours ago, this bit of rug I'm standing on would have been my final resting place. Now, the bookshelves are propping me up. My journey no longer needs to end here. Without looking back, I inch my way to the stairwell.

I keep my goals small—just one tread at a time. I can do this. Time is of no consequence as I half-crawl, half-pull myself up the spiral stairs. There is a burgeoning sense of wonder inside of me as I make my way across the living room and then, at last, into the kitchen. Once there, I can't stop the upper half of my body from collapsing across the counter. I just need to rest a moment, but the moment stretches into minutes, and my strength is evaporating. I'm too exhausted to pick my head off of the counter, and my eyelids fall shut.

I'm not sure how much time has passed, but I'm annoyed that someone is shining bright green lights directly into my eyes. My left hand moves to shield them from the glare. Nothing changes. I realize this is the work of R.B. inside my head. *You can do it. Use our strength. You must drink some nutrition. Now!*

An electric jolt runs through me, and I move. I'm not sure if I'm the one controlling my limbs, but somehow the blender produces a shake with almond milk, protein powder, and a banana. It's strange not to experience hunger anymore—and to not have the slightest desire to eat. I should be ravenous, but I feel nothing. There is only my muddled brain telling me that I need nutrition to continue surviving. The liquid slides down my throat and, after a few minutes, I feel bits of energy returning.

The fog lifts from my mind, and it's clearer than it has been in a long while. The most important challenge I face right now is how I'm going to take in enough food to stay alive. My digestive system isn't capable of absorbing nutrients from solids or moving them through my body. Every time I try to eat solid food, it sits in my stomach for days and remains undigested. The resulting cramps in my intestines are unbearable.

It barely registers that J.D. is lightly touching my right shoulder; when it finally does, the fear recedes. *Liquid nutrition is the key. Juicing food is the way,* he explains.

I agree, but I don't have the energy to figure this out on my own. I need help. No sooner does my request appear as a thought in my mind than my cell phone rings. My fingers are maddeningly slow in retrieving it from my pocket, and I'm worried I'll miss the call.

"Hi, Hol. How are you doing?" It's Jay. Relief washes over me. If anyone can find the right person to help me with a nutrition plan, it would be my brother—the research king. This is right up his alley.

"Jay! It's good to hear your voice. I'm so glad you called." I cringe inwardly at the hint of desperation in my voice.

"Are you okay? What's going on?" He goes on alert.

I know that my brother would do anything for me, but I hesitate before I respond. Why is it so hard for me to ask for help? I'm on death's door, for Pete's sake. "I really need your help right now," I admit finally.

"You got it. Anything. What do you need?" He says almost before I can finish my sentence.

I take another sip of my shake to give me the energy I need to speak. "I think the way for me to go is to juice. I need to find a really good nutritionist who could set up a plan for me." I lean against the counter for support and keep going. "But my brain isn't firing on all four cylinders, and the task seems too daunting for me to handle alone. Can you find me someone? I don't have the energy to look online or call around." My long-winded speech leaves me drained. I barely make it over to one of Sofia's dining room chairs and collapse on it.

"You can relax. Your younger brother's on the job. I'll get on it and find someone by tomorrow. Count on it."

"Thanks, Jay. You're a lifesaver." I sigh with relief. The mountain I've been carrying on my shoulders suddenly doesn't seem as heavy.

"That's what brothers are for. Hang in there, okay?"

I click the end button on my phone, and my mind is blessedly turned off as well. My brother is on the job. I don't have to do anything right now. I don't have to think about anything other than drinking my protein shake. How wondrous. It carries me through the night.

Shortly before noon the next day, I haven't made it off my bed yet when the phone rings. "Well, Hol, your fabulous brother has found 'the man' for you. You can go online and check him out. His name is Dr. Mercola. He's a guru of nutrition and natural healing, and it looks like he's a fanatic about juicing. I just know you're going to like him." He pauses. "But there's just one thing ..."

"What?" I ask slowly. Why is there always a "but?"

"He's in Chicago," Jay finally spits out. My heart sinks. "But maybe you can call him up, and he can set you up over the phone or maybe he can refer you to someone local. I think he's a great place to start. If you want, I'll talk to him about you."

"No. Thanks, but I should talk to him. I can tell him exactly how I feel, and maybe he can help me over the phone. Jay, you're awesome, having to figure this out was way too overwhelming for me."

"I want you to get well, Hol. I'll do anything for you. You know that," his voice shakes, and it touches my heart.

I pinch my own leg hard so I won't cry as I say, "I know. Thanks. I love you."

"I love you too. Let me know how it goes. If you don't think he can help, I'll find someone else for you. Call me anytime, okay?"

"Okay," I answer. As soon as I hang up, I roll onto my side and hug a pillow in despair. Chicago! Why can't this Mercola guy be local? This

35

isn't fair. It's taken numerous miracles already to keep me from my Glock and get me this far. I don't doubt that Jay found exactly who I need to see, but Chicago might as well be a planet on the outer rim of our galaxy. I barely had the strength to crawl upstairs and make a protein shake. I have no clue how I'm going to get halfway across the country.

CHAPTER SEVEN

FLIGHT TO CHICAGO

The journey of a thousand miles must begin with a single step.
–Lao Tzu

I hear the sounds of birds chirping their good morning, but my eyelids are fighting my efforts to open them. Maybe my gremlin friends have sewn them shut in the middle of the night, just to keep my life interesting. There's a nagging reason, somewhere in the back of my mind, that tells me I must keep trying. Something important is happening today. I can see there is a thought working its way through my mental fog. Ah, there it is. Today *is* a big day. I'm flying to Chicago to see Dr. Mercola. Now that I know what is on my agenda for the day, I'm relieved that I spent all of yesterday getting my suitcase packed and upstairs by the door.

It's imperative for me to go on this trip, but the massive butterflies in my stomach could give Mothra a run for its money. For months, I've rarely left my room, venturing outside only when I need to stock up on cans of Ensure. How do I think I'm going to manage flying to Chicago?

"Stop it. Get a grip," I admonish myself. My voice sounds more like a croak, but this line of reasoning won't help me at all. Once again, I make my breath the focal point. It acts as an anchor pulling me past the worry and fear to safety. My lungs expand deeply and ever more slowly until I'm calm enough to create the door to the room in my mind, my sanctuary. When I step inside, it's dark and hard to see anything, but I feel pleasantly warm. I send out a request for my guides; in moments, J.D. is standing next to me. I face him.

How can I do this? Who am I kidding? I don't have the physical stamina or strength to get myself to Chicago. What can I do? I throw my thoughts at him as my fears bubble to the surface. J.D. raises his arm and points toward a patch of light in front of us. I'm intrigued that I can so clearly smell the leather jacket he's wearing. I even hear the sound of it when he moves. Leather is tough and durable; it's protection. It's what *I* need.

Suddenly, I'm wearing my black motorcycle leathers: my jacket, pants, boots, and even my studded gloves. I glance down at my outfit. This is cool. J.D. touches my arm and points again toward the light. Sitting in the center of it is my last motorcycle, a Honda Interceptor. I smile at my guide. It's dark, but I can still make out the twinkle in his eyes. When I nod my head, I find myself instantly sitting on my dark blue Interceptor racing along an empty highway. J.D. is seated behind me. I can feel one arm wrapped around my waist and his other hand on my right shoulder. I crank on the accelerator, and the additional burst of speed is exhilarating. There are no limits to how fast I can go. Strength and power are pouring into me.

You have support all around you, from so many; you can do this. Just concentrate on one small thing at a time. The bigger picture will take care of itself, J.D. purrs calmly in my ear.

Just by shifting my thoughts, the motorcycle slows and then dissolves. Suddenly, I'm no longer in my sanctuary, but my adrenalin is flowing. I am pumped.

My eyelids flutter open. A glance at my clock tells me I have many hours before the taxi arrives to pick me up. Good. I can concentrate on the task at hand—taking a shower. My muscles are burning, and it's a tediously slow trek into the bathroom. But it is worth every bit of the effort once I'm standing in the shower. It's counterintuitive, but warm water actually helps soothe the flames and loosen my suit of armor. I visualize my muscles as perfectly flexible. Although I'm in less pain, it's taken all of my energy to remain standing in the shower. I plunk down on the edge of the tub to dry myself off. Afterwards, I'm unable to get up again. It's back to "my life as a turtle" with a laborious crawl to where my clothes are laid out next to my bed.

Once I reach them, all I can do is collapse on my back and stress out. Getting dressed is one of the things I dread the most. My hands are almost frozen into a half-open position from the scleroderma. Using them to touch anything results in unadulterated pain. Once again, I tell myself to stop it. All I need to do is handle things one miniscule step at a time. While I'm sprawled on the carpet recovering from my shower, I work on reducing the throbbing in my hands. I visualize them gently soaking in a stream of pink love while absorbing a cooling blue foam into every cell. Slowly, the pulsing ache abates.

A twinkling light shines into my eyes and pulls me out of my healing ritual. A clear quartz crystal on the window sill is refracting light into a rainbow that is dancing around the walls of my room. I'm grateful for the timeliness of the light show. It reminds me that I need to stay focused on getting dressed. While I manage to slide into my jeans successfully, putting on my shirt doesn't go as well. I get stuck with it halfway pulled down. Somehow, part of it has become rolled into a ball above my ribs. My fingers hurt too much to get them under this big knot, and repeated attempts end in agonizing failure. My heart starts to feel squeezed with frustration and despair. How can I have become this helpless? I have the absurd idea that my shirt is alive and deliberately refusing to allow me to get dressed. The sharp, barking laughter sounds strange to my ears, despite the fact that it's my own. *I've lost it.* I'm riding the razor's edge of sanity.

Breathe. I clearly hear the word separate itself from the chaos inside my head. It's J.D. The command disrupts the strange mental fit I'm having. Three deep, slow breaths later, I'm able to let go of a time limit to fix my problem. I try again. As I slowly work my hand under the twisted lump, something has shifted and my shirt unravels; at long last I'm dressed. This calls for a celebration, and I have just the thing. It takes two hands to hold it, but I raise a can of Ensure in a brief salute to my morning's victory and then carefully sip my breakfast.

Following my morning meditation, which has infused me with courage, I'm ready to get myself upstairs. I would have bartered a kidney for an elevator on the ensuing journey up the spiral staircase into the living room. But I make it! At the top, I wisely refrain from dancing a jig. The day's accomplishments don't stop there. The next rabbit I pull out of my hat is opening the front door. This is no small feat using fingers that won't close and scream bloody murder at the slightest touch. I lean happily against the doorframe. The sun is shining, and the air is warm on my skin. It smells clean, a nice change from the slightly damp and musty air in my bedroom. I could stand in this doorway forever, soaking in the sun and breathing fresh air. However, it's not long before the taxi arrives to take me to the airport. I manage to pick up my backpack—barely. Now begins the nerve-racking descent down the flight and a half of cement steps to reach the street.

Thankfully, the driver notices how slowly I'm moving and races up to help me. First, he takes my backpack, and then he carefully escorts me down the stairs and into the cab. Once I'm settled, he jogs back up to fetch my suitcase. I'm exhausted. My body feels heavy enough to sink down through the seat and into the ground. I'm pleasantly surprised that the taxi is spotless and doesn't smell like smoke. In fact, it has a pleasant floral aroma.

"What airline, madam?" the driver asks after he slides back behind the wheel.

"United, please," my response is barely above a whisper. Looking at the rearview mirror, I can see concern in his eyes. Once we're underway, my eyelids are far too heavy to remain open, so I stop trying. It's a relief to have someone else in control of my destination for a short while. All too soon, however, the cab pulls up next to the United curbside check-in. The driver jumps out and retrieves my suitcase from the trunk, but I'm still not ready to move. Reluctantly, I slide my body slowly toward the door. The driver opens the car door and extends a hand toward me.

"Let me help you, madam." His voice is kind and gently insistent. Gratefully, I accept his offer. I would never have dreamed of doing that in the not-too-distant past. The driver helps me over to the check-in stand and then fetches my suitcase, which he gives to the check-in attendant. I manage to fish my plane ticket and I.D. out of my pocket and also hand them over. When I realize I still haven't paid the driver, it takes another moment to carefully gather some cash together.

While I'm working on that, the driver calls out to the attendant with my ticket. "Would you please order a wheelchair for this kind lady? She should not be walking through the airport."

The protest—that, of course, I don't need a wheelchair—dies before I can utter a single word. I turn toward the driver to pay him. "Here you are, and I can't thank you enough for all your help. You've been so kind to me." Our eyes meet, and I'm surprised by the intensity of the emotions I can see in them.

The driver hesitates before speaking but quickly gathers himself. "On the contrary, madam, it is to you that I owe a debt of gratitude. You did not hesitate, even for a moment, to get into my taxi. There was no doubt within you that I would get you to the airport. My name is Yusuf, and you have restored my faith."

Comprehension suddenly hits me like a ton of bricks. I did see that my driver had a beard and that he was wearing a turban, but I didn't care. September 11 wasn't that long ago. I can only imagine how difficult life must be now for someone like Yusuf. Here we are, two total strangers, and both our lives have been irrevocably altered by the same terrible event—one that happened more than three thousand miles away. We are connected.

"It's nice to meet you, Yusuf." I smile back at him. "My name is Holly." My throat tightens with the lump that has formed there. I'm nearly useless with this illness, but an opportunity to help someone still appeared, even while he was helping me.

"Anytime you need a taxi—it doesn't matter what time—you call me, and I will come." Yusuf hands me his business card. "I wish you a safe flight and a good journey." He bows his head slightly before leaving.

How auspicious—the trip has barely started, and miracles are already occurring. All I need to concentrate on right now is getting to my gate. Right on cue, the sliding doors open, and an airport attendant comes through pushing a wheelchair. He sees me and immediately heads in my direction. My first flash of emotion is humiliation at looking like I need help. This quickly gives way to gratitude, and I feel like crying again.

"Thank you so much," my voice cracks a little, and I'm embarrassed again.

"Not a problem ma'am. I'm glad to be of service," the young black man smiles at me.

Never in a million years would I have dreamed I would need a wheelchair to get me anywhere. My burning leg muscles are ecstatic at not having to carry me through the airport. As we pass through the automatic glass doors into the terminal, I'm pummeled by the intensity of everything. The sheer number of people moving every which way, the glaring bright lights, the noise level—it's all a sensory overload. By the time we get through security, I'm feeling faint and nauseous. I put my elbows on my thighs and rest my head in my hands.

"Are you okay, ma'am?" the airport attendant leans closer in concern.

"There's too much noise and lights; it's making me ill." My voice is weak and barely audible.

"I think I can help with that," the kind attendant turns the chair around gently. We head for an elevator and take it down a few levels. At the end of a short corridor, he wheels me through some restricted access doors. In the blink of an eye, we've left the mad rush of people and noises behind. We pass through darker, mostly deserted, hallways. My stomach starts to settle down. I even find the energy to look around.

"This is so much better. Wow. I had no idea there's another hidden world at the airport," I remark with astonishment.

"Oh, you'd be amazed at what we have down here," he says with a laugh. As if to punctuate his words, he pushes me through a wide metal door. Suddenly, we're outside and heading down a quiet alley between buildings. A short distance later, we're back inside, where we ride another elevator. In no time at all, we've arrived at my gate. The attendant parks me in an out-of-the-way corner near the windows looking onto the tarmac. "You'll be boarding shortly, and the flight crew will take you on early to help get you situated." He gives me a light pat on the shoulder.

"You've been terrific. Thank you," I reply.

He smiles and waves before heading off to rescue someone else in need.

I've got an excellent view of our plane outside the window. Studying it distracts me from the cacophony of hustle and bustle. Fortunately, I don't have long to wait before a motherly looking flight attendant approaches me.

"We can get you on board now if you'd like," she offers pleasantly.

"That would be wonderful," I reply gratefully. She wheels me down the ramp to the door of the airplane, which means that it's time for me to move. It takes forever to hoist myself carefully out of the wheelchair and shuffle down the aisle of the plane. I'm awash in humiliation. It worries me how much my muscles are already burning and how tender my skin feels as I settle into my seat. It's not long before the rest of the passengers come bounding down the aisles. I wince every time I'm jostled as they pass by.

The air is blowing a little too strongly directly onto my head, but I don't have the energy to try to reach up to turn it down. It's a miracle when everyone is finally settled. Then it dawns on me that no one is sitting next to me. I feel like bursting into song and singing my good fortune from the highest of hilltops. Our plane is quick to take off, and it feels heavenly to close my eyes. I take the time to create the empty room in my mind. Once there, I stay inside my quiet retreat until the plane lands in Chicago. I wonder what new adventure awaits me there.

CHAPTER EIGHT
MISSION MERCOLA

*I have yet to meet a single person from our culture,
no matter what his or her educational background,
IQ, and specific training, who has had powerful
transpersonal experiences and continues to subscribe
to the materialistic monism of Western science.*
–Albert Einstein

"Welcome to the Optimal Wellness Center. My name is Mary," a stylish young woman says from behind the reception desk. She looks like she just stepped off the cover of *Vogue*. I feel so pathetic and embarrassed when I barely manage to whisper my name before leaning against the counter for support. Heels notwithstanding, Mary is at my side in an instant, gently guiding me to a cushioned chair in the waiting room.

"Just rest here a minute, dear. I'll get you in to have your blood work right away." She's young, but I sense the concern in her voice is genuine.

Our eyes meet, and I hope mine register the gratitude I feel because I can't muster the strength to utter a sound. It's a miracle that I made it to Chicago at all, let alone arrive safely and intact to Dr. Mercola's office. Any sane person would have simply hired a taxi to get from their hotel to the clinic. But not me! Oh no, that would be too easy. I have to have a rental car and drive myself. What was I thinking? Attempting to navigate in a strange city, with barely enough strength to hang onto the steering wheel, was harrowing and self-inflicted idiocy. In spite of my best efforts to the contrary, I did make it.

I arrive for the first day of three consecutive scheduled appointment days. Today is all about lab tests: blood work, hair analysis, and live blood cell analysis. A wave of dizziness hits me. I wish I could drink one of the cans of Ensure in my backpack, but I can't. The appointment nurse had told me to fast before the blood work. I concentrate on hanging on for a little while longer.

My head has fallen forward on my chest, which gives me an unobstructed view of the white tiled floor. My attention is completely taken up by a cluster of scuff marks on the tile in front of my feet. It resembles the shape of a dragon, and the longer I watch it, the more I'm convinced it's moving. In the martial arts world, the dragon represents power accumulated through patience and wisdom, as well as a link to heavenly energy. To me, however, it is a neon billboard from the universe, encouraging me to endure.

It takes me a moment to comprehend that my dragon has been obscured by a pair of white leather nurse shoes. Curiosity urges me to lift my head just the necessary amount to see who is standing before me. My eyes travel up, taking in a white lab coat and blonde hair arranged in a perfect bun, before coming to rest upon a pair of kind blue eyes.

"It's nice to meet you, Holly. I'm Kathy, and I'm here to help you get your blood work over with." Her voice is blessedly soft on my ears. She reaches out to expertly assist me to my feet. The aura around her body appears as a soft, pleasing pink, and I like her immediately. My legs burn with the effort of walking, but Kathy extends an arm that I use for support. She patiently moves at my pace. The hallway is infinitely long, and I become frustrated with my progress. A tortoise with a broken leg could have stopped for tea and still beaten me to the lab.

When we finally arrive, I'm barely conscious of Kathy leading me over to a chair with a custom armrest. I study the design with appreciation; it places my arm in a comfortable position for drawing blood. While she's filling multiple test tubes with my blood, I feel myself starting to black out. I can see her lips moving, but I only hear fragments of her friendly banter. I force myself to look at her face, which reflects only kindness and compassion. It's an anchor that pulls me back into my body. By the time she caps off the last tube of blood, I've managed to work a smile onto my lips.

"Wow. That was really painless," I mumble gratefully. I'm rewarded with a shower of pink energy droplets as Kathy returns my smile and tapes a ball of cotton onto the needle site at my elbow.

"You're welcome. The worst part of your visit is over, and now the fun part begins."

I want to weep with gratitude when she places one of my cans of Ensure in front of me. "Kathy, you're awesome. Thanks."

"Hey Kath, is your patient ready for me yet?" We both look up at the sound of the deep masculine voice.

Kathy smiles at the newcomer. "Holly, this is John. He's going to take over and do a live blood cell analysis for you."

John flashes me a grin, and then he and his white lab coat are a blur of motion. He quickly prepares a slide of my blood and moves to a large microscope on the counter along the wall opposite my chair. After inserting the slide under the microscope, John gestures toward a large flat screen monitor on the wall. The screen is split into two views, and anxiety grows in the pit of my stomach as he explains what I'm seeing. The view on the left contains my blood cells, and the right view is of normal, healthy blood cells. It's hard for me to look at what my blood cells have become. They are all dark, bent, and twisted like weird mutations out of a science fiction movie. My cells bear no relation to the bright red and perfectly round healthy cells dancing on the right half of the monitor. I wince in pain and realize that I've been unconsciously squeezing the armrest.

"Why did I think I could do this?" I mutter under my breath.

John has been quietly studying me. "Anything's possible, you know. I came from where you are now." He moves in front of the monitor to block my view and lightly taps his chest with one hand. "Take me, for example. I had cancer, and it was bad. No one thought I was going to make it. But I didn't let anyone else tell me what I could or couldn't do. Holistic medicine worked for me, and here I am, alive and defying all the odds."

His exuberance is like water in the desert. I want to crawl toward it. His story has created a connection between us, and I want to share how I feel. "My doctors think I'm crazy for quitting Western drugs ... but they were killing me, right along with the MCTD. I know that the holistic approach is right for me, but sometimes it feels like I'm walking this path alone."

John grabs a stool from against the wall and sits down on it in front of me. My eyes finally have a chance to focus. I see he is a clean-cut man in his early thirties with the lean, hard frame of a marathoner. "Everyone here is going to support you. We know you're on the right path." He smiles at me, his eyes sparkling. "I found this place after I was already well on my way to becoming healthy again, but their philosophy mirrored my own. I can see you feel the same way or you wouldn't be here." His sentiments buoy me. When I nod in agreement, he continues, "This place is why I trained to become a lab tech, and it's the only place I wanted to work." John looks down and flips through my paperwork. I feel my body releasing some of its pent-up tension. I don't feel as heavy as I did a moment ago, and my breathing is deeper. He glances back at me. "Your appointment with Dr. Mercola is tomorrow, right?"

"Yes, that's right."

"You're going to like him and what he has to say." His expression changes to a knowing smile. "I'd be willing to place a large wager on that."

I desperately hope he's right. It's that tiny strand of hope that pulls me along in fits and starts until the next day when I arrive back at the Optimal Wellness Center. There's so much riding on this one meeting. I'm nervous as I follow Mary down the hall for my appointment.

Dr. Mercola's office is bright, and sunlight streams through the large picture window on the far side of the office. I'm sitting in a comfortable leather chair on the patient side of his wooden desk. His bookshelves are filled to capacity and line all the walls. The décor is typical of a doctor's office. What isn't typical is that they contain not only Western medical references, but also countless volumes of alternative healing and nutrition. I'm pleased to see *Nutrition with the Seasons, Acupuncture and Herbal References, Healing with Light Therapy,* and many more. Their presence is a source of comfort to me.

Part of me dares to feel hopeful anticipation, but the rest is scared. I don't want to hear anything that will take away the little hope I have left. My eyelids are heavy, and they gradually fall shut. The sunlight feels warm on my face and neck. My nerves are frayed, and I breathe deeply to calm myself. After a time, the familiar presence of J.D. touches my mind and the waiting loses its sharp edge.

My eyes open at the same time as the office door. The balding, middle-aged man who enters is tan, with a lean, athletic body, and a dazzling white smile. I'm quickly basking in the glowing vitality that completely surrounds him. It's quite an entrance. He gently takes my hand. "It's a pleasure to meet you, Holly. I'm Dr. Mercola. It's wonderful you were able to make it out here. I know the trip must have been difficult." His tone rings with compassion, and I'm thrilled he's aware enough not to squeeze my inflamed hand.

"It wasn't easy, that's for sure, but I do need help and, most especially, nutritional guidance. Everything I've read about your natural healing philosophy runs parallel to my own, and I'm hoping you can help me." I glance up at him, hoping I managed to keep most of the desperation out of my voice.

Dr. Mercola smiles and the room brightens by an order of magnitude. "I've read your history and looked at your test results. But before I start talking, what I'd like is for you to tell me your story. Please tell me what happened and how you've progressed up until your arrival here." He settles back in his chair, patiently waiting for me to start.

I like this man. He's put me at ease and given me his full attention. As the words pour out of me, relief pours into me. It feels good to be heard. I talk about my life before, during, and after MCTD, right up until the present. Dr. Mercola listens attentively, politely asking for clarification on a few things, but he is content to let me tell my whole story in my own way. It feels like a bonus mini-therapy session. After I've finished talking, I slump back in my chair, feeling drained but more at peace.

Dr. Mercola leans forward across his desk, his eyes bright with intensity. When he speaks, his words resonate in my mind, and each one is made of pure gold. "The first thing I want you to hear from me, Holly, is that I know, without a doubt, you're going to be well again." The shock of his confident declaration reverberates throughout my entire being. I know that tears are rolling when Dr. Mercola kindly slides a box of tissues toward my hand. I grab a few and dab my eyes. How I had longed to hear someone other than my spirit-guides tell me I could be well. One simple statement was worth the effort it had taken to get me here.

"Thank you. You're the first doctor to tell me that." My voice shakes. When Dr. Mercola's eyes light up, I wish there were many more doctors like him. Fury surges within me over my past Western medical experiences. "It makes me angry to be told I have no hope. Who are they to tell me what I can and can't do?" I blurt out.

Dr. Mercola nods his head. "Everyone has the potential to become well." He taps my file for emphasis before continuing. "It takes a deep commitment and willingness to change, but from listening to your story, I can see you have that in spades. And you're already a big step ahead of the game."

Now it's my turn to lean forward in my chair. "Really? How so?" I want to hear about any edge I might have.

"Because you've already weaned yourself off of those harmful drugs you were on. That's huge. Most of my patients don't start out that way, and it takes a lot longer to get results."

I let out a sigh. At long last, a Western doctor who realizes the negative impact of long-term drug use. How often had I been prescribed one drug to counter the side effects of another until I was on a toxic spiral of medication? I had felt like a lab rat. My experiences had convinced me that while drugs are useful for certain conditions, they should always be a last resort and stopped as soon as humanly possible. I see a kindred spirit sitting on the other side of the desk.

"Doc, it wasn't easy, but MCTD is bad enough without the drugs joining the party to finish me off." My voice drips with disdain.

"Once you get going on your nutritional plan, you're going to be amazed at how rapidly you improve." Dr. Mercola pats my hand gently.

Anticipation is building inside of me, and it feels good. Every cell in my body is lighting up with expectations of the rewards of juicing. "I can't wait to start juicing. I know it's what I need," I declare vehemently.

"Your juicer is going to become your best friend." Dr. Mercola chuckles and leans back. "The amount of nutrition that your body is screaming for is only possible through juicing large quantities of fruits and vegetables. It takes away the work of digestion, which your system is not up to doing right now. And the concentrated nutrition is absorbed immediately and almost without effort. Once your body starts getting what it needs, you will start experiencing little miracles of recovery every day," he says. His expression becomes a bit more serious as he pulls some papers from my file and slides them toward me. I'm back on alert. "I want to chat with you about the hair analysis results." He pauses while I turn the papers over. He points to a section of the page, and I peer closely at the results. "You have extremely high levels of arsenic, mercury, cadmium, and aluminum in your system."

My mouth falls open in astonishment, and it's a good thing there aren't any flies in the room. "You're kidding?" I gasp. "That could explain a lot." My right hand hurts, and I look down to see I'm squeezing my leg. I use my left to pry it open.

"Yes, you're right. Just a single one of these toxins at the level they are in your body can wreak havoc with the immune system," he adds.

I've always considered myself fit, with a healthy diet. "How the hell can this happen?" I ask.

"It's easier and more common than you think. Many deodorants contain aluminum. Pesticides on food contain all the toxins I just listed, not to mention many other common everyday items: cleaning products, tap water, body products and cosmetics, cigarette smoke, building materials that off-gas hazardous chemicals, the list goes on and on."

My mind is spinning. I've never even looked at the ingredients in my deodorant, body products, or cleaning products. I did eat healthy foods, but I only ate organic foods occasionally—and I didn't filter my water.

"Oh, boy, I've got some changes to make there—that's for sure." I look up with determination.

"Don't be too hard on yourself. Our society has been misled and misinformed about many health hazards, and these are simple changes to make really," he says to comfort me.

"How do I get out the toxins that are in me already?" I can feel my heart beating faster, and my anxiety builds.

"The juicing is naturally chelating; over time, your body will eliminate these toxins on its own."

"Is that enough?" I look up from my test results.

"Absolutely. Let your body regain its balance naturally—in your own best time. Don't try to rush things. Your job is to focus on pouring liquid nutrients into your body." Dr. Mercola's confidence in my body's ability to handle the job is exactly what I want to hear. My heart rate slows as my thoughts return to the healing potential of juicing. "And keep doing what you've been doing," he adds with a grin.

I'm confused. "Okay. Just so we're in sync, which things are you referring to?"

"Well, you've already changed your thought patterns to become more positive, and you're working with visualizations and meditation. These are all critical components of any comprehensive wellness plan. Keep doing what you're doing, and when you add the nutrition component, you're off to the races."

I'm going to do this. I will be well. In my mind's eye, I can see myself drinking my juice, and it appears as if I'm drinking a rainbow. It's a rainbow that flows easily inside of me, nourishing every cell of my body. When my visualization is finished, I ask another very pressing question. "What about exercising? I'm so frail. I feel like I could break simply by running into something. It's a horrible feeling. I was so strong before. Physical activity was at the core of my self-esteem." My tone sounds more like a moan. The growing lump in my throat makes it impossible to say anything more.

Dr. Mercola rolls his chair around to my side of his desk and gently takes my hands in his. His eyes are kind but determined—a beacon in my fog of despair. "Holly, it's easy to see that you're attuned to your body and where it is. Again, this is a skill that I usually have to teach my patients, but you already have it. Use your body awareness to do what you can and do more when your body tells you it can. Trust yourself. You have all you need to do this. You created a miracle to get here and you're going to keep on creating them until you're well," he says slowly and with absolute conviction.

The dam breaks again. Dr. Mercola releases my hands so I can reach for the box of tissues. To hear someone else express their faith in me and my ability to heal myself is food for my starving soul. My soul is now strong enough to open the door of determination.

Dr. Mercola and I spend more time reviewing the details of my plan. When all my questions are answered, it winds up being the longest doctor's appointment I've ever had. It's also the first time I've been sad to reach the end of one. When I stand up to leave, Dr. Mercola steps toward me and gives me a gentle hug. I don't feel quite so alone. I have a nutrition plan and confirmation about the steps that I've already taken. The knowledge that many others before me have become well also strengthens me. Outside the Optimal Wellness Center, the sun is shining—and so am I.

CHAPTER NINE
JUICE OF LIFE

Most of us, swimming against the tides of trouble,
that the world knows nothing about, need only a bit of
praise or encouragement, and we will make the goal.
–Jerome Fleishman

Yesterday, I flew home from my trip to Chicago to see Dr. Mercola. It took a lot out of me, but also gave me a bigger gift: hope. And today is going to be a game-changer. I'm absolutely certain of it. I'm about to make my first juice. I feel excitement and pressure at the same time, like I'm about to play in a national championship rugby game. However, before the whistle blows to start the action, I need to catch my breath. My body is leaning against the granite countertop next to Sofia's kitchen sink, which offers an excellent vantage point to survey the field of play. To my right, another large granite countertop separates Sofia's kitchen from her living room. It's presently covered by a mountain of vegetables and fruit. On the other side of the sink is my juicer, the Green Star 2000. She is the superwoman of juicers. Although not faster than a locomotive or able to leap tall buildings in a single bound, she can extract juice from just about anything without even breaking a sweat. I'm glad she's on my team.

Breathing deeply, I inhale the leafy aroma of fresh vegetables mixed with a hint of dirt. It brings back pleasant childhood memories of helping Dad tend our half-acre garden. There were few things I loved more than crawling along the rows of vegetables and pulling weeds with the smell of rich soil in my nostrils and the sun on my back. Our family garden was my own little piece of heaven on earth. My reverie is broken when a head of lettuce tumbles partway down the mountain. The opposing team is signaling its impatience to start. Okay, I'm ready.

While I scan the vegetables for a likely target, a drumroll plays in my head. It ends with a resounding cymbal clash when I zero in on several

51

wayward carrots at the edge of the counter. In a flash, I'm off and running. Well, I wouldn't say running. All right, I wouldn't say walking either, but it's the fastest shuffle this side of the Mississippi.

A smug feeling appears when I scoop the unsuspecting carrots into my hands. My smugness is extremely short lived. There is a searing pain as I bang my fingers on the granite surface upon turning around. Not wanting to drop my treasure, I grit my teeth and hang on for dear life. It's no mean feat to keep this two-ton load of lead-filled carrots cradled against my body as I voyage across the kitchen floor. My next task is to wash the carrots and lay them out on the cutting board. Pausing to rest and catch my breath, I detect the tiniest of flaws in my game plan. Carrots are hard enough to cut with normal hands. Mine are severely inflamed, and I can't push down on the knife hard enough to slice through the carrot. How on earth am I ever going to manage this?

I lean against the counter and study the problem. This task is going to require several things: leverage, logic, and a bigger knife. Fortunately, Sofia has one that's about the size of a small machete. I return to the defiant carrot, brandishing my upgraded equipment and a sly smile on my face. Making sure that my fingers are out of harm's way, I press the machete down firmly with both hands.

"Frackin' hell!" I yell. The knife clangs against the countertop as I squeeze my hand shut, hoping to stem the flow of blood. The searing pain in my MCTD-inflamed fingers leads me to believe that perhaps I mistakenly had the sharp edge of the knife facing up. Plucking up my courage, I pry open one finger at a time to survey the damage. Miraculously, I'm unscathed.

Clearly, this calls for Plan B, which involves placing an oven mitt on the back of the knife to protect my hand. After much grunting and swearing, I lift up the oven mitt to check on my progress. Lo and behold, the machete has broken through the outer layer. I've made progress. This is fantastic! But if I'm ever going to slice completely through this adamantine carrot, I need to go to Plan C. I'm running out of ideas; my final plan just has to work.

I'm grateful, almost to the point of tears, that Sofia keeps a low stepstool in the corner of the kitchen. Once I'm standing on it, I can add the weight of my entire upper body to my efforts. At long last, there is a satisfying *snap* as the knife cuts the rest of the way through. It's also a miracle that I manage not to fall off of the stool. With renewed enthusiasm, I get to work on the rest of the carrots. When I finally finish, I complete a slow circle while raising my machete in victory. I'm feeling pretty darned proud of myself.

My tired arms struggle to lift the heaviest carrot in existence. When I finally get the damned thing into the juicer, it takes both hands on the wooden plunger and all of my strength to work it through the grinding gears. Although, once the Green Star 2000 gets a good grip on it, my teammate doesn't let me down. I'm rewarded with a stream of juice pouring out of the spout and into a large bowl. I'm spellbound by the most vibrant shade of perfect orange flowing from my juicer. It's accompanied by the sweet aroma of crushed carrot, which fills the air around me. It's hard to tear my eyes away from the bowl, but I must. The game has just gotten underway. One piece at a time, the Green Star 2000 and I keep going until the pile of carrots is gone. One vegetable is done with only twenty-three more to go. I glance at Sofia's clock on the wall. Not bad. All of that only took an hour.

My talented teammate, the Green Star 2000, and I stare at the mountain of produce. We both wonder which of our remaining opponents is going to challenge us next. As it happens, the dinosaur kale, which has been resting at the summit, makes the first move. It cackles in defiance and starts to teeter precariously, stirring several of its teammates into action. I'm horrified as the kale begins a slow-motion plummet down to the bottom of the mountain. I shuffle as fast as I can to stop the impending avalanche. Once there, I use my momentum to fling my arms around the base of the mountain, cringing at the potential for disaster. The parsley bounces off my forehead, and then lands uninjured on the counter, mocking me with its curly leaves. It's my turn to smirk when I manage to halt the careening head of romaine with my chin. The sprinting apples are the hardest to catch, but fortunately they're blocked from escaping by my forearm. My sigh of relief is premature, however, as an unruly red beet somehow manages to squirm through the gap under my armpit and roll off the edge of the bar.

"Danger, danger, Will Robinson!" I can just hear "Robot," from the TV series *Lost in Space*, waving his arms and shouting. There's nothing I can do to stop the beet from hitting my knee and then bouncing against my ankle. I grit my teeth, trying not to cry out from the pain, and remain on my feet. A part of my mind admires the combination of strikes as an efficient martial arts takedown, even if it was executed by a red beet. My legs are shaking with the effort of holding me up. After a brief struggle, they give way and my body slides to the floor. I'm forced to take an injury timeout. In a heap, I assess my situation.

It's not good. The juice is barely even started, and I've only gotten through one vegetable. What was I thinking? I'll never be able to juice all of these fruits and vegetables—it's just not possible. I see my nemesis, the rogue red beet, just a few feet away. It's laughing at me. I want to smack the smile off of its gnarly red face. Unfortunately, it is out of reach of any immediate retribution. My knee and ankle are throbbing while the cold from the floor is seeping into my bones, draining my strength and sapping my will. I feel paralyzed and unable to move. My eyelids are too heavy to remain open and slowly droop until they're closed. J.D. is there in my mind, but he's far away, and I can't hear him. I'm tired, so tired. I tell myself that I shouldn't give up so easily, but there's an exhaustion spreading within me. I feel like I'm becoming a lump of hardened glue.

I want to surrender and let myself slide into oblivion, right where I am, but something in my mind is nudging me, wanting attention. It's annoying—like being poked repeatedly with a stick. J.D. wants me to watch something. Okay, I'll see what it is, and maybe then I'll have some peace. A rugby game flashes before my mind's eye. In fact, it's my old team, the Berkeley Women's All Blues. Moving closer, I'm swept into the action. Abruptly, I'm in the middle of the field, running after the opposing team player who has the ball. Breaking away from the pack with a burst of speed, I tackle my opponent, but she's already passed the ball. Without skipping a beat, I get up and sprint to catch the receiver. I dive for another tackle, but again the ball has already been passed on. This series of missed tackles continues down the rugby pitch until my opponent crosses the goal line. My last leap lands me squarely in the middle of a mud puddle. Well, that is certainly an apt metaphor for my day. Is J.D. having a good laugh at my expense?

A hand appears out of nowhere, reaching down to grab my arm and help me up. I come face to face with the twinkling eyes and wide, conspiratorial grin of Alison, one of our best players. She's slightly shorter than I am, but fast, and an absolute bulldozer on the field. Aside from being one of the nicest people I've ever met, Alison has an indomitable spirit. With her powerful war cry, she can rally our team in a heartbeat. When Alison lets loose with her can of whoop ass, look out! My spirit is quickly buoyed up by her presence. She puts her hand on my shoulder. *Come on, Hol. They've had their turn. Now it's ours. I'm with you.* Her enthusiasm is contagious.

Thanks, Alison. I need to win this one, I pant, trying to catch my breath.

I'm right here, Hol. I've got your back. You're not alone. She glows with confidence. Alison squeezes my shoulder, and it sends a jolt of electricity running through me. The effect is instantaneous. My physical eyes snap wide open. I'm still on the floor, but my body is tingling all over.

Come on, Hol. Let's go get 'em! I hear her shout in my mind, and I'm not sure if I'm hallucinating. Maybe I am, but with Alison in the game, I'm going to finish this juice.

The first thing I decide to do is take on the red beet bully who knocked me to the ground. Extending my right leg, I manage to hook it with my foot and drag it toward me. All the while, the beet struggles to get away. Once I have it firmly in hand, however, my next challenge is to get up. I'm not surprised when it seems as if I can actually see Alison reaching out her hand to help me up. After all, has anything about this illness been mundane or ordinary? There is a connection between us; her powerful spirit is lifting me up. I'm grateful for the help. With Alison at my side, I know the juice will get made.

I make my peace with linear time; it is no longer my adversary. The juicing shifts from a game to a meditation. This process will take as long as it takes. Cutting the red beet is simply what I'm doing now. Cutting, lifting, and pushing the pieces into the juicer. Time is segmented into infinitesimal moments. I exist only within each tiny moment, and each tiny moment has a tiny, reachable goal. My reward is to see the glorious deep red liquid from the beet mixing with the fluorescent orange of the carrots. It turns into a delightful pink. The carrot and the beet have joined together to produce the healing color of pink. That's one of the colors associated with the heart chakra—very interesting. While I'm washing the leaves of kale, it squirms in my hands as if tickled. It brings a smile to my lips. One can't help but admire the deep forest green of its leaves. I'm already craving the vitality locked within that is bursting to be released.

It occurs to me that I've been wrong with regard to the produce as the opposing team. The vegetables and fruit are my friends, my co-creators of wellness. They willingly enter the juicer to share their gift of life with me. It doesn't take long for the kale to become one with the carrot and the beet. The heady aroma encourages me to breathe deeply. It seems to provide me with enough energy to move onto the next vegetable, and then the next. It's hard to tear my eyes away from the kaleidoscope of colors dancing around my bowl: the ruby red from the beets, the pumpkin orange from the carrots, the dark forest green of the kale, byzantium purple from the cabbage, and sunburst yellow from a pepper. The multicolored chard produces an iridescent waterfall that enchants me. It's a dazzling rainbow of nourishment being created before my very eyes. My body is yearning to absorb it all.

Finally, I toss the last piece of apple into the Green Star—and, at long last, my juice is done! I'm running on fumes. I need to drink it *now*. It's all I can do to fill my largest mug with the precious liquid. Not a second too soon. My legs give out. I desperately cling to my treasure with both hands while I slow my descent, using the friction of my back against the counter. Miraculously, not a single drop of the priceless stuff is spilled. Now that I'm safely on the floor, I can win the game. After another look at Sofia's clock, I'm glad that I'm sitting down. I'm shocked to see that it says 8:30p.m. Incredible. It has taken me ten hours to make my first juice.

The mug hovers under my nose. It smells absolutely divine, so fresh and full of the magic of life. Reverently, I place the mug to my lips and take the first sip. Even with parts of my mouth being numb, there is an explosion of flavor—the likes of which I've never experienced. I hesitate before swallowing. I want to allow each individual vegetable and fruit enough time to identify itself and dazzle my taste buds. Each wondrous sip is a slow, lingering walk among my friends. I take the time to greet each one before sending them fondly down my esophagus. A heavenly cascade of perfect nutrition is flowing into my body. I visualize my cells receiving and easily absorbing every last molecule of this "juice of life." I hold in my hands—the Nectar of the Gods—and it is sheer bliss.

Who knows how long I've been sitting on the floor, drinking my juice? One hour, perhaps two? I don't care. Life is stirring within my body, and it feels good. At some point, I decide to get up. I gently massage my quads in preparation. It takes me a second to realize that they aren't in flames any longer; it is more of a low simmer. I can even feel a bit of strength in them. It's wondrous. I shift them around. It's astonishing how little effort it takes to position them under me. I do believe I'll be able to stand up. Here goes nothing. I'm rendered speechless when my legs propel me upwards, albeit a bit bumpily, until I'm standing. Once I'm upright, I wait with bated breath to see if my legs will continue to hold my weight. They do!

This is a miracle. After the marathon juicing session, I expected to need a forklift. I'm giddy with excitement. My body is still craving more, and I pour myself a refill. I'm all set to continue my delicious dining experience. My legs proudly escort me over to Sofia's couch where I sink peacefully into its cozy depths. All is well. This calls for a bit of reflection. So much has happened to bring me to this moment of victory. A common thread weaves it way through everything. It's all been metaphysically inspired.

CHAPTER TEN

STIRRINGS OF CHANGE

You have to leave the city of your comfort and go into
the wilderness of your intuition. What you'll discover
will be wonderful. What you'll discover is yourself.
—Alan Alda

When I was twenty-eight, someone taking a peek at my life from the outside might think I was doing very well. I was an MIT graduate with a BS in electrical engineering and had a lucrative job as a software engineer. My career afforded me the opportunity to own a two-bedroom Craftsman style home in Berkeley, CA. My social calendar was full. I was playing rugby for the Berkeley All Blues, and we had just won the Western Territorial Championship, which meant that we qualified to play in Nationals. I was also training four days a week in Choy Lay Fut Kung Fu, which was very different from my original style of Tae Kwon Do. Recently, I had passed my black belt test—the second one I'd earned.

With a plethora of material and social abundance, I should have been happy and satisfied. But I wasn't. I felt that something wasn't right with my life. There was a distinct aching in my heart that kept growing stronger—as if a part of me was dying a little bit more every day. It didn't make sense to me. What more could I ask for? I didn't know, but I desperately needed to find out.

My favorite place to meditate indoors was cross-legged on my black leather couch in the living room. My question was burning to be answered, and so I prepared for a powerful session. As soon as I placed my hands in my lap, calmness pervaded my body. My breathing deepened automatically as I focused on the power center at my navel. In a few short minutes, I experienced a natural physical high, like the endorphin rush I used to get doing laps in the pool for an hour. Most of the time I spent in meditation was used to collect and enhance my reserves of qi. It was a technique I had learned many years earlier as part of my martial arts training.

Today was different. Instead of building and circulating energy, I was seeking a reason for the gnawing ache in my heart that refused to be ignored any longer. I cleared my thoughts and became an empty vessel. After I formed the question in my mind, I let it go and waited. My focus returned to my deep breathing. I was one with my breath, traveling with it down to my navel and then up and out of my body. After a while, an image of me formed in my mind. I saw myself running across a field, and then I leapt into the air and flew straight up into the sky. I felt a rush of adrenalin and the feeling that I could do anything. I watched myself fly over a forest fire and snuff it out using my speed to steal the oxygen away from the flames. As soon as the fire had gone out, I saw the forest turn green and watched the animals as they happily returned home. The scene changed in my mind, and I saw myself in front of a computer at a desk. I looked bored. I put my head on my desk and fell asleep. The image of me faded into blackness. Gradually, my awareness returned to my breathing and then to my body on the black leather sofa. My eyes opened slowly. The room seemed different. I was seeing things, or rather me, for the first time in a long time. My body tingled all over. I understood what was going on. I didn't have a purpose, and my passion was gone.

After I graduated from college, I had been certain I was going to help solve some major social issue. I had wanted to do something big, like develop technology to improve the health of people around the world. That certainty had given me my spark, my drive to be more. I had wanted my existence to be beneficial for the planet. In reality, I wasn't doing anything like that. What I was doing right now didn't benefit society; it was just a job. I designed firmware for computer graphics display cards. How did that solve any global issue? If I continued on my present course, I was setting myself up for a comfortable, ordinary life. I didn't want ordinary, I wanted to reach beyond my tiny circle of influence and make big ripples in the pond of my life. I needed to make some changes.

One day shortly after my revelation, I came across an ad in a New Age magazine. It was for classes in acupressure. This was interesting. It talked about manipulating points on the body to balance qi energy and promote healing. My martial arts training had already taught me how to manipulate my own qi to accomplish difficult physical feats. The thought of learning how to use it to heal stoked a little fire within. This kind of skill was something that could really help people. The ad also mentioned that acupressure was based on the theories of Traditional Chinese Medicine, or TCM, and utilized the same points as acupuncture. This also appealed to me, since I'd already had experience receiving acupuncture treatments myself. The first time was as a child at my Tae Kwon Do school, when Master Park treated my sprained ankle with needles. More recently, I received acupuncture for a knee injury I sustained while playing rugby. By the time I finished reading, my heart was vibrating with a satisfied fullness. I had no inkling then of how pivotal a decision this would turn out to be.

My first day of class fell on a warm, sunny Saturday in March. I walked briskly along Shattuck Avenue in Berkeley, wanting to be early for my first class. Finally! I had something new in my life with unknown potential. Anything could happen. I was bursting at the seams with curiosity and anticipation. Then I saw it. The Acupressure Institute was located in an older, two-story, sand-colored building with wood siding, which was set back from the busy street. As soon as I stepped through the door, I felt at home. It was as if I had been there many times before and was being greeted by the warm, welcoming energy of an old friend.

From the first day, the quality of the instruction impressed me. Each subject was taught by an instructor that glowed with passion for healing. It was contagious. While the classroom atmosphere was relaxed, there was an undercurrent of excitement for the material that was presented. Even better, we practiced the techniques we were learning on each other. Once we got started, I could feel the classroom literally sizzling with healing energy. A discovery I made in the first week of classes was worth the entire tuition I paid to attend the school. I learned that a part of me I had considered a social handicap could actually be used to great advantage in healing.

My self-revelation began in a partner treatment exercise in the Jin Shin Do class, which was the style of acupressure we studied. Our instructor, Kathy, was a petite powerhouse with brown hair that was almost as long as she was tall. She asked us to pair up and practice the acupressure point combinations we had just learned. My initial reaction was apprehension at having to work closely with a relative stranger, but it quickly faded. In this unique environment where absolutely nothing was considered strange, I allowed myself to be different. Or, perhaps, I allowed myself to be more *me*. It was okay to expose the fluffy, New Age side of myself that I hadn't truly realized I possessed. It felt kind of good and natural. Who knew?

I was standing next to one of the many treatment tables in the classroom, and it didn't take long for someone to materialize. I recognized Tina, a gangly blond, whom I had spoken to once before. "Would you like to partner up?" she asked shyly.

"Sure," I replied. "Do you mind if I'm the practitioner first?" I added quickly, wanting to dive past my performance jitters. She nodded, and I motioned for her to get on the table, facing up. Since acupressure is practiced with the patient fully clothed, there was none of the awkwardness that might occur with a typical massage session. Tina shifted around until she was comfortable, and I slid a pillow under her knees. When I was ready to begin, she closed her eyes. Standing next to the table on Tina's right side, I rested one hand gently on her right shoulder to establish an energetic connection. There was a perceptible increase in the heaviness of my hand, as if it was held in place by an unseen force. Then I slid my other hand under her low back to practice our assigned point combination. Almost immediately, I was filled with anxiety. That was weird. I wondered what happened to my calm, centered focus. The feelings were so strong that it took me a minute to realize they weren't coming from me.

It was then that I knew they must be Tina's. This was confirmed by the wrinkled frown that had appeared on her face. For a few minutes, I wondered whether to say anything, but then my curiosity got the best of me. "Tina, are you worried or upset about something?" I asked softly.

Her eyes flew open. "What? Why do you ask?" She looked startled.

I gently squeezed her shoulder for reassurance. "I didn't mean to disturb you, but I'm getting this intense, worried feeling, and I know it's not mine."

"That's freaky," she blurted, and I took my hand off her shoulder. "Sorry, I don't mean that in a bad way," she said quickly. "It's kind of amazing. You're right on. I had a huge fight with my boyfriend last night, and I'm just waiting for the guy to decide that he wants to break up with me." She lowered her voice enough that I had to lean closer to hear her.

I felt her tension blocking the flow of qi in her back. "How about you just concentrate on being here on the table? Try to imagine what it feels like for your low back to release all of its tension into the ground," I suggested.

Tina closed her eyes again, and I applied finger pressure to her low back points. Gradually and slowly, I dug deeper until I felt the congestion in her muscles release. While I was working on her, I remembered when I had helped the wounded robin. It gave me an idea I wanted to try. In my mind's eye, I imagined seeing a dark energy flowing out of Tina's body and into the ground. As I did that, her frown softened, and a small sigh escaped her lips. The anxiety I had been receiving from her dissolved until I didn't feel it at all anymore. It turned out to be perfect timing. Kathy called out for us to switch places with our partners.

"That was incredible. I'm not anxious anymore. Can you normally sense what others are feeling?" Tina asked as she got off the table.

This was the first time I recalled ever talking to anyone about sensing other people's emotions, and I hesitated. By the time I got up on the table for my turn, I had decided that if I couldn't talk about it here, there was nowhere else. I was nervous, but I sucked it up and poked my head out of the metaphysical closet.

"Yes, actually I can. Although, I think this is the first time I consciously put it to good use. Normally, I need to constantly remind myself that what I'm feeling may not be mine. Crowds are especially hard for me to deal with. It's like being in the middle of an emotional maelstrom." I stopped talking, apprehensive about her answer.

Thankfully, she appeared excited as she held acupressure points on my shoulder. "Holly, I hear you. You've had a difficult time with your gift, but just think about the ways it can help you become a better healer."

How about that? My empathic sense was something I had battled for most of my life. I'd never considered it could be a gift! I closed my eyes and let myself relax. I remembered how hard it had been for me as a kid around groups of people or at parties.

Mom always loved to throw parties. Christmas Eve was her favorite and biggest party event of the year. It was common for well over a hundred people to show up. Every year our house was packed with relatives, friends, and neighbors. Mom cooked for days to prepare the lavish banquet. Dad enjoyed his job of opening the wine cabinet and pulling out his most expensive liquor. The Christmas Eve party was full of boisterous conversations, raucous laughter, and people gorging on delicious food accompanied by lots of drinking. It was the epitome of a perfect party, but it had always been a bittersweet occasion for me.

Before every one of these parties, I usually spent hours in my room, mentally bracing myself for the onslaught. Then I headed downstairs straight into an emotional hailstorm. It felt like I was being pelted with everyone's big emotions. Fortunately, our guests had always had a good time, but even too much of a good thing had been too much. I had no way of avoiding the hailstones, but I could usually run the gauntlet long enough to greet my relatives and people that I knew. Inevitably, when I had been unable to take any more pounding, I had retreated upstairs to the solitude of my bedroom. While I hadn't discovered an off switch for my empathic sense, at least in my bedroom, the volume was down to a tolerable level. It was there that I had been able to sense and enjoy people's good spirits. My room had been my sanctuary.

The hardest part of those parties came after Mom realized I was no longer among the guests. She usually found me sitting in the farthest corner of my room, which had been the most tolerable spot for me. I always hated to let Mom down, and it was torture to try to explain why I wasn't downstairs in the middle of the party. One time she had been particularly insistent.

"Honey, what are you doing upstairs all alone in your room? Come downstairs and enjoy the party," she pleaded.

I hated seeing the disappointment in her eyes. "I'm having a good time enjoying the party from up here, Mom. It's too hard for me to be down there." I knew my response sounded silly.

"Come on, honey. I know you're shy, but it's good for you to mingle with people. There are some friends of your father's that I want you to meet. You'll like them." When I didn't move, she became more insistent, "It's really rude to hole yourself up in your room like this," With a frown, she reached out to take my hand.

Hearing words like that coming from her was a knife stroke in my heart. I struggled to my feet and went downstairs with her—back into the lion's den of emotions. As soon as I could, I snuck back upstairs.

"Hey, Holly, did you fall asleep? We need to get to our next class," Tina called.

I thanked her for my treatment and stuffed my books into my backpack. I continued thinking about having an empathic ability that was always on. As a result, in many social settings, I was painfully shy. I didn't want to be the recipient of negative emotions directed at me, such as dislike, disdain, or just plain disinterest. It was hard enough to deal with people's general feelings of random anger, frustration, or sadness. It was impossible for me to maintain a conversation with someone whose words were polite if they radiated annoyance or the need to escape. I felt vulnerable all the time. I became the stereotypical wallflower who studied the potted plant in the corner of the room.

In this place, I could be different. Tina's words had opened my mind. Being empathic was an advantage to a healer, not a liability. I made a point to tune into what each of my practice partners was feeling and then see how I could use it to enhance their healing. For the first time in my life, being empathic was actually fun.

A few weeks later, during a sunny, Saturday afternoon class, my abilities moved to the next level. We were studying acupuncture meridians, or energy pathways, and the most commonly used points for treatments. Debbie was the instructor. What struck me the most about her were her piercing green eyes and the fact that she was a walking encyclopedia of medical knowledge. When she looked at you, it felt as if she was diagnosing an obviously serious medical condition. I wasn't surprised at all when I found out she was a licensed acupuncturist with a thriving practice. That day our lecture topic was the liver meridian. Debbie was kneeling on a mat in the center of the room next to a student volunteer. While she was demonstrating various point location methods, the rest of us sat in a circle on the floor. I relaxed with my back against a wall, but I was focused on the lecture.

I became aware of an intense energy being directed at me and looked up to find the source. My gaze locked onto a woman directly across from me. She was tall, physically fit, and had short, wavy black hair and discerning brown eyes. I admired her designer T-shirt and jeans, a good style for her. I'd seen her before, but we hadn't been partners yet. She was staring directly at me, but when I looked in her direction, she quickly smiled and waved hello. I smiled back, returning her wave. A short while later, Debbie asked us to pair up and practice working on the liver meridian. I glimpsed the woman who had been staring at me; she was making a beeline straight over to me.

"Hi, my name is Tatiana. Would you like to be my partner for this exercise?" she asked, extending her hand.

"Sure. It's good to meet you. My name's Holly," I said with a smile. A tingling feeling ran up my arm when I grasped her hand, as if electrical energy was dancing all around her. Her accent was thick and sounded European. "I love your accent. Where are you from?" I asked.

"Thank you. I'm from Hamburg, Germany." Her dark eyes sparkled as she answered. "It's strange. I know we've never met, but I feel as if I know you somehow."

Tatiana had stepped closer to me than I was used to. Physical proximity made it harder for me to block the emotions from other people, and I fought the urge to step back. To my surprise, I discovered that she was right. She felt familiar to me as well, as if we were already friends. My tension melted away. We pulled a mat cushion from the pile along the side of the room and found an empty spot on the floor to practice. Tatiana positioned herself face up on the center of the mat. A comfortable silence ensued as I applied pressure to points on her liver meridian, which runs along the thigh. After a few minutes, I felt myself getting increasingly more irritated. I felt like it wasn't coming from me; it was the same thing that had happened with Tina. Just as I was about to say something to Tatiana, images sprang into my mind. It was like a movie short, and I decided to let it play out in my head.

The first scene was of a group of people jumping up and down in unison, kind of like they were line dancing. It ended abruptly, dissolving into two people gesticulating wildly at each other. And while I didn't hear anything, the expressions on their faces left no room for doubt that it was an argument. I shook my head in confusion and wondered what was going on.

Tatiana had her eyes closed, but she didn't look relaxed. I had to find out if what had happened had anything to do with her.

"Tatiana, are you okay? Are you thinking about some kind of argument?" I whispered.

"Is there something written on my face? How did you know what I was thinking?"

I described the images I had seen.

"You are so right on the money. I'm an aerobics instructor, so you saw one of my classes. The argument was one I had with my business partner right before I left Germany. It was about the gym we own together. I was replaying it in my head and getting angrier by the minute." She grinned and shook her head in wonder.

This was fascinating to me. "You know, I felt your anger first and then I saw the images." I was curious. There was something—some connection that needed to be made—but I wasn't seeing it yet.

"Amazing. Does this sort of thing happen to you often?" Tatiana asked, staring at me with fascination.

"Well, it sure seems to happen a lot in this place," I answered, shrugging my shoulders. "I've always been sensitive to emotions, but this is the first time I've been aware of something visual." All of a sudden, it hit me, and

I snapped my fingers. "This all makes sense. I was working on your liver meridian when you recalled the argument and became angry."

"How does that make sense?" Tatiana looked puzzled.

"What's the emotion associated with the liver?" I asked, tapping the meridian on her thigh.

I could almost see the light bulb flash over her head. "Of course! It's anger. This is such cool stuff," she said, breaking into a huge grin.

As we continued to explore the mind-body-spirit connection in our classes, I felt a lot like Alice in Wonderland. I was discovering an entirely new and different side of myself—and I liked it. I enjoyed all of the material I was learning. My favorite class was the one teaching us about the chakras. It was taught by an amazing woman who was aptly named Alice. She was slightly plump with shoulder-length, graying brown hair and mesmerizing dark brown eyes. My eyes followed her as she glided around the room, checking on our progress. She radiated a nurturing energy combined with an ancient wisdom. She was fascinating to me, and I couldn't get enough of her marvelous teaching.

Alice taught us several methods of detecting and balancing the chakras—the key energy vortexes located on the centerline of the body through which universal source energy flows into us. She emphasized that this would aid us in healing on all levels of being: spiritual, emotional, mental, and physical. The material felt so familiar. It was as if I was being reminded of things I already knew but somehow had forgotten along the way. Not surprisingly, I was irresistibly drawn to my next step during one of Alice's chakra classes.

We were learning how to detect imbalances in the chakras. Alice suddenly stared directly at me, and it was hard not to look away from her penetrating gaze. "Holly, would you come up here and allow me to demonstrate the technique on you?"

I lay down on her practice table, and my whole body was tingling. She held her hands over my body; wherever they moved, I felt heavy pressure—as if she were actually touching me. She moved her hands in a smooth flowing motion, pausing over each of the seven major chakras to balance it. As she worked, I felt progressively lighter. It was as if my body was being cleansed of eons of garbage. By the time Alice finished her demonstration, I was nearly floating above the table. I felt fantastic.

"All right, class. I'd like you to pair up and practice this balancing technique," she instructed.

Excited to get started, Tatiana and I quickly grabbed each other and found an empty table. She hopped up and lay face up while I held my hands, palms down, about a foot and a half above her body. Starting at head level, I concentrated on feeling the energy emanating from her chakras. I moved my hands first farther away from Tatiana's body and then lower and closer. As I did this, I was clearly able to distinguish an energy boundary. There was a warm, thickening of the air that came and went as I slowly moved my hands along her centerline. The warmer spots corresponded with the location of her chakras. Her third chakra, at her solar plexus, felt different from the others. The air was significantly cooler, and the energy felt thin. So thin, in fact, that my hands fell very close to her body before I felt anything of substance. Tatiana was watching me closely.

"Well, your third chakra is weak," I reported. "I'm going to try something. Let me know if you feel anything." I waited for her acknowledgement before closing my eyes. Then I visualized a healing yellow energy, the color for the third chakra, flowing into it. At some point, it simply felt complete.

"My chakra is warm now, and I feel energized. Thanks," she said when I opened my eyes.

I was curious to see if I could find a connection between her third chakra and a current experience. "Have you been feeling a little insecure or having a loss of confidence about anything lately?"

"Will you cut it out? It seems like I can't go through anything without you finding out about it," She started chuckling. "Yes. To answer your question, I've been feeling overwhelmed with the language barrier and how much we need to learn. I feel a step behind all the time."

"Sorry, but your third chakra is the self-confidence chakra, so I had to ask." I grinned back at her. "Anyway, it feels much stronger now. So, I hope the treatment helps."

"Nice work. I can see Tatiana's third chakra spinning normally now. It was quite contracted and barely moving a minute ago," Alice's voice came out of nowhere.

Startled, Tatiana and I turned our heads toward the sound. I hadn't noticed Alice approach our table. When our eyes met, I was suddenly held motionless and subjected to an intense scrutiny. More than anything, I wanted to measure up to her expectations. At long last, she simply smiled and nodded before she moved on to the next table. Released from my invisible bonds, I stared after her. An idea slowly formed in my mind.

At the end of class, I packed up my books as slowly as I could and waited until only Alice was left in the room. I felt intimidated about approaching her, but fortunately for me, I was able to gather my courage. Alice looked up at my approach and smiled warmly. This sent a gentle wave of calmness over me. Her energy was inviting me closer, like a lovely warm, aromatherapy bath.

"Hello, Holly. How can I help you?"

The moment felt intense, and I was tingling again. I wasn't sure I was even in my body. "Your class is fascinating, and it seems like this is just the tip of a really huge iceberg, and well ... do you teach any classes that are more in-depth than this one? I would love to learn more from you, if you do," I said in a self-conscious rush.

Alice studied me with her all-seeing gaze. Under her scrutiny, I couldn't breathe, and my body tensed. "I used to teach a private metaphysical class, but I'm no longer taking on any more students," she said finally.

My shoulders slumped, and I knew my face registered the disappointment that I felt. I started to thank her, wanting to excuse myself to run and crawl under a rock. Before I could get the words out, she said, "However, in your case, I feel strongly drawn to offer you a session of formal initiation into the world of metaphysics." She paused for effect, and it was perfect, "That is, if you are interested." She raised an eyebrow.

"Are you kidding? I'm incredibly honored. Thank you." I was excited—and didn't quite believe my good fortune.

Alice told me to come to her house the very next Saturday after classes were over. The week couldn't pass quickly enough.

CHAPTER ELEVEN
DOWN THE RABBIT HOLE

The most beautiful thing we can experience is the
mystical. It is the source of all true art and science.
–Albert Einstein

As I reached out to ring Alice's doorbell, I was so nervous that my hand was shaking. Her house reminded me of a large ski chalet. It fit perfectly that she lived in a densely wooded area of the Oakland Hills, and that it was accessible only by driving for miles along a narrow, winding road. When she opened the door, the first thing I noticed was her lovely lavender silk pantsuit. It suited her well. Then my eyes were irresistibly drawn to the three strands of amethyst crystal forming her necklace. They seemed to glow with an inner light. The longer I watched, the more her necklace seemed alive. I was certain that it was somehow tuned into her and awaiting her commands.

"Please do come in. I'm glad that you're here," she said, smiling as she gestured for me to enter. Her smooth, melodious voice created words that were imbued with a nurturing, protective quality. My tension evaporated. She moved aside to let me pass by, but I stopped short after only a few steps inside. I couldn't help gawking at what I saw.

There was a large Buddha statue in the corner of her sizeable entryway. It was almost as large as I was. Then my nose caught the scent of jasmine incense, one of my favorites. My lungs expanded automatically, filling with the divinely calming scent. My entire body relaxed. Alice stepped past me and waved for me to follow her. We walked in silence down a dimly lit hallway on the left. At the end of the hall, a flight of stairs went down into the darkness. Right about then, I had the distinct feeling that I was, indeed, about to follow Alice down the rabbit hole.

The short hallway downstairs was dimly illuminated by candles burning on a table next to a partially open door. This was our destination.

We entered a lavender room, where soothing meditation music was playing and more jasmine incense was burning. The only source of light was from additional candles placed on shelves around the room. A black table positioned against one wall was covered with crystals of every color and shape, while each corner of the room contained a towering amethyst crystal at least two feet tall. There was a treatment table in the center of the room. It all felt absolutely magical. Even the air in the room seemed to vibrate. I felt energy flowing into me and creating a sensation of physical lightness and spiritual repleteness in a way I'd never experienced before.

"This room is amazing. I feel fantastic," I said.

Alice walked to the head of the treatment table and turned to face me with an amused grin on her face. "That's because I energetically prepared this room for our session, and what you feel is clear creative source energy filling a space, without the normal barrage of emotional garbage," she explained.

"Alice, what is this session going to be like?" I was brimming with curiosity.

She motioned for me to come closer. "It's clear that you're seeking the path of your heart, your life purpose. I think you know, intuitively, that you're a healer and a teacher, but you haven't been expressing that side of yourself until recently. At the Acupressure Institute, you've been introduced to the metaphysical world and you're blossoming. Today, I'm going to teach you a few tools to help you on your journey." She patted the table for me to climb on up.

"That would be fantastic. Thank you, Alice." We hadn't even started, and already I felt more excited than a kid in a Costco-sized candy store, holding a credit card with no limit on it.

"Wonderful. Well then, first I'm going to balance your chakras and open your third eye. This will help you receive guidance from your higher self and spirit-guides more easily," she explained as I hopped up on the table. Once there, I consciously slowed my breathing. "First thing we need to do, my dear, is to ground you and bring you back down to Mother Earth." She moved to the foot of the table and held some points on my feet. I felt safe, and I trusted her completely. My body gradually became heavier until I felt solidly connected to the earthly realm. She continued to hold various acupressure points for several minutes and then balanced my chakras.

When Alice reached the head of the table, she touched my third eye, the point between my eyebrows, with one hand and the top of my head with the other. It felt as if an electric current was directed through my body, and it brought a feeling of euphoria. My eyes closed of their own accord, and the world disappeared. The only thing I was aware of was the sound of Alice's voice.

"Let's begin by meeting any of your higher spirit-guides, here for your highest good, who wish to come forth. Are you ready?" she asked softly.

"Yes." I was barely aware of myself answering.

"You are completely safe, calm, and relaxed, breathing deeply and easily." Her voice was soft and hypnotic. "You're walking along an empty street, feeling happy and enjoying the beautiful, warm, sunny day. You see a tall building in front of you. Its energy is inviting, and you feel drawn to enter. Once inside the lobby, you see an elevator. I want you to head over to it, push the call button, and describe to me what happens." Alice's voice sounded far away.

I had no trouble seeing myself push the up button. After I heard the elevator bell ding, the doors opened. "The elevator isn't empty. There's someone in there," I reported. I wasn't nervous, only curious, so I stepped inside it. I looked over at my companion, and he pressed the button for the top floor. The elevator started moving.

"Please tell me what you see," Alice gently urged.

"I see a tall man with short black hair wearing a whole lot of black leather. He's got on a black leather jacket, pants, and boots. Nice outfit, much nicer than my motorcycle gear. His is definitely tailored to form fit. And he's smiling at me." I was surprised. The man was so real that I could smell his leather outfit. "Hey, he just winked at me. He feels familiar to me, as if I've known him a long time. In fact, he seems like he's some kind of protective older brother." The more I described, the more I felt drawn in.

"I'm receiving the message that this spirit-guide definitely feels motivated to protect you. He's always by your side, ready to help you. He wants you to call on him, whenever you need support or strength to follow your heart," Alice said.

My spirit-guide nodded his head and extended his hand toward me. I reached out to take it and was surprised by the sense of power that flooded into me. "Thank you," I told him.

At my words, he bowed his head slightly and faded away until I was alone in the elevator. I heard the elevator ding, signaling my arrival at the top floor. The doors slid open to reveal the diaphanous form of a beautiful woman hovering slightly above the ground. I was transfixed by the glowing rainbow of soft light that surrounded her. I continued to describe what I was seeing to Alice as it happened.

The woman gestured for me to follow her out onto the roof and then pointed up into the night sky. My gaze followed her hand, and I was mesmerized by the vastness of it all. I instinctively felt each of those countless stars as a metaphor for a new and different possibility. My beautiful rainbow guide touched my third eye gently and smiled. I watched her as she drifted up and eventually dissolved into the night. The elevator dinged again. When the doors opened, I turned around and stepped in, and it took me back down to the lobby. What a trip!

"Take your time and ask me anything when you're ready," Alice whispered softly. Then she moved to the side of the table where I could see her.

I opened my eyes and gushed, "Wow, is an understatement! That felt real. Tell me, Alice. Do I really have a motorcycle gang member and 'Glinda, the Good Witch of the East' as my spirit-guides?"

"Guides appear differently for different people and have distinct personalities. Sometimes, it takes a little getting used to," she said with a laugh.

Alice sure wasn't kidding. The music for *The Twilight Zone* was playing in my head.

"What happened with my second guide? I felt she was trying to tell me something profound." I was very curious. Alice seemed to zone out, and I instinctively knew she was asking for information.

"She is one of your highest guides and was telling you to keep exploring your metaphysical universe. You will discover your heart's desire and follow it, and you will learn to fly."

"They don't think small, do they?" I grinned at her.

Once again, Alice's eyes took on a faraway look. After a brief moment, she refocused on me. "I'm being asked to show you a technique for doing a reading. Are you up for it?" she asked excitedly.

"I'm a sponge. Let's do it." I shifted around to make myself more comfortable.

Alice moved back to the head of the table and placed her hands the same as before, one on my third eye and one on the top of my head. "All right, begin by closing your eyes. Take deep breaths and relax." She waited until my breathing slowed. "Now, imagine a blank drawing board in the center of your mind's eye. On it will appear the answer to any question you choose to ask your guides, higher self, or source energy." Alice paused again while I did as she instructed. "Okay. I want you to tell me what you see on the drawing board when I ask you how Jennifer Woodrow is doing."

The question startled me, but an image was already forming itself on my drawing board. "There are two boulders, and one is larger than the other. They just appeared flying in from opposite directions and slammed into each other really hard. That's intense." I have a desire to draw away from the scene.

"Don't make any judgments on what you see—simply describe it to me," Alice said gently.

After a deep breath, I concentrated on neutrality. "Okay. Now, they're simply sitting on the ground but still connected. A stream of water is beginning to flow over the two rocks. It's flowing between them where they're joined together."

"Do you sense any emotions, hear anything, or instinctively know something about the water and the rocks?"

I scanned my senses. "Yes, the water is trying to soothe and heal the rocks where they crashed together. I'm getting a feeling of frustration and a deep tiredness." It was fascinating to receive such strong emotions from my visualization.

"If you chose one of those objects to represent Jennifer, which one would it be?" Alice quietly asked.

As soon as she asked the question, the water glowed brightly on the drawing board. Well, that was clear enough. "It's most definitely, the water," I answered firmly.

"Nice. Now, imagine a waterfall of rainbow light washing over your chalkboard and erasing it completely. See this rainbow light flow off of your chalkboard and into the ground, taking with it all emotions, thoughts, attachments, and judgments that may have arisen."

I did as she asked. By the time the rainbow light had all been absorbed into the ground, I felt calm, cleansed, and refreshed. Then she moved to the foot of the table and held the points on my feet. My body was rooted back to the earth. I felt complete.

"Excellent, now you can thank your guides and open your eyes when you're ready," Alice said.

When I opened my eyes, she was smiling at me. "You've just performed your first psychic reading, and you've given me some very valuable information." There was a hint of pride in her voice.

"Alice, how could watching two rocks crash together with water flowing over them be valuable information?" I was confused.

"Hang on." She grabbed a stool from the corner and sat down next to me. "Okay, that's much better."

When our eyes met again, hers were sparkling with an electric intensity. I felt some of that electricity leap into me and experienced a rush of energy from head to toe. Time seemed to stop. I was acutely aware of everything in the room: the soothing music, the flickering light, the calming aroma of incense, and even our breathing. The spell was broken when Alice leaned forward and spoke. "Now my dear, I would love to explain what just happened."

Just then, I wouldn't have been surprised in the slightest if the Cheshire Cat popped into existence above us to join the session. I gave myself a mental pinch to pay attention and focus on Alice.

"First, I asked you how Jennifer Woodrow was doing. Well, Jennifer is my sister," Alice said and smiled at my suddenly surprised expression. "I used her so I would be able to personally validate any information you received. The two rocks you saw were my sister's husband, Jack, and their son, Bobby, butting heads and getting into another clash." Alice held her hands up as fists and smacked them together. "You also saw the water, representing my sister, trying to soothe and heal the rocks." Alice dropped her hands. "That is an accurate description of my sister's biggest problem right now. Her husband and son are constantly fighting, and she's always in the middle trying to fix it. You also said she's feeling frustrated and tired, which lets me know…" Alice patted my arm, "…that I need to give her a call after our session and lend some moral support. Thank you." When she finished her explanation, she waited for it all to sink in.

"You're welcome, Alice," I replied with a crooked smile. "But I would never have been able to interpret that on my own."

"Not yet, no." She shook her head. "But even if you never went beyond your current level, your job is simply to relay any information exactly as you experience it. If the recipient is ready to receive it, they will understand the message. Sometimes the meaning will become clear in time. The best thing you can do is to leave your interpretations out of it."

I *did* follow Alice down the rabbit hole, and this *was* Wonderland. I felt as if I had been lost, wandering down a hallway of infinite doors, and Alice had just come dancing past and opened the door I was searching for all along. "Alice, I'm blown away, and so grateful. You've allowed me to glimpse an entirely new world, and I want to develop this." I could barely contain my growing excitement.

"I'm pleased that you want to learn more." Her eyes twinkled. "And I can honestly tell you, if you practice speaking with your guides when you meditate and work with your drawing board, you can receive information and guidance about anything, including your own path. I've only shown you a few tools to whet your appetite. As your imagination is limitless, so are the tools and techniques available for you to discover and develop." Her words tasted better than chocolate.

"Alice, I know you said before that you weren't accepting new students. Is there a chance you might reconsider?" She was my hero, and I wanted to be just like her when I grew up.

She hesitated for a long moment. "I'm sorry, Holly. I did ask my higher guides, but I'm not meant to fill that role for you. I'm truly honored, however, to be the one to give you a glimpse through the metaphysical 'door of possibilities.' Now, it's up to you to walk through that door. Along the way, I promise you, your next teachers will appear. Your destiny will unfold perfectly before you," she proclaimed almost forcefully. "Thank you for allowing me to play a small part in it."

I looked up at her and tried not to appear as bummed as I felt. Then I mentally willed myself to snap out of it. This experience was amazing, and I wanted to savor it. I also knew that I was only catching the merest glimpse of the profound significance of the experience. I hoped that, with time, I would understand more. I slid off the table.

"Alice, I'm overwhelmed. I can't thank you enough for this incredible gift." My voice was a bit shaky.

Both of us were teary-eyed as we exchanged a warm hug and said our good-byes. I felt different. I had seen through the looking glass. I didn't know what was to come next, but I knew I couldn't keep living the same life I had led before. I drove home, thrilled and scared at the same time, knowing that everything was about to change.

CHAPTER TWELVE
WALKABOUT

*Be patient toward all that is unsolved in your heart and
try to love the questions themselves. Do not now seek the
answers, because you would not be able to live them. Live the
questions now. Perhaps you will find them gradually, without
noticing it, and live along some distant day into the answer.*
—Rainer Maria Rilke, *Letters to a Young Poet*

I'm torn between two worlds. One is practical, lucrative, and respected.
The other is wild, magical, and on the fringe. It's January of 1994,
and it's been almost two years since my metaphysical initiation with
Alice. I'm increasingly impatient to find the path of my heart, rather
than my head. I'm not sure exactly what that translates into in terms of
a career. However, I'm convinced I'm not meant to be a programmer
for the rest of my life. I'm confused and conflicted. Sofia is my sounding
board.

I follow Sofia into her living room and sit down on the carpeted floor.
She hops onto her tan fabric sofa and pulls her legs up onto the seat. I
brace myself for impact when I see her new Doberman puppy, Cinnamon,
racing toward me. Sofia cracks up when her puppy launches into the
air, confident that "Aunty Holly" will catch her. While I'm fending off
Cinnamon's attempted kisses, I realize how much I miss having a faithful
canine companion. The last time I had a dog, I was a teenager and living
with my parents.

"So, Hol, what's up? You said you needed to talk about something
important." Sofia is the one to bring us back on topic.

I wasn't nervous before, but I am now. I need her to understand my
dilemma and not think I'm nuts. I suck it up and meet her questioning
eyes. Here goes.

"Look Sofia, you know I've been restless as a programmer. Well, I've decided I need to do something different, something more with my life," I start out tentatively.

"Oh no! Don't tell me you're going to take another foo-foo candle-making class?" Sofia exclaims, rolling her eyes.

Ouch! That hits a nerve. I put Cinnamon down on the floor and hold her away with one hand. "Sofia, cut it out. I didn't take a candle-making class. It was called acupressure, and it was amazing. It changed my life. I need you to let me get this out. Okay?" I'm annoyed before I even get started.

"Sorry, Hol. I didn't mean to jump on you. Go ahead. I'll hold my tongue." Sofia puts her hands up and backs off, looking contrite. I get off the floor and join her on the sofa, sitting cross-legged at the opposite end. Moving gives me a chance to align my thoughts.

I try again. "Look, Sofia. I know I have a good job with a good salary. It's even intellectually stimulating and challenging, but it's not enough. There's a gaping hole in my heart because I'm not happy. I'm meant for something else." That was harder to admit publicly than I thought. I have to give Sofia credit, I can see she's dying to respond. Instead she merely nods and gestures for me to keep going. "I know you think some of the things that I learned at the Acupressure Institute are foo-foo, New Age baloney. But they're not. I actually learned how to work with energy, auras, and acupressure points on the body. That kind of alternative treatment is effective in healing all sorts of issues." I'm still feeling defensive and want her to be more open minded.

She grins when Cinnamon unexpectedly jumps onto her lap. It breaks the tension. Sofia's expression softens, and I can see she's willing to be more receptive. "But I'm not sure that I want to start a practice clearing chakras and reading auras just yet. For me, energy work is really personal, and besides, I'm only a novice. I'm not ready." As soon as I say it, it rings true.

"Thank goodness!" Sofia blurts out, unable to restrain herself any longer. She immediately claps a hand over her mouth and then makes the zipped gesture across her lips. Cinnamon takes my side and nips Sofia's hand. "Ouch! All right, Cinnamon. Momma is still listening to her friend." The puppy cocks her head and sits down next to the couch. "Sorry, Hol. Please continue."

I cross my arms over my chest. I'm not sure why it's so important for me to convince Sofia of anything, but I'm determined to try. "Look, I don't know *what* I want, but right now I know what I *don't* want. I don't want to stay the same. I want to shake things up and see what happens before I wake up and it's thirty years from now." Wow! Up until now, I didn't realize just how strongly I felt.

Sofia raises her eyebrows questioningly, and I nod to signal it's her turn to speak. "I hear you. I understand what's it's like to have a job that makes good money but isn't a driving passion. I'm in one. But why don't you take more classes? Take your time to figure out what you want. Maybe you can get what you need without having to give up such a great job."

I barely register her words. All of a sudden, things seem crystal clear. "That's not good enough. If I don't do something right now to change my direction, then it will never happen." I'm talking entirely to myself now. "I've got some money saved up. I'm going to go on a walkabout and see what opportunities appear!" I proclaim. Sofia is nonplussed, but I've got a satisfied smile.

Things move rapidly once I've made my decision. First, I give notice at work. My boss surprises me by saying I can come back if I ever change my mind. That part was too easy. My parents are another story. I dread telling them what I'm about to do. I'm positive they won't understand, and the thought of having to shoulder their disappointment is a huge obstacle for me to overcome. It takes a supreme act of will to call home.

I'm relieved when Mom answers the phone. If she's on my side, I've got it made. "Hi, Mom. How's it going?" I ask nonchalantly.

"Is anything wrong, honey?" I know she detects something in my voice. She always could do that.

"Well … yes and no." Oh boy. Here I go again.

"What do you mean? What's wrong?"

I really don't want to have to explain myself, but I owe it to my parents.

"Nothing's wrong in a bad way, Mom. I've just decided to make some changes in my life. It's not a big deal. I've left my job, and I'm going to drive around the country for a few months." How lame! I roll my eyes to the heavens. That sounded ridiculous—even to me. There's dead silence on the other end of the phone. I'm quick to try to fill it. "It's really not a big deal. I just need to figure myself out. I can always go back to my old job. My boss told me so. I'll be fine." I ramble on nervously and then stop, waiting on pins and needles.

"Clearly you've already made up your mind, and clearly you've already left your perfectly good job to do this. So, I guess it's pointless for me to argue with you. I do have one request, however," she says at long last. Mom is amazing. She can always manage to surprise me.

"Okay, what?" I'm dying to hear her request.

"Why don't you end your journey at home? You can stay here and take all the time you need. Then at least, you won't be using up all your hard-earned savings while you find yourself, or whatever."

I'm relieved she can't see my mouth fall open. "You've got a deal!" I figure I'd best quit while I was way ahead.

I put my house on the market immediately so that I will be absolutely free to go wherever I want for however long I want. While I'm waiting for a buyer to appear, I make one of the best decisions of my life. I get a dog. Shika is an adorable Rottweiler who looks just like a pudgy teddy bear. She's going to be my traveling companion as I journey across the country in my Nissan Pathfinder, with no particular destination in mind.

CHAPTER THIRTEEN

HOMECOMING

*Families are the compass that guides us. They
are the inspiration to reach great heights,
and our comfort when we occasionally falter.*
–Brad Henry

"Shika, this is it girl. We're almost there!" I shouted.

Shika had been lying down in the back of my Pathfinder but got up and poked her head over my shoulder to see what the fuss was about. Our three-month, cross-country journey was about to be over. I was relieved to have a break from wandering, but I was *über* nervous about coming home. I still didn't know where my life was headed, which meant that I wasn't any closer to figuring out my next career move. It had been my hope that somewhere along my travels I'd have an epiphany that would illuminate my hidden destiny. Unfortunately, no light bulbs had appeared above my head. I wound up coming back to my childhood home. It was a step that felt tantamount to failure at life. What was it going to be like to live with my parents again? My musings came to an abrupt halt as we rounded a curve, and my old house came into view.

When I saw the large, well-tended yard and the circular flowerbed bursting with Mom's signature petunias at the end of our driveway, all was right with the world. I loved this home. It had always been heaven on earth. I pulled into the tree-lined driveway and parked behind Mom's faded light green Cadillac. I couldn't help but smile when I saw it. She'd had that beat-up beast for at least twenty years, but she loved it. She had always said she felt safe in it because it was a car that was still made with real metal in the frame, and not plastic.

At the far right edge of the driveway and almost on the grass was Dad's red Bronco pickup truck. He rarely drove it, except in winter; it was his winter toy. The Bronco had a snowplow on the front, and Dad loved nothing better than to drive around after a big winter storm and rescue people that were snowed in. He had never asked for money; he just liked to help people. I had had a blast riding around with him as his helper. Sometimes, he had even let me run the controls for the plow.

Shika nudged my shoulder with her nose and licked my cheek. "All right, girl. I get the idea. Let's go." I laughed, ruffling the fur on her neck. I got out of the car and took a deep breath. The air was hot and humid but filled with the smell of freshly mown lawn mixed with a hint of honeysuckle. Heavenly! I looked around at the large yard dotted with oak, maple, and dogwood trees and fondly acknowledged some of my favorite childhood tree friends. It was good to see the forest that surrounded our yard was still thick and lush with undergrowth. A large part of my youth was spent running barefoot through those woods.

My shoulders relaxed, and a sigh of contentment escaped my lips. It was good to be home; it had always been the place where I felt the most love and magic in my life. I smiled after Shika as she raced off into the woods to explore her new surroundings. I turned back toward my parents' stately, split-level home and admired the handsome facade. The lower half was stone, while the upper half was wood siding. The feature I loved best, however, was the three-foot-high stone flowerbed, which ran halfway along the front of the house. I was happy to see Mom had it filled to overflowing with more of her petunias. She had planted flowers all around the house, but this flowerbed was her masterpiece. It was like having Christmas lights on in the summer. Suddenly, I wanted to see her more than anything.

I ran around to the back door knowing it would be unlocked. Mom's favorite place to be was the kitchen. That's where I went first. She stood up when I charged up the stairs into the kitchen, all five feet of her, and gave me the best hug I'd had in years. It felt so good to hold her. I noticed she was wearing her usual floral print cotton top and loose blue fabric pants. Her hair was the same shoulder length curly brown style that she'd had for as long as I could remember.

When we separated, there were tears in her eyes. "It's wonderful to see you, honey. I'm glad you're here," she said.

I stepped closer and hugged her again. "Thanks, Mom. It's good to be home." I sighed in contentment. Held tightly in her arms; all was right in the world. If there was anything that could top one of her special hugs, I sure couldn't think of it.

It took me a good hour to unpack my car and haul my belongings into my old bedroom. Mom hadn't changed a thing. That fact pleased me more than I thought it would. The walls were still powder blue, and my white wooden dresser looked completely untouched. Things were exactly as I had left them: from the colorful music box that Dad had given me one Christmas to an old issue of *Kung Fu* magazine on top of it. When I opened the dresser drawer, all of my old T-shirts and jeans stared back at me. It was all there. I felt so loved that Mom wanted to keep my things as I had left them. I walked around my four-poster, queen-size canopy bed and scanned my bookshelves. Awesome! My entire collection of *Star Trek* and other sci-fi novels was completely intact. It looked like I'd have a chance to reread some of my favorites while I was home.

After poking around my room, I started to unpack. When I opened up my suitcase and grabbed a pile of clothes, a book slid out of my bundle and onto the floor. As I scooped it up, I glanced at the title—*The Lightworker's Way*. At first it didn't ring a bell, but then I remembered why I had it. Tina, one of my acupressure classmates, had raved about it and said that I absolutely must read it. She had told me it was about a woman who learned to develop her spiritual skills to help others, and I would definitely relate to her. Just before I left California, I had picked it up at a metaphysical book store, but I hadn't had a chance to get to it. Now that I was home, maybe, I could finally read it. I put it on top of my dresser and continued unpacking.

After I arranged my things, I went downstairs and plopped down on the bottom step between the kitchen and the living room. It was the widest step on the stairway, and I used to spend a lot of time thinking there when I was a kid. It was perfect. You had a clear view into the kitchen and the entire living room. From there, I could chat with Mom, who was inevitably in the kitchen, or stare out through the bay window in the living room and watch the birds and the squirrels playing in our yard. Shika lay down at my feet, content to be wherever I was. I took a deep breath and filled my lungs with the heavenly aroma of Mom's cooking. Today, it was her famous pot roast, one of my all-time favorite meals.

She sat at the kitchen table, busily poring over the accounting ledger she used for her and Dad's taxi business. Despite all the good nostalgia associated with coming home, I was nervous. How could I explain myself to her? She and Dad had worked hard to help put me through MIT, and here I was apparently throwing away my expensive education and lucrative career. I couldn't bear the thought of them being disappointed in me. Mom stopped working and glanced over at me on the bottom step. "Did you find enough space to put things away in your room?"

I let out my breath in a rush. I hadn't realized I'd been holding it. I appreciated Mom finding a benign way to cut through my anxiety. "Yes, I did. Thanks."

Her "work chair" had wheels, and she swiveled it around to face me. I saw only love and concern in her eyes. "It's nice to have you here, honey. I've missed you a lot. I know you're trying to figure things out. But I'm not sure I understand why you quit your job. I thought you were doing so well. It came as big shock to your father and me. Was it really necessary?"

I had asked myself the same question often while driving aimlessly across the country. What I came to realize was that it had been necessary. Only something drastic could have given me the contrast I needed to gain perspective. I tried to tell her how I felt. "Simply taking time off wouldn't have changed anything for me. I needed to do something bigger than that. I'm not sure what's going on with me. But I do know I need to be doing something different, something more with my life."

"What do you mean more? You were always so busy," she said, looking confused.

I shook my head. She wasn't getting it. I reached down to pet Shika. She stared back at me with adoring eyes—eyes that were telling me to speak from my heart. I gathered myself as I stroked Shika's back; she gave me strength.

Mom was watching me, patiently waiting for me to continue. "That's not it. Programming is mentally stimulating, and I put in long hours, but it's not my passion. It's like there's an empty hole in my heart. I'm not doing what I'm meant to be doing, and it's not okay anymore. I feel driven."

She looked slightly surprised but didn't say anything. Instead, she got up from her chair and went to the stove to check on her pot roast. It was part of her normal routine in the kitchen, so I knew I still had her full attention. But it was hard to sit there without a clue as to how she was taking my words. I shifted anxiously off the step and onto the carpet next to Shika. If Mom didn't react well to what I was saying, Dad was going to be a nightmare. She turned around after she finished turning the meat. "How do you mean driven? Driven to do what?"

At least she hadn't thrown a fit. I decided to spill the foo-foo beans. "I feel driven to make a difference; I want my life to mean something. I want to help people change their lives for the better. I just haven't figured out what that means for me yet," I said and held my breath.

82

She quietly took it in and leaned back against the counter. Her expression was carefully neutral and hard to read. I felt my anxiety meter climb a bit.

"Am I sounding crazy to you?" I asked abruptly.

She remained silent while she pulled two glasses from the cupboard and poured us both a glass of her homemade spearmint iced tea. It was my favorite drink. I smiled when she handed me one.

"Thanks, Mom. I've really missed your tea. It's the best anywhere."

"You're welcome, honey," she replied warmly and set her glass on the kitchen table before sitting back down in her chair. Her smile had shifted into a more serious look. It was unlike her to be so agonizingly slow with a response. I didn't know if I was about to get a huge lecture—or what—and the suspense was hard to take. "No, you're not crazy, far from it. In fact, you remind me of me." She grinned conspiratorially at me.

It took me by surprise. If I wasn't already sitting on the floor, I would have fallen down with shock. I set my glass down, afraid I might drop it. This wasn't at all what I expected. "Really? How?" I asked, my curiosity piqued.

"Well … when I was sixteen, I knew what I wanted for myself, and I went after it. I didn't let anything stop me," she replied matter-of-factly, but her eyes sparkled with self-amusement.

"What was it?" I asked, leaning back and resting my elbows on the bottom step. This sounded like it was going to be a good story.

Her eyes took on a faraway look. "I knew I wanted to marry your father. We went to the same high school, and not only was he a nice guy, but at sixteen he was already managing his father's taxi company. He even had plans to buy it." Mom closed the accounting ledger on the kitchen table and then looked up at me. "More than anything, I wanted to be married to a kind, hard-working man like that. Even more than that, I wanted to have children." Her voice was full of yearning. I'd never heard her talk about pursuing Dad before. I'd assumed it was the other way around. She sipped some tea and continued her story. "I chased your father and my dream, never losing sight of what I wanted. We fell in love and married when we were just nineteen. And can you believe it, by then he had already bought the taxi company from his father," she said proudly.

"Wow, Mom. Way to go!"

She lost her faraway look. "That was only half of my dream. After that, we tried to have children. I had a lot of difficulty and many miscarriages. It was a miracle that after eight long years we were finally blessed with you

83

by adoption, and in the very same year your brother was born by caesarian section." She leaned toward me, deliberately seeking my gaze. "I did chase my rainbow, and I couldn't be happier. You, your brother, and your father are my pot of gold. So, whatever you decide your passion is, go for it. I may not understand what you're seeking, but I will always love you and support you in whatever you do."

I had been so worried about the possibility of her rejection. A huge weight lifted from my shoulders. It didn't matter what I did with my life because she would always love me. I felt that the sky truly was the limit. I got up and wrapped my arms around her. She smelled of gardenias; it was her favorite perfume. I breathed deeply to drink it in. It was divine, and it was Mom. "Thanks, Mom. I love you."

She gave me an extra squeeze. "I love you too. Don't worry, honey. I have no doubt that you'll find your way, and you can stay here for as long as you need to."

Dad didn't come home until dinnertime. I was sure Mom had probably called him and told him to go easy on me because the lecture I expected never materialized. Dad looked good. He had lost a bit of his potbelly, which made me feel better about his health. Baldness ran in his family, but Dad still had a full head of hair, although gray was now his predominant color.

Mom and I were sitting at the kitchen table when Dad walked in. He made a beeline for me and gave me a huge hug.

"It's great to have you home, honey," he said.

"Thanks, Dad," I replied with a contented sigh.

When we separated and he opened his mouth to speak, I braced myself for the inevitable lecture. "So, tomorrow I was wondering if you might want to help me out with some chores. I've got a load of firewood for the coming winter that I'd like to have split, and the lawn could sure use some mowing," he suggested casually.

Awesome! I let out a sigh of relief. Chores, not words, were how Dad and I connected. He was reaching out to me, letting me know everything was okay. When I glanced at Mom, sitting behind Dad, she winked and flashed another conspiratorial grin. "I'd love to, Dad," I said happily.

As the weeks passed, I gradually established a daily routine. After breakfast, I'd head into the woods behind my house and then across the huge field to my favorite old oak tree. It was the very same tree that the robin had been perched on when Bradley the bully hit him with a stone from his slingshot. Sitting under that huge old oak was therapeutic. I felt watched over and protected while I meditated.

Once I cleared my thoughts, I would imagine a blank slate in my mind and ask for help finding my way. Nothing had appeared yet, but I was calmer and more centered with myself. I let go of the need to know, right then, what I was supposed to do. I had a strong sense, a knowing, that something would appear sooner or later. My morning meditations were followed by doing whatever chores Dad had lined up. I loved it. Working outside, chopping wood, mowing the lawn, or tending the garden was my idea of a well spent and satisfying day. After dinner with Mom and Dad, I usually headed over to my former Shotokan Karate studio for an intense physical workout. I lost track of the passage of time until one day, a direction presented itself in a very unlikely way.

Dad had just come home for a quick dinner before heading back to his taxicab company. My parents owned the Lansdale Yellow Cab Company. While Mom was the bookkeeper, Dad managed the drivers and kept the cars running. They were always working. Most mornings, Dad got up at 4:30. Aside from rushed meals at home, he often didn't get back until ten or eleven at night. Dad had worked hard his entire life and didn't know any other way to exist.

When he walked into the kitchen, I was reading the paper at the table. I had been hanging out with Mom while she made her famous homemade vegetable beef soup from scratch. It smelled heavenly. I was glad that Dad was here since my stomach was rumbling and my mouth was already watering. I got up from my chair when he came over to give me a hug.

"Hi, honey," he said, squeezing me hard. Dad was wearing his usual dark blue cotton work shirt and heavily worn denim jeans. His pants had fresh oil stains on them, and I knew he had probably been lending his mechanic a hand fixing one of his taxis. When I hugged him back, his clothes smelled of smoke, oil, and gasoline. Not smells I enjoyed, but they were Dad's signature and always served to remind me of how hard he worked every day.

"Hi, Dad," I replied, giving him an extra squeeze. I hoped he would understand how much I appreciated him. Dad looked pleased and then walked over to the stove. Mom was stirring her soup as she added a pinch of spices to it. She turned her head toward him so he could give her a kiss on the cheek. Then he leaned closer and took a big prolonged sniff of her soup.

"Hi, Shirl. That smells great. I'm starved," he said while trying to steal a spoonful.

"Cut that out, Jimmy. Go wash your hands and then sit down. It's ready now." She shooed him over to the kitchen table, pretending to be irritated. Dad and I sat down while Mom set the food on the table. I could hardly wait to taste it. I'd smelled the soup cooking all day long.

Dad dove into his bowl. He swallowed big mouthfuls while talking excitedly to Mom at the same time. "Shirl, that's the second time that Joe missed his shift this month, without a phone call or anything. I just can't depend on the guy to show up. He's a good driver when he's there, but I need him to be there."

I tuned out of the conversation to continue thinking about my career possibilities. Dad was chewing rapidly and preparing to continue his tirade about the unreliable help. All of a sudden, he stopped talking and his eyes opened really wide. He grabbed at his throat but couldn't speak.

Mom was seated closest to him and jumped up, knocking her chair over in a panic. "Jimmy! He's choking!" she yelled. She tried to get her arms around him, but Dad's stomach was too large. She couldn't lock her hands together. He struggled hard and broke Mom's grip. All of this happened in just a few seconds, but during that time, a switch flipped inside of me.

"I've got it, Mom," I said firmly. My mind was absolutely clear, and I felt an extraordinary sense of calm. I pulled her away from Dad and took her place. Time slowed to a crawl. As I wrapped my arms around Dad's midsection, he seemed to hover motionless. Clasping my hands firmly together, just under his sternum, I executed several quick, hard thrusts. Mom kept shouting for me to save Dad, giving in completely to her fear. Fortunately, my focus remained on the task at hand. I was devoid of all emotion and stray thoughts.

Dad was thrashing around a lot, but I was extremely strong from my martial arts training and weightlifting. Nothing was going to break my grip—not until Dad could breathe. Finally, his throat cleared enough for him to take a partial breath. I gave him one more thrust, which fully dislodged the beef he was choking on. I led Dad over to the sink and rubbed his back while he spit out the beef and took deep breaths. Then I turned back to Mom.

"Mom, it's okay. Dad's okay; he's breathing. He's going to be fine," I said. Tears were flowing down her face, but I could see that she heard me.

"Haven't I been telling you to slow down when you eat, Jimmy? You eat way too fast. Are you going to listen to me now?"

When Mom scolded Dad, I knew she was going to be all right. She was still crying as she came over to me and gave me a hug so hard it hurt. "I don't know what I would have done. It was a miracle you were here." I'd never seen her panicked before; it was a huge first. I felt her fear radiating out in all directions.

I patted her arm. "It's your turn to breathe, Mom. Everything's okay," I said.

She let out a sigh of relief and sank into a kitchen chair in a mild state of shock. Dad was breathing normally now, and I led him back over to his kitchen chair. "You're doing good, Dad. Just relax and take nice slow breaths." I continued to gently rub his back while sending calming energy into him.

Nobody said anything for a long while. We all just sat at the kitchen table, recovering in shocked silence.

Suddenly, Mom looked at me and smiled. "I had a thought for you, honey. Remember when you were first deciding on colleges and were thinking about going to medical school? Why not consider some aspect of the health care profession? Now there's a wide open career path for you to explore. In fact, you could get started by volunteering with a local ambulance crew. They're all volunteers, and you get to take classes in emergency medicine for free."

By this time, Dad was fully recovered and jumped in right after Mom finished. "Seeing as how you just saved your dear old Dad's life, I think your mother has a fantastic idea. You certainly have a cool head on your shoulders, honey," he gushed proudly.

In my mind's eye, I could see a door opening wide. "That *is* a great idea," I replied, noticing that my body was tingling all over. "I'll see about volunteering tomorrow."

And so began a new adventure.

CHAPTER FOURTEEN
FIRST RESPONDER

I am only one, but I am one. I cannot do everything,
but I can do something. And I will not let what
I cannot do interfere with what I can do.
–Edward Everett Hale

The Sellersville Volunteer Ambulance Corporation was granted the use of a large brick building on the ample grounds of the Grand View Hospital Complex. The operation was well funded by individuals and local businesses. This enabled them to purchase four large, state-of-the-art ambulances, which were stocked to the brim with medical supplies. Everything was kept in immaculate condition: the building; the equipment; and of course, the ambulances. I was impressed. Gail—the friendly administrative staff member who gave me a tour—was excited that I wanted to volunteer and signed me up immediately.

My timing was perfect; two classes were set to begin on the upcoming weekend. I enrolled in both. They were "First Responder," an advanced first aid class, and "Vehicle Rescue." Before I left, Gail provided me with the standard uniform. It was the bomb. I felt extremely official in my multi-pocketed blue jumpsuit and the accompanying jacket with Sellersville Ambulance patches on the sleeves. The weekend couldn't arrive fast enough.

First Responder was an extremely well taught, no-nonsense class, but Vehicle Rescue was pure unadulterated fun. I was quickly caught up in the fever of power tool mania. Our job was to tear apart cars with all manner of machinery—powered or otherwise. The very first day, I learned how to stabilize an overturned vehicle and punch a hole in the door with a screwdriver to get inside. On another day, I sawed an entire car in half with the "Jaws of Life." I was the only woman in the class and shocked the hell out of most of my macho male classmates. I could hoist up my

88

"Jaws" and rip up practice cars with the best of them. It didn't take me long to get inducted as an honorary member of the "Boys with Hydraulic Toys" club.

As the freshest newbie at the station, I was assigned to the graveyard shift from ten until six. I didn't mind. I was part of a four-person team and was eager to learn. Janet and Dan were both EMTs, while the crew leader, David, was a paramedic. Dan, the designated ambulance driver, was the quiet, nerdy type and would typically be found in the crew lounge with his head buried in a medical manual. David was a big guy with a beer belly and a perpetual scowl on his face. I quickly learned to avoid him as much as possible. Janet, on the other hand, was a delight to be around. She topped out at a hair under six feet but didn't have an ounce of extra weight anywhere—and she smiled as much as David frowned. I was delighted when she took it upon herself to bring me up to speed on all the equipment and procedures. She had a habit of cracking hilarious one-liners at every opportunity. We hit it off right away.

One thing that I learned early on about being on an ambulance crew was that it involved a *lot* of waiting around interspersed with bursts of frenetic activity when a call came in. The first several incidents that our crew responded to weren't life threatening. These minor injuries were good opportunities to gain more first aid knowledge while I learned how to benefit the team. Dan and Janet worked together like a well-oiled machine, efficiency in motion. I studied their every move and quickly began to anticipate their needs. This earned me coveted nods of appreciation, and I started to feel a sense of belonging.

David, on the other hand, irritated the hell out of me. His imperious behavior was hard to stomach. On our emergency runs, he usually stood off to the side, commanding the rest of us as if we were his indentured servants. At the station, I kept my eyes peeled while walking down hallways. If I saw him turn a corner, I would duck into the nearest empty room to avoid the inevitably unpleasant encounter. I fervently wished he would undergo a personality makeover.

During our down time, there was always some kind of prep work that could be done. I was intrigued to discover that I enjoyed restocking and organizing supplies as well as cleaning and polishing the equipment. It was satisfying to see my reflection in the chrome trim of the ambulances after a good polishing. Several times, David caught me unawares in the ambulance bay while I was hard at work.

"What do you think you're doing?" David shouted at my back.

I had been shining the underside of the chrome bumper and jumped up from being on my knees. I was so startled I dropped the polish, and it spilled on the ground. David's expression was one of mad glee. Now he really had something to berate me for. "What a klutz! Obviously you can't be left alone to clean an ambulance!"

I glared back at him as he towered over me. I found something new about him to dislike every time I looked. Today, it was that his crooked teeth were too small for his mouth. Concentrating on his faults enabled me to bite off the retort that was dying to fly from my lips. No good would come from a scene. I had just found out from Janet that David was the son of the chairman of the board of directors—and that was why he could get away with anything. I was seething but held it together and knelt down to pick up the fallen polish. "Don't forget to clean up your mess. It's a hazard," David launched his parting shot at my back.

I twisted the rag in my hands and tried to calm down. It helped when I imagined shoving the rag into his mouth and duct-taping it shut. After I finished cleaning up my mess, I found Janet alone watching TV in the crew lounge. She saw the furious look on my face and asked what happened. It was like popping the cork on a champagne bottle. I paced around, waving my hands in the air and venting my frustrations.

"You're right. David is an arrogant ass," Janet said. That helped lower my temperature enough to join her on the couch. "Unfortunately, he's likely here to stay. I do my best to ignore his histrionics and focus on helping people with Dan and now you." She winked at me and picked up her coffee mug to take a sip. I felt my anger diffusing even more and leaned back on the couch.

"Thanks, Janet. Helping others is why I'm here, but if you weren't on my crew, I'd be gone," I confessed.

Janet set her cup down and faced me. "Just remember that Dan and I appreciate your contributions. You've got a level head on your shoulders, and I hope you stay."

It was what I needed to hear. I did enjoy everything that I was doing— all of it—except working with David. I decided to stick it out a while longer to see what happened. As it turned out, I didn't have to wait long.

One evening, Janet and I were hanging out in the crew lounge. We were passing the time by having her quiz me on emergency procedures for different scenarios. Suddenly, a call came in. It was for an elderly woman, described by the dispatcher as being short of breath. We dropped everything and leapt into action. When I hopped into the back of the ambulance with Janet, I had the immediate sense that something was different this time. Something was wrong. My heart felt constricted, and I was uncharacteristically anxious. Oddly, I just knew that I would encounter my first real test on this call.

It was a wild five-minute ride across town. Our lights blazed a trail through the darkness as we raced to the rescue. We screeched to a halt in front of a small, single-story brick home with a well-kept front yard. David met me at the back of the ambulance just as I opened the door to hand him his emergency kit. He paused, staring intently at me as if sizing me up.

"Holly, come inside while I perform an assessment. Janet, you and Dan wait here. If I need anything, I'll send Holly out to get you," he ordered gruffly. Janet and I exchanged shocked looks, but I was excited for the opportunity. I quickly jumped down to follow David up the long sidewalk to the front steps. The front door opened just as he was reaching for the doorbell. I glimpsed a thin and balding elderly man, probably in his seventies. His brow was wrinkled with concern, and there was fear in his eyes.

"Thank goodness you're here! I'm Don Tenney, the one who called. It's my wife, Sarah. She's over there in the living room. Please help her. She's having a really hard time breathing." His voice sounded on the verge of panic, and my heart went out to the distraught man. I put my hand on his shoulder as David swept by him, almost bowling him over on his way into the living room.

"We're here to help, Mr. Tenney. Try to relax, and we'll see that your wife gets the care she needs," I said to divert his attention and comfort him as David prepared to assess his wife.

"Thank you. Thank you. I know you will. I'm just so worried." Mr. Tenney patted my hand nervously.

In the living room, David was pulling his stethoscope out of the emergency kit. Sarah was a frail woman with a head of completely white, disheveled hair. She was hunched forward on the edge of a dark brown sofa, gasping for air. I could feel the fear, rolling off of her body in intense waves, as she worked hard for every molecule of oxygen. My own lungs felt like they were struggling to take in air, and I willed David to move faster. Couldn't he see how much this woman was suffering? He sat down beside Sarah and listened to her chest with his stethoscope. Then after what seemed an eternity and without a word of comfort to Sarah, he stood up and looked at me.

"Well, there's a little congestion in her lungs, so I think we'll take her in, but she'll be fine." His voice was devoid of sympathy.

Sarah looked up, with terror written all over her face. "Please. Can you give me something to help me breathe? I … can't get enough … air."

"There's oxygen in the ambulance, so as soon as you walk out there you'll get some." David's response was short and abrupt, and I wanted to slap him. Sarah was in a panic and reached out for her husband. He took her hand and tried to help her up. She almost collapsed, but somehow she managed to stay upright. The sounds of her tortured breathing were heart-wrenching. She took a few steps toward the door and then stopped short, hanging onto her husband for support.

"I don't think … I can walk. I can't breathe." She struggled to speak, and her lungs were heaving.

David had grabbed his medical kit and brushed past them on his way toward the door. "It can't be that hard. I'm sure you can walk a few more steps to the ambulance." His words were contemptuous. I was so stunned by his outrageous behavior that I couldn't react for a few seconds. He had completely transformed from Dr. Jekyll into Mr. Hyde. When I heard Sarah gasp again, I had had enough. I quickly stepped in front of her and her husband and put my hand up to stop them.

"Don't worry, ma'am. You stay right here. I'll run out and get the gurney," I said firmly.

Sarah and her husband looked at me with intense gratitude on their faces. But David grabbed my arm.

"*I'm* the team leader, and *I* say we don't need one. She's making a big deal out of nothing," he spat out at me.

I jerked my arm free. It was all I could do not to strike him. "You're wrong, and I won't add to this woman's suffering," I hissed. My tone was filled with deadly venom. David was momentarily taken aback, which gave me the opportunity to run past him and out the front door.

I sprinted to the ambulance. "Janet, we need the gurney and fast. David is a brute, trying to make that poor woman walk when she can't breathe!" I called out to her as I tore open the back door of the ambulance. I could have wept with gratitude when she saw my face and didn't argue. Instead, she kicked it into high gear. In less than a minute, we were rushing back to the house with the gurney. In the meantime, Mr. Hyde had stayed behind trying to cajole the distressed woman to walk further. It was a nightmare.

As Janet and I bounded up the steps with the gurney, I threw poison-tipped daggers of anger at David with my eyes—a look that would have stopped a charging lion dead in its tracks. It was sufficient to cause David to spin on his heels and stalk back to the ambulance. I heaved a sigh of relief.

Janet and I worked quickly to wheel Sarah out to the ambulance and get her set up on oxygen. There was a look of pure hatred on David's face as he slammed the ambulance door shut on us. I was relieved when he chose to simply get in the front seat without saying a word. I was seething, but I forced myself to focus on Sarah. I knelt beside the gurney and held her hand. Her panicked eyes locked onto mine. She was desperately afraid.

"You're going to be okay," I said. "We'll get you to the hospital in just a few minutes. You're going to be fine." I concentrated on sending calming energy into her as we roared down the road to the hospital with lights flashing and sirens blaring.

After we arrived and Sarah was admitted to the emergency room, David charged toward me like a wild beast. "You are the lowest member of this crew. You have no say and no authority. You will never disobey me like that again—do you hear me? Better yet, you're off my crew. I don't want you on it!" He screamed at me like a banshee. His face was beet red with fury.

I didn't back down a single inch. "That woman was suffering, gasping for air, and you made her walk. Are you completely insane?" I struggled to keep my clenched fists down at my sides.

"Don't you know that old woman was pulling a fast one? Old people like that just want the attention, the ride in the ambulance. It's thrilling and gives them something to do," David ranted like a lunatic.

My mouth fell to the floor in shock. I knew we were attracting attention. Out of the corner of my eyes, I saw people stopping to stare at us. "You are a brute, devoid of compassion. You're a paramedic and your job description is to help people, not torture them," I shouted, not caring who heard.

Just then we were approached by the emergency room physician assigned to Sarah. He had an annoyed look on his face. "Keep your voices down. This is inappropriate here." His voice held irritation as he scolded both of us. Then he swung his head toward David, and his eyes were flashing. "Your patient was suffering from congestive heart failure, and her lungs were almost completely filled with fluid." He kept his voice low, but his tone was steel. That shut David up. The doctor stepped forward and locked his fierce blue eyes onto David's. "She described how you treated her, and your actions needlessly exacerbated her condition. I'm going to write a formal letter of reprimand to the Ambulance Corp."

I crossed my arms and kept quiet, thoroughly enjoying David's well-deserved comeuppance. He sputtered and started to speak. The doctor tapped the file he was holding against David's chest. "I don't ever want to hear about a repeat of today—or I will make damn sure you won't even be able to change bedpans at any hospital, let alone be a paramedic."

The doctor's pager went off. He gave it a quick glance before shooting David one final look of reproach and then hurried off. It was immensely satisfying to see David's face turn a lovely shade of fuchsia. Without another word to me, he stormed out of the hospital. I was absorbed in watching him go and didn't notice that Janet had appeared at my side. She put a comforting hand on my arm.

"I'm proud of how you stood up to David. That wasn't an easy thing to do. He put that woman's life in jeopardy."

"Thanks, Janet. At last he got some payback," I replied with satisfaction.

"I've realized I was wrong for not reporting his behavior before something like this happened." Janet dropped her hand and looked down at the floor. "I'm just as responsible."

"Don't be too hard on yourself. I'm sure you would have done the same thing if you had been in the house with him while he was torturing that poor woman," I said to console her.

"I'd like to think so." Janet looked grateful, and I gave her a hug. "What's that for?" she asked.

"It's a thank you for all that I've learned from you, and it's a good-bye. I'm not coming back," I told her.

She hugged me hard. We left the hospital together, and then I headed home.

Although David had just been deflated by several notches, I knew he wasn't gone. He had kicked me off his crew. If I wanted to stay on the team, I'd have to fight him. Then I'd have to watch my back constantly because he certainly would be looking to exploit every opportunity to make my life miserable and discredit my work. And that wasn't all, I'd have to watch him like a hawk to make sure he didn't abuse any other patients or cause them serious harm. Besides, with Daddy on the board of directors, my protests weren't going to count for much. However I looked at it, trying to stay on the crew promised to be a monumental battle. It was one I didn't have the inclination or the time to wage. I would have to trust that Janet and Dan would be able to watchdog their sociopathic ambulance leader. It was time for me to move on.

CHAPTER FIFTEEN
A DAY IN THE ER

I expect to pass through life but once. If therefore, there
be any kindness I can show, or any good thing I can
do to any fellow being, let me do it now, and not defer
or neglect it, as I shall not pass this way again.
–William Penn

After I burned my bridges with David and the ambulance crew, I felt
like I was back at square one and needed to work off some steam.
Fortunately, I knew just the place—my old Shotokan karate studio. It
was there that I reconnected with Lauren, a dear old friend and fellow
classmate. After I brought her up to speed on my career search, she spun
through her rolodex of contacts, found someone I might be interested in
meeting, and arranged a dinner meeting.

Tori, a casual acquaintance of hers, just happened to be a physician's
assistant. I found it quite serendipitous that she worked in an emergency
room. We all met up at a local restaurant where Lauren introduced me to
an elegant woman with short brown hair that framed her angular face in a
pleasing manner. While we chatted at dinner, Tori was more than happy to
talk about her work, radiating self-confidence and pride about being able to
help people. As she regaled us with stories of her emergency room adventures,
I sat mesmerized, content to listen and observe, until Lauren prompted me to
tell Tori a bit of my own story and the search for my next career path.

"It really sounds like you should check out what it's like to be a PA. I
love it." Tori's eyes sparkled with enthusiasm. "It brings you higher status
than a nurse, and I'm trained to perform many procedures that used to be
solely the realm of the physician," she said proudly. "I work in the ER at
Thomas Jefferson Hospital in downtown Philly. If you're interested, I'm
pretty sure that I can get permission from my supervisor to let you tag
along on one of my shifts."

95

"Are you kidding? Thanks—that's an amazing thing for you to do for me," I replied gratefully.

"Hey, no problem, really." Tori shrugged her shoulders. "When I was looking for a career, someone helped me out. It feels good to be able to return the favor," she explained, looking a bit embarrassed.

True to her word, Tori called me back a few days later with good news. Her supervisor had granted permission for me to follow her on rounds the following week. I thanked her profusely, not quite believing my good fortune.

On the day of my shift, I made sure I arrived promptly at the ER. When I gave my name to the emergency room receptionist, she led me back into the treatment room area without a hitch. The harried nurse paged Tori for me and dashed back to her desk to continue admitting patients. While I was waiting, I took a minute to scan my surroundings and acclimate to the sensory overload: the brightness of the fluorescent lighting, the harsh antiseptic smell mixed with subtle undertones of blood and sweat, the restless sea of sounds, and the hurried movement. I closed my eyes and listened. There was a discordant symphony playing all around me. It was made up of beeping monitors, moaning patients, talking nurses, and sliding doors opening and closing. It was all accented by the occasional ding of the elevators.

When I opened my eyes, I saw Tori come through the sliding doors and stride toward me. There was a welcoming smile on her elegant face.

"I'm so glad you could make it. There's no place to work quite like a hospital ER. I hope you're ready to rock," she said hurriedly while handing me a pristine white hospital lab coat. "I brought you this to wear." When I slipped it on, I felt like I was part of the machinery and not a visible outsider.

"Thanks, Tori. I'm ready to do whatever you need."

"Okay, then let's get started on our rounds." She whirled around, gesturing for me to follow. Reading from a pile of charts while we walked, Tori gave me a rundown of our first patient. "We've been assigned to check on Becky, a twelve-year-old girl. She was admitted for an asthma attack and has already been given an Albuterol inhaler. We just need to check on her progress and update the chart." She stopped abruptly, pointing at a door ahead of us.

We entered a small room that contained some cabinets filled with medical supplies, a single small sink, and one treatment table pushed against the opposite wall. A frightened young girl was sitting on it with the inhaler strapped over her mouth and nose. Her visible struggle to breathe and the fear on her face brought my recent experience with Sarah flooding back into my mind. I swallowed hard to help keep my emotions in check. Impulsively, I moved straight to her side. When her eyes met mine, I saw Sarah's eyes, and my heart went out to her. I wanted to comfort her however I could.

"Hi, Becky. My name's Holly." I smiled at her, trying to establish a connection. "I know it's scary to have trouble breathing, but you're going to be okay. The medicine will help you. I promise. Just try to breathe normally." I kept my voice soft and soothing. It seemed to comfort her, and I saw her shoulders relax slightly. I continued to run on instinct as I gently rubbed her back while I visualized projecting calm energy through my hands. At the same time, I pictured her breathing easily and deeply. I felt the tension in her thin body decrease even more. Her wide brown eyes registered relief.

Tori had been watching me with Becky, and she waved for me to continue. Then she pulled the stethoscope from around her neck and moved beside me. "Hello, Becky. My name's Tori, and I'm a physician's assistant. I'm just going to listen to your lungs so I can make sure you're getting enough medicine to help you breathe. Is that okay?" She used the same soft tone as I had used.

When Becky looked up at me for reassurance, I smiled and nodded. Then Becky turned her doe eyes toward Tori and nodded too. Tori's examination was quick and efficient. She quickly jotted some notes down on Becky's chart and glanced at me when she finished. "I think the dosage is fine, and I can hear the air passing more easily through her bronchial tubes."

I smiled at Becky with what I hoped was my most reassuring expression. "That's wonderful, Becky! Your lungs are opening up. Look at you. I hear you breathing easier already," I exclaimed cheerfully. It was true. Becky had almost ceased her struggle to breathe. She reached out and squeezed my hand. There was gratitude in her adorable puppy dog eyes. I almost melted with joy and a sense of accomplishment. After Tori and I said our good-byes, we moved on to our next patient.

"Nice work. You have a great bedside manner. It really helped that little girl in there," Tori said as we walked.

"Thanks. I just did what I felt she needed," I replied, feeling a warm glow inside of me.

"Good. Keep it up." Tori paused before we entered our next treatment room. "Okay, our next patient is Tray. He has an abscess on his thigh that needs to be tended."

We stepped into an exact duplicate of the previous room, but a doctor was still in the room with the patient. Tray was on the treatment table, wearing a hospital gown and worn, black socks. He looked to be in his early twenties with a head of dirty, tangled blond hair and an emaciated body. He looked up briefly as we entered the room; when his eyes met mine, they were devoid of life, as if I was looking into a dark, empty cave. Then he dropped his head toward his chest, losing interest in us.

"Dr. Marks, this is Holly, the woman I was telling you about. She's following me on rounds today."

Dr. Marks was reading Tray's charts. He wasn't much taller than me and had a thick waistline that strained the buttons on his white lab coat. He slowly scrutinized me from head to toe. "So, you're the MIT grad that's looking for a career change?" he said brusquely.

"Yes, that would be me." I was startled, but I kept my voice neutral. Dr. Marks didn't respond; instead, he waved both of us closer to the exam table. Without asking permission from the patient, he slid the hospital gown up high enough to expose a large, festering sore. Then Dr. Marks started talking to us about Tray as if he weren't even there.

"This patient has developed an abscess in his leg from repeatedly injecting himself with unsterile needles. It will need to be cleaned, with the necrotic tissue removed, and accompanied by a round of antibiotics, along with a tetanus shot. Given this patient's history, it's likely the condition will continue to recur, possibly leading to limited use or loss of the leg," he droned. The doctor could just as easily have been describing a rock.

Although Tray didn't register that he'd heard anything, I instantly developed a healthy dislike for Dr. Marks. I tried to keep a bland expression on my face when he turned to Tori and issued his directives in a peremptory tone.

"Tori, get this leg cleaned and treated, fast. We can only do so much for *this* kind of patient. Catch up to us when you're done," he ordered, and then waved for me to follow him. I glanced uncertainly at Tori. She shrugged and nodded briefly.

I felt uneasy as I fell into step beside Dr. Marks. "You don't need to waste your time following a PA," he practically spat with contempt. "Someone with your background, you've clearly got the brains to be a physician. Why waste your time at the bottom?"

I fumed internally. It was the same kind of obnoxious behavior and utter lack of compassion I had felt from David. Since I wanted to finish out my day in the ER, I chose to keep my mouth shut. Dr. Marks waved impatiently at a male PA who was leaning against the counter at the nurse's station. He was busily jotting notes on a patient's chart. "Jerry, what the hell is taking you so long to get me those charts? I haven't got all day. Let's have them!" he barked rudely.

Jerry leapt to attention and hurried over to us; his face flushed a bright red. "Sorry, Dr. Marks, but this next patient has a lot going on. Here you are," he stammered.

Dr. Marks snatched the proffered chart and read it over quickly while Jerry stood by, nervously waiting. When Dr. Marks finished, he glared at Jerry. "Go fetch Tori. Finish up for her if she's not done. Just tell her to bring a suture kit and join us in treatment room five." When Jerry hesitated, Dr. Marks yelled, "Well, what are you doing just standing there? Move it!"

Jerry turned beet red and dashed off. He barely avoided crashing into a nurse pushing an equipment cart. "What a moron. I can't believe he's come this far," he mumbled under his breath.

My body tensed when I heard it. It was hard to squelch the retort that wanted to fly out of my mouth as we continued quickly down the hall. Luckily, I became distracted when I saw two police officers standing guard at the door to treatment room five. They nodded at us politely as we passed between them. Inside there was a young black man who looked barely out of his teens. He was lying on the treatment table with one arm handcuffed to the railing. The first thing I saw was his head, which was a bloody mess. Then I noticed a spreading patch of blood oozing through his hospital gown at the level of his right upper thigh. His face was contracted in a grimace of pain.

Dr. Marks already had his latex gloves on and stepped over to the patient's head. He pulled aside the thick, dark hair to expose a deep gash that extended from the temple to the back of the head. His prodding caused the patient to moan and pull away.

"Be still, young man. I need to assess the mess you got yourself into," Dr. Marks said impatiently.

Tori walked into the room just as he was pulling up the hospital gown to examine the leg wound. He gestured for me to move closer. "This is actually a fairly clean gunshot wound. You can see the entry point here on the medial side of the quadriceps and then the exit wound on the opposite side," he said, pointing out the details of the injury. Then he extracted an X-ray from the chart folder and held it up to the light for me to see. "You can obviously see here that there was no bone involvement. These injuries can be dealt with simply," he concluded and waved at Tori. "Clean this guy up and suture his wounds. You know the drill—antibiotics, tetanus—and come get me when you're done."

Tori nodded and hurried over to the supply cabinets. She rifled through the drawer and began to lay out gauze and other supplies. Dr. Marks strode to the door and then glanced back at me. "Holly, you might want to observe Tori's suturing; she's fairly decent at it," he suggested begrudgingly.

"Thank you, Dr. Marks. I'd love to observe her technique," I replied, immediately jumping at the chance to escape the presence of this extraordinarily rude man. As he turned to leave the treatment room, I wanted to flip him the bird, but I managed to restrain myself.

The room brightened noticeably after he left, and Tori and I exchanged relieved smiles. She arranged her instruments neatly on the tray stand next to the treatment table. When she turned toward the patient with a syringe in hand, he quickly pulled his head away. A look of distrust was written all over his face.

Tori froze. "This will help you. I'm going to inject an anesthetic around your head wound. You might feel some pricks at first, but then the pain should disappear altogether."

Satisfied, he moved his head back down on the bed. I moved into his line of vision at the side of the treatment table. "Your name's Ben, right?" I'd seen his name on the X-ray film and thought that it might be a good idea to distract him while Tori worked. "Would you like to tell us what happened?"

Ben rolled his eyes; at first, I thought it was a rebuff, but then he said, "Talk about being stupid. I tried to stop a fight between my friend Randle and two other punks." The soft, melodic quality of his voice surprised me. "One of them bashed me on the head with a piece of wood, and I went down. Randle ran after them, but one of them pulled a gun and fired. It missed Randle and hit me in the leg, while I was still on the ground. Everyone ran away when the cops showed up, 'cept me, I wasn't going anywhere. Pretty stupid, huh?"

By this time, Tori had moved around me and down to Ben's thigh so she could inject the anesthetic around his gunshot wound.

Ben glanced over at her and said, "Hey man, thanks. My head doesn't hurt anymore." When Tori nodded, Ben looked back at me, obviously waiting for some kind of response. It was hard to know how to be helpful, but I gave it a shot.

"Well, I think the fact you think the whole event was stupid tells me you already learned something useful. So, tell me Ben, what *did* you get out of this?" I asked curiously.

Ben closed his eyes. I wasn't sure whether it was to ponder my question or ignore me. Tori was busily cleaning Ben's head in preparation for sutures. She smiled and nodded for me to continue. Ben's eyes remained closed for a few minutes. This gave me the opportunity to watch her expertly sew up his head wound. I admired the tiny perfect sutures. After several minutes, Ben's soft voice broke the silence. "I don't want to die. The whole thing was shit. Randle started that fight, and who got tagged? Me. Why me?" he moaned.

A sudden warm feeling spread within my heart chakra. Without conscious thought, words began to spill from my lips. "Because you're special, Ben. Consider the possibility that maybe the universe deflected the bullet that shot you." A tiny part of my mind thought that I sounded a bit corny, but I felt no desire to edit my words. They weren't mine to edit. "It moved the bullet away from somewhere that might kill you, because you're special," I reiterated. While his expression was dubious, he remained silent. "There's no one on this planet quite like you. You have a purpose. You *matter,* Ben, and the universe isn't ready to let you go. You've already demonstrated admirable qualities of loyalty, friendship, and bravery. But now it's time for you to follow your heart, not what anyone else tells you to do," I said and leaned closer, holding his gaze, "Because, as you saw for yourself, in the end—it's *you* who will take the bullet." The words stopped coming, and my mouth closed of its own accord. I stood still and simply waited.

Tori had paused to listen, but she returned to her suturing with a thoughtful expression on her face.

Ben's eyes were wide. His mouth moved as if he was trying to speak, but no words came out. It took several minutes before he finally did. "You sound like my grandma—she talks like you. You both make me feel like I'm something, like I can be something," he said.

I patted his leg affectionately, realizing that I genuinely liked this troubled young man. "You already are, Ben," I said, and I meant it.

Tori finished placing the bandage on his leg. "Well, young man, you're all patched up. I can honestly say that I hope I never see you in here again. Stay out of trouble," she said. This time her voice seemed friendlier.

Tori preceded me out of the treatment room, but I turned around when I heard Ben's voice behind me. "Hey uh, wait, umm."

I instinctively knew what to answer. "My name's Holly." I smiled back at him.

"Thanks, Holly."

"You're welcome, Ben."

I caught back up with Tori at the nurse's station. She was picking up another handful of patient charts. She looked up and grinned when I stood beside her.

"Perhaps you should consider psychology. You have a knack for connecting with people," she observed.

While I waited for her to review the charts, I glimpsed Dr. Marks at the end of the hall. He was gesticulating wildly at a nurse. Suddenly, she turned and ran toward us a few steps and then disappeared into a side corridor with a horrified expression on her face. My whole body tensed in annoyance.

"I'm sorry if this offends you, but Dr. Marks is an ass," I growled. Tori tore her eyes away from the charts and looked at me when she heard the irritation in my voice.

"He is, but it's not hard to see why. In med school, you need a massive ego to engage in the cutthroat competition with your peers. Not to mention that being given the power to make life and death decisions leads to a superiority complex," Tori explained. "But you need to realize that for about six to eight years, the typical med school student burns the oil at both ends, piles up massive college debt, and is driven like a slave during their internship. It's not surprising that many turn out to be angry, arrogant brutes. It's one reason that I chose to be a PA," she said, shrugging her shoulders.

It was then that all hell broke loose. The admitting doors burst open, and two nurses ran through, leading a young, panicked couple into the ER. The disheveled man carried a young girl, perhaps no more than five or six years old. He was holding her tightly in his arms while the woman running beside him held onto one of the little girl's arms.

"Help us—help my baby girl! Help her now!" the woman screamed.

A tall, balding doctor, whom I'd seen only from a distance, ran over to the couple. Within seconds, he was shouting for the crash cart.

The entire group headed our way; as they came closer, it seemed as if their movements slowed way down. I saw that their legs were running, but somehow they were only covering distance at a slow crawl. Suddenly, I was aware that I wasn't hearing anything—not the doctors, not the nurses, not even the screaming mother whose mouth was still wide open. All I could focus on was the little girl, or rather, the shimmering brightness that hovered above her head. I didn't know how I knew, but I instinctively felt that I was seeing her spirit and that there was no life in her physical body. It felt like I had tunnel vision. All I could focus on was that beautiful sparkle of light. I stood there mesmerized. I was tempted to reach for it as it slowly passed by. It seemed like a connection formed between myself and the little girl's spirit. I sensed that she had concern for her parents and couldn't understand why her mother was screaming. She wanted to help her parents, but she didn't know how. The connection was broken when Tori touched my arm; time shifted back to normal.

Abruptly, the world erupted into noise and movement. "I've got to assist. You can watch if you want, but stay out of the way," Tori spoke quickly into my ear. Then she was off, sprinting toward the room that everyone had disappeared into. I followed her, keeping a respectful distance. I felt strangely calm and detached. It helped that I already knew that, although the little girl's body was empty, her spirit was still close and she was okay. It took four nurses, two of them male, to drag the distraught parents from the treatment room. The mother screamed all the way down the hall.

I surprised myself by staying to watch the frantic activity taking place in the trauma room. Dr. Marks and another doctor rushed in to help. The girl's body was quickly intubated, hooked up with monitors, and injected with drugs. Dr. Marks yelled for everyone to stand clear while he shocked the tiny body with the defibrillator. Her body jumped wildly on the table. He kept doing it, twice, three times, four times—all with no response.

I wanted to tell them to stop, that they were wasting their time, but I kept silent. Then the other doctor inserted a long needle into the girl's leg while the nurses set up several IVs. Her limp body had turned a dull shade of gray-blue, but still they continued to work. The doctors argued with each other over what to do, all the while shouting at the nurses. It took them an hour to decide that it was over.

I quietly withdrew to the nurse's station. It was hard not to feel the agony of the parents when they were allowed into the room. It was impossible when the screaming began again.

Tori appeared a short while later, looking tired and defeated, and told me what had happened. The little girl had come down with a cold or flu, and the parents had given her several kinds of medications to try to help. They gave her adult doses of several medications, thinking that more was better. She reacted badly and started having trouble breathing. Her parents rushed her to the ER, but it was too late. I stood silently while

Tori spoke and felt myself moving from shock and pain into anger. What an unnecessary tragedy.

I focused my mind on the image of the little girl's beautiful spirit energy, and I felt a gentle blanket of calm settle around my shoulders. I sighed in relief as my heart relaxed.

"I hope this wasn't too much, too soon for you, but this is just how it is some days. It's probably a good thing that our shift is over," Tori said, putting her hand on my shoulder. I couldn't have agreed more. Suddenly, I needed more than anything to be away from this place and alone with my thoughts.

Outside the hospital building, the night air was hot and humid. It was like stepping from a refrigerator into a sauna. Even so, I immediately took a deep breath. It was a relief to breathe fresh air, however muggy, that was untainted by chemicals or sickness. I headed toward my car, which was at the far end of the massive west parking lot. When I rounded the corner of the hospital, I passed by a small group of nurses who were chatting and quite obviously on a smoking break. How ironic. I held my tongue and simply nodded in greeting as I quickened my pace to get past them. It was quite a hoof across the lot, and it took several minutes to reach my car. There was no one else around, and I was blessedly alone at last.

Instead of starting up the car, I rested my elbows on the steering wheel and put my chin in my hands. So much had happened, and so many feelings were racing around inside of me. The first emotion that separated itself from the pack was anger. That little girl's death was completely unnecessary. She merely had some cold or flu, nothing one should have to die from. I blamed the pharmaceutical companies first. They spent billions on advertisements that enticed people to put dangerous chemicals into their bodies. In this case, it was worse since it wasn't the little girl's choice; it was her parents' decision. A decision based on ignorance and misinformation that cut short her life before it even began. It was madness! The look of sheer agony on the faces of her parents filled my mind. I felt their unbearable grief all over again and knew they were probably going to suffer from guilt for the rest of their lives. Compassion for them finally broke through my anger. Losing a child was horrific. Their pain was mine. I shuddered and gripped the steering wheel ever tighter until my hands throbbed. It was like surfing a wave. I needed to stay balanced long enough to get to the end of the ride.

It occurred to me to use a grounding technique I learned at the Acupressure Institute. I imagined roots extending from my feet that burrowed into ground all the way to the center of the earth. Then I imagined all the pain and suffering that I was feeling as a black mist inside of me. I willed the blackness to flow out of me, down the roots from my feet, and into the ground. Slowly, the inky mist did as I asked and left my body. My heart untwisted, and it was a blessed relief.

Even though a little girl had died, I'd also experienced a miracle. I needed to acknowledge that too. When I thought of seeing the light of the girl's spirit hovering over her body, something flashed in my mind, and I was back there again. I watched the light flow toward me as I reached out to her. Then I was filled with joy, her joy. There was no suffering, only beauty. I could have stayed like that forever. Eventually, I had to let it go and returned to my body, which was sitting in my Pathfinder in the middle of a huge hospital parking lot in downtown Philly, late at night.

Released from my vision, I leaned back in my seat. For a split second, I questioned my own veracity. No! My hand smacked the steering wheel. I believed my experience was real. My connection to her spirit had felt palpable. No one could tell me otherwise. It was like the "Authorized Personnel Only" door opened, and for a few incredible moments, I was allowed inside. I felt awed and humbled. It was a shame I couldn't somehow share my experience with the little girl's parents, but I knew that would be entirely out of the question. I had learned a long time ago to keep my mouth shut about my spiritual beliefs.

CHAPTER SIXTEEN
SPIRITUAL DIVERGENCE

*Believe nothing, no matter where you read it, or who
said it, no matter if I have said it, unless it agrees
with your own reason and your own common sense.*
–Buddha

From the age of five until I was about nine, Mom made me go to Sunday school at her Baptist church. I called it hers because I never felt that I belonged there. She wanted me to like it, and I tried for her sake, but all to no avail. Religion was important to her. She felt it provided the foundation for creating a strong moral compass. I believed that she got a lot out of it, but even at such a young age, I didn't like anyone dictating what I should believe. I was willing to listen, but I made up my own mind about things. What was worse, though, was that every time I walked into church, I was overwhelmed with feelings of fear. It was a pervasive sense that someone was going to appear at any moment and hurt me. It was hard for me to understand why it felt so wrong. A church was supposed to be a good place, and all of the people there were very nice to me. At any rate, every week I could hardly wait for Sunday school to be over. As soon as I stepped outside of the church, the crushing weight of oppression would lift, and I felt light again.

From a young age, I was an avid reader. I read everything I could get my hands on, including the Bible. However for me, the Bible was simply a book. It had things in it that I agreed with and things that I considered to be rubbish. Even as a child, I knew when I heard an important truth. If it resonated inside of me and felt right, then it was.

For the most part, I toed the line in Sunday school and kept my mouth shut. It was easier that way. One Sunday, however, when I was just seven years old, I slipped up. Mrs. Weismann, the plump, middle-aged woman who taught my Sunday school class, was nice. I liked her, even if I didn't agree with half of what she taught us. On this Sunday, she was lecturing about the awful place that we would go after we died—that is, if we were bad people. I already knew the place that she was trying so hard not to name was called hell. I also knew that I would get into trouble if I used the word out loud. It was one of those words that adults got extremely upset about if a kid used it.

At seven, I already had a strong opinion about the existence of hell. In my mind, I was convinced that it didn't exist. It was boring listening to Mrs. Weismann drone on and on about something I didn't believe in. I made the mistake of looking obvious about not paying attention. She *loved* to call on kids who looked like they weren't paying attention. Suddenly, I realized she was standing in front of me. Her lips were moving, and I knew that she asking me a question, but I didn't quite catch it. *Oh boy! I'm in trouble now.* I looked up but couldn't meet her eyes. Instead, I fixed my gaze on her hair, which was curled up into a perfect bun.

I swallowed hard to get enough saliva to speak. "I'm sorry, Mrs. Weismann. Can you repeat the question?" When I heard snickers from some of the other kids, my embarrassment increased. Mrs. Weismann gave them all a hard stare, and the room fell silent immediately. I was grateful that she chose not to lecture me about paying attention in class.

She hovered over me with an authoritative air that made me want to slide under my desk. "The question that I asked was: is it important to you to live your life doing good deeds so that you won't go to that very bad place when you die?" She pursed her lips when she spoke and crossed her arms over her chest.

"No, it isn't." I was too embarrassed to think about censoring my response, and I simply answered her question. There was a collective gasp from every single one of the twenty or so other kids in the class. I was in for it now.

At first, Mrs. Weismann was too stunned to say anything, but then she finally asked, "Why isn't it important for you to do good deeds?"

It annoyed me that she changed her question. She made it seem like I didn't want to be a good person. I needed to make her understand, and right away. I sat up straighter and gathered my courage. "I didn't say it wasn't important for me to do good deeds. I think that's very important. But that's not what you asked me."

"It wasn't? Would you like to tell me what you *think* I asked you then?" Mrs. Weismann's left eyebrow tilted up in surprise, and her voice was a touch shrill as she responded.

It sure felt like I was getting picked on now, and my stubborn side was digging in its heels. If she wanted to know, then I was going to tell her. "You asked me if it was important to do good deeds so I wouldn't go to that bad place when I die. Well, since I don't believe in hell…" I knew I had used a bad word, and I hoped I wasn't going to get in trouble, but I needed to make my point, "…it's not important to do good deeds for that reason. I think it's important to do good deeds because that's how I want to live my life." I stared up at her, waiting to see what would happen. Her mouth fell open far enough that I could count four fillings. Then my classmates all started talking at once. I caught the word "hell" and the phrase "in trouble" several times. Why couldn't I just keep my mouth shut?

"All right now. Everyone, settle down." Mrs. Weismann raised her hands to quiet the class. She looked down at me with a smugly righteous expression, and I was sure that my face must be beet red. "Well, Miss Reese, I do want to hear why *you* don't believe in that bad place, especially since, it's written about in the Bible. And please, let's not use the 'h' word again."

If she wanted an answer, she was going to get one. I took a deep breath and jumped into the fire. "There is no bad place after you die. That's just made up to scare people. It doesn't make sense otherwise. I think the only real bad place is what people make for themselves," I said defiantly.

To her credit, Mrs. Weismann didn't explode or lose her temper, although she did turn an interesting shade of pink for a minute or two. I wondered whether she was going to tell my parents and if I was going to get in trouble. I didn't care. She asked me what I believed, and so I told her. There was nothing wrong with that. I crossed my arms over my chest and braced myself for the onslaught.

"We know there is a *bad* place after you die because the *Bible* tells us so. The *Bible* contains the *truth*. *You* are a little too *young* to have such strong *opinions* about such a *big* subject. I suggest you *think* upon that." Mrs. Weismann kept her voice calm for the most part, but every few words, that shrill tone snuck back in.

I kept my arms crossed and stared back at her with my stubborn face, as Mom called it. No one was going to tell me what to believe, especially about something so important. I trusted what I felt and knew was right for me. I didn't care if anyone else believed what I did or not, but it taught me to keep my beliefs to myself in the future.

CHAPTER SEVENTEEN
OUTSIDE THE BOX

*Twenty years from now, you will be more disappointed
by the things you didn't do than by the ones you did.
So throw off the bowlines. Sail away from the safe
harbor. Catch the trade winds in your sails.
Explore, dream, discover.*
—Mark Twain

The day after my ER shift, my emotions were all over the map. It was hard to digest all that had happened in the last twenty-four hours. Shika sensed my restlessness. She pushed her head against my hand as I stretched out on my bedroom carpet. Then she plopped her butt down on my legs and stared at me with soul reader eyes. I ignored her until she woofed at me.

"All right all ready. I hear you," I said, looking at her with exasperation, but it didn't last. It never did with her—it couldn't. Her entire world revolved around figuring out what she could do for me. "You're right as usual, sweet pea. Mama needs to get out of the house. Want to go for a walk?"

There was no hesitation; she leapt up and raced to the bedroom door.

We went for a long hike through the woods. Shika bounded around, sniffing everything and occasionally stopping to wildly paw a hole in the ground, hoping to catch a mole. It was a warm autumn day, and a walk was just the thing to help me sort out my thoughts. I replayed the ER shift in my mind. The encounter with that little girl's spirit was, beyond a doubt, one of the most extraordinary experiences of my life. I viewed it as a gift. I also treasured the time I had spent with Becky and Ben. I felt I had made a connection with them and a positive difference. It was deeply satisfying.

Shika and I arrived at a tiny glade lit up with sunlight. It was an inviting spot to continue my introspection for a while. I sat down with my back against an old, gnarled oak. Perhaps this grandfather of the forest might choose to illuminate me? Shika assigned herself guard duty and quietly circled the edge of the woods. I leaned my head against the tree and watched a lone cloud moving in the patch of blue sky above me. It reminded me of a mad bull that was charging something to rip it apart. I thought it an apt metaphor for the interpersonal skills of Dr. Marks. His raging ego and callous behavior repulsed me. Then there was David the paramedic, whose delusions of grandeur were crowned with an appalling lack of empathy. Were these men simply aberrations or were they the norm in a system in which doctors were practically deified? The longer I stewed over it, the angrier I got. Looking back, it was an all-too-familiar scenario.

Two of my parents' best friends had been a married couple. Paul was a prominent obstetrician, who had delivered most of the kids in my town, and Ann was a nurse. They both had worked at our local hospital. Our families had often gotten together for pool parties over at Paul and Ann's house. Paul had been one of my real-life heroes; after all, he helped bring life into the world. He was well-respected, drove one of the few BMW's in town, and wore the only solid gold watch I'd ever seen. Many times, I had ridden my bicycle to the hospital to visit him on a shift. I had felt so important asking the duty nurse to page Dr. Paul—and even more so when he had come striding down the hall in hospital scrubs to meet me. He had even taken me with him into "personnel only" places. Nurses and orderlies parted like the Red Sea before us wherever we went. He had introduced me to his colleagues as his special assistant for the day, and I had floated on cloud nine from all the attention. That had been the good part. The rest now came flooding back to me.

What I had conveniently buried in my subconscious was the actual behavior I had witnessed at the hospital. My young eyes had clearly seen the apprehension on the faces of the nurses as we walked by, but my mind somehow twisted it into respect. My young ears had heard the condescending tones used by the physicians to speak to their staff. My young heart had felt wrongness about the way patients were talked about so dismissively. I had rejected the negative aspects of my experiences because they just didn't compute. After all, doctors were supposed to be the good guys. Doctors were my heroes. Nothing was going to interfere with that certainty.

As an adult searching for my true path, the thought of working in an arrogant environment where patients were routinely treated as soulless objects was totally repugnant. It wasn't right, and it wasn't me. It was the cold reality of our medical system, and there was no way to ignore it. I felt the shock of a cold nose touching my neck and jerked my head.

"Shika, you startled me!"

She had crept around from behind my oak tree to greet me and looked slightly abashed at my response. She knew how to work it.

I felt like a brute. "Oh, sweetie. I'm sorry. You're a good girl."

She leaned closer and licked my cheek before breaking into one of her huge Rottweiler grins.

I wrapped my arms around her muscled neck and hugged hard. "Thank you, precious. Let's get going," I said laughing, and we chased each other all the way home.

Mom took my decision not to pursue Western medicine in stride, but Dad was really disappointed. It turned out he had been secretly pleased about the prospect of having a doctor in the family. While I knew in my heart that my decision was the right one for me, I had subconsciously pinned all my hopes on finding a career in the medical field. I wanted to help save lives. Why did the environment have to be so intolerable? Why couldn't I have my cake and eat it too?

I moped around the house for days, rarely leaving my bedroom. At first, I lost myself in some of my old science fiction novels, but then they suddenly lost their appeal. I finally picked up *The Lightworker's Way* from my dresser. In the first few pages, I discovered that I was a lightworker: someone who felt called to heal others or solve the world's problems, perhaps have had metaphysical experiences, and felt they had a higher purpose, even if they didn't know what it was. I was hooked. It was all about the life of a fascinating woman named Doreen who had endured many hardships before walking her true path of being a metaphysical teacher and a healer. I loved it! In one insightful passage of her book, I finally understood why I had quit my job to find my true path. It read:

> When our purpose remains dormant, a horribly painful pressure bubbles in one's solar plexus, near the stomach. There's a terrible feeling that you are forgetting to do something—which you are, if you are not working on fulfilling your life purpose. One of the greatest fears that we Lightworkers suffer from, perhaps the only fear, is that we won't fulfill the purpose for which we came to Earth.

It described exactly what I had been and still was feeling to a T. I'd reached the point where I couldn't settle for a job that wasn't part of my life's purpose. I wasn't the only one, and I wasn't nuts! Except, if I wasn't going to pursue Western medicine, then once again, I was back to square one.

Eventually, I was drawn to be with Mom near her nurturing energy. I emerged from my room and slunk downstairs to sit across from her at the kitchen table. My elbows were on the table with my chin resting on my hands. I stared off into nothingness as I replayed the hospital scene in my mind. I couldn't stop thinking about how that little girl's death shouldn't have happened. Her parents had given her adult doses of over-the-counter cold medications, thinking that more must be better.

People were woefully uneducated about the risks of drugs and way too quick to use them without question. Drug companies were in business to make money, and they spent billions of dollars on advertising to get people to use their products. They didn't care if their products had a list of side effects that were often worse than the original conditions they were supposed to treat. They didn't care if their products could kill. It was criminal.

Mom glanced up from her accounting books and peered at me over the rim of her reading glasses. I knew she wanted me to stop sulking, but I couldn't help it. Why couldn't I just be content with my old programming job? Why was I so complicated?

It was slightly annoying when she interrupted my reflection and self-pity. "Honey, why don't you give yourself a break and get outside? It's a gorgeous day."

She was right, but I wasn't ready to let go of my mood that easily. "Thanks, Mom, but I'm bumming right now. I guess I had high expectations about finding something in Western medicine. But the system is too flawed for me to be a part of it."

Mom pushed her chair away from the table and stood up stiffly, rubbing her side to ease an ache. She always worked so hard. It bothered me to see her in any discomfort. I watched as she pulled two glasses out of the dishwasher and poured us each a cup of mint iced tea from the pitcher on the counter.

I smiled at her when she set the glass in front of me. "Thanks, Mom." She knew if anything could cheer me up, her iced tea could. I savored the burst of spearmint exploding in my mouth and appreciated her attempt to help me feel better.

She sat back down and picked up her pen to jot something down in her book. She winced slightly and set the pen down to massage her right hand. "Is your hand bothering you, Mom?"

"Just a bit of arthritis kicking up. It's okay," she said as she picked up a pile of invoices to sort. She always made light of it, but I knew it was painful. She'd suffered for years with it in her hands and feet. I wished I could help her somehow. "Don't worry so much, honey. There are plenty of alternatives to Western medicine." I felt selfish. She had a ton of work to do, her arthritis was flaring up, and she was still trying to cheer me up. "Why don't you come outside and sit on the patio with me?" Without waiting for my response, she stood up and walked over to the kitchen door.

I stared at her back with my mouth hanging open. Mom *never* took breaks. She got up at 4:30 every morning with Dad, and then cooked, cleaned, ran errands, and did the books all day long—often until ten or eleven at night.

She put her hand up to push open the screen door, but all of a sudden, she froze. That piqued my curiosity, and I wondered what she was staring at. Before I could move, Mom turned around and beckoned to me to come to the door. She put her finger to her lips, indicating that I should be quiet. I popped out of my chair quickly but was careful not to make a sound. When I stepped beside her, I could see she was aglow with excitement. She pointed to the picnic table on the patio where she always kept a well-stocked birdfeeder. Just then it had some visitors.

There were four birds pecking at the seed. At first I wasn't sure why this warranted all the fuss. And then it hit me. They were all robins, beautiful bright red males! I'd never seen that many male robins in one place together without a fight. We shared a look of disbelief. Bird watching was a passionate hobby of Mom's—and one she enjoyed sharing with me. Robins were one of our favorite birds. They were fiercely territorial when mating or feeding. It was common for them to chase each other and squabble over the seed in our birdfeeder. If two alpha males clashed and neither bird backed down, it would swiftly escalate into violent pecking until one of them beat a hasty retreat. I couldn't believe my eyes, but the four red male robins at the feeder were hopping around each other like the best of buddies.

The largest one was quite a handsome fellow, parading around with his fiery orange belly, and he appeared to be the "law in town." The two scrawniest robins knocked into each other while hopping for the same pile of seeds and then bounced apart like a couple of stooges. I braced myself for all hell to break loose, but the "sheriff" wedged himself between them as if he were bellying up to the bar, and nonchalantly started pecking at the seed pile. Without skipping a beat, the little ones hopped aside good-naturedly to give him space. Then they all went back about their business as if it was the most natural thing in the world.

Mom giggled quietly, and I cracked a grin. My arm slipped around her shoulders, and I gave her a squeeze. She put her arm around my waist and leaned against me. I was supremely grateful that she had called me over so that we could witness this miraculous little scene together. My worries faded into the background for a time.

"Thanks, Mom," I whispered.

By and by, the robins finished their little sideshow and flew off, looking sated. We went outside to sit on the patio lounge chairs and enjoy a sunny afternoon. Mom settled herself comfortably and plunged into her latest detective mystery novel with obvious delight. It was difficult not to stare at her relaxing outside on a recliner. She was doing it for me, and I was extremely touched. I leaned back on my own lounge chair and closed my eyes. It was pleasurable to breathe in the fresh clean air laced with the heady scent of sweet honeysuckle.

As I let go of my worries, the scene of the robins returned to me. Something about them was nagging at me. Gradually, a memory welled to the surface—a childhood memory of the injured robin I had saved. I had sat next to it for hours, patiently pouring healing energy into it through my hands. That experience had affected me deeply. In my child's mind, I felt I had forged an energetic connection with my little bird patient. That was the kind of healing I had always wanted to do. My eyes snapped open. There was my answer!

My thoughts raced. Mom was right. There *were* plenty of alternatives. I wanted to explore medicine—but not the way it was practiced in the Western world. So, what about the Eastern world? I had already taken classes in acupressure, energy healing, and herbs. Eastern medicine treated patients as people, not objects. The art of healing was achieved through a mutual collaboration between the patient and the practitioner. It was holistic, and their theories revolved around the concept of qi, or life energy.

I believed in it—I'd seen it work. All my years of martial arts had developed my qi and refined my ability to direct it. Acupressure and acupuncture manipulated it to restore health. Why hadn't I seen this as my logical next step? Instead, I had turned away and moved toward the antithesis of everything I believed in. My path had been there all along—right before my eyes. How could I have been so blind? Maybe it was because I was still trying to find my path among the more socially accepted careers. But every time I did, I wasn't happy. I needed to let go and follow my own truth, no matter where it led. It was the only way. I sat up quickly, thrilled about my revelation.

"What's wrong, honey?" Mom was startled by the suddenness of my movement.

Instead of answering right away, I jumped up and twirled around in a complete circle before I ran over and grabbed her in a huge hug. "Nothing. Mom you're fantastic! I know what I want to do. And it's all thanks to you!"

"Me? You do? What?" she sputtered breathlessly. In the time it took to utter four words, her expression evolved from confusion to curiosity to excitement.

"I'm going to study acupuncture," I declared happily.

That shut her mouth. I could see the wheels turning on that one. After a very lengthy pause, she suddenly grinned and winked at me. "Wow. I guess that's one *alternative* I hadn't considered."

We both started laughing and didn't stop for a long time.

CHAPTER EIGHTEEN
PATHS TAKEN

"Study the past if you would define the future."
—Confucius

What can I say? I adore Whole Foods market. Yet another Toyota Prius circles the crowded parking lot, hunting for a space. I'm sitting in my parked car near the familiar tri-colored recycling containers to the right of the entrance. I take the time to center myself and visualize a successful excursion to procure the organic vegetables and fruits I need for my "juice of life." This will be the first time I've gone shopping for myself, since I embarked on my juicing program almost three months ago. The very same day I flew back from my visit with Dr. Mercola in Chicago, I drove myself to Whole Foods. It was an insane thing to do. I was so exhausted and weak that several times, I nearly collapsed in the store. My shopping cart became my life buoy as I hung on to it and stubbornly kept going. I was desperate to start my juicing program, and nothing was going to keep me from it. Somehow, I made it through my ordeal. I don't even have a clear memory of how I drove home that day. It was surely due to the protection of my spirit-guides, and I sent them my gratitude for helping me. However, after that initial near-catastrophe, my friend Kae, bless her soul, has been doing the shopping for me. Now, I feel strong enough to try again.

With growing optimism, I nudge the shopping cart slowly toward the produce section. Instead of clinging to the cart for dear life, I only need to place a fraction of my weight onto the cart handle to glide it forward. What a victory! Standing in the midst of the organic fruits and vegetables, my eyes drink in the abundance, and my heart sings a greeting to my allies of wellness; they are critical to my continued existence. Reverently, I pick up a bunch of deep, forest green, dinosaur kale. A powerhouse of healing nutrition, it's packed with vitamins A, B, C, E, K, along with calcium, iron, magnesium, protein, and many anti-inflammatory phytonutrients. I walk along the organic produce aisle, filling my cart with life. Normally, I go to great lengths to avoid shopping of any kind — I'd rather pull out my teeth one by one with a rusty crescent wrench than set foot in a store with any intention of shopping. But, to my surprise, I'm actually enjoying myself — the universe works in mysterious ways.

On my way to the aisle containing my pea and spirulina protein powder, I pass by a shelf with incense. I pause and inhale deeply. I can smell lavender, sandalwood, amber, and other relaxing scents similar to the ones I use when meditating. I've spent countless hours sitting in front of my incense burner, watching a thin line of smoke curl up in intricate, ethereal patterns while performing my healing rituals. It's conditioned me to the point where the merest whiff of my incense immediately elicits a state of deep tranquility. If not for my healing meditations, I would not be walking down this produce aisle. Then again, I probably wouldn't be walking period. I'm grateful for the choices I've made that have led me to explore metaphysics and awaken the spiritual side of myself. It has saved my life. I hover over the incense, sniffing through the medley of aromas before selecting an exceptionally calming Tibetan Amber.

Passing by the aisle containing the environmentally friendly and non-toxic cleaning products, I'm grateful once again for the existence of Whole Foods market. I don't think I could force myself to walk down the cleaning product aisle at a traditional supermarket like Safeway; all the harsh, chemical smells would nauseate me. It feels good to know that now my own body products and cleaning supplies are no longer poisoning me. And, that my "juice of life" is slowly cleansing the high levels of accumulated toxins from my body. I locate my protein powder on aisle four and toss it into the cart.

Fully loaded, I'm ready to check out. When I reach the end of the aisle, I pause a moment to rest. What a difference this excursion is compared to my last one! Not only am I still standing upright, but I've managed to finish in forty-five minutes, as opposed to the grueling three hour marathon of my first Whole Foods expedition! I survey the many aisles before me and note that all my needs have been met by the contents of just two. Two priceless aisles filled with the diamonds, rubies, and emeralds of the plant world. Since I still can't digest solid food yet, I have no use for meat, or dairy, or bread, or pasta, or cereal, or a host of other food items. But it no longer matters. Remarkably, my body is flourishing, even without these revered staples of the traditional American diet. My pea protein powder and dark, leafy greens provide all the protein, calcium, magnesium, vitamins and other minerals that I need. How many people spend only the briefest of moments in the produce section or perhaps never even visit it at all? Every grocery aisle we steer down reveals our life choices, which can transform our lives for the better or for worse.

"Excuse me. Would you mind grabbing me a bottle of that Kombucha just on that shelf near your shoulder?" My thoughts are interrupted by the voice of a young woman directly behind me.

"Not at all." I respond, and when I turn to hand her the juice, I glimpse what must be her five or six year old daughter peeping up at me from behind her mother's leg. I smile at her, and instantly she pops out of sight like a startled, little mouse.

"Thank you so much." The young mother says, and strolls on past me with her daughter trailing behind her. The little girl is wearing faded jeans, blue sneakers, and a light blue t-shirt. I smile to myself as I take in her tomboy clothes and unruly, shoulder length, blond hair; that was me at that age.

The little girl stops abruptly and snatches a light brown cereal box off a low shelf. Enthralled by her new acquisition, she studies it lovingly from every angle. Then she shakes the unsuspecting box of granola. Delighting in the rattling sound it produces, she shakes it again and again. She's so fixated on it that she's oblivious to the fact that her mother has turned up the third aisle ahead of her. It's only a matter of time before the little girl notices that she's all alone. I debate whether to approach her and point her back to her mother. I take too long. The little girl sets the box down and turns around to the place where she expects her mother to be, but her mother is gone. Her shocked expression quickly turns to panic. She races around the corner of the closest aisle and out of my line of sight. A few seconds later, she sprints back into view, darting toward the next aisle. I want to step in and help, but I feel as if I'm frozen in place, unable to move or speak. It's as if I'm in the iron grip of some unseen force that wants me to remain a spectator of the scene unfolding before me. I realize that I'm seeing myself.

Racing wildly for the next aisle, the little girl slips on the polished floor tiles and goes down in a sprawling heap. Silent until now, she finally lets loose with an ear-shattering roar, "MOM!"

Her mother appears almost instantly and gathers her wailing daughter into her arms. "It's all right, honey. I'm here. You're ok."

"You went away!" The girl sobs.

"I'm here. I'll always be close by." She reassures, gently rocking her daughter.

Gazing at the child's tear-streaked face, I empathize with her completely. The feelings are all too familiar. The little girl had experienced only a fleeting perception of loss, and yet, her pain was as real as if she had physically broken her arm. How often do we overlook our emotional pain and dismiss it as being less significant than our physical pain? How often did I? Our need for love and a sense of belonging is as essential to our health as our body's need for nutrition. Love is the nourishment of our souls. Love is life. The choices I've made, the paths taken, swirl around in my mind like puzzle pieces. How had I starved or fed my soul? When faced with loss, had I nurtured or had I abandoned myself?

I had witnessed patients come through my acupuncture practice who repeatedly sabotaged their own healing because they weren't prepared to change some of their life behaviors. When faced with the urgent need to make choices for my own healing, did I act any differently? The puzzle pieces that involve my journey toward wellness, light, and life look and feel more solid to me now. But, there was so much more to what happened to me. The complex web of my illness was woven from many different threads, some physical, some emotional and spiritual, all combining to form the unique pattern of my disorder. My illness didn't begin with my medical diagnosis, nor did it begin with that first feeling of numbness in my cheek. I want to understand the whole picture. It will help me to move forward. To do that, I need to rewind the film and play it back again. When did I first embark upon the dark path, which led to my eventual downward spiral? When did I first stumble? Mom was the linchpin. But I'm getting ahead of myself. It all started shortly after I had begun my acupuncture practice.

CHAPTER NINETEEN
THE PRACTICE BEGINS

Think not of yourself as the architect of your career,
but as the sculptor. Expect to have to do a lot of
hard hammering and chiseling and scraping and polishing.
—B. C. Forbes

"Welcome, Dr. Perry, it's good to see you again." I smile as we shake hands in the waiting room of my office and then gesture behind me toward the treatment room. "Please go on in and have a seat."

I'm heartened that my first acupuncture patient is not only an MD, but also that he had been a guest lecturer at Meiji College, and had deliberately sought me out as soon as I had a space. It's odd to see Dr. Perry casually dressed in a tan Polo shirt, jeans, and loafers instead of his usual tailored suit. I'm a few steps behind as he walks stiffly through the door. Watching him sit down as gingerly as a ninety-year-old with a broken hip contrasts sharply with his marathon runner's physique and George Clooney good looks.

The thick scent of sandalwood incense pervades my treatment room. I feel a twinge of anxiety and hope it doesn't bother him. My healing altar is on the wooden table next to his chair, and suddenly, I'm self-conscious of the rose quartz and amethyst crystals arranged around a brass statue of Quan Yin. When Dr. Perry shifts uncomfortably on the wooden Ikea chair, it's my cue to tend to the patient. I breathe deeply and ground myself. This isn't about me. I sit down at my desk and swivel my chair around to face him.

"How can I help you, doctor?" I ask.

"I just want you to know that I feel like I've run out of rope with my back pain." I hear the desperation in his voice. "I hate having to take painkillers, and I don't want surgery," Dr. Perry said while sitting straighter and rubbing his back.

I recall the years of suffering I endured from several fractured vertebrae in college and empathize completely. I nod my head and wait for him to finish. "This is a last-ditch effort before I decide to have my back fused. Please don't take it personally, but I'm skeptical whether this can help at all," he says with a forlorn look on his handsome face. There's nothing like piling on a little pressure with one's first professional patient. There were already huge butterflies doing acrobatic maneuvers in my stomach—even before he added that last bit.

Despite my nerves, I'm excited for this opportunity to demonstrate the benefits of Eastern medicine to a Western medical practitioner. "Well, I'm not going to make any promises, but ... I've had excellent results treating back pain in our clinic."

"Yes, that's what I heard from one of your patients. That's why I'm here." His pleading eyes cry out for hope.

"I'll do my best. Why don't you start by telling me what happened?"

Dr. Perry tells me about his skiing accident five years ago. It involved skidding on ice, hitting a tree, and being wrenched in several directions at once. He didn't fracture anything, but he'd suffered with intense low back pain ever since. While he's relating his story, I've unconsciously tuned myself into his pain. My own back starts to ache. I'm careful to clear it and separate myself energetically from him. I leave the room so he can change into a gown and use the extra time to ground myself and let go of my performance anxiety.

When I reenter the treatment room, I find him staring at the table with apprehension. "Acupuncture needles are finer than a hair, so this is nothing like receiving a shot with a hypodermic needle." I try to reassure him with a smile. "Please." I gesture for him to climb on the table. "Your only job is to relax and keep breathing." I slip a cushion under his legs. "Let me know if you're uncomfortable at any time. It's easy to adjust the needles so you don't feel anything. Are you ready?"

"As ready as I'll ever be. Let's do this." Since he is face down on the table, his response is slightly muffled. *Here we go.*

The first points I choose are distal ones on his ankles and hands. It's a traditional combination for low back pain. I palpate each point before I needle and have him breathe out during the insertion—an effective method for nearly painless acupuncture. When I add both UB 40's—the urinary bladder meridian points behind his knees, which work wonders for acute back pain—his body noticeably relaxes on the table. I brush his aura clear of stagnant energy and then hold my hands over his low back. At the same time, I visualize green healing light pouring from my hands into the problem area. His breathing is calm, and I feel it's time for the big guns.

During my clinical internship at Meiji College, I became fascinated with older needling techniques. My favorites were "Setting the Mountain on Fire" and the "Penetrating Heavenly Cooling" methods. They involved layered insertion depths combined with needle rotation in specific directions. They were extremely effective for all manner of complaints. I employed them for my particular passion of treating trauma and chronic pain. I achieved excellent results; when I experimented with my own modifications, they got even better.

I use a variation of the "Penetrating Heavenly Cooling" on Dr. Perry, starting farther away from the center of his pain and then working my way slowly toward it. While I'm manipulating my needles, I visualize him skiing happily down a snow-covered mountain slope with not a trace of pain. I'm feeling increasingly more confident since he hasn't complained once during the treatment. I smile to myself when I occasionally hear snoring. After his session is over and I've removed the needles, I help him to sit up slowly. He slides off the table in a single fluid motion.

"Wow! Okay. I'm taking this as a good sign. Right now my back doesn't hurt at all," he exclaims in surprise while he feels his back with both hands. A weight falls from my shoulders. "What a relief! However long this treatment lasts, I'm grateful for a few pain-free moments. Thank you." He extends his hand, and I shake it.

"You're welcome. I'd like to see you again if you're willing."

"Absolutely, I'm committed to see this through," he replies enthusiastically, and I leave him to get changed.

We shake hands again in the waiting room. "I'd like you to keep track of how long your back feels good. It's also quite common that, as the stagnation is released in your back, you may feel worse for a time and then improve. Please call me anytime if you have any questions or concerns."

After I give him my parting instructions, I notice there is a slight spring in his step as he walks out the door.

Dr. Perry comes to see me once a week. His low back improves steadily, right along with his enthusiasm. On his fifth visit, he informs me that he's going out of town for a month, and he's concerned that his progress will disappear.

"It's possible, but I don't believe so. We've been breaking down the traumatized tissue and stimulating the growth of new healthy tissue in your low back. I'd be surprised if you slide, unless of course, this is a skiing vacation," I joke.

"No, no, it's not," he says with a laugh. "It's simply a long overdue visit with relatives."

I've gradually increased the amount of needle stimulation used during his treatments, and today, something inside of me tells me that he's ready for a more advanced session. "If you're willing, I'd like to use much stronger stimulation this time around," I say.

"Go for it. You're the boss!" He doesn't hesitate, and I'm touched.

During the time that Dr. Perry is gone, I have a productive chat with Dr. Brown, the chiropractor who shares the waiting room with me. He's curious about the effectiveness of acupuncture for migraines. When I tell him that I had helped three patients eliminate their migraines at my college clinic, he becomes excited and tells me to expect a few phone calls.

In the following weeks, I'm on pins and needles waiting for Dr. Perry to return from his trip. On the day of his appointment, he strides jauntily into my room. I'm initially worried because his expression looks serious. Then he breaks into an ear-splitting grin and catches me up in a tight bear hug. I'm slightly winded when he releases me, but he can't stop smiling.

"I can't thank you enough. My back feels terrific. Although, the first week after my last session it was pretty sore, but a different kind of sore—not sharp, just achier. Then it was simply gone. I haven't used any painkillers all month, and I'm ecstatic." He plops unceremoniously down onto a white chair without a hint of discomfort. I breathe a sigh of relief over his success and feel a wonderful warm glow inside.

"That's fantastic, Doc!" I exclaim, raising my fist in victory. "Well, today we'll give you one more treatment for good measure, and then it will be as needed."

Dr. Perry calls me once more after several months—just to let me know he's doing great. He's canceled his plans for surgery and feels his back is healed. He says he will recommend me to anyone with chronic pain seeking alternative therapy.

As I hang up the phone, I'm pleased to have made some inroads for Eastern medicine in the Western world. As referrals start to trickle in from Dr. Brown, I soon find I have my work cut out for me in breaking through the wall of propaganda debunking alternative medicine.

I know I've got a tough sell as soon as my next new patient steps hurriedly into my treatment room. She's one of Dr. Brown's migraine referrals. Karen is dressed in an elegant gray business suit with perfect hair pulled back into a tight bun. I'm amused to note that she's carrying a Prada handbag. She checks her watch as she sits down on a chair and speaks in a tense, harried voice.

"I'd like you to know up front that I've never tried acupuncture before, and I don't have any great expectations. I'm going to give it a try because Dr. Brown can't seem to help my headaches, and I'm at my wit's end. I'm getting a migraine about three to five times a week, and it's ruining my life." She purses her lips and puts an imaginary stray hair back in place.

I pick up my session notebook and take a deep, slow breath. In my mind, I'm picturing a calm ocean on a sunny day with a warm, pleasant breeze. I can do this.

"I'm glad you called, Karen, and that you are open to giving acupuncture a try. From our phone conversation, you indicated the migraines started after a car accident you had several years ago. Is that correct?"

"Yes, they did. Is this going to hurt? I really don't like needles," Karen says impatiently while rubbing her neck and looking uncomfortable. "Maybe this wasn't such a good idea."

Calm ocean, pleasant day. I tell myself as I visualize blue energy soothing her fiery aura.

"Don't worry. Acupuncture needles are relatively painless and easily adjusted. I can see that you're suffering quite a bit. Why not give this a try since you're here now?" I keep my voice pleasant but confident. Karen rubs her right temple, looking distraught, but she decides to go ahead with the treatment. After an abbreviated history, I get her on the table as quickly as possible. Since she is face down, I can unobtrusively check her condition energetically by running my hands over her aura. The area over her neck and upper back feels empty, devoid of energy—almost like a black hole. When I gently palpate the area, I can feel that her neck muscles are extremely tense. It feels as if I'm touching a plate of steel. No wonder she's having migraines. I lay my hand softly on her mid-back and send healing green energy. I imagine her tight muscles melting and becoming soft and pliable.

"Karen, I can feel the problem areas, and I'm ready to get started. Your only task during this session is to relax and take nice, slow, deep breaths. Think of things that can make you smile. And if it's all right, I'd like to put on some soothing music."

"Okay, but not too loud please."

I let the irritation in her voice bounce off of me and into the ground. The first few needle insertions are a little stressful since Karen complains about feeling them. Eventually, she starts to get used to them. I gently remind her to simply relax and breathe and let me do the work. It's necessary to stimulate the needles much more slowly than with Dr. Perry because her tissue is exceptionally tight.

After a while, I can feel her muscles relaxing, and the needles rotate more easily. It's an encouraging sign when Karen falls asleep on my table. I take this opportunity to perform an entire chakra clearing and aura cleansing. She wakes up as I'm taking out the last few needles. I'm curious to hear what she has to say about the session, but I wait until she's finished changing and settled back in a chair.

"How do you feel after the treatment?"

Karen has the typical, zoned-out look after a session.

"I must say I didn't know what to expect, and it was certainly a different experience for me. Right now my head doesn't hurt," she says, reaching up to touch her right temple. "That's amazing because I was starting to get a headache when I walked in here. Actually, I feel quite good. Thank you."

I'm happy to hear that her voice has lost the tense quality it had earlier.

Before I can respond, Karen checks her watch, and I can see her body tense. "I must go. I'm running late," she announces suddenly. Then, as if she flips off an emotional switch inside of herself, Karen stands abruptly and straightens her suit before picking up her handbag. Not wanting to get in her way, I quickly open the door for her.

"I'm happy to hear that. Please keep me posted on how you do this week, and I'll see you again next week," I call out to her retreating back.

When Karen returns the next week for her appointment, she enters my treatment room and sits down with her business-like demeanor. I'm relieved that her face softens when I ask her how she's doing. "I don't know if last week was related to my treatment, but instead of my usual three to five migraines, I had only one. I got so much accomplished. It was wonderful." She touches her temple with a hint of incredulity on her face. "So, I would like to do this again and see what happens," she announces firmly. *It's back to business.*

After I get her on the table, I can feel the quality of her traumatized neck and shoulder muscles has changed. It's not nearly as hard as it was the week before, and I'm extremely encouraged by her mild migraine week.

"Karen, the area of injury feels much better. Your body is responding rapidly to the needling. I have a feeling you're not going to need many more treatments to solve your migraine problem," I say enthusiastically.

"Oh, if only you're right." She lets out a long sigh. "It would change my life."

As it turns out, she needs only three more sessions before her migraines stop completely. I consider it a success when I don't hear from her again after that.

However, my next migraine patient is an entirely different story. Debra is a workaholic attorney and gets a migraine once a week like clockwork. Her migraines aren't due to trauma, so it requires an extensive history-taking session with her before I can pry out the cause. She reluctantly admits to having several cups of coffee in the morning and afternoon and snacking on candy bars all day long. This is followed by nightly glasses of red wine with cheese and crackers to unwind. Combined with her crazy, fast-paced lifestyle, it's a textbook recipe for migraines.

When I optimistically present Debra with the solution, her response surprises me. She looks at me as if I had turned red and grown horns.

"That's impossible! I *can't* give up coffee. I absolutely *need* it to function," she whines and shakes her head repeatedly. "And chocolate? Oh no, no, no. I've got to have my chocolate. And I absolutely need my wine at night; it helps me relax. I could maybe cut down on the cheese, but that's it," she sputters while nervously smoothing a wrinkle from her dark blue business skirt.

With an attitude like this, I know I have an uphill battle to get Debra to change. I make some notes in her file, which gives me enough time to compose myself. "Some migraines can be caused by any one of or a combination of stress, caffeine, cheese, dehydration, and nitrites in red wine and preserved foods. Your lifestyle has them all. If you can start cutting down on these things, you will be able to eliminate the migraines." I explain my suggestions slowly while maintaining a neutral expression.

"Can't you just give me something—perhaps some herbs—to make them stop?" Debra looks exasperated with me as if I'm holding something back.

I count to ten in my head before I answer and try my best to keep emotion out of my response. "It's possible we could find a strong enough combination of herbs, but I wouldn't want to help you create another dependency without working on the root cause." My position is firm.

Debra argues with me throughout her treatment session. I select extra points to needle, known for calming the spirit and relaxing the body. Thankfully, by the end of her treatment, she has stopped talking. I know it's not good for business, but I'm not willing to string her along if she's not going to change.

After she is dressed and ready to leave, I let her know how I feel. "I'm sorry, Debra, but if you're not willing to make lifestyle changes, I'm afraid there's not much more I can do for you." I brace myself for the backlash.

Debra's expression is one of shock and surprise. She's obviously used to getting her way, and she's not going down quietly. "Well, this is certainly not what I expected. Dr. Brown said you could help me. I will certainly be sure to tell him that you weren't up to the task." She storms past me out of the office.

I fervently hope I don't encounter many more like her in my practice. The experience leaves me feeling out of sorts for the rest of the day. I leave early and head to the gym for a heavy lifting day. My mood is only slightly improved when my brother calls later that evening. It's been several weeks since I last heard from him, and I'm glad to hear his voice.

"Hey, Hol, have you talked to Dad?" Jay rarely starts a conversation by mentioning Mom or Dad unless something is wrong.

"No, why? What's up?" My DefCon level jumps from five down to three in a fraction of a second.

"Look, don't worry. Things are under control, but I wanted to let you know what's going on," he says to allay my concern.

"Jay, what are you talking about?" I'm irritated now. One thing I dislike is to be told not to worry, especially when I don't know what it is that I'm not supposed to worry about.

The deep sigh on the other end of the phone agitates me even more.

After a long pause, Jay says, "Mom's been placed on the liver transplant list."

CHAPTER TWENTY

TICK TOCK

Our most basic instinct is not for survival but for family. Most of us would give our own life for the survival of a family member, yet we lead our daily life too often as if we take our family for granted.
—Paul Pearsall

"Damn it!" I yell and then wing my cell phone at the pillow on the living room sofa. My thoughts are racing, and my heart is in my throat.

Mom had contracted hepatitis more than two decades ago from a bad blood transfusion. Could that have caught up with her? Shika had been outside on the back deck and pokes her head around the kitchen door. When I stretch out my hand toward her, she noses open the door and sprints over to me. I drop to my knees and wrap my arms around her neck. She stands still and wags her bobbed tail, happy that I need her. Her love is a tranquilizer for my fears.

I retrieve my cell phone and sit down on the floor with my back against the couch. Shika lies down beside me and rests her head on my leg. I'm calm enough to dial my parents' number, but my hands still shake.

"Hi, honey. How are you doing? How's acupuncture going?" Mom sounds normal, and relief washes over me. My heart rate slows by an order of magnitude.

"Just fine Mom, but how are you? I just talked to Jay. What's going on?" I ask, gripping the phone tightly in one hand while keeping the other on Shika's back.

"I'm okay. My doctor says that I'll need a new liver eventually and wanted to get me on the list. Sometimes it takes a while. Enough about me, I'd much rather hear about you." Her voice sounds unconcerned, but it doesn't align with the underlying sense of worry that I can feel coming from her—or the sinking sensation in my heart chakra.

Her evasiveness annoys me, and my jaw clenches tighter. "Mom, please. This is not a little thing. Are you in pain? What kinds of symptoms are you having?" I ask, not bothering to hide my concern anymore.

"I am a little tired all the time," she says with the tiniest hint of strain in her voice. "But I'll make do. What bothers me more is that I'm bloated. It makes me look so fat."

"Mom, come on! You're told you need a new liver, but what bothers you is that you think you look fat?" I roll my eyes in exasperation, and press her for more details. She insists that there really isn't anything else that bothers her. "How about if I came out to see you? Then I could get a better idea of how to help you."

"Oh honey, don't do that." She is quick to brush my offer aside. "Your practice has just started to pick up. Don't worry. I'm in good hands. I have great doctors—just focus on you and come home for Christmas." I open my mouth to protest, but she continues, "I want everyone to come this year; it's going to be special. Promise me you'll come, and everything will be fine."

"Of course I'll be home for Christmas," I say, but deep down I know I should drop everything and head home. Christmas is six months away; I need to do something now. "What if I get you a referral to an acupuncturist out there? Will you go?"

"If you think it's a good idea, I'll give it a try." She sounds relieved—and that worries me even more. "Enough of me, I'm so happy you'll be home for Christmas. I can't wait. I love you." Her voice goes back to her happy, normal tone.

"I love you too, Mom. I'll get back to you with a referral. Just tell me if you feel any worse, and I'll come right out. I want to know if anything changes. Okay?" I feel uneasy saying good-bye.

"Of course, honey." She beats a hasty retreat off the phone.

I contact Dr. Nguyen, my favorite instructor from Meiji College, for a referral. As luck would have it, a colleague of his has a practice in Philadelphia. But it's a haul for Mom to get there, and at first, she gives me a hard time about going. I'm ecstatic when her older sister agrees to go with her. Aunt Dot is my favorite aunt. She's also a lot like Mom: short, topping out at five feet; whip-smart; and with a heart of pure gold. Mom, Aunt Dot, and Grandmom Edna had always formed a powerful matriarchal triad of wisdom and goodness. They had a profound impact on everyone whose lives they touched. Mom and Aunt Dot grew up so poor that often they were sent off to school with only an onion between two slices of bread for lunch. Although they barely had enough food for themselves, Grandmom was always sewing clothes for and sharing food with those less fortunate.

I'm in the kitchen feeding Shika dinner when Mom calls. It's the evening after her first appointment with Dr. Chan in Philadelphia.

"Honey, Dr. Chan was great. It was amazing. You'll never guess what happened," she gushes.

Hearing her excited voice makes me feel like I've won the lottery. The vise of worry around my heart loosens its grip. "You sound good. What happened? Tell me everything."

"Well, I wasn't looking forward to going into Philly for this appointment, but since Dotty went with me, I wanted to give it a try. We made a day of it and took the train to downtown. It wasn't too far to Dr. Chan's office, but I had to walk up a flight of stairs to get there, and my knees hurt so much I didn't think I could do it."

"Oh Mom, I'm sorry it was so difficult." I picture her struggling up the stairs in pain, and my heart hurts.

"It's okay, honey. Dotty helped me, and I made it," She quickly reassures me. "Dr. Chan doesn't speak much English, but she is very nice. I didn't feel like anything was happening when she put the needles in, and then the appointment was over. It wasn't until I was standing on the street that Dotty said, 'Shirl, look at you! You just walked down the steps normally, and you didn't even notice!' Can you believe it? I didn't feel any pain. Then I felt so great we walked up the street to see a flower show. I had so much fun."

"Mom, that's fantastic! I'm so proud of you for going." I punch the air with excitement. I mouth a silent, "All Right!" at Shika. She wags her tail, pleased that I'm pleased. Mom thanks me and promises to continue to see Dr. Chan. It's a relief to know that she's willing to be treated with more than just Western methods.

Being on an organ transplant list almost entirely consists of waiting around for a phone call. Jay and I stay in touch and remain on standby, ready to leap on a plane for home if Mom gets notice that a liver is available. It's a nagging worry that hangs out on the periphery of my thoughts. As the year progresses, I try to keep tabs on her condition, but she rarely admits to anything that's bothering her. She deftly avoids talking about herself and always wants to hear about me instead. In retrospect, I'm probably as elusive with Mom talking about myself. I've been on a low simmer all summer over the building tension between Dr. Brown and myself. But I don't want to tell her about the more negative aspects of my practice; it would only add unneeded stress to her life.

One afternoon I'm prepping my treatment room for my next client, and Dr. Brown sticks his head inside the door. "Hey, you got a minute?" he asks.

"Sure," I say cautiously, not wanting to talk, but knowing I don't really have a choice. I lean against the corner of my desk and cross my arms. Dr. Brown takes a couple of steps inside and then covers his mouth and coughs, frowning at the incense on my crystal healing altar. My body tenses.

"It smells kind of strong in here, don't you think?" he remarks. I'm not taking the bait and remain silent. "Yes, well, I wanted to share some concerns that have come up about your … umm … unique treatment style, shall we say?" he says with a gratuitous smirk on his face.

I'm not in the mood for this. "What concerns? Nothing inside my treatment room is discernible from the outside." I get to his point for him. It's hard work to keep my tone light and my expression neutral.

Dr. Brown is visibly irritated and runs a hand across his army-style crew cut. "Look, I wanted to have an acupuncturist in my office, but this…" he waves his hand around in the air, "is too weird." He steps closer to me. "I don't exactly feel comfortable referring my patients." He uses a confiding tone. I look up at the clock on the wall. My next patient, who happens to be a referral from Dr. Brown, is due any minute.

"I appreciate your candor, doctor. I'm sorry you're uncomfortable with my *style*. I do think most of your referrals are quite happy with it. But, if you'll excuse me, I've got an appointment in a few minutes."

I step toward the door and herd him outside. I close it after him and turn on some of my meditation music to soothe my nerves. It helps that my next patient, Darryl, is one of my success stories. He's had chronic hip pain for years, but it's almost resolved; soon he won't need my services any longer. These positive experiences of success keep me going, but for every Dr. Perry or Darryl, there is inevitably another Debra.

Tina is my last session of the day. I meet her in the waiting area and show her into my treatment room. She's not tall, but she's wide—just bordering on obese. My Ikea chair squeaks when she drops down heavily on it. I have her file in hand and spin my desk chair around to face her. "What can I help you with, Tina?"

She digs a tissue out of her black leather purse and dabs her face with it. "It's hot in here," she says. I simply wait for her to continue. "I'd like to lose some weight, and I heard acupuncture was good for that. So, whatever you can do, I want to start right away." She sounds motivated.

"Okay then. Acupuncture can be an important part of a weight-loss program. It can help with food cravings and work toward balancing the metabolism and improving digestion. In combination with proper diet and exercise, significant results can be achieved over time." I explain it all in textbook style, and then I hand her one of my detailed diet-and-lifestyle questionnaires. "Please fill this out, and then I can make some dietary recommendations along with an exercise plan to get you started."

Tina reads over the questionnaire and looks up at me with a frown. "Look, I didn't come here for you to give me any exercises; I hate exercise. I have a problem with both knees, and I can't really do anything anyway," she says impatiently.

"Actually, there are many exercises you can do that won't hurt your knees and are aerobic at the same time." I try to keep my tone helpful, but Tina is having none of it.

"I don't think you understand what I want. If you could just give me some sessions and speed up my metabolism, then I'll be happy. I haven't been gaining weight. So any change has got to be an improvement, right?" She wipes her neck with a tissue again. "Damn, it's hot in here." Her annoyed look suggests that I should do something about that.

I count to ten slowly, but I'm short on patience today. "Tina, it's important that you hear this. Losing weight involves a well-balanced approach that *must* include diet and exercise along with the acupuncture and herbs to help restore balance. If that's not something you're willing to do, then acupuncture alone won't help you get the results you want." My voice is firm and matter of fact.

"So, are you saying you won't help me?" Tina looks shocked.

I put her file back on my desk and stand up. It gives me a few seconds to get a hold of myself and make a decision. "What I'm saying is that if you won't help yourself, then nothing I do will matter." I smile politely.

Tina mutters something unintelligible under her breath and heaves herself off the chair. "This was a waste of my time," she huffs and slams the door as she leaves.

I sink back down on my chair, feeling drained. Why was I so stubborn with her? I could have taken more time and worked a lot harder to convince her about a proper program. Maybe she would have come around—or maybe not. I don't want to be the one to beg her to do the right thing for herself. I want to be there for clients who want to do the work. I've got more important things to worry about, like Mom.

I glance at the clock; six-thirty is a little too late to call her. I'll have to check in tomorrow. I'm annoyed I missed talking to Mom over a wasted session. I need to get out of my office and decide to grab a bite to eat at the Thai restaurant near my house. As I'm headed down MacArthur Boulevard in Oakland, a window sign catches my eye. Although I've seen the martial arts studio many times before, I've yet to stop in to check it out. Today is different. Something compels me to stop.

As I walk into the Wun Hop Kuen Do Studio, a wave of calm washes over my entire body. I hear myself sigh in contentment. It's been over a year since I've had a dojo to train in. I've been too busy getting my practice started. Martial arts have always been a huge part of my life, and I don't feel complete without a place to train. While I'm standing just inside the door, absorbing the good energy, I survey the studio. There are two small sofas in the entry area, which is separated from the main training floor by a chest-high white wooden wall. It runs three quarters of the width of the room.

I move close enough to see several people watching the class from a wooden bench. My observations are interrupted by an intense energy being directed at me. I look up into the eyes of the instructor. He's a handsome, middle-aged black man, not much taller than me, with short curly black hair, and a stocky, muscular build. But it's his eyes that hold me. They sparkle with enthusiasm. There's an instant connection between us. I smile and wave at him. The instructor's face breaks into a huge grin, and he gestures for me to take a seat on the bench. I respectfully dip my head in a slight bow and sit down.

With the instructor's attention back on his class, I watch intently as he puts the class through their paces. He offers a steady stream of encouragement to his students to finish their rigorous kicking drills. By the end of it, there isn't a single one of the twenty or so students that isn't dripping with sweat and panting with exhaustion. As soon as the training session ends, the instructor jogs over to where I'm sitting and extends his hand in greeting. When I clasp it, he pulls me into a friendly bear hug and pats me on the back. I'm even more surprised when he releases me and says, "It's good to see you again. How've you been? Are you ready to train?"

It's strange. He does seem familiar to me, in a long-lost-brother kind of way. "I'm sorry, but I think you might have me confused with someone else. I've never been here before. My name's Holly."

He studies me intently. "I could have sworn we knew each other." He shakes his head and shrugs. "I'm Sifu Doug Jones, and it's a pleasure to meet you." He bobs his head and then touches my arm. "What did you think about my class?" he asks curiously. He is glowing with an innate vitality, and there's nothing I want more than to sprint out onto the training floor.

"It's refreshingly traditional in intensity, but modern in technique." I stroke my chin and put on a studious expression. Before Sifu can respond, I wink and add, "In other words, a kick-ass class—sign me up!"

Sifu Doug bursts into laughter and gives me a playful slap on the back.

Joining the school turns out to be the best decision I've made in quite a while. I'm able to channel my anxiety over Mom and my practice into Sifu Doug's body-blasting workouts. From our encounter the first day, Sifu and I are strongly bonded. It is as if we've known each other for many lifetimes—not just this one. Both of us are tuned in to the same martial arts wavelength, and oftentimes, we communicate entire volumes to each other with just our eyes. I take refuge at the school as often as possible. Inside Sifu's studio, my worries are shrouded and my mind is peaceful.

Outside of class, the threat of impending surgery looms ever closer, especially when Mom tells me that Dad bought a suitcase-sized satellite phone that is guaranteed to receive phone calls anywhere in the world. He carries it with him everywhere, determined not to miss "the call" from the surgeon when a liver becomes available. Dr. Brown hasn't referred any new clients in several weeks, and I wonder whether it makes sense to start looking for a new office location.

My weekly status check with Mom is invariably the same—still no word from the doctor. I try not to think about it, but I feel the Sword of Damocles swinging ever closer. The clock slowly ticks down to Christmas. Tick tock.

CHAPTER TWENTY ONE

THE CLOUDS ARE GATHERING

My soul is full of whispered song; my blindness is my sight;
the shadows that I feared so long are all alive with light.
—Alice Cary, *Dying Hymn*

Christmas week eventually arrives. It's been a turbulent summer and fall, and I'm feeling anxious as I board the plane for Pennsylvania. Potential homecoming scenarios continue playing in my head during the entire flight. After we land, it doesn't help that the airport is swarming with travelers rushing around like frenetic chickens. Only a tiny part of my brain is in the moment, which makes it a challenge to get through baggage claim unscathed. My mental fog continues until I roll my suitcase outside. I'm greeted by an arctic blast of frigid air. It's an abrupt reminder that I'm no longer in California.

Thankfully, Dad arrives at curbside just a few minutes later. I toss my suitcase in the trunk and dive into the front seat of his pleasantly warm, white Lincoln Town car. "Hi honey, it's good to have you home." He shifts in the driver seat to give me a big hug. He doesn't release me until the airport security guard taps on his window and waves for us to move on. I settle back on the passenger side and bask in the warmth from the vent heater blowing directly at me.

"It's great to see you, Dad. Thanks for picking me up," I say once we've gotten underway.

"Sure thing, honey," he replies and then focuses his attention on weaving through the busy airport traffic.

I have a million questions about Mom, but I'm fairly certain that he won't have the answers I need. I settle on one simple one. "How's Mom?"

He doesn't take his eyes off the traffic. "She's doing okay. The arthritis in her hands and knees is hurting her a bit," he answers tersely.

That was particularly unhelpful. After a deep calming breath, I try again. "Dad, I meant what do the doctors say about her liver and how she's doing?"

Before he has a chance to answer, he suddenly hits the accelerator and shoots ahead of three cars converging into the same lane. Dad chuckles with amusement, and I can't stop myself from grinning either—once a taxi driver, always a taxi driver.

"The doctors say she's doing pretty well. She still needs a new one, but once she gets it, she'll be fine. The important thing is that your Mom's really excited about everyone coming home for Christmas; it means a lot to her." He glances over at me. When I start to ask him another question, the discomfort in his eyes signals me not to press him any further. We continue the drive home with sporadic chitchat.

Dad has always been old school when it comes to health issues. His philosophy is that if a doctor tells you to take drugs or that you need surgery, then that is what you do. Doctors know best. Mom's doctors will fix her; it's their job. Many years ago, I learned that Dad flips on the denial switch in any emergency involving Mom.

She had been dutifully taking an aspirin a day for many, many years— ever since her doctor prescribed it. Her physician had told her it would not only improve her arthritis, but that it would also keep her heart healthy. However, there was one potential side effect he had failed to mention, and that was the hole that it eventually burned in her esophageal sphincter.

One night, while she was taking a shower and Dad was putting on his pajamas in the bedroom, he heard a crash. He ran into the bathroom and found that Mom had fallen and passed out on the shower floor. Instead of calling 911, Dad had tried to haul her back to the bed. She came to and started to throw up a brown substance. Dad had panicked but wound up doing the next best thing by calling Aunt Dot.

Aunt Dot had shifted into high gear and raced over to our house in minutes. She had gotten on the phone to 911 as soon as she saw Mom and had recognized that the brown substance was blood. The ambulance had arrived quickly and rushed Mom to the hospital. As it turned out, her stomach had been bleeding from an ulcer. She had bled out more than half of her body's blood supply and almost died. Fortunately, the ER doctor had placed her on a transfusion immediately, which had saved her life. If Aunt Dot hadn't gone over to the house, I'm certain Mom would've died.

We turn into the driveway, and I'm pulled back to the present. My heart skips a beat. Every time I see it, my childhood home fills me with love and wonderful memories. Unlike the chilly exhaust-filled air at the airport, breathing deeply here is like breathing in peace and contentment. While Dad pulls my suitcase off of the backseat, I pause to admire the beauty of the woods surrounding our split-level brick home. The white Christmas lights are up, framing all the windows. I can almost hear Mom micro-managing Dad until he got them just right. Then it hits me. I'm home, and Mom is inside.

Unable to wait for Dad, I sprint through the unlocked den door and up the stairs, taking them two at a time. I run straight into the kitchen, knowing that's where I'll find Mom, and I'm not disappointed. She is sitting at the kitchen table with her usual pile of accounting paperwork spread all over it. In the few seconds it takes for me to reach her, several things happen all at once. It's the middle of winter, so it's normal for her to be wearing one of her baggy button-down sweaters, but the sweater fits too tightly around her middle. Even though she's sitting down, I can see that her stomach is massively distended. I comprehend immediately that her illness has advanced much further than my ability to help her alone. I try hard not to react, but my face must be registering some amount of shock.

Mom's expression changes from her initial ecstatic smile to one of embarrassment. I wrap my arms around her. My heart goes out to her, and I embrace her even more tightly.

"Mom, I love you. It's great to see you." It's hard to get the words past my constricted throat. She hugs me back, harder than I think I've ever felt before. I radiate my love into her through my entire body.

"I love you too, honey. I'm so glad you're home. I've missed you so much. When your brother gets here, it will all be perfect," she whispers fiercely.

I can see she's been busy, preparing for the holiday. She's got an apple and a cherry pie cooling down on top of the stove. My mouth waters automatically at the sight of them, and it smells like she's got some chocolate chip cookies baking in the oven. It's hard to believe I'm finally seeing her. Relief spreads within me. Somehow, now that I'm home, things are going to be okay. They always are.

I hang onto my hug a long time until Mom releases me first. I pretend not to notice as she pulls her chair as close to the table as she can. I know she's trying to hide her stomach. The amount of water retention around her midsection tells me that her liver is not doing well at all. It sets off a roller coaster of emotions. Not trusting myself to speak yet, I busy myself by pouring a cup of her home-brewed mint iced tea, which she always has ready in the fridge. I move slowly, giving myself time to calm down and get a grip. Pitcher in hand, I shut the refrigerator door. It closes with a soft thunk.

"Mom, how long have you been retaining this much fluid? What are the doctors saying and doing for you?" It takes a supreme act of will to keep my voice calm and my face neutral.

She's uncomfortable and fidgets with her sweater. "My stomach's been gradually getting bigger. The doctor says it happens with liver problems and has me on lots of pills. One of them is supposed to help reduce the bloating, but he says there's not too much that can be done. I hate being so fat." Her lip trembles, and I want to scream bloody murder over the injustice of her suffering.

"Mom, it's not fat. What you have is called ascites, and it's caused by blood and fluid that's leaking into your tissues. We need to address this right away. I think we should have you get a second opinion. There's got to be something more we can do." I try to comfort her while stressing the seriousness of the situation.

"Look, let's not talk about this, now. I'm excited to have you home and I just want to enjoy it." She is distraught and starts shuffling through her paperwork on the table. I don't want to upset her any further; it's tearing my heart up as well.

"What would you like to talk about?" I pull my legs up on a kitchen chair and sit cross-legged, just like I always did as a kid.

"Tell me about your acupuncture practice. I'd love to hear about how you're helping people." Her worried eyes beg me to say something positive.

I take a big swig of iced tea, hoping it will somehow soothe the lump in my throat. I can't bear to see her suffering, and I want to make it go away immediately. I also want to read her doctor the riot act. How could he let her get to this stage? I have the overpowering urge to pore over my acupuncture notes on the liver; maybe there's something that will help.

But I'll do anything for her, and she wanted to hear something good. How could I deny her this one small thing?

"Okay. Actually, I can tell you about the guy I've been treating for chronic insomnia. He's had it for fourteen years." I manage to inject some enthusiasm into my voice.

"Really? What happened?" Her entire face lights up as I relate one of my recent success stories. It's all I can do not to cry.

Fortunately, Dad finally appears in the kitchen doorway. He's still wearing his thick yellow down jacket, and his cheeks are red with cold.

"I put your bags in your room, honey," he says, smiling at me like nothing is wrong. Then he glances at Mom. "Shirl, I'll be at the cab office for a few hours and then be home for dinner."

"Thanks, Dad. I'll see you later." I stand up and give him a hug good-bye. After he leaves, I turn back to Mom. I need to do something, anything, and the least I can do is try to reduce her pain. "How about I give you an acupuncture treatment?"

"I would like that very much, honey. Thank you." She actually looks excited. I offer her my arm and help her struggle up to her bedroom for the treatment. She winces as she walks, and a knife stabs my heart. I want to make it stop.

I dash back to my room and return with my needles. Mom is shifting restlessly on the bed.

"Try to relax." I put a pillow under her knees to make her more comfortable. "Tell me what hurts the most for you." I pray that there's something I can do for her.

"It's my knees and my ankles; they hurt so much I can hardly stand it," she says, almost in tears.

I would sell my soul for an off button to this nightmare. I fumble with my box of needles and then tell myself to calm down. I'm no good to her if I can't even hold a needle steady. That helps me. This is all about Mom, not me.

"You're in luck. Knee and ankle pain are something I can help you with." I force a casual and confident tone into my voice, but my stomach is busy doing flips.

She closes her eyes. "Thanks, honey." She sighs, settling her head back on her pillow. I insert the needles quickly. I want her to have them in as long as possible until dinner. I could weep with gratitude when she falls asleep and starts to snore. I slide down onto the carpet beside her bed and rest my head on my knees. The tears fall, and I don't bother to wipe them away.

I must have dozed off as well, but I'm alert as soon as I feel the bed shake. Mom is shifting around. I quickly dry my eyes on my sleeve and spring up from the floor. "Mom, don't squirm around. You'll disturb the needles," I tell her softly. She's looking at the clock on her bed stand.

"Oh my goodness. I fell asleep for an hour. Can you take out the needles? I've got to get some dinner heated up. Your father will be home soon," she says anxiously.

"Hold your horses. I'll have them out in a second." I pull them out quickly. "All right, you're free, but be careful getting up. Here, let me help you." I hold out my arm, and she hangs onto it as she sits up. I'm nervous when she freezes in place after she stands up.

"Are you okay, Mom?"

"Oh, this is *nice!* Thank you so much, honey. My knees and ankles are feeling much better." She gives me a hug and heads downstairs. I follow, keeping a close eye on her. She negotiates the stairs with ease, barely touching the railing, and I sigh in gratitude.

The next day, my brother's family arrives. Jay has brought his wife, Mica, and their three kids. They instantly fill the house with noise and activity. Mom can't contain her joy at being able to dote over her grandchildren. I want to get Jay alone so I can talk to him about her. Before I have a chance, Aunt Dot stops by. She arrives bearing ample supplies for our annual Christmas Eve party. It's always a huge affair with dozens of friends, family, and neighbors dropping by to eat, drink, and celebrate. I'm excited to see Aunt Dot. She and Mom are about as close as two sisters can get. When they get going at a party, it's like a free ticket to a comedy show.

It's easy to use the distraction of Jay's arrival to get Aunt Dot alone. I signal her to follow me with a quick glance, and we head downstairs into the den. She hasn't even had a chance to take off her coat. She starts unzipping her thick blue parka, but I can't wait any longer. Fit to burst, I pounce.

"Aunt Dot, how long has Mom been like this? I can't believe her doctors aren't more concerned. And her arthritis, it's hard to see her in so much pain." I try to keep my voice low so I'm not overheard.

Aunt Dot throws her coat on the couch and leans against the arm. "I have to tell you, Holly, that I'm as shocked over your mom's condition as you are. Until this week, she hasn't wanted me to come over to the house. She's been insisting that I just call her on the phone," she whispers. Her eyes are full of concern. "Did you know that she doesn't ever leave the house—not even to go shopping anymore?" Her answer hits me like a tidal wave.

"What?" I exclaim loudly, and then I glance at the stairs to make sure no one's in earshot. "No, I didn't know." I speak softly again. My knees feel weak.

Aunt Dot leans closer to me. "I think that she's really embarrassed about how big her stomach is. When we were young, your mom was always the pretty girl at school. How she looks really bothers her, and she refuses to admit to anyone just how much she's suffering." Aunt Dot's forehead is wrinkled with worry.

"She needs more urgent care from her doctors," I reply. It's harder than ever to quell the rising tide of fear inside of me.

Aunt Dot nods vigorously. "Another problem is that she's terrified of doctors and hospitals. Ever since she got Hepatitis C from her hysterectomy, your mom puts up a big fuss about going to see any doctor," she says and then checks the stairs before continuing. "Your father is not much help when it comes to these things. If she's not complaining to him about a problem, he won't notice it."

"Damn it!" I groan.

"I'm really worried about her, and I'm glad you kids are here. Maybe you can convince her to get more help." Aunt Dot touches my arm, and her expression reflects the desperation I feel.

"I'll try, that's for damn sure," I promise.

Mom was stubborn; she had always been the first one to help others—but the last to help herself. I require backup. It takes a while to isolate Jay from the rest of the family, but I finally get him alone in my bedroom. I'm trying hard not to panic, but I need him with me.

"Jay, what the hell are we going to do about Mom?" I ask urgently.

"Hol, I've been researching the best liver specialists." I can always count on Jay to be on top of things. "And there's one in Philly we should have Mom see. Don't worry. We'll get her the care she needs. It's going to be okay." He is a solid pillar of reassurance. It's what I yearned to hear, and a weight falls from my shoulders. Jay, Aunt Dot, and I are together on this; somehow, we'll find a way to help Mom. My spirits are lifted even further when Mica's mother, Minerva, arrives and lights up our house with her vivacious personality. She and Mom are good friends; Minerva showers her with much-needed nurturing and attention.

On Christmas Eve, everyone pitches in to get the food and decorations set up for the party. By the early afternoon, Mom has tuckered herself out and goes upstairs to rest before the evening's festivities. Aunt Dot has the remaining food preparations handled, so I take the opportunity to give Mom another treatment before the guests begin to arrive.

It's like a machete is slashing at my heart when I walk into her bedroom and witness her grimace of pain before she can hide it. Once again, I pretend not to notice, trying to shield her from further stress.

"Hey Mom, can I give you a pain treatment before the party?"

"Thanks honey, I'd like that." She smiles gratefully at me. "I'm so happy that all of you are here for Christmas. I haven't been feeling well, and it's really important to me that you're all here. I want *this* Christmas to be special," she says pointedly as she watches me insert the first needle. I'm focused on the treatment and only partially absorb the significance of her words.

"I'm glad I'm here too. But I wish you weren't in so much pain. I should have been here more to help you," I admit sadly, looking up at her obvious distress.

Mom quickly interrupts me. "You have helped me so much already. Your treatments help me, but being here is the best present you can give me." She pats my hand. I'm lost in worried concentration while I finish inserting the needles.

Afterwards, I pull a chair next to the bed. "Mom, I've done a lot of reading about liver transplants. Once you're through the operation and are recovering, which I can help with, you're going to feel like a brand-new person." I try to convey as much optimism as I can. Instead of comforting her, I see that my words only agitate her. "What's wrong?" I ask quietly, touching her arm.

She's silent for several long moments. "I don't want to go through with the operation. I'm tired of the pain and tired of fighting all the time. I just want my children and my grandchildren here with me. I want my last Christmas to be special," she says quietly. There's a real resignation in her eyes.

I've never heard Mom voice surrender before—about anything. It's hard to keep my hands from shaking as I adjust her needles. "Mom, don't talk nonsense. This is not your last Christmas." Denial is my only option. "We're all here to help you. I know operations are scary, but you will really feel like a new person after it's over." I keep my voice light. She simply closes her eyes, and we spend the rest of the session in uncomfortable silence. Each of us is alone with our thoughts.

As I'm taking out the last needle, Minerva bounces into the bedroom. She brings her usual bundle of happy energy with her. Her presence is a welcome relief. She's wearing a bright green apron with red Christmas balls all over it, and it flaps in the air as she dances over to Mom's side.

"Here you are, Mama Shirley! Are you ready to have lots of fun tonight?" She takes Mom's hand in hers. "Your house is looking wonderful, and the food, *oh the food,* is looking and smelling *soooo* good. I can't wait to get started." Minerva is bubbling over with enthusiasm.

Mom and I look at each other. Our walls of pain and suffering have temporarily been breached, and we smile.

Minerva pats Mom's hand. "Are you ready, Mama Shirley? We are missing you downstairs."

"I'm as ready as I'll ever be." Mom finally laughs and lets Minerva help her off the bed.

Minerva escorts her downstairs and sets her up on a kitchen chair in the central hub of the house. From there, she can see people arriving through the front door and anyone entering the living room or dining room, where the food is piled high. This is where I find Aunt Dot and my cousins, Sue and Beverly, setting out the plates and silverware.

The roast turkey smells delicious, and I decide to fill a plate before it gets really crowded with guests. I see Mom has made her decadent scalloped potatoes and scoop a hearty portion onto my plate. The table is overloaded with dishes piled high with food: potato salad, baked beans, green beans, coleslaw, carrots, sweet potatoes, ham, turkey, and so much more. I find I need to double up on my paper plate, just to hold everything. I decide to eat in the kitchen with Mom.

I'm happy to see her laughing and chatting with her brother, my Uncle Butch, and his son, Doug. I plant myself on the other side of the table. It's just in time. Before long the house is filled with cousins, aunts, uncles, friends, and neighbors. Mom is wearing a red cardigan over her favorite flowered top, and it suits her. It has a slimming effect, and she isn't acting overly self-conscious about her swollen stomach. I suddenly realize that she hasn't eaten anything yet.

"Mom, can I get you a plate?" I ask, interrupting her conversation with Mr. and Mrs. Fredericks, a couple of our longtime neighbors. They're laughing about something, and it warms my heart to see Mom's eyes sparkle with delight.

"Thank you, honey. I would love a plate," she replies, and I hop up from the table. "And can you ask Jimmie to make me a whiskey sour?" she adds nonchalantly.

"Sure," I answer. It's not until I've picked up a paper plate do I realize that Mom with her failing liver just asked me for hard alcohol. I shake my head, chuckling to myself, and take it as a good omen. She's having a good time and isn't thinking. When I return to the kitchen, she's surrounded by a fresh group of guests, and Minerva has taken up watch in my old chair. Minerva winks at me, as I politely squeeze in-between Mr. and Mrs. Curtis and set the plate down in front of Mom. "Here you go," I tell her, and then I dash downstairs to fill the rest of her order.

Dad had had an actual bar built downstairs in our rec room, and his favorite job was to be the bartender for their parties. I find him busy blending some margaritas for Uncle Terry and Cousin Hugh. The rec room is full of people, and in the background, I can hear Jay answering the front door again. Dad hands over the two giant margaritas and smiles when he sees me. "What can I get you, honey?" he asks.

I hop onto an empty barstool and spin around once. "Well, for starters, Mom would like a whiskey sour," I say when I come to rest, facing the bar. Dad had grabbed a clean glass but stopped in mid-motion with a surprised expression. "I know, Dad." I laugh. "Just make it a virgin whiskey sour. I think she's just having a good time."

"Okay. That's no problem. I'm glad your mom's enjoying herself. This party means everything to her," he replies as he mixes her drink.

I take a roundabout route through the house on my way back to the kitchen with her drink. There's close to a hundred people packed into our house. I need to push through a crowd to get back to her. I hear Uncle Bill raving about her apple pie. She beams happily at me when I hand her the glass. In the midst of it all, she sits proudly like the beloved queen of her castle.

The party doesn't break up until the wee hours of the morning. Eventually, only a handful of people remain. Minerva puts Mom to bed. Aunt Dot, Sue, and Beverly stay to help clean up, along with Minerva and Mica. We make short work of it. I hug Aunt Dot and my cousins good-bye while Minerva heads off to bed. She has Jay's old room while he and his family find places to sleep on sofas and scattered in rooms around the house. I collapse on my bed and quickly crash.

In the morning, we gather around the Christmas tree in the living room for our traditional gift-giving event. People find places to sit in a circle around the Christmas tree. Mom is ensconced in her favorite Nakashima rocking chair, opposite the Christmas tree, with her habitual morning cup of coffee in hand. Mica and Jay are seated on a wooden loveseat on Mom's left. Dad is in his usual brown armchair next to the tree, and Minerva is on the sofa to Mom's right. Jay's kids, Jacob, Nick and Juliette, ages seven, five, and three, are sprawled on the carpet in front of the tree, eagerly awaiting their bounty. Juliette is a ray of sunshine, toddling about in her butterfly pajamas. The boys are wearing matching blue pajamas with trains on them. They start punching each other, but when I step between them, they look up at Tia Holly's stern face and stop messing around.

There is a massive pile of presents surrounding the Christmas tree. I stand beside it and look over at Mom. She nods, giving me the go ahead, and I raise my hands for attention.

"Okay, is everybody ready?" I raise an eyebrow questioningly at the kids.

"Yes!" they shout all at once, bobbing their heads vigorously.

"Okay then. Here we go!" I clap my hands and rummage through the presents, looking at the name tags. My designated job is to hand out the presents from around the tree. I find one present for each of the kids and make them wait until everyone is watching. Mom has her camera ready. "Okay, go!" I laugh as the kids rip open their presents, chattering with delight. The glow on Mom's face as she watches the antics of her grandchildren has me feeling as if I've already opened my present.

Mom's image flickers, and then I see Grandmom Edna sitting in the same Nakashima rocking chair. Just like Mom, it was always her favorite place to be on Christmas mornings. She and Mom look so much alike. I remember Grandmom sitting in the exact same chair, smiling contentedly as Jay and I tore open our presents one Christmas morning when we were children. Shortly thereafter, Grandmom had fallen into a diabetic coma. She never recovered. A year later, she had died.

I shake my head to clear the image from my mind. I don't want to go there and force myself to focus on Jay's children. Nick has just gotten his box open and pulls out a yellow bulldozer. "Vrrrrrooom, vroom!" He giggles and starts to push it across the floor toward Mom.

She quickly snaps a picture. "Show Grandmom what you got, Nick," she says excitedly.

"Look Grandmom—a bulldozer!" Nick proudly holds it up for her to see.

"Oh, that's wonderful!" she coos.

Not to be outdone, Jacob holds up his red dump truck. "Grandmom, see I've got a neat truck too!" he shouts. Mom laughs and compliments Jacob's truck as well.

The kids are soon surrounded by a small mountain of toys, and Christmas day is off to a good start. The rest of it proves just as pleasant; Aunt Dot, her husband George, and my cousins Beverly and Sue arrive to play card games and polish off the party's leftovers. All in all, Mom gets her wish: Christmas is a success.

The remainder of our visit is a flurry of activity. Jay contacts a prominent liver specialist, and I track down an acupuncturist much closer to home. Mom agrees to get a second opinion from Jay's specialist and to see the acupuncturist—provided Aunt Dot will accompany her, of course.

Leaving Mom is difficult; I can't stand the thought of her being in pain. I know I can be of help to her, but I need to get back to the Bay Area to make preparations for an extended absence. As soon as the new liver becomes available, I will have to drop everything and rush back. I want to be at Mom's side during surgery and then stay and nurse her through her recovery.

Shortly after my return to California, she receives her second opinion. Her new doctor places her on a much higher priority level for a new liver. Our concerns are proven justified, and I'm eternally grateful that Jay has picked a proactive physician. I'm hopeful that it won't be long before Mom will have the transplant—and everything will be okay.

CHAPTER TWENTY TWO
THE STORM

A mother's love's a blessing, no matter where you roam.
Keep her while she's living, you'll miss her when she's
gone. Love her as in childhood, though feeble, old
and grey, for you'll never miss a mother's love,
till she's buried beneath the clay.
–Thomas P. Keenan

"Hol, I think we need to go to Pennsylvania," Jay blurts out apprehensively when I answer the phone.

"What's going on?" I ask anxiously, already picking up his fear.

"It's Mom." His voice cracks, and dread wraps its cold fingers around my heart. "Dad just called and said that she's in the hospital. He said she's okay, but they're running some tests. Her liver isn't doing so great."

"Shit, what does that mean? It hasn't been doing great for a while. Did Dad tell you anything useful?" I'm instantly regretful of my tone. Jay doesn't deserve my wrath.

"You know Dad—he's doesn't really get it. He told me not to worry." Jay sighs, and I feel his frustration as well as my own. "He wasn't going to call me at all, but Aunt Dot insisted we should know that Mom's in the hospital. He said he'll call us if anything changes, but I'm jumping on a red eye flight."

My mind races through the things I need to do in order to get on a plane, which includes arranging for Shika to be taken care of as well as notifying my patients. "Jay, if you get there tomorrow morning, I think I can get the red eye tomorrow night and be there Saturday morning. Just give me a call when you see her and let me know the real story, okay?"

"Not a problem. Don't worry, we'll get through this." His flow of support is my anchor.

I start making arrangements to leave as soon as I get off the phone. Sofia agrees to look after Shika without hesitation. I spend the rest of my time cancelling my patient appointments and packing for the red eye Friday night. I'm on pins and needles until Jay calls me late Friday morning.

"I'm here at the hospital, and I've just seen Mom. She's hooked up to a bunch of monitors, but she's talking, and Dad has even brought her some accounting to work on." Jay sounds fairly upbeat, and my relief is palpable.

It takes a few seconds for the secondary surge of anger. "What? What do you mean Dad brought her some accounting? Can't he give her a break? She's in the hospital, damn it. Would you please tell her to rest easy, and let the work go until she's out?"

"You know Mom. *She's* not going to let a little thing like being in the hospital keep her from working. Dad was probably just following orders." Jay chuckles. "Hey, don't worry. I'll call you in a bit. First, I've got to find a doctor. They seem pretty scarce around here." He sounds amused.

My body relaxes a bit. If Jay can feel that way, then maybe things aren't too bad. I'm grateful he's there; he'll make certain Mom is taken care of.

Shortly before I leave for the airport, I receive another phone call from Jay.

"What's your arrival time tomorrow morning?" His voice is unsteady, and my heart flies into my throat the instant I hear it.

"I'll be there early morning—6:30. How's Mom?" I ask quickly.

Jay hesitates only slightly, but it feels as if an entire century passes in that moment. "Mom's developed some kind of staph infection, and she's slipped into a coma. They've got her on all kinds of machines to keep her organs functioning."

"She's in a coma?" I fall to my knees. This can't be happening. "But how is that possible? You were just talking to her; she was even working on the accounting. What the hell happened?" I gasp. I'm having trouble breathing. My worst nightmare has just been realized.

"I don't know. She was okay—and then she wasn't. Hurry, Hol," he says, but all I hear is fear.

I hang up. Anger erupts like burning acid within me—anger at myself. "Damn it. Damn it! I *knew* I should have gone sooner!" I shout out loud. I can't stop berating myself while I race around the house to finish packing. My thoughts keep screaming out to the universe: *This isn't happening! Wait, Mom! Please wait! I'm coming.*

The flight to Pennsylvania is the longest five and a half hours of my life. Beverly picks me up at the airport, and we race to the hospital. When I walk into Mom's hospital room, Jay and Dad are talking quietly on the opposite side of the room. Aunt Dot is there also. She immediately comes over to give me a tight hug. When she looks at me, her eyes mirror the shocked disbelief that I'm feeling.

"I'm so glad you're here," she says. "I'm going to let you guys have a little space. I'll be just outside with Beverly." She squeezes my arm before she goes.

When I look at Mom for the first time, my throat closes down and an iron vise around my chest tightens until I can scarcely breathe. She's on a ventilator and is hooked up to a bunch of monitors as well as several IV's. Her eyes are closed, and her chest is rising and falling in concert with the pumping of the ventilator. I'm not sure how long I stand there staring at her—completely at a loss for words.

Dad comes over and gives me a hug. "Thanks for coming, honey. Mom isn't doing that well right now, but the doctors are doing everything they can." I look into his worried eyes, but I still can't speak. "I'm going outside now. I'll be back shortly," he says.

The room is spinning—maybe this is simply a nightmare? When I look over at Jay, he's moved to a chair. He has his laptop on his knees and is furiously tapping away at the keyboard. Somehow, I make it over to Mom's side and touch her hand. Her life energy is so low that I almost can't detect it. I lean down close to her ghastly pale face. It's hard to get the words past the lump in my throat. "Hi, Mom. It's Holly. I'm here. I love you Mom," I whisper.

Jay closes his laptop and slides it back into his briefcase. He stands up slowly, and I see that his clothes are disheveled as though he's slept in them. His face looks haggard, and he has a five o'clock shadow. His eyes are filled with a grim determination, and although he's looking straight at me, I don't think he truly sees me. I've never seen my brother like this before. "I've been doing some research on liver transplants, and Mom can still have one. She's just got to hang on." His words tumble out in a rush, and each one strikes me like a hammer on an anvil.

"Jay, what happened?" My knees feel like they're about to buckle. "I thought you were talking to her?"

"I believe I can explain your mother's condition," a deep baritone voice interjects from behind me. I turn around to look at the speaker. "Hello, I'm Dr. Mackey." A tall, distinguished doctor with short graying black hair is standing in the doorway. He extends his hand toward me. When our hands touch, I'm aware of an aura of compassion around him. Jay stands next to me as we listen to what he has to say. "I'm sorry to have to tell you this, but your mother's liver has reached a critical point, whereby her other organs are also beginning to fail. We have her on the ventilator to assist her breathing, and we're giving her drugs that keep her blood pressure high enough to keep her kidneys working." He pauses—maybe because of the horror on my face. "However, the news isn't all bad. We've received word that there may be a liver available for your mother."

My emotions leap at his words of hope, but then he continues.

"We're attempting to keep her stable, but what concerns me right now is the low-grade staph infection that she's developed."

My heart plummets; I know that an infection will prevent surgery.

"What are you doing for it?" Although I don't feel it, I force calm into my voice.

"We need to clear that up before we can operate, so we're giving her strong antibiotics. Hold onto your hope, your mom's a fighter," he says. His pager goes off, and he pauses to check it. "If you'll excuse me, I'll be back later. I'll keep you informed of any progress." When I nod my head, he spins on his heels and hurries out the door.

Jay grabs me in the tightest hug I've ever felt from him. His whole body shakes, and I hug him back just as fiercely. We cling together for a long time. He finally releases me, and our eyes meet. I see determination take hold in his, and it gives me something to hang onto to.

"Mom's going to get a new liver," he says. "Maybe it's been done before with an infection. I'm going to see if there's any new drug—or something that can help." He races back to his chair. In seconds, his laptop is out of the briefcase, and he's typing furiously on the keyboard.

I numbly turn back to Mom and watch the ventilator breathing for her. With all my strength, I will her to open her eyes, make a noise, or move a finger. I would give anything to make contact with her spirit, but there is nothing. I feel strange, so helpless, so lost. Mom has to recover—she's a fighter, and we all love her and need her. I want to snap my fingers and make it all go away.

Dad, Jay, Aunt Dot, and I spend the day rotating in and out of her room. The nurses in the intensive care unit are exceptionally kind, accommodating our constant presence, and they check on her frequently. A steady stream of relatives and friends come and go as the hours tick by.

It is early evening the next time Dr. Mackey returns. Dad and Aunt Dot are in the room with Mom, while Jay and I are standing in the hallway. The doctor strides up to my brother and me.

"I wanted to let you know that we feel the available liver is a good match for your mother, and we're having it flown in tonight. Now if we can get her fever and this infection down, we can perform the transplant. Let's keep our fingers crossed."

Jay glances at me, and we silently cradle a precious ray of hope between us. It's maddening that there's nothing for us to do but wait until morning to see if her fever improves. Dad and I head home to sleep, but Jay stays and crashes in the hospital lounge.

Early the next morning, we rush back to the hospital. Dr. Mackey shows up shortly after we arrive and waves us into the hall outside Mom's room. "Unfortunately, your mother's fever hasn't abated, and I'm afraid we have to give the liver to someone else." I feel as if I've been clubbed over the head. "Our goal now is to keep her stable and get this infection under control. Then she will be able to receive the next one that becomes available."

Dad, Jay and I look at each other in a dumbstruck silence. Eventually, Dad simply turns around and heads back into Mom's room.

Jay says, "Why can't you operate anyway? I mean, given the circumstances, can't you just go ahead with the transplant and worry about the infection later?"

"I wish we could, James, but we can't. It's too risky that we'd lose both. I'm sorry. But we haven't given up trying—not by a longshot," the doctor replies—and this time he's visibly upset.

I can't trust myself to speak without bursting into tears or becoming enraged. I press my lips together tightly and say nothing. Dr. Mackey slowly turns around and walks away. I hold my heart in my hand, ripped from my chest, and stare after our only hope that is now receding down the hallway.

Jay sprints back into Mom's room to grab his laptop and continue his quest for a miracle. I follow him into the room and see Dad sitting quietly by Mom's side, holding her hand. My heart hurts so badly I can't breathe. I have to get out of here.

At first, I wander aimlessly down the hallway, but then I decide to head for the waiting room. I zero in on the bank of public phones against the far wall. My hand is shaking as I dial the Colorado area code and phone number for Donna. She's one of my parents' closest friends. Donna had come with Aunt Dot to Mom's rescue when she collapsed from the bleeding ulcer. She also happens to be a metaphysical intuitive and healer that I admire and respect. I desperately need to make contact with Mom somehow, and maybe Donna can do it.

"Holly, how are you hanging in there?"

It's a relief to hear her compassionate voice. "It's not good, Donna. Can you come out?" My constricted throat makes it difficult to speak.

She hesitates before she answers. In the meantime, I slide down into the chair next to the phone.

"Oh, hon. I love your mom so very much, but I can't see her in the hospital. I need to keep my memories of her laughing, full of life and happy. I hope you can understand. I want to help you any way I can," she replies, noticeably upset.

My shoulders slump a little further, but I understand how she feels. Maybe she can still help me. "Donna, can you make a connection with Mom and tell me what she says?" I ask cautiously, knowing that my request is a double-edged sword.

"Actually, just before you called, I connected with her spirit and asked what she wants to do," Donna says slowly. My stomach leaps into my throat. "She stands with her back to me and won't turn around to talk. I'm not sure she knows yet. I think the best thing you can do right now is just be with her and send her your love—she'll receive it," she says soothingly.

It's not exactly what I want to hear, but a tiny ray of light still shines. I wander the halls but eventually return to Mom's room and find myself standing next to Dad. He grabs my hand, squeezes it, and leaves to take a break. Jay is still typing forcefully on his laptop. He doesn't know I'm there. I hear him talking to himself, using medical terminology and names of drugs I've never heard of. I take over Dad's empty chair and hold Mom's hand. I send her love and desperately hope she feels my presence.

The days crawl by with little change in Mom's condition. Sitting next to her bedside hour after hour, I become obsessed with watching her life sign monitors. I watch for every fluctuation in blood pressure, changes in body temperature or heartbeat, and even the amount of liquid in the urine bag. I mentally will the signs to become normal and healthy. Every drop that flows into the urine bag means Mom's kidneys still have life. And no matter how hard I try, I can't keep my breathing from matching the pace of the ventilator.

After several days, I give up trying. Time no longer has any meaning; my life becomes my connection with the medical monitors. If only I'm able to make them do what I want, Mom will be all right. During the moments when I force myself to let go of the monitors and connect with Mom's spirit, I sense a presence hovering around her head, but from her body, there is nothing.

On Thursday, Dr. Mackey gathers us together. Dad, Jay, Aunt Dot, and I follow him into a medical conference room. We all sit down around the table. I notice a circular water stain on the oak table and fixate on it, unable to look at the doctor. The air is thick with despair.

"I know this is a really hard time for you all, and I'm so sorry," the doctor pauses, as if searching for the right words. "But I think it's time to start thinking about what's best for Shirley right now. At this point, she's being kept alive by machines and drugs, the infection has spread unabated, and her organs have failed." Every word he utters is another nail in her coffin. "I think it's time that you consider letting her go," he urges us, sealing the lid tightly.

Dad starts to sob, and Jay reaches across the table to hold his hand.

Dr. Mackey rises, looking uncomfortable and helpless. "I'm going to let you all alone to talk to each other. I'll be outside if you need me."

After Dr. Mackey closes the door behind him, it's hard for me to breathe; my lungs don't want to expand. There are tears running down Jay's face, and Dad is trying to say something but can't quite get anything out. Strangely, I hear myself speaking—but I'm not sure how that's possible.

"I don't think Mom would want us to keep her going like this. I think she would want us to let her go," I say, forcing myself to look at my grief-stricken family.

"I think we need to make a family decision, all of us. I don't think Shirl would want to stay like this, either." Dad continues sobbing, his words coming out in spurts.

Jay says, "I agree with Dad and Hol." The tears are streaming down his face.

Aunt Dot simply nods her head in abject misery. We all join hands around the table and share our worst nightmare. For me, there is an audible click as the vise in my chest is padlocked in place. My eyes are oddly dry as I watch everyone else cry. I don't feel anything. Why can't I feel anything? Where are my emotions?

I get up to inform Dr. Mackey of our decision.

He touches my arm in sympathy. "I understand how hard this is, but there is no chance for her to come back. Her body has failed. It's her time, but you are all here for your mother, and she knows that." His voice breaks as he tries to comfort me.

I'm startled by his loss of control and then touched when I realize he had become emotionally involved with our case.

We shuffle slowly into Mom's room, like the walking dead, to say our final good-byes before the ventilator is disconnected. Dad sits in the chair on the left side near the head of the bed and takes her hand. Jay kneels down next to Dad, and Aunt Dot moves to the foot of the bed. I walk to the head of the bed on the right side and take her other hand. It's not long before several nurses come into the room and begin to turn off the machines. As each one is silenced, a part of me goes dark. The silence becomes deafening within moments.

Jay's shoulders shake with sobs.

The strange sensation of detachment continues to wash over me. I'm looking at Mom, but I know with a certainty that she is not in her body at all. When I glance at Dad and Jay, I see a soft glow surrounding their heads and, somehow, I know she is trying to comfort them. The glow expands to include Aunt Dot as she joins Dad and Jay in their lament.

I experience a single—wildly out of place—rush of joy as the glowing light touches me as well. But then, in the blink of an eye, it's gone. On my side of the bed, I see blood pouring from Mom's neck. I catch the attention of a nurse with my eyes and then nod toward it. She moves quickly to cover the blood, and I'm grateful no one else notices.

Inside myself, I can see a black box engulfing my heart. I have become an observer simply watching the scene unfold before me. Mom is gone, and so am I.

CHAPTER TWENTY THREE

THE CRUCIBLE

Give sorrow words; the grief that does not speak
whispers the o'er-fraught heart and bids it break.
–William Shakespeare

I stumble out of Mom's hospital room and into the hallway. The floor undulates beneath my feet, and I lean against the wall for support. My vision flickers like a dying light bulb.

A nurse approaches and says, "I'm so sorry for your loss. We need to make arrangements. Do you know which funeral home you'd like to use?" Her words are muffled and indistinct as if I were underwater. She doesn't go away when her lips stop moving and hovers expectantly. I sigh inwardly and reluctantly swim to the surface; they don't waste any time, do they?

"I don't know, but I'll find out and let you know," I mumble.

Aunt Dot appears at my side, and I'm relieved that she knows the answer. I feel myself rising, cocooned in some kind of bubble. My body is an empty shell, but it continues to function as if preprogrammed. It walks back into the hospital room, while I float along behind.

I don't remember the drive home, but somehow, Dad, Jay, and I arrive there in one piece. We all file in through the den door in silence. Dad suddenly announces that he wants the memorial service to be held in a week. Then his eyes go blank, and he trudges upstairs to his bedroom. When I look at Jay, I can see his eyes tearing up again. He slumps onto the sofa and dials his wife back in California. The agony in his voice sears a hole in my bubble. Abruptly, I'm reintegrated with my body. I quietly withdraw upstairs to the kitchen.

This room is special. Her presence is everywhere; this is her domain. I gravitate automatically toward her work chair, half slid under the table. The worn, green fabric cushion that Mom always sat on is still in place. Just poking out from under the table is the little wooden foot stool that

Mom propped her feet on since her legs were too short to reach the floor. There's a knife stabbing my heart, but I ignore it.

Some of her accounting paperwork is still scattered on the table. It's as if she had just stepped out of the room and could be back at any time. There's a yellow post–it note on the top page. I can't help myself and pick it up. It simply says: need milk, eggs, loaf of bread. It's Mom's handwriting. A boulder materializes in my throat, and I can't swallow. My hand shakes as I realize this may be the last thing she did before she went to the hospital. My vision darkens, and I collapse with a thump in Mom's chair. An irritating voice in my head pleads with me to stay present. I can't be consumed by the tidal wave of loss. I *can't*. Not yet. There's too much to do.

That first night with Mom gone seems as if it will never end. I lie awake on my bed, listening to my heartbeat. Jay is in his room, and Dad is in his. I hear the muffled sounds of their combined snoring through the walls. I would give anything to escape into the state of unconsciousness, but it continues to elude me.

I slip noiselessly out of my room, head downstairs to the living room, and sit on the floor in front of the large bay window. She had loved this window and how it had let so much light inside and looked impressive from the street. My parents had had this house built from scratch. It was one of the first houses on the block. It had been Mom's dream home, and she had chosen the split–level design and many extras: the large patio outside the kitchen, the wide spiral staircase in the center of the house, the layout of the kitchen, and the massive living room bay window. I was only four years old when we moved in, but I remember her dancing around this very room; she was so happy. This was Mom's house; without her in it, it's bereft of life.

I hug my knees and stare forlornly at the stars. I used to think that starlight was magical and could grant my wish if I stood in its nightly radiance. Oh, if only that were so. Unable to stand the torture of the living room any longer, I return to my bedroom. Exhausted, yet unable to sleep, I yank one of my old science fiction novels from my bookshelf. It's one from the original *Star Trek* series. I read until sunrise; thankfully, caught up in phaser fights and saving alien worlds from destruction.

Although Dad wants the service in a week, he's incapable of helping. In fact, he stays in his room, sleeping almost around the clock and seldom emerging. He answers my questions in short monosyllables. Anything requiring more of him is pointless; he just mentally drifts away. Jay is also mired in grief and focuses his time on making the arrangements to bring his wife and kids to Pennsylvania for the memorial. When I ask him to come to the funeral home with me, he says he can't. His eyes plead with me to let him be. He has reached his emotional limit, and I don't want to push my brother past it. The memorial preparations are left to me.

The kitchen becomes my command post. I had no idea how much needs to be done when someone dies, and I have so little time in which to do it. The phone has been ringing off the hook. My parents never upgraded their obsolete rotary telephones, and the one in the kitchen is mounted on the wall above the table. Whenever someone calls, the anachronistic sound of its ring reverberates throughout the house. The receiver is attached to a long cord that's become tangled around my arm and chair like unwanted ivy.

I'm seated across the table from Mom's chair, rapidly scribbling down notes with the phone receiver pressed to my ear. My head is pounding. I've been on it answering questions from Pastor Denton. He leads the congregation at my parent's church and has agreed to do her service. I switch the phone to my other ear.

"Thank you for your help, Pastor Denton. I'll get back to you with the final list of hymns and scripture passages and the rest of the agenda shortly." As soon as I hang up, it rings again. I rub my temples and answer it. "Hello, this is Holly," I intone mechanically.

"Oh Holly, I'm *so* sorry dear. This is Dr. Nessler." It's yet another neighbor. I take a deep breath and do my best to tune out. "I've just heard the terrible news about your mom. How are you holding up?"

I want to scream, "How do you *think* I'm holding up? The most important person in my life is *gone*!" But instead, I opt for the canned copy. "I'm hanging in there as best as I can. Thank you so much for calling, Dr. Nessler. We all appreciate it." I click off, wondering how many more times I'll have to repeat my speech. The phone rings again, and I glare at it with loathing. After ten rings, I can't ignore it any longer.

"Hello, is Ms. Reese there? This is Tammy with Bradley Caterers," the woman's voice is sing-song, like she's calling about party arrangements. I'm tempted to hang up on her, but I'm feeling masochistic.

"Yes, this is she." I can't quite get the growl out of my voice. Fortunately, or not, Tammy doesn't notice.

"I had a couple of menu questions. Did you want some sausage with the meatballs in the spaghetti sauce? We have a tasty sweet sausage that works well," she rattles on happily. "And then for the sauerkraut, did you want Kielbasa, Bratwurst, or Polish sausage?"

It's a pity I can't send an electric shock over the telephone wire. After a slow count to ten, I feel it's safe to speak. "Yes, please add the tasty sweet sausage and use Kielbasa. Thank you," I reply as cordially as I can. How much more inane can it get? The phone rings again, and I feel positively dangerous.

"Yes?" I answer curtly.

"Mrs. Reese, this is Dan over at Dan's Auto Parts. I'm calling personally to find out why you haven't paid your parts bill. It's over two weeks late. I was shocked to discover this—and I'm *sure* you are too. So, I hope that we can get this straightened out right away."

That does it for me. I load both barrels. "This is Holly Reese, her daughter. You haven't been paid because my mom is *dead*. Resend the bill and get in line." I slam the receiver into its wall cradle above the table. All I can do is stand and seethe for several minutes. Great, there's yet another problem.

Mom has left paperwork piled up in the kitchen, the dining room, the den, and even in her bedroom. She had solely managed the finances for the taxi business as well as their home. I stay up into the wee hours of the night sorting through several years of paperwork, trying to figure out Mom's system for paying bills. She had one that worked well, but I have no clue what it was. Neither does Dad. He was entirely dependent on her and is completely helpless without her. I'm exhausted, and my body feels like lead. The Olympian task before me seems insurmountable. If not for Aunt Dot, who guides me through the necessary arrangements, I would have drifted hopelessly out to sea. Somehow, it all gets done.

The Pennbrook Baptist Church is an unassuming two-story building with worn white siding and a slender steeple. It looks exactly the same as it did when I was a kid. Churches had always made me uncomfortable, and now, walking up the front steps, my heart is coated with an icy dread. Aunt Dot is with me, and while I feel her love supporting me, I can also sense her own private agony over the loss of her sister and closest confidante. Inside, the air is musky with that familiar old church smell. I want to bolt out the door, out of the stifling oppression, and into the free air. I've got to hold it together and get through this day. The memorial isn't for a few hours, but there's still much to be done. Aunt Dot disappears to find Pastor Denton, and I'm left alone in the vestibule.

It's been a long time since I've been inside this church—ever since my Sunday school days. Even though people had always been friendly, I resented the attempts to shape me with their cookie-cutter ideas, and I had felt like an alien. A flash of light in my eyes makes me squint. Tiny fragments of red, blue, and yellow light are shimmering on the wall in front of me. I turn around and look up at the large stained glass window on the outside wall of the vestibule. The colors taunt me with false promises of hope and happiness. I have a strong desire to find a ladder and nail a blanket over the window—the only color I can see right now is black.

I've been holding a box with Mom's pictures, and its weight reminds me I have work to do. I walk through the main archway into the nave and quickly down the aisle, past the many rows of pews. All I can think about is how horrendously uncomfortable it had been to sit on them. I'm not looking forward to sitting on them again. I want to cry when I reach the altar table, where the florist has already placed a colorful assortment of wildflowers. I imagine Mom in our backyard, kneeling down beside her beloved wildflowers patiently pulling out the stubborn weeds. The sudden longing to see her again sears through me like a hot iron and steals the air from my lungs. The box with Mom's pictures starts to fall from my hands. I quickly juggle it onto the table and breathe a sigh of relief. When I set up the poster-sized portrait of her in the center, I avert my eyes. I can't bear to look at her picture right now; it would be my undoing. I visualize an impenetrable stone wall surrounding my heart. The resulting numbness is a welcome respite.

This church had meant a lot to Mom. She and Dad had been married there, and they had both served as officials on the executive board for many years. She had had a lot of friends here. There's no question in my mind that this is where she would want her memorial. I can get through this for Mom; this is a day to honor her. I grit my teeth and hold on.

Aunt Dot returns with Pastor Denton and a surprise guest. Pastor Masley had led the church throughout my childhood. He's in his eighties now and blind, but his mind remains as sharp as ever. Aunt Dot has his arm and guides him over to me.

"Pastor Masley, it's wonderful of you to come." I'm deeply touched, and take his outstretched hand in mine.

His pupils are clouded, but his old sparkle isn't. "I've known your folks since they were born. If it's all right with you, I'd love to say some words about Shirley during the service," he says, squeezing my hand gently.

I know he can't see my expression, so I return his squeeze. "Thank you, Pastor Masley. I know Mom would love that."

My cousins—Beverly, Sue, Doug, Robyn, Leigh Ann, Debbie, Carol, and more—all come to help. Suddenly, I've got ushers and set-up staff en masse. The gratitude and relief I feel is beyond any words. When Jay and his family arrive with Dad, I walk over to meet them in the vestibule.

"I can't stay out here," Dad mumbles and then hurries into the nave and plants himself on the front pew.

Mica thoughtfully leads her kids away toward Aunt Dot, leaving Jay and me alone. When he faces me, his eyes are clear and focused. And when the guests start arriving, we stand shoulder to shoulder, receiving their condolences together. People pour into the church: friends, neighbors, extended family, and employees of my parents. The church is filling up fast, and there's still a line out the door.

I feel someone shaking my hand vigorously, and I stare up into the familiar blue eyes of Harvey, one of my parent's most trusted and longest-serving drivers. I hadn't seen him in more than ten years, and he could still pass for the scarecrow in the *Wizard of Oz*.

He grabs me in a crushing hug and says, "I'm so sorry for your loss. Shirley was like a second mom to me. I can't believe she's not here anymore." He releases me and pulls out a plaid red kerchief to blow his nose before moving on to shake Jay's hand. Harvey is replaced by another employee, and then another, all voicing similar sentiments. People keep coming, even after the nave is filled beyond capacity. The love that all these people felt for Mom slips through the cracks in my stone wall and touches my heart.

During the service, Dad sits on Jay's right side while I'm on his left. My dear friend Lauren, from Shotokan Karate School, sits on my left. Pastor Masley's remembrances of Mom move many to tears. I can hear scattered sobs throughout the church. Lauren squeezes my hand, and I draw upon her strength to keep their emotions at bay. Pastor Denton ends his eulogy by asking if anyone would like to say a few words about her. I turn my head to see Ted, a neighbor and childhood friend, stand up.

"When I was a teenager, I felt lost and alone, but Mrs. Reese was there for me. She would always invite me into her kitchen, feed me, and listen to whatever was bothering me. She didn't judge me, and she did her best to help me. She was a wonderful lady." Ted gets choked up and sits back down.

After Ted, friends and family stand to tell their stories about how Mom helped or inspired them in some profound way. I've got a crushing grip on Lauren's hand as I desperately try to keep my wall from crumbling. Pastor Denton reads several letters honoring Mom. My brother's kids, Jacob, Nicholas, and Juliette all write about how much they love and miss Grandmom Shirley. I had also written a piece, and he reads mine last.

Pastor Denton holds my letter a moment in silence and then gazes at me with eyes full of compassion. I shudder involuntarily and brace myself.

"I've saved this letter for last and I think you will all understand why when you hear it," he says and waits while the entire congregation falls silent. Then he begins reading:

Mom, I miss you so much. Before you left, I didn't have the chance to tell you how much I love you and what it meant to me to have you as my mom. If I had the entire world to choose from, I would choose you every time. When I was sad, your hugs were boundless. When I needed encouragement, you gave it to me. When you didn't understand me, you still stood by me. When I doubted myself, you did not. When I was happy, you celebrated with me. When I asked for guidance, you offered it gladly. When I made mistakes, you did not judge.

Pastor Denton's deep baritone resounds throughout the nave. I hear several people sobbing. A sledgehammer pounds my stone wall with every word, obliterating it a chunk at a time. Stone pieces are flying. I'm terrified of losing control and squeeze my eyes shut. My breath comes in tiny broken spurts, but my ears can still hear the pastor.

You encouraged me to be me, and to pursue my grandest dreams. You loved me unconditionally and asked for nothing in return. If there was anything that I would change about you if I could, it would be that you were still here and in perfect health. I love you, Mom, your loving daughter, Holly.

As the pastor reads my final words, I open my eyes to find him watching me as if he can see the thunderstorm raging within me. My wall crumbles, and I burst into tears. They're the first physical tears that I've shed since Mom's passing.

Jay wraps an arm around my shoulders, and Dad puts his arm on top of Jay's. We cry together. Pastor Denton steps down from the sanctuary and reverently places my letter next to Mom's picture on the altar.

CHAPTER TWENTY FOUR

THE AFTERMATH

If you're going through hell, keep going.
–Winston Churchill

V-o-i-d ...

My fingers balk on the keyboard, and I stare back at the screen, too tired to shake off the irony of those four letters. Somewhere in my head, a professorial narrator rattles off the textbook definition. "Void: a C language keyword signifying a procedure that returns nothing." How apt ... how absolutely, perfectly fitting!

The cursor blinks insipidly while it waits for me to type the next line of code, but the words on the computer screen in front of me start to blur. I rub my tired eyes; they need a break from the monotony of programming as much as I do. I lean back in my cushy, yet ergonomically correct desk chair and prop my feet up on my desk. My stark white office is about as sparse as they come: a large wooden desk, a chair, a desktop computer, and a single bookshelf.

I mull over the absurdity of the sole architectural feature—a large picture window that consumes half of the wall directly across from my desk. It looks out onto the long dimly lit hallway, which is completely deserted, except for my single office. But the detail that really bothers me about the window is that it's tinted. Why on earth would anyone want to tint an indoor office window that only looks onto a hallway tunneling through the center of a warehouse-like office building? It resembles a rectangular black hole. Perhaps if I were to leap through it, I'd be transported to a different galaxy? Just about anywhere else would be more preferable than here; my latest software contract job has me designing a custom e-mail list application.

I sigh with the reality of a quickly approaching deadline and refocus on the lines of code on my monitor. Where was I? Oh yeah, I was splitting the e-mail header from the body. My feet drop back down on floor, and my fingers start typing where I left off.

> *void header (FILE *fp) { while ((fgets (line, MAX, fp)) != NULL)*
> *{ if (strstr (line, "FROM")) (state = IN); ...*

As my fingers tap away on autopilot, my thoughts play out the events over the last nine months that have led me here, contracting for a high tech firm in the Bay Area.

After the memorial, Jay was only able to stay another week in Pennsylvania. I missed him terribly when he left. We'd only just scratched the surface of discovering how much Mom actually did to run the business, let alone their house. She had paid all the bills and made the financial decisions. It blew my mind when I found out that Dad didn't know how to balance his checkbook or even write a check. It was probably the first time in my life that I taught something to him, instead of the other way around.

I wound up staying in Pennsylvania another five months to help him sort out his affairs and sell the taxi business. Talking to buyers and negotiating on behalf of Dad over his and Mom's life work was a daunting task, especially since everything about the taxi business reminded me of her. My grief was still new and raw, but there was no time for mourning. Each day brought a steady stream of salt pouring onto the open wound in my chest. In time, although the pain wasn't gone, it seemed to fade into a kind of white noise.

Before her death, Mom had wanted to sell the business. My parents had toiled in the taxi industry for more than forty years, working ten-to-twenty-hour days. They had been planning to spend their retirement in ease. If only they had managed to sell it then—at least, they would have had a few years of enjoying life together. Mom had sacrificed too much of herself. She had scrimped and saved. She had given up her opportunity for writing. She had chosen not to pursue higher education and had muted her creative talents—all for a dreamed-of-moment that she would never live to enjoy. She was only sixty-four. Life isn't fair.

After months of haggling with a neighboring taxi firm, I was finally able to negotiate a price that Dad was willing accept. Instead of feeling relief, I felt an overwhelming sadness. Dad agreed to the new terms of the offer, although it took a few more weeks before the sale was completed. After he settled into a daily routine, it was time for me to leave.

The phone on my desk rings loudly, and I glare at it with annoyance. It can only be Tom, my boss. He's one of the rudest people I've ever met. I mentally steel myself before I answer it. "Yes, Tom, what can I do for you?"

"What the hell is this piece of *crap* you sent me?" he shouts into the phone loudly enough to cause me to hold the receiver two feet away from my ear. I take several deep breaths and ask myself again why I took this contract job.

"Excuse me?" I reply coldly.

"You heard me. I asked you to create a feature to let me sort the list recipients by interest categories and then tabulate their click-through results. I don't see it anywhere on the control panel." His voice drips with venom.

I'm thankful that he never comes to my office in person; otherwise, I might be tempted to practice the new takedown I learned in my martial arts class. Instead, I force myself to reply in a professional monotone. "Did you use the new install application that I sent along with the control panel app?"

"What? An install application? There was *no* install application. What the hell are you...," he breaks off berating me, no doubt scanning the files I sent him. I remain silent and crack my knuckles while I wait for him to finish. "...Oh, well, okay I see it. Next time be clearer, and don't waste my time." He abruptly hangs up.

My feet go back up on my desk, and I push my chair back a foot so I can rest my head against the wall behind my desk. The black hole looks even more appealing right now. I feel I should be more upset than I am, but Tom and his inane behavior are merely annoying pebbles that have worked their way inside my shoe. I'm here for the paycheck, nothing more. It all feels like a copout to my path of being a healer, but I just can't seem to muster the energy or desire to treat others.

When I returned from Pennsylvania, I had tried to revive my acupuncture practice, to reclaim the life I had put on hold all those months after Mom's death, but it was pointless. My heart just wasn't in it. I had nothing to give anyone else. How could I call myself a healer when I couldn't even heal my own mother? The simple truth is that I had failed the most important person in my life. How could I ever forgive myself?

Over and over, like an infinite loop in my software, I race down the endless white hospital corridor to get to Mom's room in time. My heart feels like someone has both hands clenched around it and is squeezing harder with every step. When at last I enter her hospital room, my world collapses. She's in a coma, breathing only because of a ventilator and tangled in a mass of tubes and wires. And I know I'm too late—too damn late! I've missed my chance to look into her eyes one last time to tell her I love her and say good-bye. If only I had gotten there sooner—if only I had gone back to Pennsylvania when this all had started to go bad—I could've helped her. If only I'd... if only... I race down the endless white hospital corridor...

My monitor goes dark for a second and then bursts into a twirling kaleidoscope of colored fractals. Just my screensaver, but it distracts me enough to pull me back to the present. It's clear I'm not going to get any more work done today. I quickly shut down my desktop and head home.

Always happy to see me, Shika greets me at the door, wagging her short tail. I reach down to pat her on the head. My answering machine is on a small coffee table just inside the front door. I can see the message light is blinking. It's another invitation from Sofia to come over for a dinner party—another one that I will invariably refuse. Ever since I came back to California, she's been doggedly determined to drag me back into the social scene. But the thought of having fun is repugnant. It hurts like hell to see other people laugh and go about their business as if everything is normal. Nothing feels normal for me. Mom was my foundation. Without her, my zest for life is gone. Colors that should be bright seem dull, my food has no taste, and I find no humor in anything. It's not my office window that's the black hole; it's me.

I drop heavily onto my living room couch. Shika lies down at my feet while I stare blankly across the room at the entertainment center on the opposite wall. Normally, I come home and race downstairs to my basement, to my full bench press, a Bowflex home gym, and a full rack of dumbbells and barbells. My lifelong pursuit of optimal fitness has grown into an obsession. I've become addicted to the muscle pain and resulting endorphin high. I pyramid my weights and crank out sets until my muscles fatigue and fail. If any part of me can still lift a weight, I'm not done with my workout. That could take two or sometimes three hours, but the time doesn't matter. On my martial arts days, I push myself hard in class, kicking and punching until I want to puke. On the weekends, I pack a bag and hike alone until I collapse from sheer exhaustion.

Reaching the point of physical pain is the goal; it's a place that affords me a brief respite. Mentally, I dive into the river of discomfort that flows through my body and swim for all I'm worth through the turbulent waters. At the same time, the ball and chain of emotional torment that has wrapped itself so tightly around my heart is pulled in beside me and somehow buoyed up by the rapids. The end result is that my heart doesn't hurt as much—at least for a short time.

But today I'm forced to wonder what the point of it all really is. By seeking ways to avoid my emotional pain, it seems as if I've only succeeded in postponing my suffering. I feel lonely. I've isolated myself from pretty much everyone. I miss my friends, but I can't force myself to pretend I'm happy. I don't want their pity. These past months I haven't been living; I've been fighting to survive. I look down at Shika, who immediately pricks up her ears, waiting to hear what I have to say.

"Something's got to change. Doesn't it, girl?" She thumps her tail and cocks her head at the sudden and annoyingly chirpy ring of my cell phone. I make a mental note to switch it to something less obnoxious. I have to hand it her—Sofia is persistent. Bless her; it's nice to know she cares. Maybe this time I'll summon the will power to accept her offer.

"*Kia ora* (Maori for hello), Holly darling. How are you getting on, love?"

I'm momentarily nonplussed to hear the melodious New Zealand accent. Hers is the last voice I had expected to hear. Yet at the same time, given a choice—the one I most wanted to hear. As usual, Keshama's timing is impeccable. I slide over to one end of the couch and flop down face-up, still holding the phone to my ear. The first real friend with whom I could share my metaphysical self, Keshama is a gifted intuitive. I know she can sense how I feel, but surprisingly, I don't have the usual urge to bury my feelings. Keshama's nurturing empathy is palpable. It's as if she's reached through the phone and put an arm around my shoulders.

My defenses finally crumble. "Oh, Keshama, this has been the worst year of my life," I blurt out before my throat constricts and tears roll down my cheeks.

"I'm so sorry, babe. I can't imagine how awful it must be for you," she says quietly.

I close my eyes and allow her sympathy to penetrate deeper, this time all the way to my heart.

"I've got an idea for you." Keshama's tone suggests it's something she's considered at length. "I'm going home for a bit. Come and visit me."

"What?" My mouth falls open.

"I'd love for you to meet Mum and my brothers," she adds.

"Come to New Zealand?" I sit bolt upright on the couch. "That's halfway around the freaking planet!"

"But it's so worth the trip, mate." She launches her full court press. "We live in the jungle, near gorgeous waterfalls and sacred Maori mountains." I have to admit, her description is enticing. "It will restore your soul."

This is so out of the blue, yet something about it feels right. I know I need something extraordinary—and didn't I just ask for it? I've actually always wanted to see New Zealand. Even from pictures, I can sense a mysticism emanating from it; like a siren's song, its pull is strong.

Suddenly, I hear a noise almost like fingers snapping. My eyes latch onto Mom's picture on the mantel. Odd, I could swear it's moved. I inhale sharply. Did Mom just do that? I want so much to see her and to connect with her spirit somehow. I would give anything to do that, to know that she's okay. Maybe that's what this is about. Maybe Mom wants me to go.

"Are you still there?" Keshama asks, and I realize she has been waiting patiently on the other end of the phone.

"Sorry, yeah. I was just thinking about your idea," I reply distractedly.

"Well, how about it?"

"When?" I ask, still staring at Mom's photo. It's almost as if her eyes are twinkling at me.

"Whenever you're ready. It's all up to you."

CHAPTER TWENTY FIVE
SHAKEN NOT STIRRED

*Life is either a daring adventure or nothing. To keep
our faces toward change and behave like free spirits
in the presence of fate is strength undefeatable.*
–Helen Keller

"Get ready for a rush!" Glen says excitedly.

I nod my head at the twenty-year-old New Zealand clone of Hugh Jackman sitting beside me.

"Oh, and if we kick our feet up toward our heads at the highest point, we'll be able to get ourselves going into 360-degree spins," he adds.

When I look up at the wild human slingshot contraption over our heads, he follows my gaze.

"Crazy, yeah?" he says.

Yes, crazy is exactly what I want—and a lot of it.

Glen checks my safety harness a final time and gives the thumbs up sign to his brother, Derek, in the control booth. There's the sound of a small motor starting up and then gears turning. With the anticipation building, I grab the bars in front of me and rattle the cage. Glen cracks up.

We're strapped onto a metal bench with headrests inside a circular metal frame, like roll bars on a dune buggy. Our cage is clamped to a raised wooden platform built between two tall metal towers about fifty feet apart, rising well over a hundred feet into the air. I tilt my head back, and my eyes travel along the upward path of the two massive bungee cords, each as thick as my leg. There is one on each side of our cage, and they extend all the way to the top of the tower. The massive device is called the Sky Screamer, and this one is fully loaded with Glen and me as the projectiles.

It's complete happenstance that I'm here awaiting the countdown to launch. I arrived in Auckland less than two hours ago. As soon as I made it through customs, I grabbed a taxi to get to my downtown hotel. The whole experience was a bit surreal, and then I saw something fly into the air above the rooftops of several tall, ultra-modern office buildings. I plastered my face against the passenger window in the taxi. "What the hell was that?" I exclaimed.

"That, mate, is called the Sky Screamer." The cabbie laughed. "You get buckled onto it and then shot into the air, like a bungee jump in reverse."

"Forget the hotel. Take me there!" I tapped the window excitedly in the direction of the Sky Screamer. It was perfect. I hopped out of the taxi, bags and all, and sprinted over to the control booth. There's nothing like a little adrenalin rush to start the day.

As the gears turn, the bungee cords become taut to the point where I think they will either snap or rip our cage from the clamp. We sit motionless, awaiting our fate. Encircling the periphery of my vision are the sparkling skyscrapers of downtown Auckland, a grand audience for my first New Zealand adventure. The sun is blazing hot, but since I was on an ice cold plane a few hours ago, my thawing body hungrily drinks in the heat. A tiny part of my brain offers up the merest hint of concern for my physical well-being. It's immediately squashed. I crave the endorphins that are currently being released into my bloodstream. They are the only thing that prevents the emotional maelstrom hidden below the surface from breaking through.

"Hang on!" Glen yells.

Instantly, I'm back in the now. Our cage is released from the clamp, and we're hurled into the air. I'm slammed back hard against the seat and gain an instantaneous comprehension of what five times the pull of gravity really means. As I'm rocketing up, I feel a sense of limitless freedom. Glen taps my arm, and we simultaneously kick our feet up over our heads. This makes our cage spin 360 degrees, head over heels, and we both scream in mad glee.

At the apex of the bungee stretch, the cage hangs in mid-air giving me time to survey the city from an inverted position. And then, as we rotate skyward once more, I glimpse Mom's smiling face for just a fraction of a second. I rapidly twist my head around, trying to hold onto her image. Then whoosh! We're yanked downward by the contraction of the giant bungee cord. I've just experienced what it feels like to be a rock taped to the leather pocket of a slingshot. We continue bouncing up and down many times before finally coming to rest halfway up the towers. My heart is pounding for more than one reason. Was that really Mom? Or am I totally bonkers?

Derek switches on the motor, and we are reeled back down. As our chair touches the ground, I'm feeling most definitely shaken, and not stirred. Glen whips off his harness and then unfastens mine. I stand up, but the ground is moving and I stagger.

Glen steadies me with a hand and says, "Welcome to New Zealand, mate!"

CHAPTER TWENTY SIX
HOTEL KESHAMA

Some people, like flowers, give pleasure, just by being.
–Ralph Waldo Emerson

Both hands are clenched in a knuckle-whitening grip on the steering wheel while I chant the mantra of the day—*drive on the left, the left is right*—over and over. My first encounter with a New Zealand rotary—a huge circle with five different roads branching off around it—is hair-raising, to say the least. I have to loop around three times and I'm honked at more than once before I finally figure out how to get the heck out of it and onto the correct road. I breathe a sigh of relief as I leave Auckland and head north toward Keshama's place in my rental car.

With the frenzied city traffic behind me, I settle in for the five-hour drive. The New Zealand countryside is breathtaking. The scenery gradually changes from rolling, emerald green hills covered with sheep into a Kauri forest with its massive trees towering straight up into the heavens. I'm mesmerized as the forest thickens and transforms into a mystical, rainforest where rainbow-covered waterfalls appear around every bend. I half expect to see faeries flitting around in the jungle canopy. It finally makes sense to me why Keshama had always appeared indifferent to what I had thought was breathtaking California countryside. Compared to New Zealand, California is about as scenic as a strip mine.

The sound of my own laughter startles me; it's something I haven't heard in quite some time. But I can't help it. The road signs I've been seeing are hilarious. Leaving Auckland, it started with one that simply said, "North," but the further north I drove, the more absurd they got. The next sign said, "Further North," and this turned into "Far North," followed by "Really Far North," and by the time I glimpse "Really Very Far North," I can't help myself and burst out laughing. The moment is quickly smothered by guilt over feeling good.

At last I arrive in Mangonui, a tiny coastal town in the "Really Very Far North." I spot the Blue Dolphin Café, which is where I've arranged to meet Keshama, and I park my car on the side of the road. The "side of the road" is along a nearly empty stretch of pristine white sand. The inviting azure water of the ocean is less than twenty paces away. It's quite a relief to get out of the car and stretch the kinks out of my legs and back. The ocean air is warm and refreshing. I stand motionless, simply taking in the raw tropical coastline stretching far into the distance. When I finally turn toward the open-air restaurant, I see Keshama smiling and waving at me from an outdoor table. She's seated with an older, dark-haired woman. Even from across the street, it's hard not to notice Keshama's stunning beauty. Her looks were invariably a subject for commentary whenever we went out together in public. She could and did—quite literally—stop traffic.

Once when we happened to be strolling along Market Street in San Francisco, a young man charged recklessly across a busy intersection just to meet her. He was shouting, "Wait a minute!" Keshama and I exchanged puzzled looks as the handsome young man in his early twenties skidded to a halt directly in front of her. Ignoring me completely, he fixed his eyes adoringly on Keshama. "I've been watching you walk down the street and I just had to tell you," he ranted breathlessly.

Keshama raised an eyebrow in curiosity. "Tell me what?" she asked.

"You are *by far* the most beautiful woman I've ever seen," the young man sputtered.

"That's so sweet of you. Thanks, mate," she replied in her kind and typically unassuming manner. Then Keshama signaled that the audience was over when she wound her arm tightly around mine. She nodded her head to the young man as we stepped around him. After we'd gone about a half a block, I glanced back. He was still standing where we had left him—an enthralled, open-mouthed, weak-kneed boy-puppy. I chuckled silently as we walked away. I privately thought the producers of *Xena: Warrior Princess* would have done better to cast *her* as Aphrodite in the hit TV series.

Now it's me running across the street to be swept up in a satisfyingly huge hug. "*Kia ora*, mate. It's bloody good to see you." Her greeting is effusive, and I feel her love pouring into me. We separate, and she gestures toward her mother, who has come around the table to greet me. "And this is my mum, Alana," she says fondly.

I'm excited to finally meet her mother, a woman Keshama holds dear to her heart. I had heard many stories of Alana's wonderful works of service. Over the years, she had selflessly shared her home with people who had nothing and needed one. Some were dying and had nowhere to go, but Alana had opened her arms, offering love and belonging to people who had had no one else. With such an amazing mother, it's not surprising that Keshama's spirit is even more beautiful than her looks.

Alana is shorter and plumper than her daughter, but the resemblance is clear. I have only a few seconds to take in the colorful, tropical wraparound skirt, beaded bracelets and bare feet before I am swept into the ample arms of Gaia, the Earth Mother herself. Her glowing pink aura of compassionate love settles around my shoulders. Suddenly my burden is lighter, and I feel safe and connected to spirit. Alana's arms tighten ever so slightly around me. "I'm bloody sorry to hear about your mum, Holly." Her deep, earthy voice gently parts the silence.

The caring energy pouring into me acts as an anesthetic, soothing the pain that bursts forth. "Thank you, Alana. That means a lot." We hold the hug for a while longer and then sit down at the table. It's strange. I feel like I've already known her a long time. "It's great that I finally get to meet you. Keshama often raves about you," I say. The warmth I'm feeling brings a smile to my lips.

"Aw yeah? Well, Keshama knows who her better half is." Alana grins mischievously. This starts a round of gentle, competitive needling between Aphrodite and Gaia. I'm content to quietly soak in the warm sun, entertained by their lilting Kiwi accents. The air around them sparkles, and sitting within their sphere of influence, I'm cocooned outside of time and buffered from grief.

Our fresh, organic salads arrive, and my fork moves automatically. The explosion of flavor that fills my mouth is unexpected. I must have made some kind of exclamation because Keshama and Alana both pause in their conversation to look at me. My mouth is full, and I cover it with a hand.

"What?" I mumble self-consciously.

"Is there something wrong with the salad?" Keshama asks.

"Are you bloody kidding? It's great," I exclaim. Since Mom had passed, food had largely lost its appeal, and I take it as a good sign that my taste buds are finally perking up again.

After lunch, Keshama walks with me to my car. "Hey, doll, I think it's best if you let me drive. The roads are a might tricky," she suggests casually. I can't conceal my look of exasperation, but Keshama merely extends her hand for the keys. "Humor me, love," she says. Blatantly ignoring my huffy grumbling, she hops into the driver's seat. I roll my eyes as she takes her sandals off and then tucks her sarong neatly around her legs. I have to chuckle as I realize my fragile ego has been bruised. I'm a conceited control freak when it comes to driving. That being said, I'm glad I listened!

We drive for miles on muddy, unpaved, unmarked roads that take us deep into the jungle. Keshama barely slows down as she tightly hugs the inside corner on sharp turns that would challenge an Indy 500 race car driver. At the same time, she confidently navigates past frequent deep ditches and small boulders. While I could have certainly managed the drive, there's no way I could match her speed and dexterity.

At long last, Keshama stops at the bottom of a dirt road turnoff that winds itself up a very steep hill. Nailed to a tree is a sign that reads: *The Hotel*. Keshama sees my quizzical expression. "Our little villa is at the top of the hill, but I don't think this bloody rental car has got enough guts to make it unless we back up and gun it."

I laugh, and then I pause when I realize I'm the only one laughing. "You're kidding, right?"

The frown of concentration on Keshama's face suggests otherwise as she backs up the car. "I most certainly am *not* bloody kidding! Hang on mate," she exclaims and floors the accelerator.

The car leaps forward, and I'm slammed back against the passenger seat. I quickly brace a foot against the dash and grab the armrest for support. Three-quarters of the way up the hill, our forward progress has slowed to a crawl. It's muddy, the wheels are spinning, and I have visions of sliding into a tree. I'm feeling quite petulant and open my mouth to protest. Before I can say anything, Keshama executes a perfect Farah Fawcett hair toss, and then she eases up on the gas for a split second before skillfully sliding over to the edge where it's less muddy. As soon as the tires grab solid ground, she punches it. We lurch forward, up and over the top of the hill. For the grand finale, Keshama expertly maneuvers the car into a controlled skid, deftly slipping us between another car and a palm tree. She winks at me as she gracefully extracts her lithe frame from the car. I hang back to pick the crow feathers from my teeth before I get out of the car.

Now that I'm finally here, it feels as if I've stepped into another world entirely. We're completely surrounded by the dense, lush tropical canopy. It wouldn't surprise me in the least if Tarzan suddenly appeared, swinging through the jungle on a vine, leisurely passing by on his way to meet Jane.

What captivates my attention now is the most unusual "home" I've ever seen. Spread about somewhat haphazardly in the small glade before us is a miniature village made up entirely of old school buses converted into living spaces. Their wheels have been removed, and they are connected with each other via numerous decks and wooden walkways.

Keshama grins at my look of stunned amazement. She grabs one of my bags and starts walking toward a half-size bus. "Come on. I'll show you to your bus."

I almost drop my bags. "I get my own bus?"

She glances back over her shoulder with twinkling eyes. "Of course, mate, only the best for our special guests." She grins and leads the way to a magical place. It's the size of a large bedroom with a queen bed against one wall and decorated in the distinctive "a la Keshama" style that I know and love. This includes beautifully colored Indian fabrics hung from the ceiling, shelves covered with artistic knickknacks, and an abundance of photos taking up every square inch of wall space. The energy is warm and welcoming.

"Keshama, this is so cool. I love it." I deposit my bags on the floor so I can look at the photos.

"Thanks. I'm glad you like it. This *is* my bus after all," she says proudly. "Come on, I'll show you around the place." She grabs my arm and pulls me out the door. We walk a short distance to the only structure that is not a bus, which turns out to be a multi-purpose workshop filled with tools and constructed of corrugated metal walls. She leads me through a door at the rear of the workshop and into a small patio area with a stone floor and wooden benches. Off to the side is another room with stone walls, a corrugated roof, and windows that look out onto the jungle. This is the shower.

I spin around on the stone floor. "This is *sweet*, mate," I exclaim, eagerly anticipating my first jungle shower.

Next we make our way along the wooden walkway that connects the other bedroom buses. Alana and her other four children, all boys, each have their own. Aradhe, a tall, lanky nineteen-year-old has the largest one, second only to Alana's master bedroom bus. The remaining buses belong to Rishe, Atama, and Hemi, who are fifteen, eleven, and nine. Keshama waves me ahead of her, and I climb up a few steps into the largest and most central bus in the village.

Alana smiles at me as I step inside. She is standing at a counter in the kitchen area of the bus, already busily chopping a massive pile of vegetables for a huge dinner salad. Just beyond Alana is the living room, complete with sofas and a TV. Keshama glides past me, taking my arm and gently pulling me through the sliding glass doors on the opposite side of the bus.

"I know I keep repeating myself, but this is amazing," I say for the umpteenth time.

Keshama has led me out onto a huge rear deck that is larger than the entire living room/kitchen bus. I walk over to the far edge and stare at the sublime jungle valley spread before me. It's accented with majestic, fog-misted mountains in the distance. The energy I sense here is primal and powerful. I feel it pulling at me—as if I've been expected.

Keshama stands beside me. "Welcome, to my home, love," she says happily.

"You mean, welcome to paradise," I whisper back.

I've arrived at the home of the Kiwi version of the Swiss Family Robinson. The rest of the day is an orientation into another world. Apparently, a normal day in the jungle includes a visit to the nearby waterfall. Keshama and Atama lead the way out onto the rocks. He is only eleven, but he already looks like a miniature Brad Pitt. Ripping off his shirt, he does a quick Maori war dance before leaping over the edge. His perfect swan dive slices cleanly into the waters of the idyllic pool below the rainbow-crowned falls. Keshama and I quickly follow suit. The air is sweltering but contrasts perfectly with the cool, crystal blue water that surrounds me. My eyes are closed as I float around on my back with my head submerged just enough so that my ears are covered—my jungle version of an isolation tank. I imagine the water is washing away my bottled-up emotions, giving me room to find me.

Later in the afternoon, Keshama, Alana, and I are relaxing out on the main deck, contentedly digesting the massive organic mega-salad that we all had for dinner. Aphrodite and Mother Gaia are sitting next to each other on a swinging bench, which is attached to an awning built onto the back of the bus. I lie down on a towel and stare up at the sky with my hands clasped behind my head. At first I think the jungle is quiet, but gradually, the sounds of birds singing and calling to each other filters into my awareness. The volume increases steadily until I'm almost ready to put my hands over my ears.

When Gaia Alana speaks, it's as if a supernatural hand has reached out and turned down the volume of the jungle. "Holly, tell me what you'd like to do while you're here." Her words penetrate straight into my heart.

It's such a simple question, and yet, it is not. I know she's asking my soul the question. I need to stand back and let it answer. Eventually, my lips move and words appear.

"I've come to connect with Mom and ask her forgiveness—and maybe try to forgive myself for not being there for her. I'd like to let go of my grief as an obstacle to life." *Holy crap—did I just say that?* I feel like some unseen hand has reached in and yanked a year's worth of therapy right out of me. I'm immediately drained, but the words that came out of my mouth are true. I've been stuck in a state of misery, unable to move on, and I've pinned all my hopes for change on this trip.

Alana and Keshama exchange knowing looks. "The energy here is powerful, and you've just set your intentions for your time here. Follow your heart and connect with the spirits in nature. They will help you heal," Alana says with certainty. As if to emphasize her words, the air around them shimmers. It feels like Gaia herself has blessed my journey.

Keshama slides off the swinging chair and lies down beside me. "I'd love one of your acupuncture tune-ups, if you're up for it, darling," she says.

Oddly enough, I am. In fact, I'm startled at how excited I am. It's something that I frequently used to do, whenever we hung out. I dash off and return with my needles. Keshama lies down on a towel, and I insert them in a basic tonifying pattern while sending her healing energy. It's not until I start to take the needles out, about forty-five minutes later, that it hits me. This is the first treatment I've given since Mom died where I've been able to freely send healing energy from my heart chakra. Keshama and Alana weren't kidding about the energy of this place!

Afterward, I decide to climb the hill overlooking their jungle valley. It's almost eight o'clock at night, but it's still quite light out. At the top is a cozy vantage point to sit down and meditate. My breathing slows easily as I descend further into the quiet void than I've gone in a long time. In my mind, an image forms itself into a deserted white sand beach that runs for miles along the edge of a placid ocean. I see myself sitting on a smooth, low rock at one end of the beach. A mild breeze accompanied by the rhythmic sound of the ocean is hypnotic. In the vision, I observe dark energy oozing out of me and being irresistibly drawn into the water. My aura grows ever brighter as it's cleansed.

I watch myself turn my head toward a magnificent chestnut stallion prancing along the beach. He slows down as he draws near me and lowers his head. His closest dark brown eye locks onto mine, and I sense he wants to tell me something. He nudges me in the chest, my heart chakra, and pain flares up. Somehow, I'm pulled into my image and I'm no longer an observer. I place my hand under the nose of the regal chestnut. He breathes in my scent and gently lips my fingers. The message I feel coming through isn't spoken, but somehow I sense it clearly.

I know I need to let go and move on. But the cement bunker around my heart has been difficult to penetrate, I respond directly to him.

He shakes his head up and down and then whinnies. Through our spiritual connection, I feel his agreement at my interpretation and a surge of support and encouragement. He touches my shoulder with his nose, and his wild horse spirit flows into me until it feels as if we're one.

After a time, the vision fades and I'm aware of my protesting calf muscles—too long in one position. My eyes open, but I don't want to move. The horse in my vision was so real; I can still smell him and feel his breath on my hand. This is the first time I've encountered an animal spirit-guide. His energy touched me so strongly that I'm still tingling. He wanted to prepare me for something; I sensed it.

I shiver with anticipation. The psychic energy here is so strong. A breeze blows and the honeyed scent of jasmine sweetens the air. In this enchanted jungle, the simple act of breathing is delicious, like I've just eaten a dessert.

Suddenly, I hear a rustling noise in the underbrush to my left and freeze. Ever so slowly, I turn my head toward the sound, and my heart skips a beat when I see a fern shaking. Before I have time to consider my options, a curious creature hops into view. I blink several times to make sure it isn't a figment of my imagination. It's a wingless bird, about the size of a pheasant, with a bright red beak that looks as if it's wearing gaudy lipstick. It casually pecks at the ground, either unconcerned or unaware of my presence. The sun glints off of its back and I stifle a gasp when I see its emerald and azure feathers luminesce. It dawns on me that I've seen a picture of this bird in my New Zealand guide book. It's called a Takehe, an endangered species endemic to New Zealand. Unbelievable!

I remain silent and unmoving until it wanders back into the brush. Then I shake my head in amazement and wonder what else the spirits of this magical place might have in store for me. Will I be ready?

CHAPTER TWENTY SEVEN
SPIRIT OF THE HORSE

*The wind of heaven is that which
blows between a horse's ears.*
—Arabian Proverb

The next morning is unlike any morning in recent memory. I awaken at the crack of dawn to find that the customary knife in my heart is missing. It's been reduced to a dull ache as if some angel of mercy had swabbed a numbing salve over the festering wound. I wonder if it has something to do with spending the night in Keshama's personal bus. Over the years, it had undoubtedly been imbued with her own special brand of healing energy. Regardless of the reason, this small relief allows me to be more present. I quietly listen to the world outside.

Suddenly, I bolt upright in bed as if struck by lightning. I can't believe what I'm hearing. It's the sound of *cicadas*! They're everywhere, and it's loud. How on earth did I miss hearing them until now? Did my cloak of mourning mask that much? Maybe since I grew up with them, the sound was automatically relegated to background noise. The *why* isn't important; I hear them now. They're a welcome link to my childhood and a time when I was happy and carefree. I sense Mom had a hand in this; perhaps it is another reason that she had wanted me to come to New Zealand.

The pressure to break out of my emotional quagmire continues to build. Change is coming. In this mystical place, it seems impossible to avoid it. A shiver of fear runs through me. I've barely managed to keep the pain of Mom's loss under a tight lockdown. If it escapes, I'm afraid it will be more than I can bear. The hum of the cicadas grows louder, and I allow myself to be pulled into its soothing embrace. My fear gradually recedes into the background. It's time to get up and see what happens.

I don't have any set plan, but after breakfast, Keshama lays out my map and suggests a few scenic routes to explore. Before I start the car and take off for the day, I close my eyes and send a query to the universe; I ask for the best direction to travel. An overhead map of the North Island appears in my head along with an arrow pointing toward the west coast. All right—west it is!

I slowly wind my way through the jungle, carefully following Keshama's intricate directions along the circuitous dirt roads. To my left, the jungle climbs up a steep, rocky slope; on the right, a sheer cliff plunges into the thick green canopy. A gushing waterfall leaps into view after rounding a sharp bend, and I quickly pull over into a narrow turnout, which was probably put there just for the purpose of gawking tourists. I get out and lean against the side of my rental car. I stare at the enormous volume of water pummeling the rocks below and imagine myself standing beneath it, allowing myself to be brutally cleansed by the primal flow.

The air is thick with the humidity, but it's pleasantly cool in the jungle. I catch the scent of jasmine laced within the dusky wood. It turns each breath into a sweet treat for my lungs. The rhythmic whirring of the cicadas can still be heard over the roar of the waterfall. I close my eyes and let their meditative hum penetrate my soul. When I open them, I'm greeted by a rainbow that has formed at the top of falls. I'm humbled by the spiritual comfort that only nature can provide.

Once I reach the main road, it's not long before I hit the west coast. While I'm passing through a small town named Ahipari, I spot a beaten wood sign nailed to a fence that runs along the side of the road. I can just make out the faded black letters that read: "Jayar Horse Treks." My body tingles all over. This isn't a coincidence. I quickly make the turn off onto a dirt road. It's a short drive to reach the stables. Once there, I'm treated with the playful antics of five of the most beautiful thoroughbreds I've ever seen, chasing each other around a field. I hop out of the car to stand near the fence, quietly watching. I'm enraptured with the grace and power of horse energy. A spirited brown gallops past me, shaking his head, and I'm reminded of Stormy, a horse I used to know.

I squint as the sunlight dazzles my eyes, and in my mind's eye, I see my cousin Kim, a ten-year-old tomboy, just like me. Her ponytail is flapping madly behind her back as she leans down from the saddle at a canter. Grinning madly, she thrusts her hand out toward me as Stormy thunders past.

"C'mon, Hol. Grab my hand!" she hollers.

I see myself reaching out to grab her hand. Our fingers make contact, and I race alongside her for a few paces before vaulting up behind her onto Stormy's back.

"Yee haw!" Our jubilant shouts echo triumphantly after us as we ride off together. "Ride 'em, cowgirl!"

A wispy cloud scuttles across the sun, temporarily casting its shadow over the corral. It's then that I see someone approaching in my peripheral vision. I sense their energy is as powerful as the horses I'm watching. When I face the newcomer, it's as if I'm watching a bear in the form of a woman walking toward me. She is completely proportional and massively muscled, but one of the largest women I've ever met.

"Good day, mate. I'm Joanna, and what can I do you for?" Her greeting booms across the distance still separating us, and I can see the grin on her face matches her bulk. I like her immediately.

"I'm Holly. I'd love to set up a ride, and I'm very hopeful it's on one of those gorgeous horses romping around in your meadow." I point toward the fence.

Joanna is close enough now that I can see a slightly mischievous glint in her eyes. "Well now, you look fit enough to get up on one of my beauties, but can you *ride*?" Her mouth stretches into an even bigger smile.

I can't help snatching the imaginary gauntlet from the ground. "With or without a saddle, take your pick," I say.

"Good on you, mate. Let's do it." Her deep belly laugh seems to shake the ground itself. "We'll see how good you are. My horses are faster than the wind itself," she boasts, and then pauses to consider. "I think I'll put you on Blazer. He can break the sound barrier—he's so bloody fast. Follow me."

With that, she whirls around and leads me behind the barn. Two horses are hitched to a post and standing quietly, already saddled up and ready to go. I glance at Joanna with surprise. "As you can see, I was expecting you," she chuckles. "Actually, I was going riding with a friend of mine, but she had to cancel, so I'm happy you showed up." Joanna unties the lead for a giant black stallion. "This is Shadow, my horse." Joanna smiles as she guides him over to a tree stump with a flat top. Moving with surprising grace for a woman of her immense size, she vaults nimbly onto the stump and then up on Shadow. I gaze in admiration at the perfectly matched pair of woman and horse.

Blazer nickers behind me, and I turn toward him. The first thing I see is a shimmering deep chestnut coat on a horse so magnificent, I almost forget to breathe. When I approach his head, he lowers it and stares into my eyes with one of his deep brown ones. I can't believe it! Blazer is the horse in my meditation, in every way. In an instant, I have goose bumps everywhere. I know I've been led here.

As soon as I settle myself on his back, Blazer shakes his head and prances sideways in anticipation of our ride. The sound of the saddle squeaking lightly as I adjust myself combined with the smell of its well-oiled leather is like a familiar friend. Feeling the power rippling through his muscular body, I give in to my own excitement. There is a strong connection between us, and he responds with just the merest hint of direction from my legs or the reins in my hands.

Joanna leads the way at a brisk walk along a heavily wooded trail. It's not long before we break into the open at one end of a seemingly endless and completely deserted white sand beach. She pauses with Shadow until I ride up beside her. "This is called Ninety Mile Beach, although it's really only about ninety kilometers long," she says, pointing off into the distance. "But here we can ride as far and as fast as we want. Are you ready to fly, mate?" She cocks an eyebrow at me in a clear challenge.

"I am," I reply as I pat Blazer on his neck. Joanna whoops happily and lightly kicks her horse.

Shadow springs forward so fast that Blazer and I are left eating their sand. Even though he flinches, my horse doesn't move. I know it's because I haven't signaled him to, and his self-control blows me away. However, as soon as I shift forward and give only the barest whisper of a leg squeeze, Blazer explodes as though shot out of a rocket. I imagine myself as the cartoon character that is left hanging in the air behind the horse that has just taken off, before being slingshot back onto the saddle again. What a rush! In short order, we are neck and neck with Joanna, racing along like the wind itself. I'm one with the beautiful horse spirit beneath me, hearing only the sound of my breathing and Blazer's hooves pounding the sand.

I'm filled with reckless abandon and urge Blazer to go even faster. He responds by turning on the afterburners. Shadow matches our speed. What I wouldn't give to run free like this forever and leave everything behind me. Joanna veers slightly to the right, away from us. I see a small gully up ahead, but I keep Blazer pointed toward it and rise up in the stirrups as he vaults over the dip with ease. When his hooves contact the ground, my boot slips in the stirrup, and it throws me slightly off balance. I squeeze my knees hard and grab his mane to steady myself. My heart is pumping wildly at the close call. Joanna has slowed her gallop and is running along the water's edge. I turn Blazer to follow, extremely grateful that I'm not sprawled in the sand behind me. I feel like I was just scolded by the universe.

Joanna gradually slows Shadow to a walk while Blazer and I match her gait. She turns toward me, and I feel a sense of camaraderie. "Brilliant riding, Holly. I had a feeling you were going to be fun." She laughs as Shadow prances around in a tight circle. "What usually happens is that most of my guests who say they can ride wind up on their ass in the sand after that first little test." She grins wickedly.

If she only knew how close I came, but then I'll just keep that one between me and Blazer. I chuckle at my own private joke. Suddenly, it dawns on me that, in this moment, I'm happy. "Blazer is, without a doubt, the fastest and most intuitive horse I've ever ridden. He's awesome!" I pat his neck affectionately, the adrenaline still pumping hard through my veins.

"Let's have another go—shall we?" Joanna says, beaming with pride.

Now it's my turn to be mischievous. I surreptitiously slide my feet out of the stirrups, my preferred riding position, and then quickly lean forward, tapping Blazer on the neck. This time it's Joanna who's eating our sand behind us. I hear a loud guffaw behind me, and suddenly, Shadow is hurtling along beside us.

"That was bloody well done, mate. Now let's see what else you've got," Joanna calls out.

We fly up the beach, challenging each other to go ever faster. I imagine myself racing toward the blackness in my heart. I'm not sure what I'm doing, and it scares me. Yet, at the same time, part of me is exhilarated. I feel merged with Blazer, as one with his strength and grace. By the time we head back to her stables several hours later, I'm thoroughly exhausted.

Just as Joanna turns onto our original trail through the woods, something tugs at me. I gently rein Blazer to a halt. There's something hovering, just at the edge of the woods, where the light fades into the shadow of the trees. I stand up in the stirrups, and Blazer jigs sideways. Then I see her. A lump immediately forms in my throat. It's Mom, or at least I think it is, and she appears to be reaching for me. I urge my horse forward, my heart pounding, but her image fades as we draw closer. I want to scream in frustration. I want to believe it was her, and I can feel she wanted to tell me something. But what? I hear Joanna calling for me, but I'm too dazed to move.

Blazer whinnies and breaks into a trot to catch up. As we pass by the spot where I think Mom was standing, I twist around in the saddle, keeping my eyes riveted on it for as long as possible. I search for some trace of a presence, any clue that might indicate she was really there. All that I have time to observe is a shadowy space between a scrub bush and the tree where I think I saw her. She *could* have been standing there.

My thoughts are racing as Joanna and I tie our horses up to a hitching post and start to undo the cinches on our saddles. That's twice now that I think I've caught a glimpse of Mom, and it seemed real. Maybe I'm hallucinating? Maybe my need to see her is so great that my mind is creating these visual images. But my heart urges me to consider otherwise. There have been too many signs: Mom's picture frame moving, the Sky Screamer, the cicadas, and now this—it's all too coincidental for me to ignore.

As I pull Blazer's saddle off of his back, Joanna is right there beside me to take it from my hands. Fortunately, my head is tilted down, and she can't see the odd look on my face. I turn around, wrap my arms around Blazer's neck, and lean against him. I sense the power flowing through his rippling muscles; through our connection, some of it flows into me. It helps me to temporarily tuck my thoughts of Mom into a safe corner of my mind. As soon as I do, I'm awash with gratitude for the most amazing ride of my life. When I finally drop my arms from Blazer's neck, Joanna has returned to see me off.

"Cheers, Holly. That was incredible fun for me. Anytime you want to come back, I'd love to ride with you again." Her huge hand engulfs my own in a powerful grip.

"I can't thank you enough, Joanna." It's difficult to keep my voice steady, but there's no way I'm going to let myself break down in front of her. "This day has been amazing for me—more than you can know." I shake her bear paw with both of my hands and manage a heartfelt smile of gratitude. Joanna grins and engulfs me in her massive arms.

Once inside my car, I feel reluctant to leave. I can't help thinking about Mom. Was that really her? It was such a brief glimpse, but she *was* standing there plain as day. I miss her so much; maybe she senses that and let me see her? What would Sofia say if I told her that Mom was trying to contact me from the other side? Oh, and in broad daylight no less, without the use of a psychic—just me having paranormal close encounters. I know exactly what she'd say: *Well, Hol, you've finally gone off the deep end.*

A nervous shiver runs through me. I take a swig of water from my thermos to try to calm down. If that really was Mom and there is even a chance of contacting her, I have to find out. It's what I want, isn't it? It's the reason I came all this way. Yes, but what would she say if I actually connected with her? What if it's not what I want to hear? Would she affirm my self-recriminations? Could I stand to hear that from Mom? My heart shrivels with the possibility, but *not* knowing might be a lot worse.

I insert the key into the ignition, getting ready to leave the stables. Out of the corner of my eye, I glimpse Joanna coming out of the barn. She's coiling a lead-rope as she strides purposefully toward the equipment shed next to the side of the barn that's closest to me. An idea flies into my head. When she waves at me, I roll down the car window and lean out.

"Hey, Joanna!" I holler over the motor's hum. "Do you know of a really good trail guide who could take me on a 'killer hike' around the Top of the North?"

Joanna's laugh booms across the gravel parking area. "Without a doubt, mate. *You* want Marty!"

CHAPTER TWENTY EIGHT
MAORI SPIRIT TREE

You will find that it is necessary to let things go;
simply for the reason that they are heavy.
So let them go, let go of them. I tie no weights to my ankles.
–C. JoyBell C.

"Good day, mate! I'm Marty. Pleased to meet you," the young man said.

I matched his firm handshake while surreptitiously studying Joanna's referral. I was immediately pleased. With his shaggy, shoulder-length blond hair, adventurous demeanor, and rock-hard body, Marty looked a lot like he could chew up and spit out Ironmen for breakfast. His eyes gleamed with enthusiasm when I asked him to put together a three-day trek that was as physically demanding as he could make it.

Two days later, it's just after sunrise, and here I am, carrying one end of our kayak on my shoulders. We're about to put it into the ocean at Matai Beach, which is just another one of those, run-of-the-mill, secluded, breathtakingly beautiful beaches that I'm quickly growing accustomed to finding in this idyllic country. The kayak is loaded with all of our camping, snorkeling, and fishing gear, but we don't waste any time getting into the water and digging in with our paddles. Our goal is to kayak around Cape KariKari, follow the coast down along the peninsula, and then return to Matai Beach before nightfall—an ambitious, eighteen-mile roundtrip.

Marty and I operate on a similar wavelength and quickly fall into an efficient rhythm with our paddles. The day is dawning crystal clear with only a slight headwind. I'm relieved that he also enjoys silence. It allows me to use the metronome-like qualities of our paddling to enter a meditative state. The energy of the ocean has always been cleansing and grounding for me. I use that quality to siphon off dark energy from myself and toss it into the clear blue water. By the time we reach the halfway point of our journey, I'm feeling open and receptive—similar to how I ended on my ride with Joanna.

At lunchtime we pull out on a tiny strip of beach surrounded by sandstone cliffs. After securing our kayaks, we chow down on several turkey sandwiches apiece. Then Marty scrambles up and grabs a fishing pole and tackle box out of the back of our kayak.

"Well, mate, I'm off to catch us some dinner for later. Relax and enjoy the day for a bit," he says cheerily and jogs away down the beach.

In no time at all, he's reached a small reef at the end of it and hops nimbly from rock to rock while toting his fishing gear. He waves at me when he reaches a large rock about halfway out. I wave back and watch him until he casts his fishing line into the ocean.

A big wave breaks and races up the beach toward me. I shift my gear away from the edge of the water, and sit cross-legged on my towel. The rhythmic crashing sound of the waves is hypnotic. The salt air is invigorating, and my lungs strain to breathe in as much as possible. It also has a cleansing effect, and I can feel my aura being energetically scrubbed until it shines.

After a while, I become aware of a presence next to me. It's as if the air has taken on a denser quality. It feels like it does when someone sits down next to you, but you happen to be looking the other way. I yearn for this presence to be Mom. I close my eyes and picture us together at the beach, like we used to on our annual vacation to the Jersey Shore. Those family trips to the ever-crowded Atlantic City beach had been one of my favorite times of the year. We would set up our beach towels, and then Jay, Dad, and I would scramble into the ocean.

Mom was content to simply watch us play in the waves. When we were hungry, she would pull out her signature roast beef sandwiches. As far as I was concerned, she made the best pot roast in the world, and I could taste the love in every bite. After a fun-filled day on the beach, we'd stroll along the boardwalk, eating salt water taffy and going on amusement rides. Those vacations ranked in my top five of happy Mom memories.

The presence beside me grows stronger. Now I'm almost certain it's Mom because I can actually feel her arm wrap around my shoulders. She holds me close. No words pass between us, but my heart fills with love and aches with loss at the same time. I screw my eyes shut, but that doesn't stop the tears.

"Mom, I'm *so* sorry," I barely manage to whisper. When I summon the courage to open my eyes, I can no longer feel her presence beside me.

Instead, I hear Marty calling my name. I quickly wipe my face before I turn around. He's smiling as he holds up several snappers and a bucket filled with mussels and abalone, or *Paua*, as the Maori call them. After he packs our dinner in an ice-filled cooler, he tosses me some snorkeling gear.

"It's time for more fun, mate. Let's see what's around," he suggests. I think it's exactly what I need.

As soon as I wade into the surf and start swimming, the warm water comforts me, cleansing my wounded heart. Marty darts past me, swimming as naturally as a fish, and I pump my fins hard to keep up. We snorkel a fair way out from shore. Suddenly, Marty stops kicking and gestures ahead of us. I follow the direction of his finger and spot a huge manta ray. At first I'm blown away by the sheer size of it, but then I notice the powerful sense of calm that emanates from it. We float, suspended in the water, watching the amazing creature swim unhurriedly away. When we can no longer see it, we pick our heads up out of the water.

"That was bloody awesome. I've never seen one in this area before, although I have further north," he says excitedly. "I think you're a bloody good luck charm." He chuckles and splashes some water at me in fun.

I splash playfully back, equally excited about our close encounter with this majestic creature of the deep. I can't help but wonder if Mom had anything to do with it. Marty and I unanimously decide to head back to shore and take off on the return leg of our trip back to our camp.

The next morning, the sun is barely peeking above the horizon when I'm awakened by the cheery chirping of birds. Marty is already up and preparing our breakfast of oatmeal with luscious mangos. While I'm hungrily attacking a huge bowl, he lets me know what's in store for us over the next two days.

"We're going to drive north to Waitiki Landing to start our hike. From there, we'll work our way overland to Spirits Bay, and then tomorrow we'll head north to Cape Reinga," he explains.

I'm relieved that today and tomorrow are hiking days since my forearms and shoulders are shredded from our grueling kayaking trip. Once we reach the trailhead at Waitiki Landing, my pride is somewhat mollified when I catch Marty wincing as he straps on his backpack. My smug moment ends when he sets off at a blistering pace, and I'm left trotting to keep up.

Our trail starts out on a low, grassy plain but quickly climbs up a hill where we enter a thick morning fog. It's hard to see more than a few feet in front of me. I begin to have the feeling that Mom is with me again. It's not long before I understand why. Climbing down the other side of the hill, the fog thins until I can see that we've entered a forest of small trees. But what stops me in my tracks is that they're all in various stages of bloom; it takes my breath away. All around us is every imaginable variation of white, red, and pink blossoms. Marty quickly realizes that I've stopped and turns around with a questioning look.

"Marty, what kind of trees are these?"

"They're tea trees. Aren't they spectacular?" He waves his hand up at them.

"That's an understatement," I reply, spinning around to take in the magnificence.

Marty continues at a slower pace. I follow him reluctantly. All I really want to do is fall onto my knees and soak in Mom's presence. Her pride and joy had been her flower garden, and she was especially fond of white, pink, and red flowers. Again, the tears flow. I'm grateful that Marty doesn't look back.

We hike for quite a while through tea trees in full bloom. That unique, not-quite-eucalyptus smell of the leaves is everywhere. It stimulates deep breathing, and I feel invigorated. Maybe Mom is reaching out to me, sending me her love. But it's hard for me to simply accept it since I don't feel worthy of it.

The rest of the day is quite arduous. We climb over countless hills, stomp across grassy plains, and even muck our way through a swamp before we reach the ocean. Through it all, the image of all those beautiful tea tree blossoms and thoughts of Mom fill my mind. Our campsite for the night is at Spirits Bay, a lovely, secluded beach at the northern tip of the island. So far, Marty and I have been alone on the hike. Staring off across the Pacific Ocean, it feels as if we are on the edge of the world—the only two people left on the planet.

After a tasty dinner of freshly caught Blue Cod and mussels, we hang out around the fire, watching an endless stream of stars blink on for the evening. I'm humbled and grateful to be here with the perfect guide for me. Marty is stretched out on the other side of the fire, staring up at the night sky.

"Hey, Marty. This hike has been great. It's as rigorous as I asked for, and more." I have an impulse to share about Mom. "I didn't tell you before, but I've been trying to connect with my mom. She passed away a year ago." Marty turns his head toward me but remains silent, patiently waiting for me to continue. "And that's happened on this hike, so I wanted to thank you. You don't know what that means for me." I speak softly, trying not to let my voice crack.

Marty smiles in acknowledgement and reflects before he answers. "You've just helped me pick the perfect place to end our hike tomorrow. It'll take a bit longer than the loop I had originally planned, but I know you'll love it." He grins. When I try to pry the destination out of him, he refuses to say anything more, preferring to keep it a mystery.

Our last day is the most arduous and also the hottest. I've lost track of the hills we've climbed and the grassy plains we've crossed. In the afternoon, the landscape changes to sand dunes—countless sand dunes stretching as far as the eye can see. It wouldn't take much to convince me that I've been transported to the Sahara Desert.

I'm the tiniest bit chagrined when Marty picks up the pace, but he's exuding an excitement that's contagious. After all, I did ask for this! Focusing on Marty's back, I concentrate on my foot placement so I don't slide back in the sand. It keeps my mind so occupied that it comes as a shock when I notice that the endless dunes have gradually been replaced by gravelly dirt and scrub trees. Marty finally stops for a break.

"Where are we?" I ask, gulping thirstily from my water bottle.

He tilts his head. "Just through these trees, and you'll see."

Not much further ahead, we encounter a paved trail and a small herd of tourists heading in the same direction as we are. We pass an information building and continue to a lookout point with a view of the very tip of the North Island.

Marty taps my shoulder and points toward the farthest point. "This place is Cape Reinga, and out there is where the Pacific Ocean meets the Tasman Sea. You can see it forms a visible line of different currents meeting each other."

I reseat my sunglasses to better block the ocean glare and nod. The line delineating the meeting of the two seas is distinct, and I feel it's also a powerful energetic convergence. The day is blazingly hot, but goose bumps form on my arms.

Marty leans closer and whispers, "Do you see that lone tree hanging out over the water right at the meeting point of the two seas?"

I squint and follow his line of sight. "Yes, I do."

"That's what I brought you here to see. It's an ancient *pohutukawa* tree, and it is sacred to the Maori." He shields his eyes with his hands to get a better look. "They believe that spirits go there after death, and that it's their jumping off point to the afterlife," he whispers reverently. "*Te Reinga* actually means the leaping place of spirits."

My goose bumps get bigger, and I feel myself surrounded by a strong presence. I'm no longer aware of the other tourists, or even Marty, standing beside me. My eyes are glued to the spirit tree—the air around it is shimmering. Mom's face slowly materializes, first in my mind, and then I'm sure I can see her standing next to the tree.

As clear as if she is right next to me, I hear her whisper, "It's time. You need to let go."

That's not what I want to hear! My mind pulls away, and the image of Mom disappears. I'm instantly pissed at myself. I reach my hand out to somehow get her back, but all I see is the tree and the ocean. I'm back standing next to Marty, who is calmly watching me.

"Messages aren't always easy to hear. Be gentle with yourself." His voice is kind as he takes my arm. We walk over to an empty bench and sit down. He fishes a toothpick out of his backpack and silently chews on it. I'm way too dazed to say anything yet, and Marty is experienced enough to recognize it. He reaches back into his backpack and hands me a fresh toothpick. "Here you go, mate. It always helps to chew on one of these."

Tears well up and threaten to fall. I wipe them dry on the tail of my T-shirt. I'm afraid that clinging to my grief is the only thing holding me together. *How can I let go? I never had the chance to say good-bye because I screwed up. I was too late. I want her back so badly that I want to hit something. She was ripped away before her time. I still need her—damn it! Don't I get a say in this? I'm not ready to let go. In fact, I downright refuse. It's not over.*

I shake myself and exhale sharply. Marty turns his head and looks at me questioningly. I manage a crooked smile and take a quick swig from my water bottle to soften the lump in my throat. We sit in silence. It's a long time before I feel like talking again.

We finally stand and pick up our backpacks. I glance back at the spirit tree one last time. Its windswept branches lean out over the ocean. It's hard to figure out how it's managed to survive so long on its precarious perch. Its roots must run deep. The air around it still shimmers, but Mom isn't there. Her words linger in my mind, but I can't do it—not yet.

CHAPTER TWENTY NINE
TO TOUCH THE VEIL

It is not all of life to live, nor yet all of death to die.
For life and death are one, and only those who will
consider the experience as one may come to understand
or comprehend what peace indeed means.
–Edgar Cayce

Driving back to Keshama's place, I keep replaying the scene with Mom at the Spirit Tree in my head. I desperately want to contact her again, to beg for forgiveness and tell her I love her. Jay arrived at the hospital in time to connect with her before she slipped into a coma, and I envy that priceless gift he was given. Missing my last moment with her was entirely my own fault, and the misery I feel is like a maggot in my heart, gnawing at me from the inside out. Over the next week, as each attempt to contact Mom fails, my need to see her increases until it morphs into a quest for my own personal holy grail.

My first thought is to repeat what worked before. I set up another horse trek at a different stable. It's a scenic ride, but the energy I felt riding with Joanna isn't there. I'm not surprised when Mom doesn't appear. Maybe I didn't get deep enough into the wild?

Next I pin my hopes on an arduous seventeen-kilometer hike along the Herekino Trail. The circuitous track ventures deep into the ancient Kauri forests of the Northland. After several hours, the trail climbs up a steep five hundred meters to the summit of the biggest mountain in the area. The panoramic view at the top is breathtaking. From there I can see both sides of the Cape Reinga Peninsula with the Tasman Sea to the west and the South Pacific to the east. I'm close enough to touch the heavens. Surely, I can reach Mom here! Unfortunately, after a lengthy meditation that takes me past my designated departure time, nothing happens.

By the time I hike back to my car, the sky is growing dark, and I'm disappointed. I have to see Mom before my trip is over. Like a petulant child, I'm not leaving until I do. Fear of failure slips into my thoughts and spreads like a pernicious weed. What can I try next?

Sifting through my large pile of adventure brochures, I spy an ad for scuba diving. I've never done it before—probably due to my very nontrivial fear of drowning. But the "Discover Scuba" option catches my eye. My own private instructor would take me on two dives in the popular Bay of Islands—no experience necessary. It scares the heck out of me, but at the same time, I have an irresistible urge to do it. It will test me and stir up my fears. I want to be tested; I want to prove myself worthy. Maybe it will lead me to Mom.

Troy hands me a fifteen-pound weight belt. When I roll my eyes at this additional ball and chain that he insists is necessary for the dive, he simply flashes me a super white grin. I reluctantly snap it around my waist. I must weigh about a million pounds with all this gear. The air tank all by its little lonesome is forty-pounds, plus the fifteen for the belt, plus the eight pounds for the buoyancy compensator vest, plus my fins, snorkel, and mask. I'm lugging around a whopping sixty-five extra pounds. I'm surprised the boat deck isn't sagging under all this weight.

Troy fiddles with my regulator and then adjusts something on my air tank. "All right, mate. You're all set. Hang on a quick minute while I get geared up." Troy, my private dive instructor, looks like he could be Marty's twin brother—young, ripped, and adventurous. In other words, he's a typical Kiwi.

I glance around the boat at the flurry of activity. There are ten other certified divers along on the trip, and they're scattered around the deck in various stages of preparation. We're currently anchored in a shady cove in the Bay of Islands, someplace called Pig's Gully. The boat rocks with the waves, and the unwieldy weight of the tank throws me off balance. I quickly grab the railing at the back of the boat to steady myself. Troy materializes from below deck, lugging his oversized gear bag.

"Hey, why don't you lower yourself into the water? I'll be right in," he says.

"That's a good idea." I let out a sigh of relief. I'm in good shape, but the mountain on my back is getting heavier by the minute.

I watch as several divers sit on the flat metal grate at the back of the boat and then slide gracefully into the water. Before I let myself have too much time to think, I mimic their actions. Once I'm in the water, I turn to face the back of the boat. The waves are rough, and I'm tossed about. It occurs to me that I'm in a worse position than when I was standing on the boat. I'm treading water with sixty-five pounds on my back; my chest is feeling squeezed and it's hard to breathe. I'm not going to last long like this. *What is taking Troy so long?*

I can see him helping a diver with her regulator. I raise my arm and wave to get his attention. He holds up two fingers, which I gather means two minutes. The two minutes turn into ten. I'm feeling like I've been through several washing machine cycles by the time he finally slides into the water next to me. My anxiety level is off the charts, and I'm questioning whether I should get out now before something else happens.

"What the heck is going on?" Speaking was a mistake. A wave chooses that precise moment to plow into me. I choke and spit out a mouthful of salt water.

"Sorry, mate. Sophie's regulator was giving her a problem, and I helped her out," he explains sheepishly, although not nearly sheepish enough, in my opinion. I wonder if it has anything to do with her fashion model looks.

Troy adjusts his mask and inserts his regulator into his mouth. He gestures for me to do the same. I battle with myself over whether to keep going as I shove the regulator in my mouth. Troy tugs at my arm and submerges.

I stop treading and let myself sink a few feet under the surface. Troy hovers in front of me, waiting to see how I do. At first, taking breathes from the regulator is hard work; I have to suck hard to get any air. I fight the urge to panic, realizing that I am actually receiving oxygen into my lungs. Troy points to my mask. I remember his instructions on the boat. My first task is a drill. I need to remove my mask, then put it back on and clear out the water. At first I decide that I probably didn't have a good seal when I submerged because my mask is already halfway full of water. But I perform the exercise successfully, and my anxiety decreases. Troy gives me the okay sign and points down. We drop another five feet, but my mask is filling with water again. This is annoying. I take it off and clear it. Troy keeps pointing down. Again, my mask fills with water. I clear it. We drop another five feet—again, the mask.

I'm anxious, exhausted, and irritated. This isn't going to work for me—feeling like this, something could go very wrong. I point up, but Troy shakes his head. I have to clear my mask *again*. I point up more insistently, but Troy continues to shake his head. That does it for me—I'm out of here. I kick upward. Suddenly, I feel Troy grab my leg and pull me down. Not the best choice for him. I punch him in the shoulder and point up. He lets me go.

I haul myself onto the metal grate and collapse. A moment later, Troy surfaces. "What was that? You never take off like that, ever," he says angrily.

"Don't even start with me, Troy. You left me treading water at the surface forever. I got bashed by waves and exhausted." I hold up my mask. "And this mask leaks big time. You think I want to go on a dive clearing my mask every thirty seconds? This is my dive—not yours." That seemed to snap Troy out of it.

"You know what? You're right. I'm sorry. I'll get you a new mask."

"Forget it. I'm whipped and actually feeling kind of seasick. I'm going to lie down at the bow of the boat."

"I understand if that's how you feel. I'll be back in a bit." He reinserts his regulator. I feel let down as Troy sinks beneath the surface.

Once I divest myself of my gear, I make my way to the bow and sprawl, exhausted and miserable, on the deck. My stomach is doing flips, and it's a struggle to hang onto its contents. I'm pissed at myself for quitting. I should have let Troy get me a new mask and kept going. Is this what I'm becoming, a quitter? I let down Mom, and this is my new trend? Things are hard, so I give up? I slap the deck in frustration. I should have gone back in the water. The sun pops out from behind the clouds, and the sudden glare off the deck hurts my eyes. I drag my towel over my head. Fortunately, it's not long before I fall into a fitful sleep.

"Holly, are you alive under there?" I hear Troy's voice quite close to my head, and I lift the towel.

"More or less," I say with a grunt.

"Hey, I'm really sorry about that first dive. I screwed up. Look, we're going to head over to Putahataha Island. It's a cool spot for a second dive." He squats down next to me. "How about if you use my mask? It's a good one. And I promise we'll be in the water first and submerge immediately." He offers me a box and a Gatorade. "Here's some lunch. Eat up, and you'll feel better. The second time's a charm, mate." He smiles as I sit up and accept the box. "It'll take us about a half hour to get there, so eat and relax."

The ham sandwich tastes quite good, and the Gatorade sliding down my throat does wonders. By the time the boat anchors in our new location, I'm feeling almost human again. I want to give it another shot; I can't let this trip end in failure.

Everything about the second dive is the opposite of the first. The sea is calm, the sun is out, and Troy has us geared up in the blink of an eye. When I slide into the water, my fear returns, but Troy is in the water only seconds behind me. Before I have time to reconsider, we insert our regulators and sink below the surface. His sleek mask is a beautiful thing. I run through my drill: remove it, put it back on, clear it—all smooth as silk. I give him the okay sign, and we drop lower. Breathing with the regulator is much easier this time; in fact, it's kind of enjoyable.

I look around and notice I'm in an entirely different world. Troy motions for me to follow him, and we kick slowly along the bottom. A school of bright yellow and blue fish barely parts as we swim through them. Troy points and I see the sinister form of a barracuda swimming casually along to our right. It's got to be about four feet long. I forget to breathe when I glimpse the razor-sharp teeth in its open mouth and have to take several huge gulps of air after he's safely past us. This is wild! However, the biggest treat is the group of small rays that we encounter, measuring at most five feet across. The manta ray I saw with Marty was at least twice as big as the largest one in this group. But size definitely doesn't matter. As they glide slowly up and down, their movements are fluid and beautiful to watch. They don't seem to mind us being there, and I'm mesmerized by the gentle flapping motion of their wings. I forget about everything until I feel Troy tug on my leg. When I turn my head, he taps on his watch and points up. It can't be over already—can it? Back on the boat, I feel a huge relief. I did it. I didn't quit this time.

Having completed the second dive, it's time to head back to the wharf in Paihia. I return to my previous spot at the bow of the boat in a very different frame of mind. I spread my towel and lie down to catch some shuteye. I'm exhausted and manage to drift off in a few short minutes.

The light pressure of the warm salt water is like a comfortable blanket wrapped gently around my body. I float, unmoving, a few meters below the surface, calmly waiting. For what, I'm not sure? The only sound I hear is my breathing as I suck oxygen in through the regulator. The water is aquamarine and so startlingly pure that it doesn't seem real. Not too far ahead of me, I notice a wide column of light angling down from the surface. Curious, I swim toward it. Once I'm inside the shaft of light, I have an overwhelming urge to follow it up. I kick hard with my fins. Breaching the surface of the ocean, I pull off my mask and spit out my regulator.

Where am I? I bob up and down with the waves while I spin full circle to get my bearings. I'm alone. Then it hits me. The boat is gone! *What happened to the boat?* I can see the shore so there's no need to get too upset—not yet anyway. Actually, there's something familiar about the shoreline. There's a tiny white sand beach to the right of a small promontory with a lone windswept tree jutting out over the water. I know this place! That's the Spirit Tree. How the heck did I get here?

I swim toward it, but the currents are surprisingly strong, and I struggle to make headway. After what seems like hours of kicking, the waves have grown rough and my strength is all but spent. When I raise my head out of the churning salt water, I can still clearly see the pohutukawa tree. It's so close! I need to reach it. It's my only hope.

My legs are fatigued from kicking, and I start to slip under the surface. There's no more air in my tank, so I unstrap it and watch it sink into the depths. I extend my hand toward the surface, but I've dropped too far to reach it. I'm too exhausted to continue and let myself sink. It isn't unpleasant; in fact, it's almost easy to let go. I'm facing up as I drop and the water remains so clear I can still see the rippling black edge of the cliff that is home to the Spirit Tree. Soon I'll be there for my own final leap across the veil and into the spirit world. Mom will be there.

Suddenly, I'm surrounded by a bright light, and a hand reaches down to grasp mine. I'm pulled toward the light. I can see the pohutukawa tree! Am I still under the water? I can't tell, but I'm almost to the tree. Abruptly, the world seems to shake, and my hand slips free. I'm falling again, and the tree is receding. No, wait! I can't leave yet.

My eyes snap open. There's a soft thud as the dive boat docks. *What the heck is going on?* I shake the sleep out of my senses, quickly realizing that I was dreaming. But it all felt so real—far more lucid and tangible than any ordinary dream. In those last moments, as I let myself slip under the water, I felt that hand grasp mine. My wrist smarts, and I rub it to ease the pain. I can still feel the vise-like grip pulling me up. If I had held on, dream or no, could I have touched the veil and made contact with Mom? Was it real or a road map pointing the way? A miniscule part of my brain shouts, "Crazy just moved into the neighborhood!"

Crazy or not, I'm convinced that if I want to reach Mom, I've got to walk the tightrope between worlds. The only way I can see to do that is to walk right up to the brink of my own mortality and reach out.

Since New Zealand offers every wild adventure conceivable, it isn't hard to line up a few death-defying exploits. But out of all the stunts in my upcoming action-packed itinerary, one of them scares me beyond reason—bungee jumping. I start shaking just thinking about it. But it's perfect! Maybe I've lost it, but I don't care. Nothing else matters except finding Mom. I will do anything. It's all or nothing. Like Evel Knievel, by the end of the week, I'll either be on the other side of the canyon or a splat on the rocks at the bottom.

Tomorrow I will head south to begin my death-defying adventures, but right now I'm taking in the view of Keshama's jungle valley from a clearing on a tiny plateau behind her villa. Externally I appear as a woman reclining lazily on a towel, perhaps to catch the afternoon sunshine. Internally my mind is girding itself for the upcoming gauntlet of fear. Part of me says, "Bring it on!" Another part lurks below it, dark and cold.

When I close my eyes and look inside my heart, I see a black mist. Concentrating on the warmth from the sun, I draw it into me and imagine its light gently dissipating the darkness inside. When I open my eyes, I feel calm. I'm not sure if that's an improvement because, without the mask of anxiety, I can perceive an undercurrent of self-destructive energy. There is a part of me that doesn't want me to come back alive. Am I really doing all this to find Mom? Or am I trying to punish myself to ease the big, bad guilt monster thrashing around inside of me. I don't quite trust myself. The realization is chilling, and I repress a shudder.

Thankfully, my dark thoughts are interrupted when I spot Keshama popping her head out of the living room bus. I wave to get her attention. She waves back and climbs up the hill toward me. I make room for her to sit on my towel; for several minutes, we share a moment of peaceful silence.

I cock my head slightly toward her. "You're not by any chance interested in coming along with me—are you?"

"Are you bloody kidding? I think not." She laughs. "I'm not into crazy."

"I thought so, but I just thought I'd ask."

Atama appears from between a couple of buses. He's wearing a pair of tan shorts, and no shirt or shoes. For a moment, he stands as still as a statue, looking as if he's waiting for something.

"Hey, Ati!" Keshama shouts to get his attention.

Atama sees us and races up the slope to join us. It's clear how much Keshama adores him. His eleven-year-old body is like a miniature Greek Adonis. There is something special about him; his spirit is a bright light that dispels all darkness. Atama leaps around us with a wild grin, making us laugh with his playful antics.

Suddenly, he freezes and slowly turns toward us with his tongue sticking out. Next he prances around beating his chest and stomping the ground with his feet. I'd seen Atama do a few moves from a *haka* at the waterfall, but it's quite a sight to see the full version of a Maori war dance. He's a marvel in motion, a perfect little warrior.

A wild thought occurs to me, and I lean in closer to Keshama. "Do you think Atama might want to go with me?" I whisper conspiratorially.

Keshama's face lights up. "He'd love it, but you'd have to run it by Mum. He'd be missing school."

We both clap in delight as Atama makes a final leap into the air, spinning in a circle to land facing us. His eyes bulge and his tongue is sticking out.

When I ask Alana's permission, she's as enthusiastic as Keshama. "That would be awesome. It's much more worthwhile to have real-life experiences than a week of bloody school."

"Cool as!" Atama's response is short and sweet.

With Atama along on my crazy ventures, I know I'm coming back. Before, I couldn't see myself returning, but now I know I can. A part of me is still clear-headed enough to realize I do need the added insurance of his presence. Being responsible for his safety means I will need to protect and watch over him. To fulfill that obligation, I'll need to survive the next few days myself. Atama will not just be my charge; he will be my guardian as well.

CHAPTER THIRTY
TAKE THE JUMP

"When I let go of what I am, I become what I might be."
–Lao Tzu

"Buzz!" The alarm clock insists that I respond. I slap the snooze button and turn my head to look at the time. The clock reads 7:00. Good. I have plenty of time to meditate and then wake Atama for today's ultimate adventure—bungee jumping. Just hearing those words in my head stirs the butterflies in my stomach. Do I really need to go through with this last crazy stunt?

Over the course of this last week, Atama and I have dangled on ropes suspended three hundred feet above the ground, squeezed ourselves through claustrophobically tight limestone tubes in caves, rafted over a waterfall and flipped upside down, tramped along seemingly bottomless crevasses deep underground, parachuted out of a plane fifteen thousand feet in the air, and more. I had thought if I could stare death in the eye, it would somehow magically hand me the key to seeing Mom again. I guess I was wrong. Perhaps, her appearance beside the Maori Spirit Tree, when she spoke to me, was my one and only moment with her? Maybe I should hold that experience close to my heart as the miracle it was and really try to do as she asked and let go.

Annoyed with the universe, I kick the sheet off and stalk over to the sliding glass doors of my room at the Redwood Lodge in Otorohanga. My balcony overlooks a dense jungle forest. A wooden recliner with teal cushions invites me to sit outside. I take a few deep breaths of the pure New Zealand air and lean back against the plush fabric.

It's time. You need to let go. That's what Mom had said. But what does that really mean for me? After she died, I let my healing practice slip away and sank into a mire of grief and guilt for over a year. Quite simply, I had given up on my life. Isn't it time to let go of that and find my own way

200

again? Am I afraid that letting go will leave me with nothing to hold onto? The hypnotic buzz of the cicadas grows louder. I concentrate on it until my mind is empty of thoughts. An image of Mom's smiling face appears in my mind. It must have taken an extraordinary effort for her to reach out to me from across the veil to help me one last time. I feel a rush of determination. I will honor her wishes.

I jump up from the recliner into a Tae Kwon Do fighting stance and raise my fist to the sky. "I'll do it, Mom!" I declare forcefully, accepting her challenge from beyond. If I can throw myself off of a tower, an act that scares me more than anything I've ever done before, will I not then find the courage to let go in my heart?

When Atama and I are in the car and on our way, I catch him watching me from the passenger seat. He raises an eyebrow to question my tense demeanor. I hesitate for a moment, not wanting to appear vulnerable to a kid. But then Atama isn't just any kid. His age belies a connection to ancient wisdom and a serenity that engenders my trust.

"You know, Atama." I let out a nervous sigh. "This is hard to admit, but I'm more terrified of bungee jumping than anything I've ever done. But I want very much to prove to myself that I can do this," I say earnestly, as much to myself as to him.

Atama doesn't laugh but considers my words quietly for a moment. "Holly, think about it like this. Every one of our adventures has been something that could kill us. What's one more? Each one changes us, and I'm happy for this experience. You've already stared death in the eye. I say let's go for it." He pumps his fist in the air.

His spirit is infectious. "Let's do it!" I slap the steering wheel with both hands. Was that psychotherapy from an eleven-year-old? Maybe I should have tried it before.

He cocks his head slightly, suggesting he can read my thoughts, and we grin conspiratorially at each other.

Our destination is called "Bungee Jumpers." We follow the signs along a winding dirt road that leads us into a small forested canyon. The track ends at a wooden shack with a sign on the door that says simply: *Office*. As soon as we step out of the car, we're met by two wildly enthusiastic Rambo types. Brian and Gregg bound out of the office door and quickly snare us in their web of daring and adventure.

Just beyond the office, the 150-foot bungee tower looms high into sky. My eyes are drawn inexorably upward, assessing the condition of every beam and bolt holding it together. The platform at the top is well above the tallest of the trees. My knees turn to jelly. There is a small stream that runs underneath the tower, but it's only a few feet deep. There would be nothing to cushion the fall if something went wrong. Atama, bless his heart, confidently walks over to Brian and announces that he would like to go first. He gives me a wink, and I swear that he looks thirty and not eleven. I want to hug him, but I know it would embarrass him.

Brian takes Atama onto a lift, and I wave at him. Gregg and I watch them rise toward the jump platform at the top of the tower. Gregg notices the look of fear in my eyes. "No need to worry, mate. You'll do fine. I know it," he says, patting me on the shoulder. "In short order, you're going to become a member of the 'bungee jumpers' club. When you jump, you change. You'll feel different, like nothing is impossible."

It seems like an eternity since Brian and Atama have reached the top, but eventually, Gregg raises his arm and points to the platform. Atama is stepping out onto what looks like a plank jutting out from the side of the tower. I hold my breath in nervous anticipation and close my eyes to visualize his jump. I imagine him soaring like a bird and then bouncing gently upward. I feel that he'll be okay.

I open my eyes just in time to see him actually leap from the tower and dive like a swan straight down. His form is perfect, and his trajectory brings him so close that I can see the crazy grin on his face, a warrior in the rapture of battle. The bungee stretches until I wonder why it doesn't snap, and then he springs back up. He bounces up and down several more times and comes to rest halfway up the tower, dangling from the end of the bungee cord. When he's lowered to the ground, Gregg grabs his hands and expertly removes the harness from his feet. The explosive exhalation of the breath I'd been holding is loud enough to startle me.

As soon as his feet are free, Atama springs up from the ground. "That was bloody excellent, Holly! I know you can do it."

Before I can change my mind, Gregg grabs my arm and conducts me firmly over to the lift. The noise of the motor propelling us up is loud and distracts me until we reach the top of the tower. At the top, I cautiously look around. The platform is surrounded by a waist-high railing, but when I glimpse the view beyond it, the world spins crazily. I focus my attention on the floor.

Gregg sits me down in the only chair and expertly begins strapping my feet into the bungee harness. As soon as my butt hits the chair, I snap out of my daze and my fear slips back in. My body starts shaking, and my stomach adds twists and somersaults to the mix. *What the hell am I doing?*

This is crazy! While he works, Gregg chats amicably about how much I'm going to love jumping. He seems completely unaware of my impending meltdown.

"Umm, Gregg? I'm not so sure I can do this," I whisper hoarsely.

"Oh, sure you can. I've almost got you done up. Hang on a moment." He tightens the last clip on my leg harness and stands up. "There. Okay, now just take a few steps over to the gate," he says, gently pulling me to my feet and scooting me to the edge of the platform.

I'm standing in front of a waist-high metal gate. Beyond it is a metal plank—just like the kind you see in pirate movies. I shiver involuntarily. I'm walking the plank! Suddenly, my feet weigh a thousand pounds, and every drop of moisture in my throat evaporates.

Gregg launches in with the bungee jumper's propaganda speech, like a flight attendant blandly reading the emergency landing protocol for the umpteenth time. *"This* is a moment to treasure, an experience you *must* have. I know it. *You* know it."

I can feel myself start to panic. My heart is pounding. The air seems much too thin. Why did I need to face my worst fear again? My mind goes blank, and I can't think of a single good reason.

I hear a voice inside my head. *Let go and trust.*

Why do I require such drastic measures in order to learn my lesson? Why couldn't I just stay home and read a self-help book like most sane, normal people?

"You can do this and join our exclusive club."

I risk a tiny peak down. Holy shit! My hands clamp onto the gate in front of me as I'm hit by a wave of vertigo. It is a *long* way down to that itty bitty stream below. I'm frozen in place, clinging fiercely to my tiny perch, like the lone pohutukawa tree. I'm one with the Spirit Tree that dangles precariously over the precipice, hovering above the line between seas, the veil between worlds. Feeling its roots as my feet and its branches as my hands, I sense its purpose is to give one the ability to touch life and death at the same time. Unlike the Spirit Tree that's bound forever to that place in between, I'm here to let go and make the leap—a leap of faith that could free me or end me. I can't move. The icy cold hand of fear is relentless, squeezing me ever tighter.

What are you more afraid of, Holly, dying or living? An inner voice says. *Your mom has her own destiny; you have yours. Don't be afraid to follow your heart.* These last words are spoken so softly I can barely hear them.

Gregg's enthusiastic pep talk fades back in. "Bungee jumpers can do anything they set their minds to do!"

I'm not sure how, but all of a sudden I find myself standing on the plank as Gregg closes the gate behind me. What the hell? I start to turn around.

"Gregg, I've really changed my mind. This isn't necessary." My hands have locked onto the gate. At any moment, I could lose my balance and fall off this toothpick of a plank. "I'm sure that now that I've stood on the edge of the abyss, there's really no need to actually dive into it—is there?" *Did I really just say that out loud? I've got to get a grip.*

Gregg makes no move to open the gate. "Holly, I want you to take a deep breath and relax. I'm going to guide you through this; all you need to do is listen to my voice." His tone is persuasive, compelling me to stop and listen.

I force myself to take a deep breath and then let it out in a rush.

"Good, that's better. You've come here to do this—to meet and master your fears—and you will do this. Now don't worry; nothing bad will happen. I'm right here. Just close your eyes for a moment." The calm certainty in Gregg's voice keeps me listening. I close my eyes and continue to breathe.

Soon this will all be over—one way or the other. I inch out a little farther along the metal plank and feel myself wobble. *Shit!* All I can feel or think about is my fear. What a scary four-letter word it is; for me it's by far the worst one of the bunch. I scrunch my eyes shut and start to mumble.

"Fear—I must not fear. Fear is the mind-killer." I recognize the words from Frank Herbert's *Litany of Fear*, and I roll my eyes at myself. *Dune?* Really? At a moment like this, poised between life and death, all I can come up with is a passage from a sci-fi novel?

The wind picks up and pushes me in the back as if it has a mind of its own. On the other hand, a sci-fi passage works just fine for me, so I let my mind continue to recite: *I must not fear. Fear is the mind-killer. Fear is the little-death that brings total obliteration. I will face my fear. I will permit it to pass over me and through me. And when it has gone past, I will turn the inner eye to see its path. Where the fear has gone there will be nothing. Only I will remain.* I concentrate on the words until that's all I see. Eventually, I feel my hands release their hold on the gate behind me.

Gregg's voice pops back into existence. "Okay, great, now open your eyes and look straight ahead. Don't look down. I'm right here, right behind you. I'm not leaving, and I won't let anything happen to you. Raise your arms out to your sides," he commands, and my arms move of their own accord. "Excellent. You're here for you. This is all about you and letting go. Trust in the universe, and trust in yourself. Now relax and go. *Now!*"

Before I'm actually aware of it, I'm falling forward off of the platform. I hear myself yelling obscenities, but another part of me is simply a silent observer. Time seems to stand still. An eternity passes as I see the itty bitty stream approaching. I feel a bit like Superman as my senses become hyper-aware. It's eerie, but somehow I can actually see the rounded pebbles underneath the water as if they were inches from my face. I can hear the water rippling as it flows gently along. The quiet, meandering stream is quite obviously unaware of the screaming woman who's about to smash her face into a million pieces when she hits the ground since it appears that there's too much slack left in the bungee cord. After all my observations, I still have time to ponder why all this is taking so long.

Miraculously, and at what appears to be mere inches from the water, I'm gently whooshed back up as the bungee cord reaches its maximum extension. There is no snap or whiplash—just an incredibly smooth bounce up and then down several times until I finally come to rest upside down. Brian is right there, reaching out to help me as I'm lowered to the ground.

Atama is skipping with excitement and greets me with a smug look of approval on his face. "I knew you could do it. Good on you, Holly," he crows, reaching out his hand and pulling me to my feet.

I'm alive? I feel strangely giddy. The reality is slowly sinking in. I did it! A rush of energy flows into me. I tilt my head up to take another look at the tower. My head spins and I still feel like I'm falling. I look down again and wiggle my toes, checking to make sure that my feet are truly and firmly connected to the ground. What could possibly be harder than that? It feels as if I leapt all the way through the veil and came out on the other side. *Where the fear has gone, there will be nothing—only I will remain.*

I watch Atama high-five Brian and raise a fist in victory. Was it he who reached out to pull me up as I was sinking in my dream on the boat? I feel more alive than I've felt in a long time. A light bulb flashes over my head, and I realize it's because I'm not afraid anymore. I can let go, and I'll be all right—just like Mom tried to tell me at the pohutukawa tree. I wonder if she's watching me right now, probably shaking her head in disbelief and calling me a "crazy ninny" for all my wild shenanigans. The thought makes me laugh out loud. Atama looks over at me, grinning from ear to ear.

"We did it—didn't we?" I smile back at him.

Gregg hops off the tower lift and emphatically waves us over. "Hey, don't forget your souvenir T-shirts!"

CHAPTER THIRTY ONE

THE READING

Whatever relationships you have attracted in your life at this moment, are precisely the ones you need in your life at this moment. There is a hidden meaning behind all events, and this hidden meaning is serving your own evolution.
—Deepak Chopra

"Hol, it's about bloody time you're back from tramping through the wilds. I've had a brilliant idea, of course, and I've been bloody dying to tell you," Keshama says.

I've just walked into the family room bus, and I'm instantly curious. "Tell me what, mate? I'm all ears," I reply, smiling at her enthusiasm.

"We're going to Auckland tomorrow, and you've got an appointment with my friend." Keshama taps me on the chest. "Joline is an amazing psychic, and I think she's just the person you need to see. What do you think about that?"

"I think that sounds perfect. Thanks, Keshama. I can't wait." Excitement bubbles to the surface. After making it through my bungee jump, I have the impression that something big is about to happen. Tomorrow can't arrive soon enough.

The next day, the drive south to Auckland seems to take forever. The closer we get, the more I excited I feel. Keshama grins like the Cheshire Cat the whole way. I'm intrigued when she announces that we've arrived after we turn into the driveway of a modest suburban home on the outskirts of Auckland. This isn't at all what I expected a psychic's house to look like. I wave good-bye to Keshama as she beeps the horn and roars off to get in some whirlwind shopping while I have my reading.

When I turn around to face the front door, Joline is standing in the entranceway. She does know how to make an impression. Her long, black hair reaches almost to her waist and shines as though polished; it's accentuated by a light purple silk skirt and blouse. As soon as she raises her arms, tiny rainbows spring forth from the crystal jewelry that adorns every finger, both wrists, and even both ankles. The *pièce de résistance* is her magnificent amethyst necklace. Her soothing aura reaches out to embrace me even before she does, and it sets me at ease. In fact, I have a strong sense of déjà vu; she reminds me of Alice from the Acupressure Institute.

"It's so nice to meet you, Holly. You know, our dear Keshama was absolutely adamant that I do a session with you, and I can already see the spirits dancing around you. Be welcome and enter," she says, graciously inviting me into her home.

The entry leads immediately into a living room of soft lavender that is accented with many crystals on shelves and tables encircling the room. It's a deeply spiritual and protected space. Joline guides me to a matching lavender couch and offers me tea before settling into the plush armchair across from me. She tilts her head at an angle, as if listening to something. "Well, I'm being encouraged to get started without delay," she says. The corner of her mouth curls up into an amused expression. "Just make yourself comfortable, and we'll begin."

I happily kick off my sneakers and pull my feet up onto the couch. Joline closes her eyes and slows her breathing. The air in the room becomes dense. I can feel its weight on my body, but it's comforting. There's also a slightly sweet taste in my mouth when I breathe. I feel wonderfully nurtured.

Joline slowly opens her eyes and stares at some point behind me. "Well, this is beautiful. There's a tremendous amount of dolphin energy surrounding you. Have you been around them recently?" Her soft voice is curious.

I'm fascinated and pleased that she picked up on the dolphins. Just before my wild weekend with Marty, I went on a catamaran tour around the Bay of Islands. The captain let me hang over the bow while a pod of dolphins swam along with us. One dolphin in particular swam a few feet away from me for a long time. Her body was turned slightly so that she could look directly at me with one eye. I felt powerful energy all around me and a deep connection between us. It felt as if I was in the presence of ancient wisdom.

I nod my head, and Joline says, "The dolphins want to give you a message. They share a strong connection with you and will play a future role in your endeavors. They're sending you love and playful energy. Lighten up and allow yourself to shine. There's so much that you want to do. Don't worry. All in good time—it will come." Her voice is powerfully hypnotic, and I have goose bumps all over. "There's more. They want you to call on the dolphin realm whenever you get too serious or need support. They're pleased that you came on this trip; they've wanted to establish a closer connection with you for some time." Joline's eyes refocus on me. "This is truly special, Holly. I rarely receive such a strong and clear message from the dolphins for a client." She smiles and raises her eyebrows.

"I'm overwhelmed and gratefully accept their help and guidance. Thank you." I smile back at Joline and let myself revel in the spiritual intensity of the moment.

Joline nods her approval. "One of my guides wishes to speak. He says that even though there are many mountains yet to climb on your journey, do not lose heart or hope. Look within, and your light will shine," she says slowly and with increasing emphasis. It's as if I can feel her words being directed into my heart chakra for later use. She pauses to let the message sink in, and we each take a sip of tea. I'm enthralled and can't wait for her to continue.

Joline sets her cup down, and her eyes become unfocused once more. "Now I'm seeing a number of spirits appearing who wish to speak with you. I'm asking for one to separate from the crowd so that I can receive their message clearly. Oh, this is interesting. I can see someone in the back of the group, jumping up and down, trying to get my attention." As soon as she says this, my heart skips a beat. I eagerly lean forward on the couch, straining to hear every word.

"This spirit is short in stature but trying desperately to be seen. Oh my goodness, what a bundle of energy it is." Joline chuckles, and my goose bumps are back in full force. "This one is elbowing the others out of the way. I can see her now. She's waving her arms at me and pushing others backward to get to the front of the crowd. Oh, what a cute, determined little woman she is." Joline claps her hands together in delight. By this time, I've shifted so far forward on the couch that I almost fall on the floor.

"She's made it out in front, a short woman with wavy brown hair. Now what is she doing? She's throwing tiny objects into the air, lots and lots of them. What are they?" Joline's forehead wrinkles in concentration. "They're beautiful and sparkle with many colors. She's waving her arms at me and stomping her foot; she wants me to tell you what they are."

Before Joline can say what she sees, I know.

"Oh, I see. They're opals, beautiful opals, and so absolutely stunning," she says in awe.

A torrent of tears is already flowing down my cheeks. My heart is about to burst with all the emotions that are flying to the surface. Joline hands me a box of tissues and waits patiently for me to speak the words that are struggling past the boulder that has materialized in my throat.

"That's Mom! She's barely five feet, and she loves opals; they're her favorite stone," I finally manage to blurt out.

Joline nods her head and raises her hand to signal she has more to say. "Your mom is nodding in an emphatic yes. She wants me to tell you that she loves you—and she's so proud of you and your accomplishments. She says that you don't need to prove anything to anybody. But, most of all, she wants you to know that she's happy where she is, very happy." Joline grabs a tissue and dabs her own eyes.

I'm shaking as the words I never got a chance to say claw their way out of my constricted throat.

"Can you tell her how sorry I am—so very sorry—that I wasn't there for her, that I wasn't around to help her when she needed me. And that I wasn't there to say good-bye or tell her how much I love her. Can you tell her how wonderful a mother she was to me and how grateful I am?" It all pours out of me in a desperate rush.

Joline waits to respond while I blow my nose and wipe my face. "Your mom is quite adamant that you hear this. You've done nothing she needs to forgive. You are her pride and joy, and she loves having you as her daughter. She asks you to please forgive yourself and live your life. She says the joy she experienced having you in her life was indescribable. She's on her journey, and she's happy. Your mom wants you to continue yours and to know always that she loves you—and she feels and knows your love for her."

My ears reverberate with the sound of my own personal mountain of guilt exploding into millions of teeny, tiny pieces. Relief floods my entire body. Mom is here, and she's happy! She loves me, and she knows I love her. Perhaps I can allow myself to use the many happy memories of her to ease my sense of loss. Perhaps at last, I can finally let go.

Joline says, "Your mom is waving at me. She says she needs to go, but she's smiling. I feel such love and joy coming from her for you. It's incredible. What a beautiful spirit your mom is."

By the time Keshama arrives to pick me up, I'm feeling so much lighter that I'm positive my feet aren't touching the ground. It's hard to find the right words to thank Joline, so I try to convey my gratitude with a hug.

Keshama drives us north to meet Alana for dinner at the Blue Dolphin Café. It's the perfect ending to a perfect day. A world of guilt has fallen from my shoulders. At long last, I have what I came to New Zealand to find, and now I'm free.

CHAPTER THIRTY TWO
READY AIM FIRE

*Some things cannot be spoken or discovered until we
have been stuck, incapacitated, or blown off course
for a while. Plain sailing is pleasant, but you are not
going to explore many unknown realms that way.*
—David Whyte

"This is the police! Stay where you are, and get your hands in the air!" The harsh words reverberating in the air leave no room for negotiation.

I slowly raise my hands above my head.

"Get down on your knees, and put your hands behind your head. *Now!*"

The abrasive voice continues barking orders at my back. Irritation and a sense of wrongness pervade my entire being; this isn't going at all the way I expected. I obey as slowly as I dare. It's humiliating to be treated in this manner, but I suppose that is the point. Police are trained to intimidate and subjugate their "perps," which is what I am. My shoulders protest as my hands are cuffed roughly behind my back, and I'm yanked to my feet.

"Recruits! Switch places."

The much louder voice of Corporal Drake slices through all the chatter around the gymnasium floor. I wait patiently while Recruit Jackson removes the handcuffs from my wrists. Now it's my turn. I raise my gun at Jackson, and hear myself shouting at him to get down on his knees. I close in fast and handcuff Jackson with smooth efficiency.

"Well done, Recruit Reese," Corporal Drake says as he saunters past me.

Praise is a rare commodity here. It should feel good to hear it, but instead my heart shrivels in my chest. An ear-piercing whistle blast from the corporal signals the end of class.

210

It's a mad dash as all the recruits race to form up into our assigned squads and stand at attention. As leader of Squad Five, it's my job to organize my team quickly and get a head count. If someone in my squad screws up, it's my neck that's on the line first. I quickly tuck in my shirt and snap to attention. Just in time.

"Squad leaders sound off!" Corporal Drake bellows.

The split second after Recruit Durbin reports in for Squad Four, I chime in, "Squad Five, all recruits are present and accounted for, sir!"

It's the end of another grueling day in the police academy. I'm lost in thought as I walk back to the women's locker room. Six months ago, it seemed that the universe was herding me here. How did I wind up as a recruit for the Berkeley Police Department? It all started after my New Zealand adventure.

I came back from my trip like a fireball shot from a cannon. My outlook had changed dramatically after Joline's reading. I finally began to forgive myself. And not only that—I seemed to be able to open myself up during meditations and reconnect with Mom's spirit when I needed to feel her love again. She was happy; it came through to me loud and clear. I felt emotionally available to practice acupuncture again, and a few days after I made the decision to start treating clients, my martial arts instructor, Sifu Doug, offered me the use of an empty room in the back of the studio.

My modus operandi was different this time. I was extremely selective about who I agreed to see. A prospective patient needed to demonstrate willingness to do the work required to heal. This mission statement for my new practice was emotionally satisfying—but not so much financially. I had a sliding scale, and more often than not, the people who needed the most help and were willing to do the work could not afford to pay much. I hated to turn anyone away. It was extremely satisfying to collaborate with clients who willingly put forth the effort required to heal. The short of it was that I needed to find a supplementary source of income.

It pained me too deeply to take on a contract programming job again. It felt like I was moving backward, and I didn't want that to happen. I was obsessed with finding the "right" career mix. What I did know was that I couldn't bring myself to do a desk job. So, it was back to the proverbial drawing board. Once again, I switched into exploration mode and opened myself to all possibilities.

It all started innocently enough. Sofia and I were lounging in the sun on my back deck. I was taking a sip of my of Earl Grey tea when she dropped a bomb.

"Sofia, please, you've got to be kidding me," I sputtered, choking on my tea.

She raised her hand, signaling me to shut up and let her continue.

I gave in reluctantly and noisily set my cup down on the deck. "Okay, I'm listening," I said grumpily, waiting for the silliness to be over.

Sofia took her time adjusting her baseball cap to shield her eyes from the sun. Finally, she was ready. "Really, Hol. I think you should think about it. I ran into a friend who's a Berkeley cop, and I told him about you."

I opened my mouth to protest, but Sofia pressed on.

"It's the *Berkeley* Police department for crying out loud! They're different from other cops, more laid back. They're actually well-liked."

I stared back at her with obvious skepticism.

Sofia was an extroverted Australian woman and the spitting image of the goddess Artemis, whose picture was hanging on my bedroom wall. We had met many years ago in the MIT gym, and we had hit it off right away. Our first conversation had ended with me talking her into joining our women's rugby team. We'd been through many adventures together, and our friendship had deepened over the years.

Not to be denied a chance to fill the silence, Sofia started up again. "Look at yourself, Hol," she said, pointing her index finger at my chest. "You don't know what you want to do, and you've been running around like Rambo ever since you came back from New Zealand more than a year ago."

I didn't like her accusatory tone and opened my mouth to protest.

She gave me an exasperated look and talked in a rush before I could object. "You joined a search-and-rescue team, you've looked into being on a Medevac team, firefighting, and who knows what other craziness. You're back doing acupuncture at your martial arts studio, but obviously it's not enough for you. So why not?"

For a split second I considered her words, but then my inner spiritual being took over, prodding and poking, urging me to protest. I quickly shook my head in dismissal. What was I thinking? The idea was ludicrous. "Come on, Sofia. For starters, I have a *major* issue with authority. Besides, I want to *help* people, not hurt them."

Sofia took a swig of her Molson ale. "Don't shoot the messenger; it's just an idea. What do you have to lose by checking it out?"

I mulled her words over in my mind; maybe I shouldn't dismiss it quite so readily. There were aspects of the idea that worked for me. I could protect victims and help people through police outreach programs. It was unlikely that I would have given this crazy notion of Sofia's further thought, but a major world event was about to unfold that would soon change my mind.

One cloudy September morning, I happened to turn on the TV in the living room. I usually didn't watch it in the morning, but I was hoping to catch the weather report. I wanted to plan a hiking trip for the upcoming weekend. Instead of a weather report, I saw a plane crashing into the World Trade Center in New York City. At first, I thought it was a prank, but then the video repeated itself, and the news announcer looked dazed and in shock. Then it sunk in what had really just happened. This was real. My knees buckled, and I almost fell over a chair as I stumbled backward. It felt like my feet were knocked out from under me, and I wanted to get up swinging. What could I do?

I opened myself up to receive the emotions radiating outward from the devastation. The emotional hurricane hit me like a Mack truck. My heart exploded—not only with the agony of all those who had died or were injured, but also with the anguish of their families and friends. It was more than I could bear, and I wasn't even there in the thick of it. But I wanted to be. I tried to send love and support to all the people who were suffering. I felt connected to them, to their lives, and to their stories. Total strangers became neighbors and fellow Americans as we all shared in their tragedy. More than anything, I wanted to reach out and protect them from any more harm.

In the weeks that followed, I turned into a news junkie. I remained glued to the tube, watching for every tidbit about the attack. I found myself pacing constantly in front of the TV, but I didn't know what to do. Stories began to emerge of the heroes of 9/11—of firefighters, police officers, and brave civilians. At least 343 firefighters and 72 police officers died trying to save the lives of others. It was estimated that the actions of these courageous souls probably saved the lives of more than 25,000 people.

Two police officers were women, Captain Kathy Mazza and Officer Moira Smith. Captain Mazza was the first female commander of the Port Authority of New York and New Jersey Police Departments. She was leading a group of people down the stairs when the building started to collapse. Using her 9mm sidearm, Captain Mazza shot out glass walls, enabling many to escape, although she herself did not. Officer Moira Smith ran into the Trade Center to help people escape and stayed inside, directing hundreds to safety until the building collapsed on top of her. They were my heroes, selfless guardians who sacrificed themselves to rescue countless victims of the attacks. It was something to feel proud about in the midst of all the horror. More than ever, I wanted to spring into some kind of action, to do something, anything. Instead, I felt utterly helpless and angry. How could we have let this happen? I felt consumed by the rage of inaction. A month after 9/11, a chance encounter with a friend from my old Wing Chun martial arts school proffered the opportunity I thought I was looking for.

I was sitting at an outside table at Café Roma in Berkeley. It was a hot Tuesday morning, and the café patio was packed with customers. I was fortunate to find an empty table and sat down to enjoy my jasmine tea. I didn't notice I was being approached until a shadow fell over my table. When I looked up, there was a police officer standing beside my table. I saw that he was holding a latte, but the sun was bright behind him, so I couldn't see his face until I shaded my eyes with a hand. I was shocked when I recognized who it was. "You're kidding? David, is that you? How the heck long have you been a cop?" I exclaimed in surprise.

David had an amused grin on his face as I reached out my hand and shook his in greeting. His grip was like iron, as I knew it would be. "It is me—can you believe it? I've been a cop for five years already." His eyes twinkled with pleasure as he answered with genuine warmth.

Actually, I could believe it. I had met David almost ten years ago, when I had trained for almost a year at a Wing Chun Kung Fu studio in downtown Oakland. He had been one of the advanced students. He had lived, eaten, and breathed Wing Chun. Not surprisingly, he had been good. David didn't look intimidating on the outside. He was lean and short, with a slightly nerdy, Clark Kent look about him. However, underneath his clothes, his body was rock hard. He had spent countless hours pounding the wooden training dummy until he had no longer gotten bruised from hitting it. It had been a pleasure to spar with him. He had always pushed me hard, but only to help me advance, and he never lost control. He was a consummate martial artist. I had worked hard to earn his respect. Just then I was happy to see him. I felt this was no ordinary coincidence.

"It's great to see you, David. Do you have a minute?" I asked hopefully. When he nodded, I waved toward the empty chair across from me. He took a second to shift his baton out of the way before he sat down.

He took a big gulp of his latte and regarded me with curiosity. "So, what's up?" he asked simply.

The three monosyllabic words flipped a switch inside of me. Suddenly, I needed to vent. The frustration I felt with myself and my indecision about what I was meant to do all came pouring out. David listened patiently, sipping his latte and casually observing the passersby. Eventually, I ran out of steam.

"I think Sofia has a good idea; you should look into being a cop. And, by the way, you'd be good at it." He leaned toward me, and I had to admit, he looked sharp in his uniform. His eyes were bright with enthusiasm. "Besides, there are many opportunities that will open up for you after you've been a cop for a while. I know I'm making a positive difference in this community, and I feel good about it. I know you would too." His confident demeanor radiated in all directions.

I had to admit I felt my position softening. David winked at me as he swallowed the last of his latte.

"Hey, you get paid for working out. What could be better?"

I couldn't help but crack a smile. Of course he just had to throw that one in, knowing I would appreciate the paid workouts. David tapped the table with his empty cup and let me mull that one over. Then his expression was smugly triumphant as he played his trump card.

"It just so happens, we're recruiting right now—*and* we're having our physical fitness and written exam this weekend. All you need to do is show up, and you can take it." Before I could react, he quickly assured me. "Don't worry, you'll pass."

I was stunned. Okay, how serendipitous was that? David stood up and reached for my hand. "It's simply a place to start, and it doesn't have to be forever. The world is wide open to you. Good luck in whatever you decide to do."

He shook my hand again, and I watched as he casually strolled up the street. He nodded and waved at almost everyone he passed. Running into David affected me deeply and kept me thinking the rest of the week about what it might be like to be a cop.

On Saturday, I took the bull by the horns and showed up for the recruit testing. It turned out to be fun. We got to leap over obstacles, climb walls, drag a dummy, and more. And the written test was trivial. It seemed as if the universe was coaxing me in that direction.

Over the next few weeks, I tried to lighten up and open my mind to the possibility. I visualized myself involving acupuncture and herbs as part of a police outreach program. Maybe, I could mold this to fit me or discover my true path along the way. I did love the idea of getting paid for working out. When at last I received an invitation to join the Berkeley Police Department, I accepted. In January of 2002, I was sent along with eleven other chosen recruits for training at the Sacramento Police Academy.

I wanted to make a good impression on my first day and arrived early for the academy orientation. It felt strange to be wearing my dark blue recruit's uniform. I hadn't looked bad in the mirror that morning. At thirty-eight years old, I was in the best physical shape of my life, and the uniform showed it. The dark blue accentuated my short, wavy blonde hair and blue eyes. Part of me couldn't believe I was doing this, and the other part was excited to be a part of this new adventure. I smiled at myself as I walked down the hall toward the classroom, most definitely a Gemini. I paused before entering the classroom and took a deep breath. I hadn't been nervous until that moment, but there was no sense turning back now. I cleared my mind of expectations and stepped inside.

The décor looked like your typical high school science class. The desks were old style wooden two-person tables. There was a chalkboard covering the front wall of the room and a large teacher's desk in front of it. Most of the desks were already occupied. Not so early after all. I swiftly realized everyone was staring at me, sizing up the newcomer. I quickly slid into an empty seat in the middle of the room. Safely out of the limelight, I peered around at my fellow recruits. I counted forty-seven. Only five were women. They all appeared to be in their early twenties—save for one pudgy male recruit who looked close to my age. I could already hear the "old lady" jokes in my mind.

I told myself to relax and focused on my breath. Closing my eyes, I expanded my senses around the room. It was absolutely silent, no rustling of papers, not a murmur. When I opened them again, I made eye contact with the man next to me. He answered my gaze with a mute shake of his head. Silence, it was then.

The door opened, and three fit, confident male officers strode purposefully into the room. The last officer to enter reminded me of a bulldog, especially when his eyes bulged as he yelled, "Recruits, on your feet! Stand at attention! What a pitiful display of respect for your commander!"

We all jumped out of our chairs and snapped to attention. It was then that the butterflies quite distinctly made their presence known in my stomach. The officer who had spoken took in the room. He glared at each and every one of us in turn. When he was finished, he gestured to the other officers standing beside him. "Recruits, this is the commander of the academy, Lieutenant Diaz and Corporal Hong. I'm Corporal Drake.

We're just a few of the instructors, who will be attempting to mold your pathetic selves into police officer material."

I knew I should be paying attention, but I couldn't help but marvel at the width of Corporal Drake's mouth. He could have easily stuffed a couple of Big Macs into it and still have room for more.

He stepped to the side as Commander Diaz took his place. The commander bellowed, "Welcome to Class 02-BR1, basic recruit training!"

And so it began. After a lengthy and berating orientation, we were divided into five squads and assigned an instructor who acted as our "counselor" during the academy training. My squad was assigned to Corporal Brendan and told to report to a classroom down the hall. The moment we all filed into the room, Corporal Brendan immediately lashed out, "Get your asses lined up against the wall!" We shuffled around each other, lining up. "Move it!"

The corporal was an intimidating package in his Arnold Schwarzenegger body. It was a shame his snarl marred the features of an otherwise handsome face. Corporal Brendan surveyed our squad with a look of disdain. When his gaze fell upon me, he stormed over to stand directly in front of me. "What are you doing here, recruit?" he demanded, shouting in my face.

Okay, here we go, I was really doing this. "Sir, I'm here to become a police officer, sir!" I yelled back, matching his steely-eyed stare with an unblinking gaze of my own.

"Do you really think you're cut out for this? I don't think you are. I think you should leave now. Leave! Now!" he roared like an angry grizzly. Fortunately for me, Corporal Brendan had good breath. My hair blew in the wind of his verbal onslaught.

"No, sir!" I answered quickly and loudly. I managed to hold my stare without flinching.

He got up in my face so close his nose was practically touching my own. "I'll be watching you, Reese. You're not going to twitch a muscle without my say-so. Is that clear?"

It was odd what thoughts pop into your head during moments like these. All that I could think about was an article I remembered reading in *Guns & Ammo* magazine. It had mentioned that it was always a good idea to thank the drill instructor for yelling at you. "Absolutely, sir. Thank you, sir."

I immediately felt silly and couldn't help rolling my eyes to the heavens once the corporal had moved on. So ridiculous! He stopped to yell at the recruit standing next to me for his dirty uniform. I was slightly comforted by the fact that he had something derogatory to say to the entire squad. It took forever. I lost track of the time waiting for Corporal Brendan to finish his tirade. Eventually, hallelujah—praise the heavens, he ran out of gas and yelled at us to report to the gym for our physical fitness assessment.

Glad to be free, I made a beeline for the women's locker room and changed into my workout uniform. I was the first one there but not for long. I looked up when the locker room door swung open. Tanya Maverick was tall, graceful, and athletic. I had met her at the physical fitness test, and we had hit it off immediately. She was an instant bright spot in my new endeavor. It pleased me that Tanya took the locker next to mine. She had a playfully evil grin on her face and patted my shoulder in greeting.

"Hey, Reese, it's good to see you. Did you have a pleasant little chat with Corporal Brendan?"

I didn't even try to soften the sarcasm in my laugh, and it felt good. I closed my locker and leaned back against it. "Doesn't all that screaming bother you?"

Tanya shook her head as she changed into her gym uniform. "I'm a sergeant in the Air Force Reserve, so I'm used to it. You just play their game, even if it seems stupid. Don't worry, this won't last forever."

"Good advice. Thanks," I replied sincerely. I liked her straightforward manner and friendly personality. Her slight Southern accent suited her just right. We both looked up as the doors swung open again. The other women in our class all filed into the locker room. From Berkeley, I recognized Janice Linnear, Nancy Devon, and Ricki Burkett. The lone Sacramento female recruit was Tina Carter.

Tanya and I nodded and shook hands with each of them, officially introducing ourselves. I studied them as they passed by. We were a motley crew, to be sure. Linnear was the stereotypical Southern California blonde and would give Bo Derek a run for her money. Devon could have passed as Whoopi Goldberg's twin, except that she was twice as tall. In fact, she was probably a good two inches taller than Tanya who checked in at five-foot-nine. Burkett was an attractive young black woman with short tight curls. She stood about my height—five-four—and was as muscular as I was. Tina Carter was a beanpole and appeared almost frail—until she shook my hand. It felt like she could crush bricks with that grip.

"All recruits have ten minutes to report to the gymnasium!" Corporal Brendan shouted outside our locker room. That broke up our bonding session, and we hurried our butts up.

Inside the main gym, we were divided into three groups for the first test called "The Wall." Tanya wasn't in my group although Burkett was.

"Group one—form a line and put your backs to the wall," Corporal Drake said and explained the test. There was a moment of shuffling around as the first group lined up against the wall. "Place your feet about two of your own foot lengths away from the wall. When I say go, slide your body down with your back against the wall until your knees are perpendicular. You will hold this position for five minutes or until you collapse. Okay, group one, go!"

As one, the recruits slid their backs down and began to hold. Tanya was in group one, and I positioned myself directly in front of her. I'd done similar exercises in my martial arts class. One minute was hard enough; five was downright insanity.

A minute dragged slowly by and Tanya's legs began to quiver. "I know you've got this, Maverick," I told her. She took a deep breath, and when our eyes met her face had a look of pure determination. I stayed directly in front her and kept up a steady stream of encouragement.

I saw a long line of straining faces and shaking knees. Tanya was starting to have a really hard time. "Stay on that wall, Maverick," I said. Her stamina was impressive. "Keep breathing and hang in there. I know you can do this!" She'd outlasted almost the entire group with only three others left on the wall. At two minutes, Tanya had reached her limit. Suddenly, a cramp seized her entire quad and she was forced to fall off the wall. I reached out a hand to steady her. "Way to go, Maverick! You beat most of the guys!"

It seemed as if the remaining male recruits were merely trying to make sure they weren't beaten by a woman. As soon as Tanya came off the wall, the rest of them fell off as well.

Corporal Drake stepped forward. "I hope this next group can do better! Use your minds, recruits. This is not a brute force exercise. It's your determination that will see you through. Group Two, you're up! Backs against the wall!"

It was my turn. Maverick and I switched places. This was my realm, and I felt confident. I slowed my breathing and quickly sank into the void. "Group Two—go!" Corporal Drake's voice sounded far away.

Tanya was standing right in front of me, and my range of vision narrowed to focus on just her. I barely noticed the first minute tick by followed by the second. My breathing remained slow and deep. I used it to pull in strength and solidarity for my legs. They were shaking a bit and the muscle burn was getting intense, but I wanted to make it to the end. Other recruits were falling off the wall right and left.

Out of the corner of my eye, I saw Burkett still on the wall. Her legs were shaking wildly, but she was trying to hang on. Tanya kneeled down in front of me so that our eyes were on the same level, and her face was close to mine. I looked deep into her eyes and used them as a point of concentration. It helped me to remain in the void. My mind was empty. Three minutes slipped by and now there were only two of us left.

"Reese, I can see you're on a whole different plane. I don't know where you are, but keep it up, it's working," she whispered.

My entire consciousness had shrunk down to reside inside Tanya's deep brown eyes. My muscles were screaming for me to stand up, but inside those eyes, all was quiet.

"Time's up, and what do you know—we've got a pair of winners! Well done, Recruits Underton and Reese, just what I like to see." Corporal Drake raised his fist in a victory sign.

I could see a gleam of excitement in his eyes when I nodded back. Corporal Drake was clearly enjoying himself. Then he turned toward the waiting group of recruits. "Now let's see if we've got any other winners in Group Three. Get your backs against the wall."

I held onto Tanya's proffered hand to help peel myself off the wall. She steadied me as I worked the kinks out of my legs. "Great job, Reese. Talk about finding the zone. That was nice work."

"Thanks, Maverick," I replied, pleased that I had won one for the women's team. We walked over to where Burkett, Linnear, and Devon were standing away from the other recruits.

I patted Burkett on the shoulder. "Hey, Burkett. That was good work."

She playfully punched me on the arm. "Thanks, Reese, but when I grow up, I want to be just like you."

The rest of the day was packed with countless physical fitness competitions. I was happily in my element and enjoyed myself. The women stuck together. We encouraged each other in every event. I'd forgotten how good it felt to share a bond with a group of likeminded women—it had been since my rugby days.

The police academy was a grueling six-month training program, and I soon discovered that I was woefully unprepared for the constant mental torture inflicted on us by the corporals. It annoyed me to no end that they screamed at us for insignificant reasons. I was berated for not having shiny enough boots or belt buckle or, heaven forbid, I had a wrinkle in my shirt! The corporals especially liked to skulk along the hallways and ambush recruits. We were supposed to snap to attention and spit out a "Good morning, Corporal So-and-So or good afternoon, Corporal So-and-So." All hell broke loose if you got the morning greeting confused with the afternoon greeting. It was simply inane.

Little by little, I was indoctrinated into the police academy environment. For every day that passed, the amount of sleep I got steadily decreased. We were up at the crack of dawn for morning fitness class. Then it was a mad dash to the gym showers since we had to present ourselves without a hair out of place in lecture classes. Afterward, it was back to the gym in the afternoon for self-defense and police manhandling tactics. In the evenings, I spent hours cleaning my gun, shining my belt and shoes, writing up my notes in perfect little block lettering, and reading for the next day's class.

We were only given forty-five minutes for lunch, and the only choices were fast-food takeout like Burger King or Taco Bell. I felt ill eating such crap, but I didn't have any time to cook for myself. Worst of all, I was too physically and mentally exhausted at the end of the day to meditate and let go of all the emotional garbage that was building up inside of me. All I could do was collapse in a comatose state for the three or four hours until I had to get up again. Deprived of my spiritual rituals, I existed in a constant state of underlying nervousness and tension.

I was grateful that the Berkeley Police Department paid for its recruits to live in an extended stay hotel during our academy training. Tanya and I had rooms next to each other, and we fell into a comfortable routine of making sure we'd each woken up in the morning. We were both early birds and formed the habit of going to the gym together. Linnear, Devon, and Burkett had formed a trio as well since they didn't mind arriving just a few minutes before our mandatory run at seven o'clock. Tanya and I were stretching out on the gym floor, prepping for a run, when I saw the trio jogging past the door into the locker room. I glanced over at Tanya and shook my head.

"Man, I can't cut it that close. Those three seem to get here later every morning," I said.

Tanya had straightened both legs and pulled herself low to loosen up her hamstrings. She turned her head to the side and winked at me. "I'm glad you like to be early, Reese. I like you watching my back."

"We do work well together," I said, smiling back.

Corporal Hong chose that moment to stomp into the gym and wave his arms at us. "Recruits, outside! On the double, move it!"

Another crazed day was about to begin.

Fortunately for me, every moment wasn't entirely stressful and tense. I particularly enjoyed the first time we were taken to the shooting range for target practice. Corporal Crawford was in charge of the academy range. He was the oldest of the instructors and had a permanent scowl on his face and a scar along his left cheek. If there had been a patch over his right eye, he could easily have passed for the captain of a pirate ship.

Corporal Crawford certainly ran a tight ship at the range. He insisted upon absolute focus for each exercise and strict adherence to safety. I liked him for that. His approach to shooting reminded me of my college pistol team days.

For once, Tanya and I were in the same group. We took up positions next to each other on the firing line. I looked over at Tanya, and we gave each other a nod of support. Corporal Crawford stood behind the class in the center of the range, master of his domain. The other instructors spread out behind us along the firing line.

"Recruits stand ready," Corporal Crawford ordered.

I felt relaxed. I'd done group target practice many times before on my pistol team. My eyes were focused on the target with my left hand positioned comfortably over my holster. My mind was empty of distractions, and I was ready.

"Fire at will!"

In one smooth motion, my pistol was in the air, and I squeezed off a shot and then another. I kept firing until my clip was empty. That felt good. My breathing was calm, and I knew I was shooting well. When we retrieved our targets, Corporal Crawford came over to inspect mine. I was quite pleased to see that the center circle was almost completely shot out of it.

"Recruit Reese!" he barked.

I snapped to attention. What could the corporal possibly find wrong with my shooting? "Yes sir, Corporal Crawford," I responded crisply and waited for the hammer to strike.

He slowly looked up from my target. "Where did you learn to shoot?" he demanded impatiently. His voice was loud and attracted the interest of the other corporals. My heart sank as they gathered in a circle around us.

"Sir! I used to hunt with my dad when I was a kid, and I was also on my college pistol team." I held my breath. If he made a crack about my dad and hunting, I was going to lose it.

Instead, his snarl morphed into something approaching a hint of a smile. "You've had some quality training. I expect to see more of the same."

The shock of a compliment from Corporal Crawford made me hesitate for a moment. He handed me back my target, and I couldn't hold back a small smile in return.

"Yes, sir. Thank you, sir. My pistol team coach taught us shooting techniques similar to yours. I look forward to more of your instruction."

It was amusing to see Corporal Crawford puff up at the praise. I saw the other corporals try unsuccessfully to hide their grins. I spun crisply on my heels and headed back to the benches behind the firing line.

When I passed by Recruit Dawson, he grabbed my arm and snagged the target from my hand. Dawson was a Southern boy with a real twang in his speech. "Well now, let's just take a look at what's got them corporals all curious," he drawled. Dawson glanced at my target and looked downright astonished before he broke into a hearty laugh. "Well, I'll be damned; this is mighty fine shootin', Reese. I reckon it's good enough to knock the fleas off of a gnat's ass." I cracked up as Dawson took my hand and shook it. "You're all right in my book, Reese."

What do you know? I was making progress with the boys.

After the shooting range, the corporals' attitudes toward me changed. Their comments held a glimmer of respect instead of derision. It was immensely satisfying. Corporal Drake even went so far as to ask for my help. Corporals Drake, Hong, and Brendan were the morning workout instructors and always accompanied us on our daily run. I made it a point to stay in the middle of the pack. Stragglers were often targeted for harassment by the corporals with a continuous barrage of invectives.

One morning, Corporal Drake jogged up the line of recruits and pulled even with me, matching my stride. I maintained my pace and looked straight ahead, determined not to succumb to any verbal assault he might launch at me.

Out of the corner of my eye, I noticed the recruits closest to us were either speeding up or slowing down. Great, they were leaving me alone in the lion's den. Soon it was just the two of us with a lot of pavement in between us and the next recruit. It was even more disconcerting when he remained silent for at least a minute. I disliked the uncertainty of his intentions. Finally, he spoke, but for once his tone wasn't a bark.

"How's it going, Recruit Reese?".

I was so surprised that I nearly lost my footing. *Was he being friendly?* "Sir! Very well, sir! Thank you, sir!" I played up the expected recruit response.

"Relax, recruit. I want to ask your opinion on how to solve a problem."

My mouth fell open, but I shut it quickly. *Was this for real? Maybe it was some kind of a test.* I decided I needed to tread carefully. "Certainly, sir. How can I help you?" I turned my head slightly and caught the corporal smiling. It seemed so out of place.

"It's about Recruits Devon and Luskin. They're both Berkeley recruits, and they're both not cutting it." I wondered where he was going with this and kept my expression carefully neutral. "They're both failing in their self-defense techniques, which are something you're good at."

The light bulb finally flashed on above my head. I felt a warm fuzzy glow for the corporal. "I can certainly help them, sir. It's not a problem."

Corporal Drake nodded his head and looked almost smug. "Excellent, Recruit Reese. The job is yours. I will be looking for improvements in their performance from now on." Now this sounded more like an order.

Oh boy. Had I just gotten in over my head? I fervently hoped, not. The corporal put on the afterburners and sprinted to the front of the pack.

After the run was over, I told Devon and Luskin about my conversation. I felt great when they both jumped at my offer of help. They had already been warned by Commander Diaz that, unless they improved, their days were numbered. Every evening after that day, I met with Luskin and Devon and drilled them on techniques until they were smooth as silk. I felt a sense of pride whenever I saw them doing drills in class.

However, as our training progressed, the exercises grew less benign. Our objective became how to injure or kill. This wasn't what I had signed up for. It wasn't me. I kept telling myself that the training was only going to last for a few more months. Once it was over, I'd be free to be me. One day in April, with only two months left to go in the academy training program, I nearly pulled myself out of a training exercise.

The shooting range at the academy was quite large. In one area, there was a makeshift building with a maze of corridors and rooms. It was something you might find on a Hollywood movie set. Some rooms were empty, and others contained life-sized cardboard figures. The figures were either bad guys holding weapons or hostages. It was just like the old TV show *S.W.A.T.* We were supposed to sweep the building with a partner, shooting all the bad guys without hitting the hostages. Our weapons were 12-gauge shotguns—not exactly the best weapon to use when you wanted precision in close quarters.

My partner was Dawson; he was excited to the point he could barely contain himself. We were the fifth team in the lineup and had plenty of time to wait before it was our turn. We stretched out and warmed up in a grassy area that was well away from the starting line. I watched with apprehension as Burkett and Underton dashed into the building. Almost immediately, shots were heard.

Dawson punched me lightly on the arm. "Reese, I'm glad to have you covering my six. This is going to be fun."

There was a sinking feeling in the pit of my stomach. "Actually, Dawson, fun isn't exactly the word I'd use to describe this," I replied quietly.

The more I considered the reality of what the exercise represented, the more I wondered if I was going to freeze and screw up the exercise. If it were real life, I could get my partner or an innocent victim killed. The stakes were high. I needed to do something to pull myself together before Dawson and I were up. The sun peeked out from behind a cloud and forced me to squint from the instant glare. I heard more shots coming from inside the building, and each one hit me like a hammer in the chest. More than anything, I wanted to run away, to be anywhere other than there.

"Reese, come on. We're next." Dawson grabbed my arm and tugged me to my feet.

I shook my head to clear it as we jogged over to the starting line and positioned ourselves to run into the building. I looked down at my weapon with dread in my heart. The loaded shotgun felt like I was carrying a deadly snake. It was something that could just as easily turn around and bite me as well as the bad guy.

Corporal Brand blew his whistle for us to start. Without conscious thought, I stayed a step behind Dawson as we charged into the building. We took up mirrored positions on either side of the first doorway. I watched with trepidation while Dawson gave a silent three count with his lips. My heart was pounding when I pushed the door open hard and swept the left side, keeping low. There was a bad guy on my side of the room, and—without thought—my finger pulled the trigger. I nodded to Dawson and ran to the left. The room was empty of other hostiles. But the bad guys had been alerted to our presence and would be ready for us.

We had to clear two more rooms before we encountered other targets. The next occupied room had three bad guys and two hostages. There was no time to think or feel. Everything was a blur as Dawson and I charged into the room and shot the bad guys. The hostage on my side of the room was too close to the two hostiles. It all happened too fast. Part of me recognized that taking the shot was risky, but I did it anyway. My shot hit the hostage in the arm as well as the hostile in the chest. My heart was screaming for me to stop. I wanted to quit that insane exercise, but instead I fired and hit the second hostile. *Who was I that I could do that?* My legs felt weak, but I kept them moving, trailing Dawson out of the room. It was all I could do to simply focus on the back of his uniform while we moved on. I kept telling myself to hang in there a little longer. It would be over soon.

By the time we were through the building, Dawson and I had neutralized eight hostiles and saved four hostages. Dawson and I each shot a hostage, mine in the arm and his in the leg. Apparently, injured hostages notwithstanding, we passed our exercise. It was small consolation. I watched dumbstruck with horror at the other recruits around me. The ones who had merely injured their hostages and not shot them in mortal locations were high-fiving each other. Did they think this was a game? It was a twisted definition of victory. I had a pain in my heart for the rest of the day.

That night, Maverick and I spent the evening studying together as usual. I was trying to finish the reading assignment on Tanya's floor, but I couldn't concentrate. I put my head down on my arms and attempted to breathe away some tension. I didn't notice that Tanya had slid down beside me until I felt her hand gently touch my shoulder.

"Reese, you okay?"

"Yeah, I'm just wound up tighter than a spring. It was intense today at the shooting range. You know, when we did those hostage exercises?" I looked at her for affirmation. When she nodded, I kept going. "Well, I nearly lost it. First, I worried about freezing up, but fortunately that didn't happen. Unfortunately, I shot a hostage during my rampage, and it doesn't make me feel any better to know it was 'only an arm wound.' It's hard enough training to kill a bad guy, let alone having to face the prospect of killing an innocent person," I blurted out in a jumbled rush.

"We're going to have to keep practicing the possibility of shooting someone. But Reese, statistically it's not likely that you'll ever have to," Tanya said, trying to allay my fears.

That didn't help me. "Doesn't mean *never*—does it?"

Maverick gave my arm a squeeze. "You're good, and you've got a cool head. I know you'll handle yourself just fine. I've got no doubt in my mind." Hearing that I'll handle myself fine isn't what I wanted to hear. I closed my books and packed up my study materials. "Hey Reese, I know you can't possibly be done, yet. What are you doing?"

"I'm taking a break. I'm going to take a hot shower to see if I can steam away some tension." My heart was heavy, and I knew it was evident in my voice.

The hot water did feel good on my tight muscles, and I imagined my stress and tension pouring down the shower drain. It was then that I noticed something strange. The tendons along my inner thighs, from my hips down to my ankles, were slowly tightening. When I reached down to touch the tendon on my right leg, it seemed to have stiffened in place. The normal pliancy wasn't there. How odd. It was a strange sensation and not anything I'd ever felt before, even with all my years of physical activity and sports. As I washed my hair, I tried to think what might be happening. Something inside of me told me that I shouldn't ignore this, that I needed to pay attention, but I wasn't sure what I should do.

The next morning, another disturbing incident occurred during our class run. I was jogging along with my classmates when I noticed that instead of holding steady in the middle of the group, I was being passed up by one recruit after another. My legs felt weak and no matter how hard I tried, I couldn't get them to move any faster. When Luskin passed me, I knew something was really wrong. He was always last. I switched on the afterburners, but there was no fuel in my tank. My usual energy reserves were nowhere to be found. I wanted to crawl under a rock when I came in dead last. The corporals looked at me in shock and dismay. Suddenly, I knew how Luskin felt every day. If only I had known how ominous a sign it actually was.

CHAPTER THIRTY THREE
BROKEN

There are no mistakes. The events we bring upon ourselves,
no matter how unpleasant, are necessary in order to learn
what we need to learn; whatever steps we take, they're
necessary to reach the places we've chosen to go.
—Richard Bach

*I*t's the middle of the night. I'm running down the deserted street as fast as I can, faster than I've ever run before, but it's not fast enough. I sense my pursuer is closing in behind me. A darkened alley is ahead on my right, and I make a mad dash for it. The sound of my black leather police boots hitting the pavement and my labored breathing are all that I can hear. There is a coldness touching my neck. I have to get away! I dart into an even darker side alley. It was the wrong decision. It's hard to see in the darkness, and I almost crash headfirst into a brick wall. Oh no, it's a dead end! I pound my fists on the wall in despair. I hear the evil laughter behind me and turn around to face it. I can't see it yet, but my heart freezes with fear. The cold stone bricks press against my back. I'm trapped, and there's no way out! Shit!

I sit bolt upright in my bed. My body is drenched in sweat, and my heart is pounding. What the heck just happened? I look around to get my bearings. I'm in the extended stay hotel at the police academy. It's another nightmare. I've been having them ever since the hostage training exercise. This isn't good. I look at the clock on the bedside table. It's 4:30. My hand is shaking as I take a sip of water from the glass next to the clock. I almost spill it setting it down and then let myself collapse onto my pillow. I stare at the roughly textured white ceiling and try to relax. It's difficult. It still feels as if I'm in the alley with my back against the wall.

It's hot, and I feel sticky in my sweat-soaked police academy T-shirt and shorts. I kick off the sheet, but I'm feeling too lethargic to get up to change. I close my eyes and try to sleep; it's no use. In martial arts terminology, I have monkey-mind and can't clear my head. The same tag line keeps playing: *There's simply no way out. I can't quit, and I can't go on.*

Wide awake, my eyes spring open again, and I flop around restlessly. It's a sauna in my room. It's unusually hot weather even for the Sacramento Valley. But there's something else. There's something familiar about the humidity—so thick it's hard to breathe—mixed in with a large dose of desperation. I've felt like this before.

It was the summer of my fifteenth year. I had recently passed my black belt test. One day after class, I was approached by Master Park, my Tae Kwon Do instructor. He told me that he'd been asked by the AAU (American Athletic Union) to recommend a female student to complete their international Tae Kwon Do team. The team was invited to compete in Seoul, Korea in one month at the Tae Kwon Do International Championship Games, but they were short one female competitor. This tournament was an important step toward getting Tae Kwon Do approved as an official sport in the Olympics.

Master Park blew my socks off by saying he wanted me to go.

I was swept up in a surreal dream from the moment I hollered, "Yes!"

Mom and Dad surprised me with their complete support. They had a passport expedited for me and didn't say a word about the mint they spent getting my plane ticket. I met up with my fellow teammates and AAU coaches at LaGuardia Airport in New York; from there, we flew to Seoul. We arrived two weeks early so that we could acclimate to and train in the Korean climate. I thought Pennsylvania was hot and humid in the summer, but it was nothing compared to the steam box that surrounded us from the moment we stepped off the plane. It was like breathing boiling water.

My left hand reaches for the water bottle on my bed stand. Damn it. It's empty. I hop out of bed and head for the sink in the tiny kitchen area of my hotel room in Sacramento. Not even bothering with a glass, I turn on the spigot and let the water pour down my throat.

While I'm at it, I let the cool water run freely over my head and neck. At least now I feel like my brain isn't overheating. As soon as I throw myself back on the bed, my thoughts return to my trip to Korea.

The four-day tournament was scheduled to be held at the Kukkiwon, the official world headquarters for the Korean Tae Kwon Do Association. It was a big deal. The sparring matches were all full contact, and I trained hard with my teammates to prepare for the event. We expected fierce competition from the more than twenty countries that were represented. With all my heart, I wanted to make a good showing and represent the United States with honor.

When the tournament began, I fought hard and won all of my fights the first day. The second day, I won my quarterfinal. It wasn't until the semifinal, that I faced my first South Korean opponent in the ring. We were well-matched, but I was on fire. I danced around the ring, blocking well, and scoring on the majority of my strikes. My opponent became frustrated and made a few mistakes that I capitalized upon. I couldn't have been prouder when the referee raised my hand in the air to signal me as the victor. My teammates swarmed around me, slapping me on the back and congratulating me. Little did I know how drastically my simplistic world view was about to change.

After the women's matches were over for the day, I was able to relax along the sidelines and watch some of the men's competition. In front of me was a fierce competition between a South Korean man and a contestant from Lesotho who towered over him. The young African man used his height to good advantage. I winced as he brought a crushing heel kick down on the collar bone of his opponent and shuddered involuntarily at the sound of the bone breaking. To my utter astonishment, the South Korean refused to end the fight—even though pain was written all over his face.

"Are you enjoying the competition?" I was startled to hear the soft masculine voice and spun my head toward the sound. I took in the exotic black eyes of the older teenager squatting next to me. A scar ran the length of his jaw on the right side of his face. I thought it was cool. The patch on his uniform told me he was on the South Korean team.

"Yes, I am," I finally answered and then pointed toward the match in front of us. "But why doesn't your teammate stop fighting? His collarbone is broken. He's getting killed out there."

"Because he would lose even more face than he already has if he quit. He must continue."

"Well, that's nuts. I don't think I can watch any more of this." I rose swiftly to my feet. Then it dawned on me that as an official representative of the United States, my manners were terrible. "I'm sorry, forgive my rudeness. My name is Holly. It's nice to meet you." I extended my hand.

"It's also nice to meet you, Holly. My name is Yung." He shook my hand and bowed his head. He waved his hand toward the gymnasium exit. "May I show you around the Kukkiwon?"

I was excited by the kind offer. Our team had been training hard right up to the start of the competition. Other than the inside of the huge gym we were standing in and a few blocks of the downtown area around our hotel, I hadn't seen anything yet.

"Thank you, Yung. I'm delighted to have an official guide." I smiled and bowed my head. I followed him out into the hall.

Yung was a talkative host. He animatedly pointed out portraits of accomplished Tae Kwon Do masters on the walls of the huge corridors and rattled off the fascinating history of their lives. As we walked along the hallways, we were so wrapped up in our discussion that I didn't notice the sound of yelling. We were passing by an office with a window, and movement in my peripheral vision caught my eye. Inside the office, I thought I recognized my South Korean opponent from the semifinals. She wasn't facing the window directly; she was turned at a slight angle away from it and me. Her head was bowed down, and a man in an immaculate black suit was gesticulating wildly and shouting in her face. He had a couple of inches on her, but he was pencil thin. I knew she could take him; she was fast and out-massed him. Then I recognized the screaming meanie as an official with the South Korean team. His yells became steadily louder. Just as it dawned on me why the woman was being berated, I saw the official slap her hard across the face.

I snapped and jumped toward the door, but Yung restrained me. He pulled me roughly past the office and shoved me against the wall, pinning my shoulders. "This is none of your concern. It is an internal matter, and you will not interfere," he said in a stern whisper.

I considered fighting Yung right then and there. If I could take him down quietly, I would have the element of surprise when I burst into the office. It was a *big* if. Instead, I opted for trying to pry more information out of him first. We locked eyes, and I fixed him with a deadly glare. "Maybe I won't interfere if you tell me what is going on in there," I said, struggling against his grip. "And let me go right now—or you will be sorry."

Yung let go and gestured for me to continue down the hallway. When I didn't move and simply crossed my arms, he sighed in exasperation. "Look, I'm sorry you saw that and I will explain, but we need to move away from here," he said anxiously.

I saw the sincerity in his eyes and, although I didn't like it, I nodded in agreement. We moved further down the hallway. "It's quite simple really. Tae Kwon Do is a *Korean* martial art, one that we have nurtured and developed for more than 2,000 years. It's in our blood, and there should be no question of which team takes the most medals."

When we could no longer hear the screaming, he stopped. "That member of our team has lost face for herself and for her country by being defeated, especially by a non-Asian. She is Korean and accepts that she needs to be punished." He pounded his right fist against his other open hand.

I wanted to scream at the absurdity of it all. It was only a stupid competition! What did it matter who won? If we had been in the States, that official could have been arrested for assault and battery. Unfortunately, it was crystal clear to me that we weren't in the States. I knew there would be cultural differences, but I had never expected to be confronted with one so personally repugnant.

We returned to the main gym. I thanked Yung for the tour and excused myself. I needed time alone to think. The sense of accomplishment and pride I had felt at winning the semifinal had vanished. It was supplanted with anger at my own naïve stupidity. Sure, I wanted to win for my team and country, but it was only a sparring match to me. I had had no idea what the stakes were for the other competitors, especially the South Koreans. I felt awful. My win had resulted in an innocent woman being beaten and humiliated. How could I make amends for that? What had started out as an amazing experience had been turned upside-down. I felt trapped—with no good options. One thing was for sure: I wasn't going to allow another woman to be assaulted because of me. It violated my sense of personal ethics, which in my mind, superseded my team obligations. An opportunity arose the next day in the final match.

Again, my opponent was South Korean. She looked extremely stressed out as we squared off to start our fight. Her hair was only a couple of inches long. I could see a bruise on her forehead and wondered whether it was from a previous match or a warning cuff from her coach. The wheels were spinning in my head. I wanted an honorable out. We exchanged a series of kicks that served merely to test the waters. She had a lot of power behind her kicks; they jarred my forearms when I blocked them. Neither one of us scored any points. Her anxious eyes stared at something, or someone, over my shoulder. My mind was racing. I couldn't quit; it would dishonor my own team and country. Yet, I refused to accept the consequences of victory. I saw a high roundhouse kick coming, and an idea popped into my head.

I hesitated, just a fraction of a second, before moving. Her foot contacted my jaw hard, and I saw stars. Ironically, that made me happy. Our eyes met, and in that brief moment she saw that I wasn't fighting to win. It spurred my opponent into high gear. She pressed her advantage and quickly landed several more blows. My prayers were answered. It had become a simple matter of staying behind in points. The match was soon decided.

My teammates looked on with incredulity as my opponent was declared the victor. They couldn't believe that I had lost the fight. I hadn't stopped to consider how devastating their disappointment in me would feel. When I was called to the victory stand to receive my silver medal, it was all I could do to make myself go. I felt like I was being summoned to my own execution. I could feel my coach watching me, but I couldn't look him in the eyes. What about Master Park and all the faith he had placed in me by entering me in this competition? How could I ever explain myself to him? I wanted to crawl under a rock and hide my face in shame.

The alarm clock buzzes annoyingly, and I slap it hard to turn it off. Terrific. I'm an emotional basket case, and the day hasn't even begun. I groan as I remember that today is baton practice.

"Hey Reese! Are you up?" I hear pounding on my door and a familiar voice. It's Maverick. Okay, let's get this day over with.

"Yeah, I'm up, Maverick. I'll meet you outside in twenty." I rub my tired eyes and sit up. Today at the gym, we're working on subduing a suspect using our batons, and I'm not looking forward to it.

"Recruit Reese, crank it up. Let's see you break some ribs with that baton," Corporal Drake hollers.

I'm hitting a dummy repeatedly across the midsection. It's a body location that is less likely to cause death. Every time I smack the sandbag, it feels as if I'm striking myself.

Corporal Drake urges me to yell louder and hit harder. Every blow is an injection of self-loathing and impending doom. I'm grateful when my turn is over and I'm allowed to move off to the side. My dream about being trapped in the alley and the memory of the tournament keep playing in my mind.

"Reese, partner up with Jackson for some throws and takedowns," Corporal Drake orders.

I walk slowly over to Recruit Jackson. My heart hurts. *What if my actions as a police officer harm an innocent victim? What if I kill someone who was simply in the wrong place at the wrong time?* I think I could live with hurting a criminal but not an innocent person. I desperately want to walk out of the gym. Instead, I face Jackson and we square off.

I'm the aggressor. The exercise is to take Jackson to the ground and allow myself to be thrown off. I grab his arm, sweep his leg, and jump on top of him. Jackson rocks his body and kicks me into the air. My job is to tuck and roll, but I know right away that my angle is wrong. I come down hard on my right shoulder. There is a popping sound followed by searing pain. It's bad. I know this is an academy-ending injury. *Did I just set myself up?* I'm disoriented for a second and imagine I'm back in the gold medal round in Korea.

A figure bends over me. At first, I think I see my coach, but then the face of Corporal Brand comes into focus.

"Reese, where are you injured?" The sound jolts me back to the present. There's a look of genuine concern in his eyes. It's unexpected. The pain is so intense I can't speak, but I manage to point to my shoulder.

Corporal Brand turns to Recruit Jackson. "Don't just stand there, recruit. Help Reese to her feet and get her to the infirmary."

After a brief examination at the infirmary, I'm taken to the hospital for an MRI and X-rays. The wait is interminably long. Finally, Dr. Boise whisks briskly into the examination room with my results.

"Recruit, you have a torn rotator cuff and will need surgery," he says almost proudly. "You won't be able to complete this session of the police academy and should return to Berkeley until you are recovered."

"The rotator cuff is not where I feel the pain; it's more medial, right at the AV joint." I argue with him, certain he's wrong. All this gets me is a haughtily raised eyebrow followed by a disdainful sniff.

"You are free to get a second opinion once you get back to Berkeley."

Corporal Drake issues the orders for me to report back to Berkeley the following day. Part of me is relieved at being able to leave, but quitting is not who I am. I'm surprised at how much it means to me when all the corporals wish me a speedy recovery.

Corporal Drake takes me aside and puts a fatherly hand on my good shoulder. "Reese, we're sorry to see you go before graduation. It's been a pleasure training you." His tone conveys pride and respect. "If you can heal up by the fall, the Sacramento Police Academy is officially extending you a special invitation to return and join our fall class. Normally, it's restricted to Sacramento recruits, but we would be proud to have you back with us," he says, breaking into a rare grin.

In this moment, the moral, emotional, and spiritual dilemma I've been suffering at the academy is shoved to the side. I feel proud to have earned the corporals' respect and am honored to be invited back.

"Yes, sir! Thank you, sir. I look forward to it," I say without hesitation.

Corporal Drake gives my good shoulder a light pat. As proud as I feel right now, a tiny voice tells me that I should just shut up and quit while I'm ahead, but I can't help myself. My stubborn pride won't let me. I still want to prove I can get through the academy.

Maverick and I hang out together for my last night. I'm in a lot of pain, physically and emotionally. We are facing each other on the floor; my back is propped up against the couch, and hers is against the bed. "Reese, I'm going to miss you terribly." Her eyes mirror the dejection I feel as well.

"I'm going to miss you too, Maverick. I shudder at the thought of doing this twice." I could easily break down and cry. Instead, I swallow hard and send my feelings of loss down into the ground.

"The corporals will most likely leave you alone and focus on the newbies. The second time around will probably fly by," she says halfheartedly.

"At least, I know that once I get through it, I'll be working with you at Berkeley," I respond. I stretch out my leg and kick her foot, trying to disperse the fog of misery we share. We talk until quite late that night, neither of us wanting our time to be over. In the morning, we exchange a lingering, heartfelt hug just before Maverick departs for class. I feel a deep sense of loss as I imagine my days without her.

Once I'm sent home, I have time to reflect on what I want. In spite of everything—no matter how wrong my choice to enter the police academy seems in retrospect—I still can't bring myself to quit. It seems too much like failure, and failure for me is not an acceptable option. I still haven't learned my lesson, but life is about to teach me.

CHAPTER THIRTY FOUR

INSTANT TRAIN WRECK

A bodily disease, which we look upon as
whole and entire within itself, may,
after all, be but a symptom of some
ailment in the spiritual part.
—Nathaniel Hawthorne, *The Scarlet Letter*

Halfway through June, it's obvious that something insidious is happening to me. It's obscenely difficult for me to get up in the morning. I'm used to a nearly inexhaustible supply of energy, and I don't understand the problem. It's odd that nothing else seems to be wrong. I just can't seem to keep my eyes open and get out of bed. I don't have a cold or flu, but I have that same tired and sleepy feeling that comes when I'm about to get sick.

At the end of June, the area of skin just above the right side of my mouth and below my nose feels numb. I tap that area with my finger and feel nothing. This is so weird. I wonder if maybe I'm having an allergic reaction to something. On July 1, 2002, my tailspin into hell begins.

I wake up and discover that my entire right cheek is numb. Actually, I wouldn't call it waking up. I can barely get out of bed. It takes a supreme act of will to simply move. I have no fever and don't feel sick in the normal way.

A few days later, my thighs begin to burn, and walking is difficult. Fortunately, I have an appointment at the workman's compensation clinic, which is where I've been receiving physical therapy for my shoulder. I have a good rapport with my PA, a pleasant young woman named Terry. I trust her enough to share what's been going on with me. Getting to the clinic is the real problem. I'm so insanely tired; it feels like I need to prop my eyelids up with toothpicks. On the drive over, I almost fall asleep at the wheel. It's purely by chance that I make it there in one piece.

While I'm waiting for Terry in the examination room, I don't even have the energy to sit up straight. I'm hunched over on the examining table with my elbows on my knees and my head in my hands. *This is not good.* I'm starting to get scared.

"What in the hell happened to you?" Terry says from the doorway.

It's all I can do to barely lift my head and tell her how I feel.

"You need to get in to see a doctor at Kaiser Permanente right away," she says. For once, I couldn't agree more.

By the time I can get an appointment at Kaiser, nearly a week later, every cell of my body is burning. It takes a huge effort to make my muscles work. And, unfortunately for me, the first Kaiser physician I see is focused solely on my facial numbness.

"This is obviously Bell's palsy. There is not really anything that we can do for you—just go home and get some rest," the prim-faced woman says. I don't have the strength to argue the absurdity of the diagnosis. It's clear I'm not getting help from Kaiser.

I remain at home on medical leave from the police department— ostensibly to rehabilitate my shoulder—but it's the least of my worries. I have a well-equipped home gym set up in my garage, but most of the time, I'm too exhausted to use it. When I can manage a workout, it's a joke. The sensation of acid burning my muscles skyrockets after only a few repetitions, which is immediately followed by my muscles seizing up and refusing to cooperate. I'm at a loss—my body has become a stranger to me.

By mid-July, the fatigue is all consuming. I'm unable to drag myself out of bed until midday. My muscles burn constantly as if I'm suspended in a vat of acid. Walking is an effort of sheer will power. I panic as my left cheek starts to go numb, but this quickly pales in comparison to the excruciating nerve pain that blasts across my face and temples like lightning bolts.

It takes Kaiser a week to return my calls; after which, I'm given an appointment to see a neurologist, Dr. Evans. I wonder why I even bothered to call; my head will probably explode long before then.

Midweek, I'm hit with an off-the-charts migraine. I try to remain calm and meditate, but it's impossible to maintain my breathing for long. My brain is operating in a fog, and the pain is so distracting I can't think clearly enough to pin down a Chinese medical diagnosis. I take a combination of herbs to support my immune system—the shotgun approach—but I know I need to do more.

Why can't I think straight? I'm used to being intimately connected with my body, of feeling powerful and in control. *Now I don't know which end is up. I can't understand what's happening to me, why my body is failing me, and I don't know what to do. I'm in uncharted territory, helpless and powerless, drifting on a rudderless boat without a paddle.*

When I drag myself in to see Dr. Evans, it's another disappointment. He listens to my story, performs some nerve testing, and then tells me he has no clue about what's wrong with me. His solution is simply to prescribe a limitless supply of morphine for the pain and a drug called Neurontin for the burning sensations. He informs me that, while Neurontin is primarily used for seizures, it may help with neuropathy. He'd like me to try it and let him know if it has any effect at all. *Great—now I'm a lab rat for a clueless physician.*

Waiting for my prescriptions to be filled at the Kaiser pharmacy is like running through my own personal gauntlet of humiliation. I want to pursue a holistic solution, but I'm desperate for some kind of respite from the pain. I can't think in the state I'm in. What does come to mind is my single-minded condemnation of the clients in my practice who didn't or couldn't embrace the holistic solution to their health issues. Maybe they were at their wit's end, like me? Maybe they just needed a break, a pause, a small moment free from suffering so they could gather strength for the long haul. Perhaps, I could have had a dollop more of compassion. The irony bites.

Unfortunately, neither the morphine nor the Neurontin has any effect on the searing nerve pain. The sad result of taking the drugs is that, along with the excruciating pain, I'm also nauseous and constipated. When all hope seems lost, alternative medicine swoops in to my rescue. I try the biofeedback and self-hypnosis techniques that I learned as a result of my martial arts training. After spending almost an entire day on my couch experimenting with my perception of the lightning bolts in my face, I'm able to loop my mind around and outside of these sensations. It's as though I'm a detached observer. Although I can still feel it, the pain becomes something that is simply there. I no longer need to stop it, destroy it, or fight it.

Kaiser subjects me to a host of MRI's, CT scans, a spinal tap, and an array of blood work to try to find an answer. They look for MS, lupus, tumors, Lyme disease, and more, but it all turns out negative. Outside of providing the continuous supply of morphine and Neurontin, Kaiser has no useful suggestions. It's frustrating, and I'm scared. My body has never failed me before. During my years of martial arts training, I pushed myself to perform amazing feats of power, speed, and agility. My physical potential was limited only by my mind saying it shouldn't be possible.

Time and again, when I changed my thoughts, I reached my goals. So, this shouldn't be happening, I've always been invincible.

By the end of July, my nausea is 24/7, and it has become difficult for me to swallow. My muscles burn and tighten when I walk. After a few steps, I can't even will them to move. The simple act of getting out of a chair has become such a newsworthy event that it should be submitted to the major channels for press release syndication.

One day I'm out on my back deck collapsed in a lounge chair. My dear friend Chris stops by to visit. I had met her about seven years earlier when I had rented her a room in my house to bring in extra income. We had gotten along very well as housemates, became friends, and stayed in touch after she had moved out. Chris knows the layout of my kitchen and quickly makes herself a cup of tea before joining me on the deck. I'm relieved that she stopped by. Chris used to manage three homes for the developmentally and physically disabled and is intimately familiar with the Western medical system.

For a brief moment, I'm jealous of her perfect health. Watching her petite, athletic frame reclining gracefully on my deck chair is a branding iron that burns the word "wretched" onto my forehead. I'm ashamed of my thoughts and shake my head to snap out of it; she's here because she's concerned about me.

Suddenly, a look of incredulity appears on her face. "Holly, look!" she exclaims, pointing at my feet.

I'm mortified to see they are a dark shade of purple. This is July in Oakland. I'm in shorts and a T-shirt because it's hot, and my feet have lost all trace of circulation. "Chris, what the hell is happening to me?" I look over at her in dismay.

"That's it." She stands determinedly and reaches for my hand. "I'm taking you to the emergency room to see what we can find out."

"What good will that do, Chris? I've already been to Kaiser and the only thing they have to offer me is morphine."

Chris leans closer and puts her hand on my leg to comfort me. "I know this may sound strange, Hol, but sometimes you can get deeper into the system and make things happen when you go to emergency." She sounds so certain that I finally agree to accompany her.

Unfortunately, it's Saturday afternoon, and we wait around for hours before we're eventually seen by an emergency room physician. Dr. Young leads us down the hall into a private treatment room. I climb slowly and painfully onto the treatment table. Of course, by this time, the circulation in my feet has returned. My exhaustion is so all pervasive that I'm happy to let Chris do all the talking. She explains to Dr. Young about all the strange symptoms that I have begun to experience. I'm listening with only half an ear as she continues on to say that I have gotten nowhere through the normal medical channels and could he please recommend a next step for me. Dr. Young is concerned and expresses a sincere desire to help. He says he is going to do some checking and will return as soon as he can.

I slump down onto the exam table and close my eyes. I lose track of time. Chris pats my leg to get my attention when he returns and helps me into a sitting position. Dr. Young waits patiently for me to get situated. He casually leans back against the supply cabinet, holding a clipboard. "I contacted a Kaiser rheumatologist that I know, Dr. Prang, and described your symptoms to him. Dr. Prang feels fairly certain that he knows what is happening." Dr. Young flips open my chart to glance at something. Chris and I exchanged surprised looks. "He ordered some nonstandard blood work that will confirm or rule out his hypothesis and recommends that I immediately prescribe a high dose of prednisone." Dr. Young pulls a prescription pad out of his lab coat and starts writing.

"What does he think it is?" I ask impatiently.

Dr. Young looks up at me. "Dr. Prang wasn't willing to put a name to it yet and would prefer to discuss it when he sees you."

I know I'm a mess when I don't even have the strength to argue. My shoulders slump lower. I know how detrimental taking steroids can be to the body. The side effects start flashing through my mind like a neon sign: bleeding stomach, ulcers, high blood pressure, increased blood sugar, heart arrhythmias, blood clots, adrenal failure, fatty liver, osteoporosis, cataracts or glaucoma, weight gain, Cushing's disease—the list goes on and on.

The sudden urge to throw up brings me back to the present moment. I'm sitting in the emergency examination room with a numb face, feeling nauseous, every muscle in my body is burning, and I've barely enough energy to talk. I decide that I'm willing to try anything.

"Thank you, doctor, I appreciate your help," I mumble, and then use the last scrap of energy I possess to get off of the table.

"Please call Kaiser tomorrow. Dr. Prang promised he will make an opening to see you right away," Dr. Young says as he follows us out the door.

I reluctantly start taking 60 mg of prednisone a day. After a week, I feel a reduction in the awful burning sensation in my muscles and have a bit more energy. It still takes two weeks before I can get in to see the rheumatologist.

I bring Chris along for support. She sits quietly in the treatment room while I climb onto the exam table and relate my saga to Dr. Prang. He faces me, making occasional notations on my chart while he listens. My head droops when I'm finished, but he wheels his chair close enough so that I find myself staring at his navy blue pinstriped tie. I'm unable to lift my head any higher.

"The blood work confirms that you have developed a relatively rare auto-immune disorder called mixed connective tissue disorder, or MCTD," he recites from my chart in an almost mechanical tone. "This disorder typically strikes active women in their middle to late thirties."

"What causes it?" I ask.

"It's not clear, but my experience suggests a combination of stress, a genetic predisposition to inflammatory conditions, and possibly some contributing environmental factors."

His words careen through my head like bumper cars slamming into each other to get my attention. I have a disorder that strikes active women, well, that would certainly describe me, and I just turned forty in June. Two bumper cars crash into each other, and I see the word "stress" in huge letters float up from between them. What about my life hasn't been stressful since college? I went from unrelenting academic pressure at MIT to the long hours and stress of a high-tech job, to the intense career search, to the rigors of a graduate degree in Oriental medicine, immediately followed by starting a new practice, then the death of my mother, culminating with 9/11 and the police academy. I wasn't sure about any contributing environmental factors, but I seem to recall that my half-sister had some kind of auto-immune health issues. That would tick the final genetic predisposition box on the check list for MCTD. If I wasn't so exhausted, I would scream out what bullshit this is. The problem is that I was the only one driving the bumper car called my life. *I* had done this.

Dr. Prang said, "MCTD can mimic other illnesses; it is sometimes mistaken for Lupus or MS, and sometimes Lyme disease. Your circulation issues are called Raynaud's syndrome, the inflammation of your muscles and joints is fibromyalgia, your facial numbness is atypical, but trigeminal neuralgia is not, your extreme lethargy is chronic fatigue syndrome, and all of these can be a part of MCTD."

I had done *this*! The bumper cars are crashing wildly around in my head; I'm afraid it's going to explode. I need him to stop talking, but nothing comes out of my mouth.

His tie disappears from view when he rises out of his chair to stand in front of me, "May I see your hands?" Without thinking, I hold them out for inspection, and he takes them in his. "Do you notice the extreme puffiness and swelling in your fingers?" I nod my head like an automaton. "This symptom is associated with the beginning of scleroderma, which is a tightening and hardening of skin and possibly organs. Have you noticed any trouble swallowing or stomach issues?" He keeps blathering, piling it all on, oblivious to the dark fog that has appeared before my eyes.

Hearing all this is too much. I want to throw up; if I do, I know where I'm aiming. "Doctor, wait. I need a moment." I feebly raise my hand, desperately trying to silence him.

He hesitates for one slim moment. "I know all this is hard to hear," he says.

I fervently wish I had the strength to smack him. He knows?

He doesn't have the slightest clue; he has about as much empathy as a rock. And the rock keeps talking. "It is more typical for someone to develop one or two symptoms over an extended period of time, years, in fact. Your case is unusual, in that, you have exhibited almost the whole spectrum in a few months." The rock with the navy blue pin-striped tie rambles on as if reading the entry from a medical encyclopedia. If only I had a roll of duct tape, I could tape his mouth. "But actually that's what helped me to immediately identify your condition."

I wonder if he's waiting for me to congratulate him. Right now there's only one thing I want to know, one thing I need to know, but dare I ask? "What's the treatment?"

The rock returns to his chair and grabs my chart off of the counter behind him. "I recommend continuing the prednisone and to begin a low dose of methotrexate."

"What is methotrexate?" I ask, already not liking the sound of its name.

"It's a drug used in chemotherapy that works to suppress your immune system."

As muddled as my brain feels, this strategy sounds absurd. "Why on earth would I want to do that?" I snap, but the rock is not disconcerted in the slightest by my skepticism.

"Your immune system is operating in reverse. Instead of protecting you, it's attacking you. I've had some success with this approach and would encourage you to consider it."

I rub my temples and try to calm myself. "If I do that, how long do you think it's going to take me to recover?"

The rock raises an eyebrow in surprise just like Mr. Spock. "First, we need to get this progression of symptoms under control and manageable, and then we can determine the most effective dosage of drugs for lifestyle maintenance."

"Maintenance isn't really what I had in mind. I mean how long will it take for me to recover completely from this illness?" I ask, bracing myself for his response.

The rock hits hard and low. "I'm really sorry, but you need to understand that this is not about recovering. You have a lifelong disorder. Maybe we can get you into a kind of remission, but this could take many years to accomplish—if it happens at all." I've just been punched in the gut, but the rock doesn't stop there, "To be blunt, your life may continue in a series of bad days mixed with a combination of worse days. Of course, we're going to try not to let that happen, but I want you to be prepared."

Thwack! My head is throbbing. Did he just smack me upside the head with a sledgehammer? My head is spinning, and the room starts to recede as his words bounce around my skull. He can't be talking about me. This is not my life. I refuse to accept this as a description of my life.

"Let's just take this one day at a time. Will you try it my way for a while?"

I'm pulled back into the room by the rock's nasally voice, but my whole body remains cramped and tense. I'm confused, exhausted, and in a considerable amount of pain. I want something to make this all go away. "Okay. I'll try the drugs, but I'm going to be pursuing other options. And I'm not settling for just maintenance. I'm going to kick this thing."

The rock morphs back into Dr. Prang, and he pats me on the back like some miscreant child being brought into line. "I'm glad you're going to give this a try. We need to get you some measure of relief and then we can reassess your situation." He stands up and closes my chart, signaling the end of my audience.

Chris drives home and patiently waits for me to break the silence. I can't say anything for several minutes. Finally, I give in to my misery.

"Chris, what the hell am I going to do? This is not acceptable. I don't want to take drugs. With all their side effects, if this MCTD doesn't kill me, they will."

Chris reaches over and puts a comforting hand on my shoulder. "I know it sounds bad, Hol, but you have a much bigger arsenal then just Western medicine that you can use." She glances at me encouragingly.

Her words cut my tailspin short. She's right. No one can tell me what I can or can't do. I feel a wee bit of spunk returning. "No one is going to tell me that recovery is not an option. I refuse that line of thinking entirely."

"I *know* you can get through this." Chris nods and gives my shoulder another squeeze.

Her words give me strength. I recovered from a fractured spine in college. That injury brought me excruciating pain for seven years, but I healed from it fully. Surely, I could tackle this.

I'm determined that I'm not going to just manage this; I'm going to be rid of it. I can do this. Whatever it takes—I'm getting my life back.

CHAPTER THIRTY FIVE
PERILS OF PREDNISONE

Confront the dark parts of yourself, and work to banish
them with illumination and forgiveness. Your willingness
to wrestle with your demons will cause your angels to sing.
Use the pain as fuel, as a reminder of your strength.
–August Wilson

My hand is shaking as I line up all the pills on the counter. I don't remember the last time I took aspirin, and now there's a whole pharmacy of pills I'm supposed to take: Methotrexate, Prednisone, Neurontin, morphine, and more. I look despairingly down at the prescription bottles and double check the doses. Difficulty swallowing is part of the MCTD, and I have to be extremely careful not to choke on the pills. Each one that slides down my esophagus feels like a betrayal of my body and my principles. The drugs are hard on my stomach. It's in constant pain, and I'm worried about adding an ulcer to my long laundry list of symptoms.

I developed an ulcer in my crazy college days when I was drinking as much as ten Tab sodas and eight cups of coffee a day. All of that was so I could stay awake and study. When the pain in my stomach became unbearable, I went to the medical center on campus, but they had nothing to offer me. I did some herbal research and eventually cured my ulcer with slippery elm powder. I've added some into my daily regimen, hoping this will protect my stomach from the onslaught of medications.

After a few weeks on Dr. Prang's program, I have enough energy to get out of bed before noon and make it through the day. The pain and inflammation are always present but tolerable. I hang onto the belief that perhaps I can gradually replace these drugs with my herbs and acupuncture or other holistic therapies. Without that hope, I can't justify taking them.

245

The Methotrexate leaves me weak and nauseous, but Prednisone is the medication I abhor the most. Aside from the unattractive puffy face it has given me, there is a far more insidious side effect—uncontrollable anger. After I choke down a pill, I can feel it being generated inside of me. It is a constant anger that has no off switch. It grows and twists inside of me like an evil alien parasite. A significant amount of my time is spent meditating to let go of it. I focus on washing it away from me and into the earth, where it is transformed into healing earth energy. I feel relief during my meditations, but as soon as I stop, it returns with a vengeance. Then, one day after an appointment with Dr. Prang, it all boils over.

I'm already on a low simmer by the time Dr. Prang walks into the office. I've been waiting for at least a half hour and I'm in considerable pain on the treatment table. I watch with what little patience I have left as he peruses my file yet again. I should think he'd have it memorized by now. Finally, I can't keep quiet any longer.

"Dr. Prang, I really need to talk to you about this intense anger that I'm feeling. I get it when I take the Prednisone and it never goes away. It's driving me crazy."

"Some people do report an increase in irritability," he responds without even looking up. "But it's an acceptable and rather trivial side effect for getting your inflammation under control."

I feel my blood pressure rising—he doesn't get it. I need to make him understand. "This goes way beyond irritability. I feel terrible. I'm angry at everything, and my meditations only help in the moment. Now that I can barely work out, I have no way to vent these feelings by exhausting myself physically."

Dr. Prang finally pries his eyes from my chart. "You're working out?" he asks, looking startled. It's the first genuine reaction I've seen from him, but at least I have his attention. I throw my hands in the air and scoff at myself.

"If you can call it that, it's pathetic. I'm losing strength, and my muscles keep locking up and failing in the middle of a set. I don't even have a chance to get physically worn out. I'm just exhausted period."

He raises his hand to silence my tirade. "I want you to stop working out immediately."

Despite the pain in my fingers, my hands close into fists. I know my blood pressure is off the charts. I'm not some child to be commanded about. "What? Doc, are you insane? My muscles are already atrophying from lack of exercise, and you want me to stop? Working out and physical activity are who I am. Without that, I can't handle this."

"If you continue to work out while your muscles are in this severely inflamed state, it will accelerate their deterioration. It won't be forever—just until we get you more stable." His tone turns soothing. Maybe he finally gets how close to the edge I'm feeling right now.

Heartbroken, I stumble out of the office. My last refuge has been taken from me. *How can I cope now?* My leg muscles are on fire, and my pace slows to a crawl. Fortunately, my car is close by. I only need to cross one street to get to it. A woman in a mustard-yellow station wagon pulls up to the stop sign and waits for me to cross the street. It takes forever for me just to get halfway. The rather large woman sitting behind the wheel has so far been fixing her makeup in the rearview mirror. She suddenly loses her patience—maybe she thinks I'm deliberately walking so slowly? She pounds her horn with a fist the size of a small ham and shouts epithets at me to get out of her way. I look into her flashing gray eyes; I see nothing but fury. There's not a speck of compassion. I want to find the nearest rock to crawl under so I can hide my shame and humiliation. As soon as I make it far enough for her to speed around me, she flashes me the finger and takes off past me. Her blaring horn and screams of rage ring in my ears long after she turns the corner.

I'm completely distraught on the drive home. My hands grip the steering wheel until the pain distracts my attention. From out of nowhere a car suddenly cuts me off, missing my bumper by inches.

"Shit!" I yell. That was the final straw. The alien parasite writhes inside of me, and a tidal wave of rage surges through my entire being. All ability for rational thought deserts me, and I speed up, chasing after the offending blue Cadillac. The driver is a young, inconsiderate punk with a purple Mohawk. He glances in his rearview mirror; when we make eye contact, he flips me the finger. Twice in one day! The alien screams in outrage and takes complete control. It's the puppet master manipulating me with strings of fury. I shake my fist and shout obscenities at the demon driver with the purple Mohawk. He needs to be punished, and I'm the punisher!

The Cadillac takes off ahead of me, and my foot punches the accelerator to maintain my pursuit. We zigzag through traffic at insanely dangerous speeds. Slowly, I'm gaining ground. When I'm right on purple Mohawk's tail, I can see his eyes watching me in his rear view mirror. *Is that a hint of fear I see?* I chuckle with malicious glee, certain of my imminent victory.

Any moment now I'm going to hear the satisfying sound of his bumper crumpling under my assault.

One homicidal maniac coming right up!

Suddenly, the Cadillac swerves two lanes to the right, narrowly missing a Ford pickup loaded with furniture. It's a move of desperation, but I will not be denied my prey so easily. I yank the steering wheel hard, aiming for an opening two lanes over. Unfortunately, an unsuspecting Toyota Camry is also merging into the same space. I hit the gas and narrowly miss clipping the front of the Camry. The terrified driver blows her horn at me—a plea from the universe for me to snap out of it.

Somehow, the sound slices through my rage, cutting the alien puppet master's strings. A tiny beacon of sanity dispels the fog. Finally, I comprehend the danger and horrible stupidity of my actions. I get off at the first exit and pull over. My entire body is shaking with fear. Tears stream down my cheeks. I came so close to hurting or even killing someone. My head rests on the steering wheel. *What kind of monster am I?* I sob despairingly.

I send a prayer of gratitude to the universe for stopping me. It takes me a long time to pull myself together. Eventually, I summon the courage to turn the key in the ignition. The motor starts up. I let it idle as I wait for my heart to stop pounding. *I need to get home. Now if I can just do that without killing anybody.*

CHAPTER THIRTY SIX
SLIDING INTO THE ABYSS

It is by going down into the abyss, that
we recover the treasures of life.
Where you stumble, there lies your treasure.
–Joseph Campbell

The months crawl by slowly and painfully. With the police academy clearly out of the picture, I decide to sell my house. Getting it ready for market becomes my reason for struggling out of bed every day,—and the only way I can prod myself into swallowing the dreaded drugs.

It's a fright fest every time I get into my car. I'm terrified of turning back into "The Punisher" if some poor unsuspecting soul chooses to cut me off. I force myself to drive slowly and move away from cars that get too close. All the while, I replay the video of my road rage episode in my mind. I'm a mentally exhausted mess at the end of each outing, but at least I manage to keep out of jail.

Shika remains by my side all day long. She shadows my moves and allows me to use her as a crutch whenever my legs lock up and won't move. With each day that passes, my muscles burn faster, my legs are weaker, and the nausea makes it more difficult to eat.

In March of 2003, I've just finished packing a box and barely make it back to the couch to collapse from fatigue. I don't know how I'm going to finish the painting and the last remaining odds and ends that need to be done. The phone rings in the middle of my quandary.

"Hello, Holly darling. How are you, love?" Keshama's voice is a pleasant surprise.

"Keshama! It's great to hear your voice. What's it been—a year since we've spoken?"

"Too bloody long is all I have to say. You know how fast time goes. I suppose you're busy chasing down the bad guys by now."

"Not exactly," I say, and my throat constricts with emotion. I take a deep breath and bring her up to date on my life. It's satisfying to have Keshama punctuate my story with her frequent exclamations of "bloody hell" and "my poor darling."

"Why didn't you call me sooner, Hol? I could have planned some trips up from L.A. to give you a hand."

"This thing has hit me so hard and fast that my head is still spinning." I am unable to admit to the humiliation I feel at having to ask anyone for help.

Keshama pauses but doesn't press me any further. "Well, love, you say you still have some painting to do?"

"Yes." I let out an exhausted sigh. My task list still seems infinitely long.

"Good. Don't lift another finger on your house. Steen and I will be up this weekend to get it done."

"Keshama, that would be wonderful. Thanks." I barely manage to stifle my sob of relief as I hang up the phone.

It's all I can do not to count the seconds until Keshama and Steen arrive. When the time draws near, I plant myself on the sofa and watch for them out my living room window. My heart sings when I see the tan pickup truck pull up in front of my house.

Keshama gets out of the passenger side, and I can't help but grin. Even while dressed in her "work outfit" of battered jeans, tan leather hiking boots, and a light blue T-shirt, she still looks like a fashion model. Steen bounds over to her side, wearing a similar outfit, except that his T-shirt is white. Steen is a character, and I adore him. He stands out with his ultra-thin, lanky body, shaved head and permanent grin. He's one of Keshama's best friends. They used to share an apartment in San Francisco, and I met him after Keshama and I became scene partners in an acting class.

When I open the door, there is a momentary flash of shock in Keshama's eyes. I know I look drawn and haggard. I'm so weak that I can't even stand up straight anymore.

"Holly, darling. It's good to see you love, it's been too bloody long." She sweeps me into a big embrace. Her love is pouring into me; for a moment, my mountain of disaster is swept aside.

"Hey, I want a piece of her, too, K," Steen says from behind her. I chuckle as she reluctantly releases me and is immediately replaced by Steen. There is a sniffing sound behind me, and when I turn my head, I catch a glimpse of Keshama dabbing her eyes with a tissue. She's never seen me look helpless before, and I know she gets it. She quickly puts the tissue back into her purse and clears her throat. I lower my eyes before she looks up; I'm too embarrassed to meet her gaze.

"Right, well, Steen let's get to it. Why don't you get the supplies up here, and I'll make Hol Bol a nice cup of tea before we start." Keshama takes my arm and walks me over to the sofa. "You just rest here, darling, and let us handle things for a while."

I'm trying hard not to cry as I turn to face Keshama before sitting on the couch. I force myself to look at her. When our eyes meet, it's torture for me to allow her to see my suffering. I don't want to be an object of pity, but I crave for someone to understand my nightmare. Keshama is an angel. I see only concern and understanding reflected back at me.

"Thanks. This means a lot to me," I say, my voice quivering.

She gently embraces me again. I rest my head on her shoulder. "I'm so sorry, babe," she replies, and her words feed me what I need. At least for a short while, I can let go of a piece of my burden. *Friends* are the pot of gold at the end of the rainbow.

Keshama and Steen work well together and entertain me with their unique blend of comic relief—Kiwi-style. It feels good to laugh. The dynamic duo finishes every task I have left to do. Unfortunately, the weekend ends all too quickly, but my friends have filled me with love and nurturing. We have one final, fierce group hug before they leave.

"I'll plan trips up from L.A. more often to check in on you, darling. Call me anytime, and Mum sends her love. She also says you're welcome to come and stay with her. She'll pour some good food and loving into you," Keshama says as they head out the door.

I wave to them as they drive off, treasuring their priceless gift of friendship. When I turn around, Shika is watching me with her big Rottweiler smile. I wrap my arms around her warm, muscular body and rest my head on her neck. She is another gift of unconditional love from the universe.

The effort of getting my house ready for market has exacted a heavy toll. Even an increased dosage of prednisone cannot stem the rising tide of inflammation and overwhelming fatigue. Dr. Prang recommends that I also increase the amount of methotrexate. Every fiber of my being rebels against taking an even larger dose of these destructive drugs, but I'm desperate to stop—or at least slow down—the physical slide.

I tell myself that this is only temporary and that I will reduce the medications as soon as my symptoms are under control. It doesn't help. I haven't taken my morning mountain of pills yet, but I can already feel the nausea building in my stomach. I force myself to swallow them anyway. My bed seems miles away from the kitchen, but I'm able to reach it and collapse in a state of exhaustion. Shika lies quietly by my side with her head resting gently on my leg. After a long while, I drift off.

My eyes spring open, and I reach for the bucket next to my bed, thankfully, grasping it to me before I vomit. Six hours later, my position remains unchanged. I'm vomiting every few minutes. I know I'm in trouble. I can barely see the numbers as I dial a friend who lives close by.

"Kae, are you in the neighborhood?"

"I'm in San Francisco at the moment. Why? What's up?"

"Nothing much," I say, and my heart sinks. "If you were around, I was going to ask for a favor, but thanks anyway."

Kae hesitates. "If you want, I can swing by after I come back to the East Bay."

I'm feeling nauseous again and need to get off the phone to figure something out. "No, that's all right. I'll talk to you later." I hang up in a hurry. Just in time as, I use the bucket for the umpteenth time. My heart is racing, and I'm scared. I need this to stop. I'm dangerously dehydrated. In the middle of a work day, I can't think of anyone who might be available to drive me to emergency. So, for the first time in my life, I dial 911 for me.

"911. What is the emergency?" The woman's voice on the other end is crisp and emotionless.

I swallow hard to control my need to use the bucket while I speak. "I think I'm having a reaction to an increase in medications. I can't stop vomiting." My words come out in a panting rush. *Is this really a description of me?* It's hard to accept this situation as real. I must be dreaming, but in case I'm not, I utter the dreaded words. "I need help. I can't drive myself to emergency."

The 911 dispatcher answers quickly. "An ambulance is on its way. It won't be long."

I'm not sure, but I think there's a minute amount of encouragement that accompanies her words. I grit my teeth and manage a quick, breathless thank you before I hang up to use the bucket again.

CHAPTER THIRTY SEVEN
THE OTHER SIDE OF THE MIRROR

We shall draw from the heart of suffering itself
the means of inspiration and survival.
–Winston Churchill

In less than two minutes, I hear the ambulance approaching. I drag myself and the bucket across the living room floor. Shika is glued to my side, and I lean on her to help me crawl. She turns her head toward me and licks my face, encouraging me to keep going. By the time the ambulance pulls up out front, my bucket and I are on the floor by the front door. I reach up and manage to pull the inner wooden door open, but the outer metal screen door is still closed. When the ambulance crew comes to the door, Shika steps over me protectively and growls menacingly. I put my hand on her neck to calm her down.

"Ma'am, you need to get the dog away from the door, or we can't get to you," the paramedic says through the screen. If the ambulance crew can't get to me, I'm afraid they might call the police, and Shika could be hurt or killed. The nausea is threatening to overwhelm me again.

Shika's in danger now, so I can't give in to panic. I need her to understand me, "Shika, my sweet girl, it's okay. They're here to help me." Her soulful eyes stare into mine searching for confirmation. "Yes, my love, it's really okay. I need to go now. I'll be okay."

Shika nudges my cheek with her nose and then reluctantly backs up so I can crawl outside the door with my bucket. She whines and licks my hand as I push the screen door closed. Our eyes meet once more. "I'll be okay, girl. I'll be back soon."

Now that Shika is safe, I try not to pass out as the two youthful paramedics lean over me. I focus on the closest one, a woman who reminds me of Meryl Streep. She attempts to gently pry the bucket out of my hands. I refuse to let go.

"I'm going to need you to let go of this, but don't worry, I'll give it back as soon as we have you settled in for the ride," she says. Her compassionate eyes engender my trust, and I release the bucket. They lift me up easily and quickly strap me onto the gurney. I grimace as the motion exacerbates my nausea.

Again, it's the young woman who makes the connection. "My name is Terry, and this is Danny. Don't worry. We'll get you situated quickly. Hang in there," she says. I draw on her strength as they load me into the ambulance and lock down the stretcher. It feels surreal to be the one strapped down and staring helplessly up at my rescuers. My eyes track them as they move efficiently about the ambulance. In record time, they've logged my vitals and have started an IV. Terry raps on the glass partition, and the driver gets underway. I'm grateful when she returns my bucket and sits beside me. She takes my hand in hers. Her compassion is a lifeline that I desperately want to cling to, but it's embarrassing to be on the other side of the mirror.

I don't want to be so pathetic in front of my fellow rescuers, an object of pity. Deep down, I still think of myself as a person who comes to the rescue of others—and not the other way around.

"I used to run with an ambulance crew in Pennsylvania. It's weird to be in this position," I say. "Thanks for helping me." She smiles sympathetically at me. It's hard to keep the pain out of my voice, "I used to be strong and healthy, like you. I shouldn't be on all these drugs. It's not me." I feel like I'm babbling. I'm embarrassed again and struggle against the straps trying to sit up.

Terry puts a comforting hand on my shoulder and gently pushes me down. "You're going to be okay. I can see you're a fighter. Relax, and let *us* help *you* for a change." Her words have the desired effect, and I stop struggling. The rest of the trip is an epic battle not to vomit again. Fortunately for me, it's a short ride to Oakland Kaiser.

Terry and Danny wheel my stretcher into a large emergency room treatment area. The sudden glare of the bright overhead lights hurts my eyes, and I squeeze them shut. My nose is assailed with the pungent hospital aroma of antiseptic floor cleaner that fails to mask the underlying smells of sweat, urine, blood, and vomit. I'm mortified as I immediately throw up into my bucket.

An emergency room nurse directs Terry to shift me onto another bed. Unfortunately, it's positioned in the middle of the room next to a large support column. While Terry is transferring my IV bag to the pole attached to the bed, I hear the nurse tell her that all of the partitioned treatment cubicles are currently in use. I have to remain in the center of the room until one is free. Terry sees the panic in my eyes and rests her hand protectively on my shoulder. I feel myself calm down.

Danny appears and whispers something in Terry's ear. She nods back at him and then glances down at me. "I'm sorry, we've got to go. Good luck, Holly. I know you're going to be okay." She pats my arm before hurrying off with her partner.

I watch my rescuers leave and try not to panic. As soon as they're out of sight, however, I need to use the bucket again. My throat is raw, and my stomach is cramping painfully with the effort. I wonder how there could possibly be anything left inside of me to get rid of.

The nurse returns and tries to take my bucket. When I adamantly refuse to let go of my only ally, she's forced to speak to me. "I simply want to exchange this for a clean pan. Please let go of the bucket," she insists, without a hint of compassion, and pulls harder. Her dark brown hair is tied up in a bun, which makes her rather large nose seem even more prominent. Her eyes are distant and cold.

I read her name tag. I'm startled when I think I see her last name is "Devil." My grip is momentarily loosened, and she pulls the bucket out of my hands. I'm about to complain—until she replaces it with a plastic pan. I see now that her name is Devon, but I think Devil would be more apt as she pauses a moment to glare at me with a smug look of victory. *Is this really happening? Did I just land in some surreal psycho ward?* I decide to keep quiet and close my eyes. It's my fervent wish that Nurse Devil will go away and leave me to my misery in peace. The heavens smile upon me, and I get my wish.

A few minutes later, I'm forced to use the plastic pan. It seems as if the whole room pauses to watch me vomit, and I wish I could crawl under a rock. This time I'm visited by a young blonde nurse with smiling eyes. She is a gift from heaven. "Oh, you poor thing, let me have that. Here's a fresh one," she says kindly. After she hands me my new pan, she scans the room as if looking for something. Suddenly, she smiles in satisfaction. "There's an empty place against the far wall, out of the spotlight. Would that suit you better than here?"

An emotional lump forms in my throat at this small act of human kindness. All I can manage in response is a nod and a grateful look. While she gently wheels my bed across the room, I manage to get a look at the nametag of my savior. It says Darlin. Okay, now I know I'm in soap opera central, undoubtedly, somewhere on the set of *General Hospital*. Any second now the director is going to yell, "Cut!" and this will all be over. Alas, the words never come.

We reach my new-and-improved resting spot, and I try to speak while Nurse Darlin locks the bed wheels. "Your name suits you. Thank you for helping me." My words sound more like a croak, but she hears me.

Nurse Darlin moves to the head of the bed where I can see her. She has an aura of white light around her head. It befits her as the angel of mercy that I believe her to be. It feels good to see her beaming at my compliment and gratitude. "Why, thank you. It's my pleasure to help you be a little more comfortable. I'm going to check on getting you somewhere a little more private. Will you be okay for a few minutes?"

"Yes, I'll manage. Thanks," I reply hoarsely.

Nurse Darlin strides away purposefully, and I relax for the first time. I'm out of the line of sight of most of the people in the room. Even the lights are dimmer in my new spot. Now that I'm no longer the main attraction in Times Square, the sound of everyone talking around me fades into white noise. My eyes close and I drift off. When Nurse Darlin returns, she brings good news.

"You're in luck, Holly. An actual treatment room is open, and Dr. Metzger is there now," she says with a wink.

"Thank you so much. You're an angel," I whisper and close my eyes.

Nurse Darlin smiles and pats my arm affectionately as she wheels me to the treatment room. "It won't be long now, and we'll get you some relief."

Dr. Metzger is young, but he examines me quickly and efficiently. It probably helps my case that I throw up as he starts writing on my chart. He glances at me and then makes some additional notations before he hands the chart to Nurse Darlin.

"Well, Miss Reese, I'm going to have Nurse Darlin add a strong anti-emetic to your IV. Are you in much pain from the MCTD?"

Up until now my concentration has been centered on not throwing up. As soon as Dr. Metzger mentions pain, my entire body seems to light up with it. I realize it's been there all along. "Yes, there's a lot of pain," I say with a grimace.

"Okay, well, then we'll add some morphine." He makes another notation on my chart and then looks at me. "That should help you. I'll be back later to see how you're responding." He spins around quickly and is out the door before I even have a chance to thank him.

In a few short minutes, Nurse Darlin adds the additional medications to my IV line. The morphine dulls my senses immediately, and I feel like I'm floating above the bed. Her angelic face appears above me, and it takes some effort to hear what she's saying.

"Try to get some rest. I'll be back to check on you in a while."

Before my brain gets any foggier, there is something I need to do. I struggle to form the thought. Then it comes to me. It's Shika. I need to make sure she's fed. I remember that my cell phone is in my pocket. Fortunately, it's in the pocket on the same side as my free arm. I know Sofia will be home from work soon.

"Holly, what's wrong?"

"I'm at Kaiser Emergency, and I'm not sure how long I'll be here. Would you mind feeding Shika for me?" I ask feebly, wishing my voice didn't sound so weak.

"Of course I will. What else do you need?"

My body relaxes slightly knowing that Shika is taken care of. "Nothing right now. I'll check in later." I hang up—not a second too soon. Another wave of nausea has me reaching quickly for the pan again.

I'm not sure, but I think I see Dr. Metzger poke his head into my room momentarily. The next few minutes, I'm too busy hunched over my plastic pan to think about it.

An older, unfamiliar nurse enters the room. She doesn't even look at me while she pulls a bottle of some medication and fills a syringe. She is an older facsimile of Nurse Devil and has the bedside manner of a rock. When she takes hold of my IV line and prepares to inject the contents of the syringe into it, I'm annoyed enough to speak.

"What are you doing?" I grunt.

She seems irritated by my question. "You're not improving, so the doctor has ordered something stronger." The sound of her grating voice matches her personality.

Almost as soon as the new drug is fed into my IV line, something is different. The room seems to darken, and I lose focus. I'm floating above my body, merely an observer of the events in the room. Watching the nurse from my new vantage point, I see her frown at the heart rate monitor and then move quickly to a cart against the wall. It's a strange sensation to watch myself from above, but it's pleasant not to feel nausea or pain any longer. I watch the nurse select another bottle, load her syringe, and then inject this new drug into my IV. I'm almost disappointed to be pulled back into my body.

Now I'm looking up at Nurse Devil Senior from the bed.

"Does that feel better?" she asks in a voice devoid of emotion.

"I guess so. What happened? I'm feeling very lightheaded."

"The new anti-emetic dropped your blood pressure too low, so I administered a stimulant."

After checking the heart rate monitor one more time, she abruptly leaves. I'm glad that she's gone, but I don't really want to be alone. Thankfully, I fall asleep for a time.

When I awaken, I have a new problem. I need to pee. There is no nurse, and I have no call button that I can find. I can see a bedpan, but it's on a table that's just out of reach. I'm getting more desperate and need to act. Maybe if I shift to the edge of the bed, I can reach it. That does get me most of the way there. I fling the lead weight that calls itself my arm and manage to touch the table with my fingertips. Stretching further pulls the IV line taut, which tugs the needle in my elbow. That hurts, but I just need to reach a little further. I imagine suction cups on my fingertips and will the table to move closer. At long last, my hand reaches the bedpan. It's all I can do to get it positioned in time. As I put it back on the cart, the tears roll down my face. This is all so pathetic.

I don't want to think about my situation. I've lost control of my body, and now the drugs are in charge. I'm on drugs to dull the pain, drugs to fight the inflammation, drugs to destroy my immune system, drugs to stop the nausea caused by the drugs destroying my immune system, and drugs to raise my blood pressure that dropped because of the drugs to stop my nausea that was caused by the drugs destroying my immune system.

The chatter in my mind is deafening. *What have I become? This is not happening. This is not my life. I'm not meant for this, but how can I accomplish anything in this condition?* Moving restlessly in the bed, I accidently pull on the IV line. It sends a shooting pain from my elbow up my arm. Anger erupts from within, and I want to rip it out of me.

I've fallen into the Western medical trap, a vicious cycle of drugs. If I keep taking them experiencing side effects, and then taking ever more drugs, I will never recover. *This is not me; it is not my way.* Right then I decide that, whatever happens, I'm done with drugs. They are my sadistic prison guards bent on slow torture until my untimely demise. The rush of anger and determination feels good. I have chosen a direction—to whatever end.

Sofia chooses that moment to walk into my little room. I pretend not to notice the brief look of horror that crosses her face. "Hol, how ya doin', mate?"

I'm hoping that was a rhetorical question. If I answer it, I'll surely cry. I pick my head up slightly. "Is Shika okay?"

Sofia moves to the foot of my bed and tries to look cheerful. "She's got a full belly, but she wants to know when her Mama's coming home."

My head drops back down onto the pillow. Knowing that Shika is okay and fed is a load off of my mind. "I'm not sure, but they'll probably release me in the wee hours of the morning. Any chance you could pick me up?"

"Not a problem—just give me a ring," Sofia says, patting my leg.

I'm too tired to talk more and remain silent. Sofia nonchalantly looks around the room. I can sense her discomfort at seeing me helpless and tell her to go since I need to rest. I can't bear being watched like this.

Alone again with my thoughts, my resolve gradually hardens into stone. I'm going to stop taking all drugs just as soon as I get home.

CHAPTER THIRTY EIGHT
COLD TURKEY

We gain strength, and courage, and confidence by each experience in which we really stop to look fear in the face... we must do that thing which we think we cannot.
—Eleanor Roosevelt

Going cold turkey is not a recommended method for getting off of the meds I'm taking, but I can't force myself to swallow another pill. Even braced for a hard impact, nothing could have prepared me for the exponential exacerbation of all my symptoms. It's hard to tell which of them are from withdrawal and which of them are from the illness.

My thoughts are muddled as if I'm moving through a fog that never clears. My days are defined by the couch in the middle of the house. If I can get up and make it there before one o'clock, I'm having a good day. It's my resting spot, my safe haven; once there, I allow myself a respite. Sinking into it gratefully, I'm one with the couch—unable to distinguish where I end and it begins. Shika, bless her heart, spends every day at my feet, never leaving my side. She wags her stumpy tail whenever I look at her. Days are rough, but nights are the hardest. The pain never lets me attain a state of true sleep.

At long last, I've finally moved into a shared house rental with Brenda, an acquaintance from my old flag football team. But in this new living situation, winter brings a new problem. Brenda's house has poor insulation and the cold seeps in from the walls, the floors, the windows, from everywhere. Every morning, I'm confronted with purple hands and feet. The thought that I could lose my fingers or toes terrifies me.

I find I'm spending most of my day with my feet and hands shoved underneath a heating pad. I lose circulation within minutes of taking them out. Before, the couch was an oasis; now I'm chained to it. My saving grace is Shika. At night, she lies next to me and lets me keep my hands underneath her warm belly.

The facial numbness has spread to encompass my entire face. Unfortunately, this also includes my nose. The numbness translates into a strange sensation of wet heaviness. The feeling never leaves; at times, it's almost maddening. However, that pales in comparison to my real problem. I can't feel air going into my nose when I breathe, and that creates the sensation that I'm suffocating. I have panic attacks about not getting enough oxygen, especially at night.

In the dark of night, the inability to feel air entering my nose makes me think I've stopped breathing. I wake up, gasping for air, but breathing through my mouth doesn't help. Often, I need to look into a mirror to prove that I must be getting oxygen. *Obviously, I am—or I'd be passed out by now.* Eventually, I calm myself enough to return to bed. Once there, I wrap my arms around Shika for warmth; sometimes I manage to fall asleep to the calming sound of her heartbeat.

My thoughts are increasingly muddled, and decisions are hard. I know I should try to find someone to come help me figure out what to do, but that would take effort and energy I can't seem to find. This time, Sofia comes to my rescue.

One day in February of 2004, I accept an invitation to meet her for tea at a nearby café. When Sofia asks me how I am, it's a desperate struggle not to cry as I vent about how miserable it is at Brenda's house.

We sip our drinks in silence for several minutes. "Hol, maybe you should consider moving into my house. The basement is renovated into a carpeted bedroom with a full bath. And—maybe best of all—it's got its own wall heater. I wouldn't care if you ran it all the time; it won't affect the upstairs."

Manna is falling from the heavens. "Sofia, thank you. I have so many issues that I'm battling. I can't tell you how wonderful it would be to be warm enough to have circulation."

"I didn't realize that things were so hard for you at Brenda's house. I'm glad I can help. You know we all need help sometimes," she says, reaching out to pat my arm.

Sofia's house has its own set of unique challenges, but it's worth it to have circulation again. Her house is set on a steep hill, and there's a flight of steps up to the front door. To reach my basement room, I must cross the living room and descend a narrow metal spiral staircase near the fireplace. The journey is difficult, but I'm determined to find a way to manage. The carpeted bedroom is much larger than my old one at Brenda's house, and the bathroom is right there. My commute to the shower is only a fraction of the daily journey I had before. And that isn't even the best part.

My first glimpse of the large in-wall gas heater is love at first sight. With adoring eyes, I gently caress the metal surface, and gratefully, turn the temperature setting to high. The warmth pouring into the room feels divine. Every cell in my body happily basks in the heat. At long last, I'm able to keep my circulation flowing.

Once I'm settled into my new digs, another problem arises. It seems only fair. After all, now that I'm no longer worried about losing my fingers and toes, I certainly have room for additional torture. This time, GERD, or gastro-esophageal reflux disease, gallops in to join the fray. My nights are now enhanced by explosions of acid. I discover that any sleeping position other than sitting upright results in flames leaping into my throat and mouth. The only solution is to stagger to my feet, deliriously tired, and shuffle slowly around in circles until the molten lava recedes.

The days pass slowly, but nights last forever. I seldom surface from my room, but through it all, Shika remains glued to my side. She is the light that shines in my life.

By the end of April, I wonder whether I'm going to need to find myself nursing care. Defeated and humiliated, I dial my dad's phone number, trying not to cry.

"Hello, honey. How are you? Feeling any better?" he asks, but there's a wheezing sound in his voice. I almost decide not to say anything. *What am I doing?* Dad has his own issues with diminished lung capacity from smoking. But I'm desperate for sympathy and advice.

"Dad, I'm not sure what to do," I admit with difficulty.

"What's wrong? You can tell me—whatever it is." His voice is full of love and concern.

"This illness I have is bad. I'm not doing well at all, Dad." I'm pinching myself hard to keep the tears back and not choke up. "I'm in a terrible amount of pain, and it's hard to get around. I can barely digest food, and I think I need more than one brain working on this problem."

Dad pauses and then says, "I'm so sorry, honey. Why didn't you tell me sooner? Look, we'll figure something out. I'm going to come out there to see how I can help you."

The love and support I feel from him overwhelm me. For a moment, I'm a little girl again, and Dad is there to sweep me in his arms and tell me everything's going to be okay. I can't stifle my sobs, but I press the phone against my chest to keep Dad from hearing them. I make a big effort to get a grip when I hear his muffled voice calling my name. As much as I want someone to take the reins and make it all go away, he isn't well either. I take a deep breath and move the phone back to my ear.

"Dad, you don't have to come out. You're not feeling all that great yourself. Maybe you, Jamie, and I can brainstorm a plan on the phone. Just the fact that you care means more to me than you can possibly know."

"I'm coming, and that's that. I'll talk to your brother, and we'll work something out as a family. I love you, and I'll call you when I have my tickets. Just try to relax, honey."

I hang up the phone and burst into a new round of crying. I want help—and I need help—but I don't want him to harm his own health trying to help me.

A short while later, Jay calls. "Dad tells me he's coming out there, and he says that you're feeling shitty. Give me the details."

It's good to hear his voice. I miss him. I take a breath and plunge in, telling him how bad things have become.

"You could have told me a little sooner, I'm really sorry you've been suffering so much. You know you can always move into my house down here in Oceanside. I've got an extra room with your name on it. I'd look after you."

"Jay, thanks. I really appreciate that. I'd like to try to get well here, but if I need to, it really helps to know that's an option," I reply, and the tears are flowing again.

"No problem. You're my sister, and that's what brothers are for." His words echo in my mind and a memory wells to the surface.

There was an incident when we were only seven or eight years old. We were sitting in the back of Mom's light blue Chrysler sedan. She had brought us along to go grocery shopping with her. Jay was sitting behind her and looking out his window at the endless row of red brick storefronts. I was on the other side of the back seat leaning against the passenger door about to nod off. When Mom turned a sharp corner, my coat pocket caught on the door handle and pulled it open. It happened so fast that I didn't even think to yell out. I was being irresistibly pulled out of the car. My right arm was pinned against the door, and all my weight was on the armrest. My legs were the only things holding me inside the car. Jay felt something happening behind him and turned around. He was only seven years old, but he leapt to my side in an instant and grabbed hold of my legs. I stopped sliding. He reached out for my free hand with his and our hands interlocked. Jay hung onto me for dear life screaming for Mom to stop the car. Afterwards, when I thanked him, he said simply, "You're my sister, and that's what brothers are for."

CHAPTER THIRTY NINE
DAD LENDS A HAND

You don't choose your family. They are
God's gift to you, as you are to them.
–Desmond Tutu

I watch from the living room window as a taxi pulls up in front of the house. Dad gets out of the car slowly, but he looks like he's sprinting compared to how fast I'm moving. I have only a few steps to get to the front door—and Dad has a flight of steps—but we arrive at our destination at the same time.

When I open the door, we're both out of breath. Dad has lost weight since I've last seen him, and even his face looks drawn. I don't think I've ever seen him this thin. I wonder if my face mirrors his shocked expression when he sees me for the first time since my illness began. I step forward and hug him before the embarrassment can reach my face.

"Hi, Dad. It's great to see you. I hope the flight was smooth," I mumble.

"It wasn't too bad. I'm glad it's over though," he wheezes, trying to catch his breath. "I'm going to sit down on the sofa if you don't mind."

We both move awkwardly and slowly over to the sofa. Even sitting down, it takes Dad a while to stop panting. I'm already feeling guilty that he's here.

"Honey, don't worry about me. I'll be fine in a few minutes. I'm here to give you a hand. You look a lot worse than I do," he says, trying to lighten the mood.

Now that sounds like Dad—direct and to the point. I do feel better.

Later, he decides to go food shopping while I take a nap. When he returns, I hear his footsteps, and then the thumping sound of something heavy being set down on the floor. It takes me several minutes to get to my window. I'm just in time to see Dad carrying some heavy boxes up the front steps. My anxiety level starts to climb. All I need is for Dad to have a heart attack while trying to help me.

By the time I make it up the stairs, he's finished unloading the car. He's bought boxes of canned food items and prepackaged meals and has them neatly stacked against the wall. When he turns around, he's wheezing again. His face is red with exertion.

"Well, honey, at least you won't starve to death for a while."

"Dad, I really appreciate this, but please sit down and rest before you fall over." I feel grateful and exasperated at the same time.

He doesn't argue with me, and we shuffle into the living room. It's fortunate that Sofia has two sofas. We each pick one and collapse onto it. Neither of us has the energy to speak for some time.

Eventually, Dad looks at his wristwatch. "When does Sofia get home? It will be nice to see her again."

"Sorry, Dad. Sofia is out of town on business. She says hello." I'm impossibly tired and barely manage to answer. "I think I need to take another nap, if you don't mind."

"No, that sounds like a good idea." He stretches out on his sofa. In no time, we're both fast asleep.

The next day, Dad decides to organize my room so the things I need on a daily basis are easy to get to. I take up position on my bed, leaning against a stack of pillows, and watch Dad study the layout of my room. He's sitting in my desk chair with a thoughtful expression on his face.

"You know, honey. I bet you only have a small number of clothes that you actually wear right now. Am I right?"

"Yeah, you are. You're thinking I can consolidate what I actually wear into one drawer—aren't you?"

"Yep, and if you tell me where those things are, I'll put it all together for you. We can do the same in the bathroom."

"Thanks, Dad. That's really helpful. I should have thought of it myself."

"Don't be too hard on yourself. It took me a long time to think of it for myself. My stuff was all spread out. By the time I got showered and dressed in the morning, I felt like I had hiked five miles to get to everything I needed. You know what they say about necessity"—we both laugh and finish the sentence together—"being the mother of invention."

After our afternoon nap, Dad says, "Honey, I know this may be hard for you to hear, but in your current condition and being unable to work,

I think you should apply for disability. Heaven knows you need it right now."

Just hearing the word makes me shudder. I would never, ever, have imagined myself needing to accept money from the government. I feel like I'm a failure. My shoulders slump a little lower. "Yeah, maybe you're right, but I don't even know where to start."

"Well, I do. I can help you apply. We can get started tomorrow." His tone is gentle. He knows how difficult this is for me. Dad spends the rest of his trip helping me get the right paperwork submitted for disability. It's a complicated, arduous process, and my self-esteem is nonexistent by the time we finish.

On the last day of his visit, Dad has one more thing on his agenda. As per our daily routine, we're back on the living room sofas. "Honey, I'm going to miss you after I go. It's been nice to see you."

"I'm going to miss you too, Dad. You've been a big help."

"I've been thinking, and there's just one thing I'd like you to consider," he says hesitantly.

"What?" I ask with trepidation; it already sounds like it's going to be something I won't want to do.

Dad looks uncomfortable. "I think you should consider going back on your medications."

"There is no way in hell that I'm going back on that Western path of destruction, Dad!" A shiver of revulsion passes through me. "Those drugs were sucking the life out of me faster than this illness ever could. I know there's a holistic way to recover, and I'll find it. I don't want to talk about it," I say harshly, and I instantly regret it.

"Okay, okay. I just thought I'd mention it." Dad sighs and puts his hands up, trying to restore the peace. "If you want to talk about it sometime, we can."

"Thanks, Dad, but it's not going to happen. Please let's drop it." I'm grateful that he doesn't bring it up again.

The next morning, I'm sad as we say our good-byes. His bags are by the door, and we wait in front of the big bay window in the living room for the taxi.

"Dad, coming out here to help me was really great. Thanks a lot. I love you, and now I hope you go back home and take care of yourself."

Dad puts his arm around my shoulder and gives me a light squeeze. "It was worth it. I love you and want you to get better. Please call me anytime. Whatever you need, honey."

"Thanks, Dad."

The taxi pulls up and honks the horn. I put my arms around him, and we hold each other tightly. We let go when the taxi honks again. I'm sad as I watch him carry his luggage down the steps.

He turns around to wave good-bye while the driver loads his bags in the trunk. I smile and wave back. As the taxi drives off, there's a sinking feeling in the pit of my stomach.

SHIKA

*I look into your great brown eyes, where love
and loyal homage shine, and wonder where the
difference lies, between your soul and mine!*
–Josiah G. Holland

A week after Dad leaves, I'm preparing a cup of tea in the kitchen when I hear a loud thump in the den.

Wondering if Shika has knocked something down, I slowly make my way there. To my horror, she is lying on her side, and her whole body is convulsing. I swallow hard to stem the rising panic. I've got to get her to the vet, but how can I possibly get an eighty-pound Rottweiler to the car? I can't lift her; I can barely lift myself. I stroke her head, sending love and healing, while I try to figure out what to do.

After a few minutes, the convulsions slow down and stop. Her eyes focus on me.

"Shika, please listen. I need you to help me. I can't lift you by myself. Please get up and help me get you to the car."

I know she understands, and by some miracle, she struggles to her feet. I grab a coat and slide it under her to help hold as much of her body weight as I can. The tears are pouring down my face as we begin to move. I don't know how we make it to the car, but we do. Fortunately, the vet is only a few miles away.

Dr. Dorsey performs an ultrasound to try to find the problem. She studies the screen intently for a few moments, and when she looks up at me, the expression on her face makes my heart grow cold and my knees weaken. "There is a tumor around Shika's heart that appears to have ruptured. I'm so sorry."

I'm having a nightmare; this can't be real. The tears continue to stream down my face. I feel as if my heart is being torn into tiny pieces. My vision blurs, and I lose all sensation in my body.

"Ann, help Holly to a seat," Dr. Dorsey says to her assistant. Hands grab me and guide me into a chair. A glass of water is placed in my hand.

"Try to take a few sips. It will help," Ann says.

I look at Dr. Dorsey. "What can be done?"

She puts a supportive hand on my shoulder. "I'm so sorry, but there really isn't anything we can do. The tumor is large and part of her heart." I slump lower. "We can drain it and attempt to remove parts, but I can tell you there would be many surgeries—and Shika would suffer greatly. She may live a few more months if we do that, at most. And her quality of life would be poor. It's my recommendation that you let her go."

"Wait. No! This can't be happening." I rub my temples with my free hand. "She was fine. I can't lose her now. It's too much!"

Dr. Dorsey sits down next to me. "I understand how hard this is. I really do. But I can tell you a story about a woman whose Labrador was my patient. Her dog had a heart tumor, like Shika, and it also burst. But this woman didn't want to let go. She had me perform surgery after surgery to try to keep her dog alive. Her dog lived for another few months, but she was in constant pain and agony. If you try to keep her alive, it won't be for her benefit—it will be for yours. Do you want Shika to spend her last days like that?"

"No. I don't." My body shakes, and I'm unable to contain the sobs.

"You can stay with her until the end of the day if you'd like." Dr. Dorsey gives my shoulder a squeeze for support before she leaves the room.

Shika is moved to a pen, and I follow behind the vet's assistant like a lost soul.

After she's settled on a blanket, I sink to my knees and wrap my arms around her. "Oh Shika, how can this be? I love you so much. I want you to stay." I cry into her neck. Shika picks her head up and licks my cheek.

Dr. Dorsey brings me a box of tissues and some more water while I remain in the pen with my arms wrapped around Shika's neck.

After a while, I hear Sofia's voice in the hallway. She had dropped everything at work and raced home when I called her. She rounds the corner and there are tears flowing down her cheeks. She sits down on the other side of Shika, and we spend the rest of the afternoon holding her. We tell her what a good dog she is.

When Dr. Dorsey comes in at the end of the day with a syringe in her hand, I look up at Sofia in panic and see new tears flowing in a steady stream down her face.

"It's best for Shika, mate," she stammers.

I kiss Shika and hold her until she is gone. *What is left for me now?* The days pass ever more slowly. Much of my time is spent on my bed, staring at pictures of Shika with tears pouring down my face. There is a hole in my chest where my heart used to be. Every so often when I look up, I'm convinced that I see her sitting on the floor watching me with her adoring brown eyes.

With Shika gone, the will to battle my illness is also gone. I rarely leave the house. The intensity of all of my symptoms keeps increasing. The stairs are an insurmountable mountain. The throbbing pain and inflammation in my hands and wrists is excruciating. My fingers and especially my thumbs are painful to bend or move. It's agony to get dressed. Putting a shirt on is nearly impossible. I can't wear any shirt that needs to be tucked in; it's simply out of the question. At times, I can't even zipper my pants or tie my shoes. There are days when I'm unable to open the front door because it's too painful to turn the doorknob. The scleroderma causes my tendons and ligaments to shrink and my hands are practically frozen in a partially opened position. I can't close them into a fist or fully open them. In fact, the fascia throughout my body is shrinking and tightening. It's as if I'm wearing a suit of armor that is slowly shrinking. Even the simple act of expanding my chest to breathe is difficult.

The fatigue is worsening, and I'm losing the desire to get out of bed at all. On the days that I do move, by the time I manage to crawl up the stairs and into the kitchen, it's well into the afternoon. I have no appetite and constant nausea; trying to force myself to eat is becoming harder. The food I do eat sits in my stomach for nearly an entire day. My digestive system is no longer moving it through my body. Even water sits in my stomach for many hours.

I've lost nearly forty pounds, and I'm becoming weaker with every day that passes. I'm a walking skeleton. My face is sunken, my muscles are gone, and my limbs are sticks. They're attached to my body only by weakened tendons and ligaments. My joints throb with a lack of supportive tissue to hold things together. I know that my time is running out, but I don't know if I care anymore.

I rarely surface from my basement room. Months of unabated torment have taken their toll. I'm deliriously tired and can't remember the last time I slept longer than ten or fifteen minutes at a stretch.

The summer of 2004 crawls by slowly and agonizingly. In July, Sofia leaves to visit her parents in Australia, and I'm alone in the house. My spirit is fading. There is too little left of me to continue. Anything is preferable to this living hell. Then it comes to me. I glance across the room at my bookcase. I know that buried behind and under a pile of books on the bottom shelf is a bag. In that bag is a small case that holds a solution—my Glock 9mm handgun and a box of bullets.

CHAPTER FORTY ONE

ON THE RISE

When the heart is enlivened again, it feels like the sun coming out after a week of rainy days. There is hope in the heart that chases the clouds away. Hope is a higher heart frequency, and as you begin to re-connect with your heart, hope is waiting to show you new possibilities and arrest the downward spiral of grief and loneliness. Listening to the still small voice in your heart will make hope into a reality.
–Sara Paddison

I have fallen into the abyss. It is an icy darkness that swallows all warmth and dims my soul until there is nothing left but a tiny sputtering spark. I reach out for something to hold onto, anything to guide my way. Everywhere I reach, I touch only walls of pain. I cling to them anyway; they are all I have. Exhaustion and despair are my bedfellows. Eternity passes. Why hold on any longer? Who will catch me if I let go? Does it matter? No. Death is coming, the ultimate solution. My spirit is but a wisp connected to my body by a fragile thought. Why do I wait? A long-forgotten belief crawls from the farthest recesses of my mind. I feel the pressure as it pushes against the darkness. A murky mass of grayness stands out in the black void and moves toward me. Almost upon me, it becomes the dimmest of lights. I stretch out my hand to touch it, and the memory releases its secret. I must be the one to ask for help, to let go and trust. A cry for help escapes my lips as I release my grip and let myself fall. I am empty of all thoughts and desires. A hand of light burns through the darkness and takes hold of mine. I feel myself rising and see my guides materialize before my eyes. I reconnect to the Oneness as the light of hope shines onto me from above. It beckons me upwards. I rise to meet it.

It's only been a little more than three months since I almost took my own life. I can still remember with absolute, chilling clarity what it felt like to lose all hope and to want to die because living was unbearable. And then at the lowest point in my life when all else had failed, I gave up. I let go of my ego, let go of my struggle, and called out for help from the universe—something I had forgotten to do until it was almost too late.

Exploring my spirituality and metaphysical abilities was what had brought me closer to myself and my true path. I had disconnected from that part of myself after Mom died, and it took a near-death-experience to put me back on track. Reconnecting with my guides saved my life and set in motion a series of miracles that brought me hope. My continued existence is a miracle, and I'm grateful for my life. It doesn't matter where I am; I know that anything is possible. If I allow myself to receive guidance and listen to my heart, I'll find the answers I seek.

I started juicing the day after I flew back from my visit with Dr. Mercola in Chicago. After a few short days, I could wake up before ten in the morning. I hadn't been able to do that in years. The fact that any change could happen that fast was mindboggling. After several weeks passed, the pain and throbbing in my hands was noticeably reduced. The amount of time I needed to spend in my healing meditations to silence the pain decreased dramatically. I actually had enough energy to stay awake an entire day. When I ventured outside to run an errand or go shopping for my juicing ingredients, I didn't need to collapse in a near-coma afterward. With every day that passed, I could feel the life slowly returning to my body.

As soon as I was able to, I took the time to sort through all my body products. The harmful chemicals listed on the labels were horrifying. The same deodorant I'd been using for more than twenty years contained aluminum. Since my eye-opening visit to Dr. Mercola, I learned that symptoms of aluminum toxicity included memory loss, learning difficulty, loss of coordination, disorientation, mental confusion, colic, heartburn, flatulence, and headaches.[1] My shampoo had so many chemicals in it that I was surprised there was room left on the label for the product name. I recognized sodium lauryl sulfate, which is the active ingredient in garage floor cleaners and engine degreasers.[2] There was a chemical called methylisothiazoline, or MIT, which was found by the National Institute for Health to cause neurological damage.[3] I saw DEA, or diethanolaminehis, a known carcinogen, on many labels. The toxic ingredient story was repeated with every item in my bathroom cabinet, ad nauseam. I dumped them all peremptorily into the trash. I had been soaking in toxic chemicals for decades. Was it any wonder my body had become a waste dump?

I also learned that manufacturers can put practically any chemical they want into shampoos—even if it's a hazardous chemical listed in the Registry of Toxic Effects of Chemical Substances database (known as RTECS) or is considered a toxic waste chemical by the EPA. The FDA allows all sorts of chemicals to be used in these products, including chemicals that are known carcinogens and that contribute to liver failure and nervous system disorders.[3] I quickly replaced my cosmetics, body products, and cleaning supplies with natural and organic (where possible) substitutes. I knew it was an important step and felt immeasurably cleaner and a lot less toxic afterward.

When I celebrated the two-month anniversary of my juicing and protein shake program, the improvements I'd made in that short amount of time simply defied the imagination. My pain level had dropped by at least a third. My mornings were nothing short of amazing. I reveled in the newfound ability to open my eyes easily, and tickle me pink with a feather because I could also get out of bed by nine—and I didn't mean crawl out of bed! I could roll over without wincing and stand up without pulling myself up with the chair. Next on the daily agenda was my morning shower, which actually was a morning shower since it could be completed before noon. Afterward, it was absolutely blissful that I no longer needed to collapse and recover.

And, right now after three months, I wake up in the morning with gratitude in my heart. My day begins with my favorite healing meditation. The one that J.D. taught me where I become friends with the parts of me that are in pain. My hands have also made astonishing progress. My fingers aren't as inflamed and swollen, and it's easier to dress. I'm able to proudly, albeit slowly and carefully, tuck my shirt in. I've also been working hard on stretching, and I can raise my arms above my shoulders. At least for a short while anyway, but every day, they go a little higher. Each success lightens my burden and my thoughts. Speaking of my thoughts, they are sharper and more focused. It's as if my brain is firing on eight cylinders instead of two. My physical body is still a weak apparition of my former self, but I'm making progress. Hope isn't a distant dream any longer and grows more tangible every day. I want to do everything I can to keep this positive flow going.

One day I have a strong desire to open a box in the corner of my room, which I haven't opened since my move. It contains my extensive collection of crystals and the personal power stones I've found and kept over the years. It's a veritable treasure trove of energetic enhancers and healing tools. My excitement grows with every piece I unwrap and set in front of me. Each of my stones has its own energetic healing properties. In the past, I was often drawn to use a specific crystal for periods of time. I would carry it around in my pocket until I felt I no longer needed its presence. One of my favorite activities was to arrange them in intuitive geometric patterns. Each type of crystal vibrates at a unique frequency and has specific healing properties. I would choose the stones that were appropriate for whatever issue I wanted to work on and set them up in a pattern around me to enhance my meditations. It's perfect that they should reappear now to strengthen and support my recovery.

Sorting through them brings a feeling of serenity and a desire to meditate. My anticipation grows as my gems practically arrange themselves around me. An outer ring of clear quartz crystals encircles me, and I use selenite to clear the space and each crystal I select. My completed layout contains crystals aligned with the energy of each chakra, creating a powerful healing circle. After connecting with the source above and the earth below, I clear my chakras, followed by visualizing a healing pink energy that travels everywhere in my body. It's not long before the morning pain and stiffness are washed away. Before I end my morning ritual, I ask a specific question of my guides. It's a request for the next best step along my healing journey.

J.D., my faithful leather-clad protector, appears almost as soon as the question is formed in my mind. He's quietly standing in front of the image of me that I project into my mind's eye. He lifts both arms out to his sides; at the same time, his leather outfit transforms into a suit of armor. I immediately comprehend what he means and couldn't agree more. I need to work on loosening my fascia. It's the connective network of tissue that runs throughout our bodies and surrounds all muscles, groups of muscles, blood vessels, and nerves. One consequence of the scleroderma is that my body's fascia has contracted and hardened to the point where it feels exactly like I'm wearing a suit of armor. In fact, the fascia around my ribs has shrunk to the point where it's hard for me to breathe. The next question that forms in my mind is simple: *How do I work on this?*

In answer, J.D. bends over and picks something up from a table that has appeared out of nowhere. It's a magazine. He opens it and begins thumbing through the pages. When he finds what he's looking for, he points at me. I get it. When I thank him for his guidance, he bows low—no longer wearing his armor.

It's obvious to me that J.D. is telling me to look in the new age magazines that I recently picked up at Whole Foods. I'm full of curiosity. The pages almost turn themselves. I scan them slowly, not quite sure what I'm looking for. Suddenly, my fingers stop turning and my attention is riveted on the ad in the middle of the page. It's one for Rolfing. I'm speechless; I know this is the perfect answer. If there is any modality that has a chance of cracking my armor, it would be Rolfing. If only my friends from MIT could see me now. Smiling to myself, I wonder what they'd think of my scientific method.

I'm encouraged when Gregg, the Rolfing practitioner listed in the ad, answers my call right away. Although I've never had Rolfing work done before, I'm not under any illusions. I know it's going to be painful. In order to remove my armor, Gregg is going to have to rip through the hardened fascia that encompasses my entire body. I'm used to pain, but I'm extremely nervous on my first visit. Gregg is a friendly young man with bright red hair and has a soft kind manner about him. By the time he's finished his initial assessment of me, I trust his instincts.

The first session involves Rolfing my back. As it turns out, I wish I had thought to bring a bullet to bite on. Gregg uses a device that resembles a thimble. With it, he digs deeply into my back muscles and then drags it in the direction of the fascia. It feels like a red-hot poker is searing into me, but I'm determined to get through this first session. He's apologetic as he works, and the compassionate tone in his voice helps me a lot. As soon as I stand up, I'm glad I did suffer through. Although my back feels like it's been tossed through a tree shredder, it's already easier to breathe. I'm convinced. I thank Gregg profusely and schedule the next appointment.

Over the next couple of months, I undergo a full series of Rolfing sessions that covers my entire body. Each time, it feels as if I am being sliced into pieces with a machete, one excruciating cut after another. Out of all the sessions, the one in which Gregg works on my hands and feet is the world-record-holder as the most painful. While he's working on my feet, it's the only time that I ask him to stop and allow me time to recover. I understand now why striking the bottom of the feet is used as a method of torture. After he finishes, I wonder whether I'll be able to walk when it's time to get off of the table. Right now though, he's about to Rolf my hands.

My whole body has broken out in a cold sweat, and Gregg asks if I want to postpone my hands for another session. I can't bear the thought of waiting another week, and I tell him to go ahead. Digging into the fascia of my hands is so excruciating that my vision dims—and I nearly pass out. When he works on my thumbs, I cry out in pain. Gregg wants to stop for the day, but I beg him to continue. I want it over and done with. When I finally do stand, my feet are thoroughly tenderized, but I can wiggle my toes separately from each other, and my ankles bend. And that's not even the best part. The best part is that I can almost close my hands.

In the days and weeks that follow, my suit of armor seems to melt away. My chest is freed from bondage, and I can breathe more deeply than since this whole thing began. Every day, I spend many hours gently stretching my body. Afterward, I dig into my hands and feet using an actual thimble to continue the work that Gregg has started.

One morning in the shower, I'm flexing my fingers and gently trying to squeeze them into a fist. My knees almost give way when my fingers close all the way. Miraculously, I'm staring at a completely and perfectly formed fist. My shouts of joy can probably be heard a block away. It's sheer pleasure to pump my tightly formed fist in the air in a raucous salute of gratitude to the universe.

My days are filled from morning until night with the task of healing. Every morning, I wake up and perform a healing meditation using my crystals to aid me. After my healing, I spend time visualizing myself as completely well. I see myself practicing martial arts, lifting in the gym, and engaging in many other activities. Every day it's getting easier to make these visualizations clearer and stronger.

Afterward, it's on to the kitchen and my beloved juicer. Once there, I make a protein shake and my priceless "juice of life." It's heavenly to feel the life energy pouring into me with each deliciously nutritious swallow. My body craves it as soon as I wake up, and it's fascinating to feel how much I'm receiving from it. Shortly after I drink a juice, a lasting energy arrives that carries me through the day. I'm also aware of a noticeable reduction in my pain and inflammation. I'm drinking more fruits and vegetables in one sitting than most people probably eat in a month. All that healing power and nutrition is completely bioavailable to my body. In juiced form, absorption of nutrition actually begins in my mouth and continues through my entire digestive tract.

Now that my fingers are flexible enough to open and close into a fist, they're dexterous enough to use acupuncture needles. It's yet another healing tool that I'm supremely grateful to have access to again. While it's an incredible boon to speed my recovery, it's always more powerful to have someone else perform the healing treatment.

I sense the universe and my guides at work when Laura, an especially gifted classmate from my acupuncture college, happens to call me up out of the blue to say hello. After hearing my story, she insists that I come to her for treatments. I'm touched by her caring and concern and gratefully surrender some of the healing work to a woman I completely trust.

In order to keep my acupuncture license current, I must take some CEUs, or continuing education units, soon. Although I've made a lot of progress, I'm concerned that I'm not up to the rigors of attending a class. The day after I start to think about it, a flyer arrives in the mail. It contains a list of upcoming CEU classes, and one of them catches my eye. The class focuses on herbs for weak and debilitated patients. The herbs commonly used for pain and inflammation and building healthy tissue are hard on the stomach. Except for slippery elm powder to protect my stomach, I haven't been taking any herbs for a while. However, with all the progress I've been making, this may be the right time to add them back into my healing program. I sign up without another moment's hesitation.

On the day of the class, I'm worried about whether my energy will last the entire time. I carefully pack up my "juice of life" and a hearty protein shake to get me through the day. As it turns out, my energy isn't the overriding issue during class. With all the weight I've lost, one item that I no longer have is a butt. In the past, I might have thought that that would be a good thing. Actually, not having a *gluteus maximus* is a big problem. Without the fat and muscle tissue to form a butt, there is nothing to protect the tailbone. This discovery has taught me to be extremely careful when sitting down. Even with precautions, my tailbone remains constantly bruised. Right now it's speaking loudly and painfully to me about the hardness of the cement block I'm sitting on, which outrageously insists upon calling itself a chair.

I'm relieved that the instructor, a Dr. Nguyen, is not only a fountain of herbal knowledge, but he is also a delightfully entertaining teacher. It's a challenge to keep my left hand writing fast enough to catch all of the droplets of herbal wisdom that fall from his lips. After an entire day of copious note-taking, my hand is throbbing, and I'm having trouble gripping my pen. However, I'm quite proud that I didn't miss a single pearl of wisdom. Sitting in one position all day has been hard on me. There's nothing I can do to disguise the stiffness in my body as I pack my bag before leaving.

Dr. Nguyen remains at the front of the class room where he's been chatting with a couple of students. When our eyes meet, he smiles and waves me over. I'm self-conscious about my slow, stiff shuffle to the front of the room. Thankfully, the other students leave before I get there. Dr. Nguyen gestures for me to sit down at a desk while he grabs a chair and sits on the other side of it. I introduce myself and let him know how much I enjoyed his class.

"Thank you. I'm glad you enjoyed it." He smiles across the desk at me. "Would you mind if I take your pulses?"

I nod and place my hands on the desk. He gently touches my wrists and looks down, concentrating on what he is feeling through his fingertips. After a few moments he looks up at me.

"I'm so sorry, my dear. You're in a great deal of pain, aren't you?"

His words are unexpected, and the lump in my throat keeps me from speaking, but I manage to nod my head. "Please tell me your story. I'm curious about what happened to you."

As I replay my tale, I can almost see the wheels turning in his mind.

"If you're interested, I believe I can help you put together a formula that will be helpful in your healing process, especially the pain and inflammation."

"Are you kidding? That would be fantastic!" I continue with a note of caution. "In the early phase of my illness, I was taking a lot of herbs, but when my stomach started to feel ulcerous, I had to stop using them."

"With the delicate condition of your digestive system, I can understand why you stopped. They are hard on the stomach. But I believe, if we start slowly and move carefully, we can begin adding them back into your daily program. You're ready for the next step," he says confidently.

I'm so grateful, and I thank him profusely.

Dr. Nguyen patiently runs through his herbal recommendations and his theories behind their conception. By the time we're finished, I feel as if I've been blessed with another mini herbal class—and all for my benefit. As I get up to leave, I'm thrilled when he hands me his card with his e-mail address and asks me to keep him posted on my progress.

I waste no time in getting started with his herbal recommendations. And, wondrously, if I mix the herbs into my protein shakes, it seems that my stomach can tolerate them. As I gradually incorporate the herbs into my daily nutrition program, there is a noticeable acceleration of my physical healing. At the end of every day, I make a point of noting my accomplishments as the tiny miracles they truly are. I walk the path of wellness.

---

1. "Heavy Metal Toxicity." Life Extension. 17 Jan. 2008
   http://www.lef.org/protocols/prtcl-156a.shtml#alum2
2. Sodium Lauryl Sulfate: http://www.naturalnews.com/025515_chemicals_
   toxic_products.html#ixzz1aboJwOhE
3. "Popular shampoos contain toxic chemicals linked to nerve damage.",
   by Mike Adams, 1/11/2005, Editor of NaturalNews.com http://www.
   naturalnews.com/003210.html#ixzz1abnqA7sS

CHAPTER FORTY TWO
FEEL THE QI

*In everyone's life, at some time, our inner fire goes
out. It is then burst into flame by an encounter with
another human being. We should all be thankful
for those people who rekindle the inner spirit.*
–Albert Schweitzer

"Mrs. Reese, I just need you to complete a few more forms." The young woman behind the reception desk called out to Mom, who was sitting beside me in the waiting room.

"Everything will be all right, honey. You'll see." She reached for my hand and gave it a supportive squeeze before getting up and heading over to the check-in nurse. I tried to muster a reassuring smile for her, knowing full well she could see right through it.

I briefly shut my eyes to eclipse the glaring white walls while trying to ignore my growing sense of panic and the uncomfortably cold, hard, plastic seat pressing against my butt.

"Excuse me. Are you Holly?"

My eyes snap open to the sound of my name being called by a different nurse in the doorway. The newcomer was quite tall, and her smile lit up the room when I nodded.

"Wonderful. I'm Nurse Beckett, and I'm here to take you back to the changing room so we can get started." She reached her hand toward me. "Would you be so kind as to come with me, young lady?"

I rose resolutely to accompany her. Mom turned around from the pile of forms in front of her and rushed over to give me a hug. "You'll be fine, honey. I'll be right out here the whole time."

"I'll have your daughter back to you in no time, Mrs. Reese. We'll take good care of her." Nurse Beckett patted my shoulder and led me back to the changing room.

My anxiety escalated as I slipped on the blue hospital gown with the gaping hole in back. What if they made the incision too deep and damaged my tendons? What if they severed my Achilles' heel? It could be a career-ending injury. I couldn't bear that—not after I'd come so far! My sixteen-year-old mind worked itself into a tizzy over preposterously dark scenarios. In reality, the benign, fleshy lump that had materialized on the arch of my foot was nowhere near my Achilles' heel. But martial arts meant everything to me, and I couldn't imagine my life without it.

After I finished changing, Nurse Beckett led me into a small waiting room with several cushioned chairs and a TV. I plopped down on one of the chairs and pulled my legs up onto the seat. My frenzied heart was beating so fast I thought it might crack a rib. I was terrified that something might go wrong and I might not be able to use my foot again properly. Nurse Beckett leaned down next to me and felt the pulse at my wrist. Her eyes softened with sympathy.

"There's no need to be frightened. This will all be over before you know it." She patted my arm gently. "I'll be right back with some pills to help you calm down." She smiled one last time before she turned and headed out of the door.

As soon as she said the word "pills," it set me to thinking. As a martial artist, I had been trained to use my thoughts to center my qi in preparation for sparring. It had a calming and grounding effect. I decided I could use that technique now. I directed my attention inward until I became aware of and then merged into one with my pounding heart. The qi was frenetic, but I began to calm it down. I invited it to gently follow my focus down to my navel, the root of power called the dan tian, in order to reside there in safety.

As I continued the centering process, I could feel a subtle electric current of motion draining from my heart down to my dan tian. My heart rate slowed, and I felt calm, relaxed, and peaceful. The feeling increased after taking a few more extremely deep breaths. I visualized my heart pumping slowly in no hurry at all; everything was fine.

When Nurse Beckett returned, she was carrying a paper cup with some pills in it and a glass of water. "Well, you look different." She paused when she saw the relaxed smile on my face. "Did someone else come in and give you something to relax you already?"

I glanced up at her perfect white uniform, admiring its complete lack of wrinkles. Even her white nurse's cap was precisely situated on top of her head with not a single stray hair escaping from her bun. I felt great.

"No. No one's been in here, since you left."

Her expression changed to one of confusion, and she leaned down again to take my pulse. "This is extraordinary," she exclaimed after she counted my heart rate. "Before I left, your pulse was over a hundred. And now it's down to sixty. What did you do?"

"I used my qi to slow my heart down and relax." My smile became even broader than before.

"I'm not sure what that means, but that is quite a handy trick you've got there." She straightened and shook her head in amazement. "I guess you won't need these," she said, flashing me the pills in her right palm. "Nice job."

She handed me the glass of water but left the room, taking the pills with her.

It's been eight months since I began my journey back to the world of the living. I'm feeling a wonderful sense of accomplishment. I've already completed my morning meditation, light stretching, and a batch of my "juice of life." Today, I'm feeling very well and I want to be around people. I decide to take a book and hang out at a local café. It turns out to be a good decision.

The café is filled with sunlight and bustling with activity. I settle in a chair by a window. The sunlight streaming through it is warm and pleasant. I close my eyes for a moment, deliciously aware of the warmth penetrating into my body. For a long time, I'm content to simply sip on my cup of chamomile tea and watch the people come and go. The café is packed with local yuppies grabbing brunch and buzzing with conversation.

What captivates my attention most is watching how people move. I'm mindful of how much I used to take for granted. Observing simple tasks like digging change out of a pocket, typing on a keyboard, or buttoning up a sweater seem like minor miracles to me. I'm spellbound when an athletic young woman struts into the café in tight black biker's shorts and a fluorescent, green-striped racing top. It's quite an eye-catching outfit and compliments her toned physique. She plucks a banana from the fruit basket on the counter and sets it down in front of herself while she orders a double espresso with foam. She's carrying her helmet in her left hand and pays with her right. It's fascinating to see the dexterity in her fingers as she deftly unzips her waist pouch, extracts a wallet, and flips out a few bills onto the counter.

I look down at my own hand cradling a full mug of tea. I'm quite pleased with my humble achievement. It wasn't so long ago that my scleroderma-hardened hands couldn't even turn a doorknob, let alone perform this minor miracle of holding a mug. Without the full use of my hands, I had been a prisoner confined to my own personal hell. I had taken my miracle-working hands for granted—but never again. I vow to appreciate all the simple, everyday tasks I am once again able to complete.

My gaze returns to the biker woman. As she picks up her espresso in her right hand, she accidentally bumps the banana, which was resting precariously on the edge of the counter. What happens next can only be described as a moment of pure Zen. In one fluid, seemingly unhurried motion, the woman lifts up her right foot and deftly catches the falling banana. She remains perfectly balanced, with the banana on her right foot, an espresso in her right hand, and her helmet still clutched in her left hand. I hold my breath in anticipation. The finale is well worth the wait. The young woman flips the banana into the air with her still raised foot and neatly catches it in her helmet. I notice with rapt admiration and just a smidgen of envy that she doesn't spill a single drop of espresso. I want to jump up and applaud this stupendous feat, but incredibly, no one else in the café seems to have noticed. The counterperson had already turned away, and everyone else has their attention elsewhere. I catch the woman's eye as she heads outside and raise my mug in salute. She smiles and winks back at me. I settle back in my chair to reflect.

She had caught the banana by pulling her foot up into a gracefully executed crane stance while maintaining perfect balance. In many martial arts styles, the crane is used as either a defensive blocking technique or as a transitional move into an offensive strike. This athletic woman had moved instinctively and spontaneously and, quite likely, without a conscious intention of performing a martial arts move. It was simply a natural expression of someone in touch with her own qi.

I'm reminded of my black belt test. At that time, I was hyper-aware of and tuned into the qi flowing in my body. It was like being connected to the electrical current running through me that propelled my every move. And it responded instantaneously to whatever demands I placed upon it without the need for conscious thought. If my mind could conceive it, my body could do it. By controlling my qi, I learned to do things like slow my heart rate, enhance my senses, regulate perspiration, or send it out to magnify the power of my strikes or blocks. I even learned to radiate it from my body and use it as a kind of proximity detector. I could sense people or objects around me without needing to see them—an essential skill for the martial artist in combat, but also, quite useful in everyday life. It's as if I had an extra sense beyond the normal five senses, and losing that connection has been tantamount to losing a limb. *How I long to feel that way again; I need to feel that way again.*

I can sense the tiniest trickle of the river of qi that used to course through me. My vitality has been drained to the extent that I feel like a walking ghost of my former self, fragile and breakable. I'm convinced I'm on the right track with my juicing and nutrition program, meditations, acupuncture, herbs, and stretching. I've come quite far in an incredibly short period of time. My chronic fatigue is practically gone. I have energy to stay up an entire day, although I tire easily. Another major milestone is that the fibromyalgia has subsided to the tiniest of tingling sensations; the searing flames of white-hot pain have, thankfully, been snuffed out. I know I'm ready to take the next step in rebuilding my physical body. The smiling face of my current Sifu, Doug Jones, flashes in my mind. The studio is just down the street. The time has come for me to return.

The Wun Hop Kuen Do studio is the middle commercial unit in a single-story concrete building on MacArthur Boulevard in Oakland. I've got nervous jitters as soon as my hand touches the metal handle on the glass door. It seems like it's been forever and a day since I've been here. Meanwhile, I've been run through the coffee grinder more than once. I need to do this for me. I glance up at the familiar quote painted in black script letters above the door: *For those who say it can't be done, step aside for those who are doing it.* Just the right enticement—I push open the door and step inside.

I can detect a slight hint of sweat that hasn't been completely eradicated by the lemon-scented air freshener. For me, the smell of a hard workout is energizing. My eyes latch onto the familiar surroundings. There is still a chest-high wooden wall that separates the entry from the training floor, and it gives me a chance to look around without being noticed. The main walls are still white with blue trim, but they're fresh as if Sifu has had them repainted in the last year. I'm pleased he's finally had the chance to get that done; it had been on his to-do list for quite a while.

I sneak a glance over the divider. Sifu Doug is teaching his teen class, and I'm a little bummed. I'd been hoping to catch him between lessons. I don't want to be seen by anyone who knew me from when I was in my prime. He must have added an extra class since I was here last. That's certainly a good sign for the school, but I wonder if I should try to come back later. I'm self-conscious enough as it is; I don't think I could handle being stared at or judged. My muscles are still quite atrophied, and I feel so inadequate and ashamed. With my tail between my legs, I turn around to slink away quietly—only to be admonished once more by the quote above the door. No, wait… I can do this. I have to do this. The familiar blue sofa is still in the far corner of the entryway. It's the perfect place to sit and gather myself before I make my presence known.

I listen to the students yelling and kicking and imagine I'm one of them. I used to be one of them. I'm filled with envy as I hear them practice. The spirit of martial arts defined who I was, and I had been so confident in myself and my abilities. *But now who am I? My essence is so weak. Could I ever get it back? Maybe I'm simply deluding myself by coming here? Here I am, wanting to dive back into class leaping and kicking, while simply walking a few blocks remains a major accomplishment. Who am I kidding?* Sifu's shouts of encouragement to his class disrupt my negative thoughts. *It's too late to turn back now.* I swallow my fear, pushing it down and into the ground, and stand up slowly.

Sifu is the first one I lay my eyes on. He's standing underneath another one of my favorite quotes: "A journey of a thousand miles begins with but a single step." *All right then, let me take that step.*

When Sifu spies me, his face lights up like a beacon in the fog. His energy reaches out and grabs hold of me. I have no choice but to stay. I head deliberately over to the bench and take a seat. I take my time, trying hard to conceal the effort it takes, so as not to attract attention. I don't want to be labeled or made an object of pity. Not here of all places! Sifu nods at me after I'm seated and then turns back to his students. Discreetly, I scan the faces in the room. I'm relieved that I don't see anyone I recognize. There's no one who would stare or pity me. The tension in my body gradually releases, which allows me to focus my attention on watching the rest of the lesson.

Sifu Doug has his students doing kicking drills from one end of the training floor to the other. By the time they complete one roundtrip across the mat, he has a frown of dissatisfaction on his face. I know what he's seeing, and it doesn't surprise me when he interrupts the exercise.

"Wait, hold up!" he shouts.

All of the young students, I count fifteen, stop what they're doing and give him their full attention.

"I see one thing that I need to correct right now. You all are moving like a herd of elephants. When you step forward, kick, and then step down, like this." He smoothly demonstrates the sliding side kick, gliding forward without a sound. "I don't want to hear a thing."

One lanky teenage boy with a big question mark imprinted on his forehead starts to raise his hand. Sifu catches the question before it's asked and faces the young man. "It's okay, Greg. It's not difficult, but it does take practice. Just remember to keep your weight centered at all times. Don't send your energy into the floor by bringing your foot down hard. Learn to step lightly."

Sifu's wiry, compact frame is grace in motion as he repeatedly fires off silent sidekicks while advancing across the floor. I can't help thinking of Kwai Chang Cain, my childhood hero. One of his challenges had been to learn how to walk upon rice paper without leaving a trace. Sifu whirls around when he reaches the other side of the mat and surveys his students with a raised eyebrow. "Make sense?" he asks.

"Yes, sir!" the students sound out in unison.

"Okay, try it again." Sifu nods in satisfaction and gestures for the class to continue the exercise.

As they work their way across the mat, he glides among them, cheering them on. The effect of the encouragement is to draw out the best effort from each student. This time, they're all much improved. Their combined enthusiasm and motivation is almost palpable. The energy of the studio courses through my veins, and I feel like I've come home. I'm bursting at the seams to join them on the mat and to feel myself gliding once again across a martial arts training floor.

Once the class is over and the students have been dismissed, Sifu jogs over to me. I stare up at him, feeling exposed and dreadfully vulnerable. It's the first time he's seen me since the illness. The last time I saw him, he was wishing me good luck for the police academy. Then my injured shoulder kept me away. And, after that, all hell broke loose.

Now here I am out of the blue. I half-expected him not to recognize me; I'd make a scarecrow look like a porker. I steel myself as a wide range of expressions flit across Sifu's face: first surprise, then sadness, followed by compassion, and finally acceptance and understanding. He gently pulls me up and sweeps me into a gentle embrace, being careful not to crush anything that I'm going to need in the near future.

"Holly, we've all missed you terribly—me especially." He gives me an extra hug, and then we sit down together. "What's happened to you? How can I help? Whatever you need, consider it done."

My fears melt away at the sound of his voice.

Sifu and I were close from the moment we first met. It was easy. It was as if our kindred souls recognized each other from another life. Both of us share a well-developed connection to our internal qi, which strengthens our common bond. Over the years, he had become like a second brother to me.

I feel foolish for allowing my stubborn pride to keep me away from my second home for so long. He listens intently while I relate the events of my life since I last saw him. When I'm finished, I stiffly remove my windbreaker and self-consciously raise my atrophied right arm to show him what I've got to work with.

Sifu reaches up and gently takes my hands in his. "I'm proud of how far you've come already." I swallow hard to hold back the tears that are threatening to roll. "There's a ways to go, but I've no doubt that you'll be back in action faster than you think." He pats my arm gently. "And now that you're here, we'll get the rest of the way there together."

Sifu's acceptance and the realization that I don't have to do this all alone is an overwhelming relief. I lean my head on his shoulder in gratitude and let out a long sigh. A heavy weight is lifted from my tired shoulders. He asks me to wait around until the few remaining dawdlers have left the studio. I'm happy to stay and absorb the invigorating martial arts atmosphere. After Sifu locks the door, he walks past me onto the training floor.

He spins around to face me. "Okay, we need to build your qi and get it moving again at the same time." He pumps his fist in the air for emphasis, and then pauses to consider. "That's it!" he says abruptly, snapping his fingers. "Okay, I want to show you a form that I think will help you a lot. It's called 'Floating Leaf.'" There's a self-satisfied smile on his face as he moves to the center of the training mat.

I'm intrigued as soon as I hear the name of the form. I like the sound of it. A snapshot of me in perfect martial arts condition flashes in my head. I want it back. My focus shifts back to Sifu as he salutes toward the front of the room then begins the form. The style is slow and elegant, similar to a Tai Chi form. It's designed to gently build qi, strengthen the core, and create a connection between balance and flowing power. Sifu's movements are silky smooth with footwork that is light and whisper silent.

For the second time today, I'm witnessing Zen in motion. I can easily imagine him as the "floating leaf" being gently blown all around the room. Yet, beneath the perfect calm on the surface, I can sense his powerful qi coursing through every technique. Sifu is a leaf that would hit you like a hammer if he was blown into you.

"That was beautiful, Sifu. It's perfect! I want to get started now."

"I thought you might." His blindingly white smile is followed by a quick bow. "Let's not waste any more time. Come on out here, and we'll get started."

I'm hopeful as I step out onto the training floor. Sifu teaches me the first few moves. Even though I'm stiff and awkward, it feels exquisite to move my body again. There is a familiar stirring within me, and for a few consecutive moves, I can sense a connection to my inner source, my qi. As I continue to move, my awareness expands to touch the flow of energy in the universe. I'm one with the infinite and no longer bound to just my limited physical form. I'm aware of my body—and of my feet touching the floor—yet, I'm also everywhere at the same time.

I perform a short series of movements, almost without thought, as pure energy in motion. It lasts only a few seconds, but they are seconds spent existing purely in the divine. I try to hang onto that fleeting accomplishment even though I'm exhausted in just a few short minutes. I stop where I am, panting for breath. *I'm so excited! This is it! It's exactly what I needed for my next step.*

"That was good work, but I think you're done for today." Sifu is by my side in a flash to help me back over to the bench. "Don't worry; you'll be back in no time." He places a reassuring hand on my shoulder.

"Thanks, Sifu. I'm starting to think I can do this." I catch myself grinning without effort, and it feels good.

"Of course you can. I have no doubt." His eyes reflect the utmost confidence in me.

I had walked into the Wun Hop Kuen Do studio embarrassed and vulnerable, ready to bolt out the door. I would have missed a golden opportunity to leap forward. Just in time, Sifu was there without judgment to reel me back into the martial arts fold—right where I belong.

I step through the doorway and out into the sunshine, feeling like I'm more than just the hollowed out survivor of a chronic disease. When I look in the mirror, I begin to catch glimpses of someone I recognize—someone I thought I had lost. I see me.

CHAPTER FORTY THREE

I CAN DO IT

Too often we underestimate the power of a touch,
a smile, a kind word, a listening ear, an honest
compliment, or the smallest act of caring, all of
which have the potential to turn a life around.
–Leo Buscaglia

My attention is riveted on the intriguing subject line of the e-mail in my inbox. It reads: "Hay House Presents—The I Can Do It Conference!"

Whoa! I wonder what it's all about. Anything that Hay House, the top self-help publisher in the world, is putting together at least deserves a quick read. I'm hooked on the very first line: "The Mind, Body, and Soul Retreat. This is it—the conference you've been waiting for!" These last three years, I've been on a non-stop physical, emotional, and spiritual roller coaster; I desperately need an emotional respite from it all.

The rest of the e-mail goes on to describe a three-day event filled with lectures and workshops given by a select host of the most renowned motivational, spiritual, and transformational speakers and healers out there. In fact, Louise Hay is one of the keynote speakers! She is the one who created Hay House, one of the most powerful media organizations promoting alternative medicine in the world. Just seeing her speak, even if there was nothing else, would be worth the trip. But that's not all!

As I scroll down through the list of speakers, it's a who's who of inspiration—Wayne Dyer, Caroline Myss, Christiane Northrup, Sylvia Browne, Jerry and Esther Hicks, and then... Doreen Virtue's name pops out at me. I can't believe it! She's my favorite metaphysical author, and she's holding a special day-long workshop introducing her Angel Therapy methods at the conference. Sign me up!

My ever-growing self-help library contains a number of Doreen's works. In fact, right now the extremely worn and dog-eared copy of my favorite one, *The Lightworker's Way*, is next to my bed. I read it after I quit my programming job and drove across country with Shika on the walkabout to find my passion. It helped me understand myself and shed light on the newly recognized metaphysical aspects of my life. I've lost count of the number of times I've thumbed through it to reread various inspirational passages. There's no doubt about it; I have to go to the conference.

The fact that it's being held at the Las Vegas Convention Center gives me slight pause. But I'm so certain about going to this event that even the formidable logistics of getting to and staying in the "City of Smoky Casinos" is not enough of a deterrent to stop me. It will be the first time in a year that I've been without my "juice of life" every day, but I'm confident that I can make it for four days.

To see me through, I'm bringing my protein powder, herbs, and a wonderful green veggie and fruit powder that I can mix into nutritious liquid meals. The prospect of an emotional and spiritual long weekend supplies the motivation necessary to make my trip happen. It will be the first time I've flown since my visit to Dr. Mercola almost a year ago. So much has changed since then. I've come so far.

The taxi drops me off curbside amid the chaotic jumble of cars dispatching people into the airport terminal. I carefully navigate the obstacle course of suitcases and their harried owners. Once I step through the automatic doors, it's even more of a madhouse. The throngs of people seem to writhe around me like a snake tightening its coils around a prey. This won't do. Before I get into the security line, I need to calm down and appreciate this moment.

The last time I had been in an airport was to catch the flight to Chicago to see Dr. Mercola. It had been a grueling ordeal, and I was barely hanging on. Now look at me. This time, I'm walking on my own, sans wheelchair, and I'm even carrying a lightweight backpack with my most indispensable herbs inside. Every step I take is a victory. I'm hyper-aware of everyone around me so that I don't get run over, but at the same time, I'm thrilled to be on this amazing adventure.

Relishing my newfound ability to participate in the hustle and bustle of the "normal" world, I make every effort to camouflage my physical challenges. An outside observer would see me as a person, simply strolling along, not in any obvious hurry to get anywhere. Several times, I need to stop and let my muscles recover, but that is easy to disguise by window-shopping on my way to the gate.

One of the most difficult aspects of my illness has been the loss of anonymity that comes with being healthy. I despise being an object of public scrutiny and speculation. It always took so much energy just to deal with the sheer intensity of the emotions being flung in my direction—and there were all kinds. Some people stared with a simple pitying curiosity, but others projected fear or open hostility, especially if I'd somehow managed to interfere with their forward progress.

When I pass a young girl with atrophied legs in a wheelchair, I smile directly at her. At first she looks startled, but then she nods and smiles shyly back at me. I discreetly perform an exercise called the "rose of compassion." I learned it many years ago in a metaphysical class. It's a quick visualization of a rose filled with love from the universe that I release and send to her for her highest good. It's a simple thing really, but I can just imagine how much love a person would receive if everyone did that.

From the moment I walk through the main entrance of the Las Vegas Convention Center, I can see why such a large venue is required. There are thousands of people pouring into the building to attend the conference. Several things strike me when I look around at all the people. The first is that my visual sense is on overload. There is a blaze of color, everywhere. Everyone's clothing is vibrant with color; people are walking rainbows of silk and shimmering crystal jewelry. I love it. I notice that the attendees are probably close to 90 percent women, but the few brave men who are there are wearing garments as brightly colored as the women. And best yet, everyone is smiling. Everyone is in a good mood, and all that wonderful, happy energy is pouring into me. After a few short minutes of standing in the middle of this sea of positive vibration, I'm practically floating above the floor.

The convention center is huge, but it's easy enough to follow the influx of attendees straight to the registration table. By the time I make my way through the line, I'm feeling a bit worn out and hoping that Doreen's workshop is in one of the closer meeting rooms.

"Hello there, and welcome to the I Can Do It Conference!" I'm enthusiastically greeted by a bouncy young woman in a neon pink blouse.

"Wow, okay. Now that's pink! I'm almost tempted to put my shades back on." I laugh and wink at her, and then spy her nametag. "Um, Debra. Can you tell me where to find Doreen's workshop?"

"Why yes I *can*!" Debra chuckles good-naturedly and returns my wink. "Here's a map of the complex, but follow the corridor to the left and hers is the first room on the right." Still smiling, I reach for the proffered map and she adds, "You *have* made the right choice. Now go and enjoy!"

As my hand touches the paper, I feel a jolt of electricity and look into her suddenly knowing eyes. "Thank you. I will." I realize that Debra deliberately gave me a boost of energy. Amazing! And the event hasn't even started. Any concerns I had about traveling so far are temporarily swept away.

My legs glide effortlessly down the hallway, and I'm filled with anticipation when I see the signage for Doreen's workshop. I walk past the beaming workshop assistants at the door and step inside a large conference room. There are enough chairs for a couple of hundred people. I'm happy to have arrived early and find a seat in the third row. It's an excellent vantage point to see the stage, which is a low platform only a couple of feet above the ground. A pleasant young woman in a light lavender silk top and skirt sits down next to me. She introduces herself as Terry from New York. The tiny woman on my right is Mary, and she's from Arkansas. I'm not surprised that Doreen draws people from all over the country. I'm fidgeting with excitement when she is finally introduced and the workshop begins.

Doreen does know how to make an entrance. She is captivating with her long blonde hair flowing down her back and a stunning floor-length royal-blue silk gown. Her outfit is simply adorned with a gold belt and a gorgeous turquoise necklace. What amazes me the most is the brilliant purple aura around her head and shoulders. I've never seen an aura so clearly before.

When Doreen takes the stage, the room becomes so quiet you could hear a pin drop. She scans the room slowly, taking in the entire audience. Then she smiles. It's almost blinding. When she begins to speak, I'm momentarily struck dumb because it's not at all what I expected. She's outrageously witty. In moments, I can't help myself and burst out laughing with the rest of the audience. Her style is refreshingly down to earth. In no time at all, the entire audience is engaged and captivated by her every word. She begins by telling us a bit about her life, her psychic experiences, and its development. Then she talks about awakening to receiving guidance from angels and spirit-guides. She mentions that there are many lightworkers in the world right now who are starting to awaken to their true purpose in life. She suggests that this is the reason for many of us choosing to come to her class today.

Doreen scans the room and seems to focus on me as she says this. Suddenly, I'm sitting up straighter in my seat. This workshop and this moment are special, and I need to pay close attention. I was guided to come here just as I was when I flew to Dr. Mercola's in Chicago. And look what miracles came out of following that direction!

Our very first class exercise is worth the rigors of my entire trip. Doreen leads us on a guided meditation to meet one of the angels who have chosen to be our personal guide. With my eyes closed and feeling high from all the positive energy, J.D. appears almost as soon as I think of him. He's wearing his customary black leather jacket and pants. I hear Doreen's voice, in the background, suggesting that we ask our guide for a name. I think the question at J.D., and then wait for him to answer.

J.D. crosses his arms and, at first, he doesn't say anything. Then a smile spreads slowly across his face. *It's Michael.*

What? You're kidding, right? I'm positive my physical jaw just hit the floor in shock. *Do you mean Archangel Michael?* I ask for clarification with my thoughts. Michael's grin gets bigger, and in my mind, his outfit transforms into brilliant purple robes.

"Holy crap!" Oops, did I say that aloud? I dart a glance to either side to see if anyone noticed. Thankfully, it doesn't appear that anyone has. I focus back onto the image in my mind. *Okay then, Michael. I'd like to thank you for all your help.*

When he bows his head slightly in acknowledgement, a question bubbles to the surface, and it's imperative for me to know the answer. *But please tell me this. Why on earth have you always appeared to me in a leather motorcycle outfit? You look more like James Dean than an archangel.*

Michael smiles mischievously and shrugs his shoulders. *And why not?*

After Doreen teaches us how she performs psychic readings, we get to practice the technique upon one another. Terry and I are partners for this exercise. Moments after I've tuned into her energy, I'm flooded with an anxiety that I identify as not being my own. The tension is accompanied by indecision and a confusing mental image. There's a woman standing on the sidewalk in front of a building. It's obvious she wants to go into the building, but there's a small crowd of people holding her back. They keep her from moving. Finally, I see the woman pull free and walk inside. She heads straight into a classroom. Once there, she sits down in the front row, facing the lectern. My mental video stops playing, so I relate what I've seen to Terry.

"Oh my goodness, that *actually* makes sense to me." She gasps. "Now that my children are grown, I've wanted to go back to school to finish my degree. But it seems as if everyone is unhappy about me wanting to do something for myself. I've been torn not wanting to upset my family. I think you've just helped me decide to go for it. Thank you," she says, squeezing my hand gratefully.

I'm excited with the success of my reading and can't quite believe it at the same time. It's the first one I've ever done without being guided through it. With all the positive energy in the room, I'm feeling euphoric. The afternoon flies by. Doreen teaches us many useful psychic exercises. Before I know it, she is thanking us for coming and wishing us the best of luck in all of our endeavors.

After I say good-bye to Terry and several others that I've worked with, my feet don't want to move toward the door. Michael's presence is still in my head, and he's urging me to stand in Doreen's book-signing line. I resist him; I'm not typically someone who stands in line to get an autograph. But this workshop has changed me. I feel I've been spiritually elevated to the next level. I want to express my gratitude. By the time I decide to wait, I'm the last person in the line.

While I'm waiting, I watch the people around me. Many of them have bright colorful auras that I can see easily. Standing in the midst of this sea of smiling faces and laughter, I feel a creeping sense of inadequacy and isolation. They all look like they've got the world by the tail, while my major accomplishment was walking through the airport from security to the gate without a wheelchair. There's so much work ahead of me. *Am I strong enough to keep the flow going?* Once I'm strong enough, will I find myself plunked back in the middle of my seemingly endless career search? My mind chatter is interrupted by the sense of being watched. I'm caught off guard when I look up and see that the person in front of me isn't there anymore. The line is gone, and Doreen is sitting on the edge of the stage, patiently waiting for me.

Our eyes meet, and Doreen breaks into one of her brilliant smiles. "Wow, you remind me of Joan of Arc. It's nice to meet you," she says.

I know it was meant as a compliment, but her words hit me like a ton of bricks. In my mind, I see myself being burned at the stake, an apt metaphor for my illness and how I've felt these last several years. My throat closes up. I can't speak and, to my utter horror, a fat tear rolls down my cheek. Doreen is calmly observing me with an expression of compassion. She pats the stage next to her. "Why don't you come over here and sit down next to me for a moment?"

It's a relief not to have to speak, and I quickly wipe the tears from my face as I sit down. I want to share with her that her work has helped me.

"Thank you, Doreen. Things have been very hard for me, and your books and your words have been so helpful."

When I meet her eyes again, they bore into me as if she sees deep into my soul.

"Holly, I want you to know that we do need you *here, now, with us.*" She answers the unspoken question that burns within me. "You are *needed* here, and we really *want* you to *stay.*" Her compelling tone propels her words straight into my heart.

A brilliant light blazes inside of me. I'm needed on the earth—in this time! All the effort to become well has been worth it, and there is a purpose for me. I'm overwhelmed. I can't speak again; instead I simply try to radiate my gratitude out through my heart chakra back to her.

Doreen smiles with a look of understanding. "Holly, is it okay if I give you a hug?" she offers spontaneously.

When I nod my head, Doreen wraps her arms around me in a loving embrace. I'm enveloped in nurturing and healing energy. I drink in her kindness. It reminds me of what it felt like to hug Mom. And in fact, maybe Mom is there too, adding her love alongside Doreen's. I feel the power of a compassion that touches the very depths of my soul. Long after she releases me, it feels as if my body is still vibrating.

While Doreen's workshop is the pinnacle, the entire weekend is packed with one inspirational speaker after the next. At one point, someone announces that there are over 5,000 participants at the conference. No wonder I've been floating through the weekend. I've never had an experience even remotely like this in my entire life. As I walk around to attend the various lectures, people are constantly smiling at me. I can feel their loving energy directed toward me as I pass by. I do my best to return the favor.

Louise Hay is given a standing ovation when she takes the stage for her keynote speech. Her voice is powerful, full of life and possibility, and her aura is such a beautiful blue I can't take my eyes off of it. Here is a woman who has cured herself of cancer through many of the same holistic methods that I've been using. She discovered that her purpose in life is to teach people how to heal. She wrote a self-help book on positive affirmations called *Heal Your Body*, but when no publisher wanted to print it, that didn't even slow her down. Louise started her own publishing company, and it flourished. She's so motivating that, by the time she's finished, I want to put on my running shorts and take a quick jog up the north face of Mt. Everest.

It's a wonderful way to end the weekend. It was filled with inspirational teaching that has replenished and uplifted my soul. As I board the flight home to San Francisco, I keep replaying all the highlights in my mind. I find myself lingering over a profound point that Wayne Dyer made at the conference. He told us that although he didn't say it first, he couldn't say it any better. "When you change the way you look at things, the things you look at change." It's such an apt phrase for how I feel. It wasn't until I learned from my guides—how to change my thoughts about my body's relationship to pain—that I really began my journey to wellness. After that, I intentionally looked for messages of guidance to lead me onward. Ordinary people, places, and objects were transformed into angels, sanctuaries, and healing tools. The conference provided me with a concentrated dose of all three.

I had been worried about managing on my own for the weekend. I didn't just survive it—I'm rejuvenated! I feel better in every way, not just physically, than I did before it started. And *that* is an undeniable miracle. Healing doesn't just take place at the physical level; our thoughts matter. We can enhance our health by changing our thoughts. It's an empowering reminder of our potential.

But that's not all. I leave the conference with something intangible, but infinitely priceless, something I thought MCTD had all but stripped from me. I leave with a renewed sense of self-worth. My life matters. It was Doreen's parting gift to me—I *am* needed, I *do* have a purpose here and now. And I'm closer to discovering it now than I have ever been before. All that I've experienced will have been worth it because it is all coming together.

The plane finally starts to move, and I tilt my head to get a better view out of the window. I watch the white edge lights start to blur as we pick up speed. As the plane lifts off and quickly gains altitude, I lean back against the headrest, close my eyes, and focus my thoughts on my new affirmation: *My life is perfect, whole, and complete. I can do it!*

CHAPTER FORTY FOUR
DEFINITELY NOT IN KANSAS ANYMORE

To see a world in a grain of sand, and
a heaven in a wild flower,
hold infinity in the palm of your hand,
and eternity in an hour.
—William Blake, *Auguries of Innocence*

I'm kneeling on the ground while I carefully remove the cloth protecting my tallest quartz crystal. Sunlight hits it as soon as it's exposed and creates a rainbow that shimmers on my body. Perfect! When I place the crystal on the ground, I make sure it's still in the sun, and the rainbow radiates out in an arc over the ground.

I reach into my backpack and pull out the rest of my crystals one at a time, arranging them along each of the bands of color in the rainbow. There's rose quartz, amethyst, jade, larimar, rainbow fluorite, turquoise, labradourite, angelite, and so many other powerful crystals. I made sure to bring all of my energetic "big guns." When I'm satisfied with the circular arrangement, I sit down on the ground and admire the display. It's dazzling. I can feel the energy flowing from them already, and I'm tingling with excitement.

This will be the first manifestation ritual I've ever done for anyone other than myself. Until now, Cory and Julie have been standing off to the side, silently watching me set up the crystals. I motion for them to take a seat on the ground on the other side of the crystal layout. They position themselves to form the other two points of a triangle.

"This is so cool. I'm already glad that we're doing this," Julie says, looking pleased as she's arranging herself into a cross-legged position. I smile back. I'm excited to have this chance to officially apply some of the skills I learned at the "I Can Do It" conference. Julie and Cory are old friends I hadn't seen since I'd been ill. It seems like decades ago that we all used to hang out and go to wild dance parties. I'd been pleasantly surprised when Julie called yesterday.

Julie had told me right away that Sofia had brought her up to speed on my health issues. She had me on speaker phone so that she and Cory could express their sympathy over my suffering.

Julie said, "Sofia also told us about the really cool workshop you went to and that you came back and dove into your 'foo-foo, crystal candles and stuff,' as she put it." She had sounded amused. I had taken it as a good sign that Julie had called the workshop "cool," so I had simply waited to hear where she was going with it. "I haven't told you that Cory and I quit working for the health club, and we've been trying to open up a studio of our own." She waited for me to say something.

I immediately felt that it was a great idea. Those two were highly skilled and charismatic personal trainers. I had no doubt they'd be successful. "That's fantastic, Julie! I'm happy for you guys."

"Actually, Cory and I are reaching the end of our rope. We can't seem to find the right location for our studio; it just doesn't seem to exist. But after talking with Sofia, I have this feeling that you can help us create the right affirmation, or do some ritual, or *something* to help us find our place. Would you consider helping us do that?" The frustration in her tone had been plainly showing; that was a rare thing.

I had almost dropped the phone because I was so thrilled by her request. "Are you kidding? I'd love to help you guys! We can do a manifestation ritual for the perfect location. This will be great. Let's do it tomorrow."

We are in a secluded meadow, surrounded by trees, after hiking several miles along a trail in the Oakland Hills. I continue setting up for the ritual, pulling out some incense and several candles. I crack a smile. I know what Sofia would say if she was here, and "foo-foo" would definitely be the word of the day.

After I light the candles, I cross my legs to get comfortable and smile at my friends to help soothe their anxiety. They're both wearing fashionable designer jeans and form-fitting tops that accentuate their muscular bodies. Cory reminds me of Uma Thurman, while Julie is more along the lines of Cameron Diaz. I wait patiently while they get settled on the blanket.

When it's time to get our ritual started, I put my fingers to my lips and signal for silence. Then I close my eyes and ground myself. The sun is warm, and I feel myself absorbing its energy. I hear birds chirping in the trees. In my mind, I invite my guides to join us and immediately feel a connection being formed with several of them. I recognize the energy presence of Raphael, Michael, and Gabriel. My breathing has slowed dramatically. As I clear our ritual space energetically and ask for assistance from my guides, a feeling of euphoria flows over me. I'm ready.

"Okay, Cory and Julie, I want you to close your eyes and slow your breathing." I wait until I see them become visibly calmer. "Imagine that a tree trunk extends from the base of your spine into the ground, and its roots travel all the way to the center of the earth. Then imagine that all your stress, anxiety, and fears gather together into a black mist that you release down into your roots to be absorbed by Mother Earth." In my mind's eye, I can see their roots grow, and then black ooze flows from their bodies down the roots and into the earth. Awesome! The energy in the circle gets lighter and brighter until it I feel it crackling with electricity. Now we're all ready.

I pull out a notepad and some pens from my backpack. "Okay, excellent job, you two. Now let's create some positive affirmations." I hand over the writing supplies. We get our own fun little think tank going as we write, rewrite, and refine their affirmations, which describe exactly what they'd like their business and location to look like. Once we're all satisfied, the papers with the affirmations are placed in the center of the ritual circle. I lead us into a group visualization of their perfect studio, complete with an abundance of happy clients. The energy of the moment is intense. The image of their studio is so clear—it seems as if I can reach out and touch it. We close the ritual with expressions of gratitude for what has already been created.

Just as we finish, three hawks fly directly over our heads, calling out at the same time. "Now that is most definitely a good sign," I exclaim as we exchange smug grins. "I have a strong sense that you will find the perfect location within a few weeks. It's going to happen fast, so get ready and hang onto your hats." I am not sure how I know, but I do.

Cory and Julie are all smiles, and I can feel their gratitude mixed with a renewed sense of hope and anticipation.

Just two weeks after our ritual, I receive an excited phone call from Julie.

"Holly, it's fantastic. We found the perfect location, in Alameda, on Park Avenue. It's a main drag. There's a lot of foot traffic, the demographics work, and the landlord is giving us a great lease—and helping with the renovations. *Thank you* for helping us. I really feel like it was our ritual that got the energy unstuck and helped this happen."

I'm ecstatic for my friends and send a big mental thank you to the universe for its help with their creation. I take pride in my role in helping

Cory and Julie. It was the first time I had put my metaphysical skills into practice for others since the conference. Little did I know that our ritual was simply an appetizer.

One morning shortly after my successful visualization session with Cory and Julie, an incredible event happens while I'm in the shower. The hot water feels wonderful as it flows over my body. I'm doing my usual regimen of massaging each finger, flexing and bending them to maintain the progress I've made. Abruptly, the bathroom is flooded with bright light. This is odd. The bathroom doesn't have a window, and the one dim fluorescent light in the room is already on.

My field of vision narrows as if I'm peering into a tunnel, and my eyes are drawn up toward this inexplicable light source shining at the end of it. With a fascinating kind of double vision, I see an image in my mind's eye as well as in this tunnel of light. There is someone approaching. My body is frozen in place. I'm unable to move, but before worry or anxiety sets in, I sense Mom's presence. It's wonderful, and she's so happy and light that I'm smiling with the joy of it. Mom turns her head to look behind her and then reaches back to grasp something. To my astonishment, she pulls my Uncle George forward to stand next to her but continues holding his hand. Uncle George has the biggest smile on his face I've ever seen. He appears younger than he is now and in excellent health.

He looks at me with his kind, patient eyes. "Tell Dot I'm okay, I love her, and I'm happy," he says in a perfectly clear voice.

I'm stunned, but I manage to nod my head. Uncle George's smile gets even wider, and the shower gets brighter. I can feel his joy, and it's intense. At the same time, part of me is thinking about just how odd this is. Did Doreen Virtue mention shower visitations during her workshop? I hope nudity isn't a requirement for mediumship!

Seeming content with my answer, George looks at Mom and bows his head slightly. Mom reaches a hand toward me, and a pink stream of love flows toward me from her fingertips. When I reach my hand toward her, Mom smiles and turns around. She wraps an arm around Uncle George's waist, and together, they walk back into the light source. The shower darkens noticeably, and I'm released from the rapture.

Holy cow, Batman! My knees are weak and shaking. I grab the shower handle as I plop unceremoniously onto the edge of the bathtub and try not to fall over. I'm in a mild state of shock as I reach for the towel and manage to wrap it around me. I shake my head in amazement. *That was by far the wildest and most existential shower I've ever had. I have no doubt in my mind that*

300

Mom and Uncle George were just here with me. I felt Mom, her presence and her love—it was her. And my favorite, Uncle George, it was him. A shiver runs up and down my spine. It's not from being cold, but I wrap the towel a little tighter anyway. My "wow-ness" meter is off the scale. I feel honored and blessed to have received this spiritual visit. I'm also pretty sure I understand why it happened.

Uncle George is married to my beloved Aunt Dot, but he has been battling cancer for many years. Six years ago, the doctors told him he wouldn't live longer than a year. I know that his kind, loving spirit and ability to live entirely in the moment helped him to continue for much longer. Up until recently, he was doing relatively well. However, the last few weeks he's been bedridden with daily visits from home hospice nurses. The fact that he just showed up in my shower with Mom can mean only one thing.

While I'm dialing Dad's number, I think of Aunt Dot and visualize holding her tightly and sending my love. "Hi, honey. I guess you're calling about George. He passed away early this morning." Dad's tearful voice confirms my fears.

A great sadness fills my heart, and I'm worried about Aunt Dot. I want to offer my love and support. "Do you think it's okay to call her—or is it too much for her right now?"

Dad suggests waiting a few days, but he lets me know that Aunt Dot is surrounded by her daughters, and many others 24/7. I hang up without mentioning my experience to Dad, but I'm determined to carry out George's last request to me. Several weeks pass before I feel the time is right to tell Aunt Dot my story.

I call her, ostensibly, to check in and see how she's doing. As we're talking, I feel a distinct nudge from my guide Michael to tell her about my visitation. I'm afraid of sounding like a nut, but Uncle George asked for my help. I can't let him down. Taking a deep breath, I gather my courage and decide to just do it. "Aunt Dot, I've wanted to tell you about what happened to me on the Sunday morning after George passed, but it hasn't seemed like the right moment until now. It involves George, and it's a good thing, but if you don't feel ready to talk about him, I'll just wait until you are," I blurt out.

There is a short pause, and I hear Aunt Dot take a deep breath. "I think I would like to hear it, especially if you think it's good and has to do with George."

My heart starts pounding. I think I assumed she would say no. I have no choice but to tell her the story. My hand is holding the phone so tightly my fingers hurt. *What if I tell her and she thinks I belong on a funny farm?* I punch my leg with my free hand. The pain gives me a little momentum from which to launch into my story.

"Okay, I'm not quite sure how to tell you this, because it may sound weird and hard to believe, but it really happened." I stop for a moment to muster the additional courage I need to continue. Aunt Dot remains silent, patiently waiting for me to resume. I punch my leg again. "Well, here goes. Something strange and wonderful happened while I was in the shower…"

As I'm relating my story, there are several quiet gasps on the other end of the phone. By the time I've finished, tears are pouring down my face, and Aunt Dot is crying on the other end. "Oh, Holly. I miss George and your mom so much, but I believe you. I think it really happened, and it's wonderful. It sounds like just the thing that Shirley would do to help me get a sense of peace and know that she and George are okay. Don't mind my crying. I'm glad you told me; it does help me. But I think I need to get off the phone and cry some more. Thank you for telling me. I love you very much."

"I love you too, Aunt Dot." I hang up the phone and sink into Sofia's sofa. I'm mentally exhausted. I'm also relieved beyond measure that she didn't call me a lunatic and hang up on me. I hope with all my heart that telling Aunt Dot brings her some measure of peace and helps her know that George is okay and happy.

My life certainly has become stranger than fiction. Metaphysics has opened up my life to possibilities and experiences I could hardly have imagined. They are almost too amazing to believe—even after they happened to me. Anything seems possible now. I imagine myself as Dorothy, skipping my way along the yellow brick road.

I turn to Toto and say, "Well Toto, we're definitely not in Kansas anymore."

CHAPTER FORTY FIVE

LIFE IS SOLID AGAIN

The wise man should consider that health
is the greatest of human blessings.
Let food be your medicine.
–Hippocrates

Over the summer of 2005, my progress is steady; my health is improving on all fronts. In fact, by the time August rolls around, I'm ready for the big test. I think it's time to bring solid foods back into my diet. It's been a year since I've started juicing. In combination with my protein shakes, that has been all I've subsisted on. I'm worried about choosing something too difficult to digest, and I start off with cooked vegetable soups. I'm relieved to discover that the cooked vegetables pass through my digestive system without any pain.

The difficulty I've had in swallowing, another aspect of my illness, turns out to be useful in my recovery. I've learned that if I cut my food into tiny pieces and then chew it into oblivion, good things happen. The first good thing is that I can swallow. Secondly, by pulverizing the food in my mouth, I can absorb more nutrition and receive a lot more energy. I know this because my body gives me explicit feedback about it. The more I chew, the less I suffer. And finally, my digestion doesn't slow down to the point where food gets stuck in my intestines. I'm a living example of why chewing your food thoroughly is beneficial. I'm taught a valuable lesson on the day I decide to further expand my menu.

I'm at Sofia's dining room table, and I've selected a few raw and uncooked items to try. My first choice is a plain bagel. It's soft and should be easy for me to chew and swallow. I tear off a small piece and chew carefully. That seems to go well, so I keep at it until I've finished half of it. Not wanting to push my luck, I pick up a book to read while my body works on digesting the bagel. To my astonishment, shortly after I eat it, my energy level drops sharply, so much so in fact, that I need to lie down on Sofia's sofa to rest. I feel that the bagel is draining my precious life energy and offering me nothing in return. It has stolen my qi.

I drag myself back into the kitchen and, this time, I pick up a carrot. After I return to the dining room table, I hesitate before taking a bite. I turn the carrot over in my hands to study it. I've seen the sunburst of orange vitality that comes out of carrots when I juice them. This is the kind of food I want to be able to eat and digest. I'm reminded of a story told to me many years ago by Sihing Masazaki, my favorite instructor at my old Choy Lay Fut Kung Fu School in San Francisco. Sihing is a martial arts title used to refer to a senior male instructor. Sihing Masazaki was as thin as a reed, but struck hard and fast like a cobra when he sparred. He had grown up in Japan, learning martial arts in the old way, with a strict instructor and brutal physical training. He had loved to share his hard-won lessons with me, and I was a sponge.

One day after class, I was stretching out on the mat when Sihing Masazaki approached. I smiled as he sat gracefully in front of me. "Hi, Sihing. What droplets of wisdom do you have for me today?"

He bowed slightly, quickly removing the smile that had started to appear, although he couldn't do anything to dull the twinkle in his eyes. "Today, grasshopper, I'm here to share the story of when I learned how to truly find the qi in my food." He bowed over his hands, which were held up in a Buddhist prayer position.

I smirked and straightened my right leg in front of me so I could massage the tightness out of my hamstring. I liked it when Sihing called me "grasshopper," which was Kwai Chang's nickname in the *Kung Fu* TV series. "I'm all ears, master."

Sihing inhaled deeply and began his tale. "My Sifu came to me one day and told me that it was a special training day. He wanted me to complete a series of drills and told me that they would take me all day. First, he sent me on a ten-mile run." Sihing chuckled. "I lit out and came back in record time. I thought that wasn't so bad, but then Sifu added that the run was just a warm up."

I switched legs to work on my other hamstring. "A ten-mile warm up? I thought our warm ups were tough. What came after the run?"

Sihing's eyes took on a faraway look. "I was tired when I finished the run, but I wanted more than anything to succeed at whatever my Sifu asked me to do. I proudly announced to him that I was ready for my next task." Sihing stared hard at me, and I stopped stretching, giving him my undivided attention. "Sifu told me that I had to do 1,000 sit-ups first, 1,000 pushups second, followed by 1,000 kicks with each leg, and end with 1,000 punches with each hand." He finished by rapid-punching the air for emphasis.

"No way, Sihing. That's insane!" My mouth fell open in astonishment.

"Yeah, it sure wiped the arrogant smile off my face." Sihing laughed. "But that's not all." He raised his index finger in the air. "Sifu reached into a bag he was holding, pulled out a carrot, and handed it to me. When I asked him what it was for, he said that the carrot was the only food I was allowed to have for the day."

"One carrot?" I asked.

Sihing nodded and shifted his legs into the lotus position. "Yes, one carrot. Sifu told me that, if I ate it correctly, it would provide me with all the qi that I needed to sustain me." He gave his chest a thump. "And let me tell you that it turned out to be the best-tasting carrot I've ever eaten." He smacked his lips, and I laughed.

"Okay, what happened?" I asked after too much silence. I was dying for him to continue.

Sihing smiled slyly. "I told Sifu that there was no way I was going to make it through the day on just a single carrot; I'd already run for ten miles." I nodded vigorously, thinking how whipped I would be if that had been me. "That was when he told me that there was an extraordinary amount of qi locked inside of the carrot, but rarely does anyone take the time to free it." Sihing deliberately slowed down, and I listened carefully to every word. "It requires that one is entirely in the present moment while chewing each bite. I must be aware of only the carrot and chew one small bite at a time, at least fifty times before swallowing. I must pulverize it completely in order to release and receive all the hidden qi." Sihing mimicked crushing something in his hand and then opened it quickly, while making the sound of an explosion.

I had a great visual of an orange cloud of energy being released from an exploding carrot. Then I tried to imagine doing all those exercises with only a single carrot for sustenance. It was precisely the kind of trial that Kwai Chang was put through during his training. Sihing was watching me intently as though he was reading my thoughts.

After a moment, he nodded his head in apparent satisfaction and said, "It took me all day, but I finished everything Sifu asked me to do. I'd never been more exhausted in my life. And you know what?"

"What, Sihing?" I asked when he stopped for too long.

"That carrot was the reason I made it. I took tiny bites and made it last the entire day. I chewed each bite into oblivion, and all I thought about was that carrot. I *did* feel the qi being released and then flowing into me. There was more flavor in that carrot than I'd ever imagined there could be. It was amazing. I've never looked at food in the same way again."

With that, Sihing abruptly jumped to his feet and left me to ponder his tale alone.

My thoughts return to the present. The carrot in my hand practically glows with vitality. I want to feel what Sihing Masazaki felt when he ate his carrot. I take another minute to study it further. The orange color is vibrant, but now I see more than a carrot, much more. It's a plutonium fuel cell of qi, and I'm the reactor. I take one tiny bite and start to chew, keeping my entire concentration on pulverizing the small piece of carrot in my mouth. Each bit that is broken down releases a tiny burst of flavor. I also notice the sweet aroma of carrot filling the air. I can feel the tiny bursts of qi being released with every nibble.

Sihing's story is true! My teeth have become a miniature Green Star 2000, and the carrot is my co-creator of life energy. By the time I've finished that single carrot, it feels as if I've just had a glass of my "juice of life."

It takes several weeks of experimentation before I work the kinks out of my new solid food diet. But I'm ecstatic! I've put together a good menu, consisting of soups, fruits, cooked vegetables, and even fish. The hours I spend researching the healing properties of food help me make further refinements. I pinpoint which foods tend to produce inflammation in the body—like turkey, wheat, and mango—and keep them out of my diet. I happily add other items that have a lot to offer, like papayas, avocados, and coconuts.

I'm delighted to be eating food again, but my "juice of life," my personal rainbow of nutrition, remains a daily, essential part of my diet. I've learned firsthand what it means to eat to *live* and not live to *eat*.

CHAPTER FORTY SIX

THE WOMEN'S CIRCLE

Have you had a kindness shown? Pass it on;
twas not given for thee alone, pass it on.
Let it travel down the years, let it wipe another's
tears, 'til in Heaven the deed appears - pass it on.
—Henry Burton, *Pass It On*

I'm strongly drawn to take another class with Doreen Virtue. This time, it will be a five-day workshop with extensive training in metaphysical tools. The Angel Therapy Practitioner, or ATP, workshop is held in Laguna Beach at the end of October.

My physical body is steadily improving, thanks to my holistic wellness regimen of juicing, acupuncture, herbs, foot reflexology, massage, meditations, and Sifu. I can feel my inner reserves of qi building, and I'm growing stronger by the day. Now when I perform the "Floating Leaf" form, I can move in one continuous flow from start to finish. I'm not quite "floating" yet, but I'm connecting to my qi for longer and longer periods of time. I feel I'm ready.

I'm buzzing with anticipation long before I step inside the large workshop space at a posh beachfront hotel. The room is arranged with many rows of folding chairs facing a low stage at the front of the room. My attention is riveted by the largest quartz crystal I've ever seen. It's on the floor in front of the stage and stands at least two feet high.

Just as in the "I Can Do It Conference," the kaleidoscope of rainbow-colored clothing and crystal jewelry returns to dazzle me. It adorns nearly everyone in the room, men and women alike. Out of 120 attendees, I notice only a handful of men. Staff members are strategically positioned around the room, and I observe them all making circular motions with their hands. I realize that they're clearing the room energetically. It's definitely working. The energy inside this space is like taking a scented bubble bath and feeling your tension melt away.

The crowd is hushed and excitedly expectant as Doreen glides into the room. She is the epitome of elegance in her magnificent purple gown, complete with a stunning amethyst necklace and bracelets. She performs her preliminary scan of the room. At the same time, it feels as if she is sending a spiritual hello to us all. Then comes the *piece de resistance* of her entrance—a fully amused grin that grows into a smile, stretching from ear to ear. It ends with a blinding flash of white as she laughs. We all can't help but laugh with her. And the fun begins.

This workshop is packed, and not a moment is wasted. Doreen dives right into our training by leading us through a ritual to awaken our third eye. This is followed by exercises that help us to recognize and receive guidance from our higher self, as well as spirit-guides, angels, and ascended masters. For each exercise, we pair up with someone different, which gives me the opportunity to learn handy new tricks and tips from each one. I'm truly enjoying myself.

Our days are filled from morning until evening with exercises that are designed to awaken and stretch our psychic skills. On the third day, we learn about psychic mediumship, and I can hardly wait until we have a chance to practice what we've learned. My exercise partner is a young woman, probably in her late twenties, named Jean. Our assignment is to clear and open our third eye, and then scan our partner and ask to receive a message from someone they know who has passed. I'm trying hard to let go of my nervousness and just be open. Jean and I turn our chairs to face each other, and then I take her hands in my own. Glancing over her shoulder, it seems as if there is some energy, a denseness, which is hovering behind her. A picture forms in my mind's eye, and I describe what I'm seeing to her.

"I see the image of a young man, wearing tight jeans, flannel shirt, and cowboy boots leaning casually against a car. He has an intriguing, almost teasing smile. He's quite charming." I break off when I see tears trickling down her face, "Jean, are you okay? Do you still want me to continue?"

"Don't mind me. Please continue." She gives my hands a squeeze. "You've just described my last boyfriend, Ron. He was killed in a car accident," she adds shakily.

I'm about to continue, but her mouth quivers as if she wants to say more.

"Can you ask him something for me?" she whispers.

"I'll do my best." I smile and give her hands a return squeeze, "What would you like to ask?"

"Well, it's been a few years since he died." Jean dabs her eyes with a tissue, and then musters her courage. "I haven't been able to date anyone until recently, but would you find out from him if it's okay if I do? Does he mind?"

When I form the question in my mind and send it toward Ron, he responds right away. "Ron is nodding his head vigorously up and down and showing me an image of himself with his arm around you. I'm getting a strong feeling of love and support."

Jean sighs loudly, and her shoulders visibly relax as if a weight has been lifted. Then she straightens in her chair. "Just one more thing, does Ron think that David and I will work out?" She smiles shyly.

"Ron is shrugging his shoulders. And now he's crossing his arms. Oh, and he's saying something. I'm getting the message: 'Babe, you'll just have to figure it out for yourself.'"

I wonder if I'm not just hallucinating.

"Oh my God!" Jean puts a hand over her mouth, "That's exactly what Ron would do and say. It's really him!" She tries unsuccessfully to stifle a laugh. "Oh, thank you so much. I've felt so guilty about wanting to move on. Thank you." More tears flow as she leans forward to give me a big hug. I'm euphoric with the success of the reading. It's uplifting to experience the extraordinary as ordinary in this workshop. Even so, I'm still unprepared for tomorrow's main event.

All of the women are asked to stay in the main room while the men are taken into another room for a male-bonding exercise led by Steven, Doreen's husband. After they leave, Doreen tells us we're going to create a "Women's Empowerment Circle." To help facilitate that, our chairs have been arranged into a large circle three rows deep. As Doreen explains the object of the exercise, I'm feeling a little anxious and decide to sit in the outermost row.

"This circle is one of my favorite moments in an ATP workshop. The object of it is to give those women who ordinarily would not speak out and talk about themselves a chance to do so." She smiles almost mischievously as she slowly moves around the circle, "I will pick the first one of you to start." Trying not to be noticed, I slink lower in my chair when Doreen passes by my side of the circle. "I want the speaker to take the microphone and stand here and tell us a story of your personal empowerment. Tell us about a moment when you moved into your feminine power and used it for your highest good."

My whole body is vibrating at her words.

"In our discussion groups, we've heard from many of you who are comfortable with speaking in front of a group, so I really want to get those wallflowers into the circle." She swings back toward my area, and my jitters increase. Is she talking to me? I lean down and pretend to get something from my backpack; anything to escape her discerning gaze. "If you are chosen, once you tell us your story, I'd like you to select a woman that you feel would rather run and hide than be in the circle."

I can feel my heart rate escalating. I don't want to stand in the middle of this circle in front of all these talented women and stumble or stutter in embarrassment. Glancing around to make sure no one is paying attention, I slide as far down in my chair as possible, hoping that I'm hidden behind the two rows of women in front of me.

Doreen chooses a woman named Sandy on the other side of the circle, and I breathe a sigh of relief. *Why am I so nervous? There's not a chance I'll get picked.* My heart goes out to the petite, middle-aged woman. She looks mortified but stands up anyway and lets Doreen lead her to the center of the circle.

It takes Sandy a minute or two before she is able to pull it together. She turns several shades of red, but then, bit by bit, she proceeds to tell us her life story. It's the story of a life of submission. Growing up, she had been abused by a controlling father, only to be bullied later by her domineering husband. She had allowed herself to be led around and told what to do for most of her life, till one day she finally snapped and said: "No more." She didn't have the support of other family members at first, but once they began to see how miserable Sandy had become, they rallied around her. She's celebrating her newly won freedom by coming to this workshop. We all clap and voice our congratulations and support as Sandy begins a slow pace around the circle looking for the next person.

When she nears my section, my stomach is doing flips—and they're accompanied by a spiritual nudge. In this workshop, it's been easy to maintain a calm, meditative state. I've felt the presence of Michael in my mind from time to time. Now I hear him send: *You need to tell your story; it's important.* I don't want to be in the center of a circle. I *detest* the spotlight; I'm too self-conscious. One on one is fine, but me with a *microphone*? No way. I'd rather go bungee jumping.

Ever since my ill-fated, third grade science project, I've avoided public speaking like the plague. Miss Saxon had assigned us all different animal science projects, which we had to present orally before the entire class.

I had made a large display box consisting of several skeletons of small mammals: a raccoon, a rabbit, and a fox. During my presentation, I had stuttered over the names of some of the bones. (Metacarpals, metatarsals—who needs them anyway?) One little smart aleck in the front row, Timmy, had started mimicking my mistakes. And then, to my utter horror, all the kids started laughing at me. I had been so embarrassed that I couldn't continue, and the teacher had to move on to the next student. It had been an absolute nightmare. I had resolved never again to expose myself to such humiliation. Of course, being nine at the time, the word "never" had seemed appropriate. Thirty-four years later, my palms still sweat just thinking about it.

I breathe a sigh of relief when Sandy hands the microphone to Terry, a tall, reed-thin woman with slightly stooped shoulders. She's an excellent choice, appearing even more timid than Sandy. I can see her hand shaking as she takes the microphone and steps into the circle. Taking a deep breath to gather her courage, Terry shares her tale of lifelong oppression by her mother. It's only recently that she's found the courage to say no and live her life on her own terms. Again, we clap and shout words of encouragement and congratulations. Two more women go on to share their stories, and the odds of me being chosen to speak substantially decrease. Just when I'm finally starting to relax, Doreen announces that there's time for one more person.

I'm aware of Michael's presence again. *Sit up and quit hiding.* He's more insistent now. *It's your turn to tell your story.* His last words are punctuated by a tiny electric jolt. That really irritates me, and I shake myself to try to get rid of him. At the same time, I imagine a mental image of me clamping my hand over his mouth. *Just keep quiet for a minute, and this will all be over soon.* I see myself whispering back through clenched teeth. Then I catch myself and roll my eyes. I'm arguing with an archangel—my life is so strange.

Thus, I'm totally unprepared when the tip of a microphone looms in front of my face. *Crap!* Linda, the woman holding the microphone, has a smug and incredibly self-satisfied look on her face. It looks like I'm not getting out of this one. I slowly stand up and trudge into the center of the circle. It's an incredibly surreal feeling to have the attention of more than a hundred women focused on me.

My hand is sweating profusely, and I'm worried I'll drop the microphone. The last time I held one was during an elementary school production of *The Wizard of Oz.* In her infinite wisdom, the drama teacher had chosen me to be the narrator. I don't need to say how that turned out. I take a deep breath, fully intending to start, but for a moment, nothing happens. Then I notice that everyone is looking at me with smiles of encouragement, and it dawns on me that they actually *want* to hear what I have to say. My fear dissipates, finally freeing my heart to speak.

"Four years ago, I was on what seemed to be a never-ending search for my true path. I was a self-admitted adrenaline junkie with a hero complex and thought a career in law enforcement might suit me. So, I joined the police academy. Aside from the fact that I was absolutely miserable, everything was going along quite smoothly. But then I couldn't get out of bed one morning ... and then the burning in my legs started ..."

As I tell my story, turning slowly to make eye contact with each woman in the circle, I feel so exposed; it's a struggle to keep going. But there's an intensity within this moment that's pushing me, and I get the sense that it's imperative to get my story out. By the time I reach my day of decision, the entire room has fallen absolutely silent. It feels as if I'm back in my basement room, reliving my moment at the bottom of the abyss.

"I knew I needed to make a decision. Was there a reason for me to stay—or should I just let go?" My voice is shaky with emotion.

I hear soft exclamations of things like: "Stay, you should stay," and "That must have been terrible. But don't go."

I glance over at Doreen, and she nods, encouraging me to proceed.

"Fortunately, I did decide to stay, and that it wasn't my time to go. And once I made this decision and opened myself up to receiving, I did receive help in so many ways from some extremely unexpected sources. I meditated, practiced qi gong, used acupuncture and herbs, created affirmations, started juicing for nutrition, and more. As I regained some strength and energy, I also started a physical rehab program. To be standing here in front of you today is nothing short of a miracle, and I'm grateful now for every day of my life. Thank you for the opportunity to share my story with you."

I lower the microphone. For a moment, there is dead silence, and I flash on the thought that maybe I've just made a huge fool of myself and everyone must think I'm an idiot. But then suddenly, to my surprise, everyone is clapping, and I see more than one person dabbing their eyes with a tissue. It feels amazing to receive their outpouring of encouragement and support. Doreen is smiling at me with a twinkle in her eyes. Inside my head, I hear a smug *I told you so* from Michael as I plop back down on my chair. Doreen stands and brings the session to a close. She thanks us for being courageous with sharing our stories and asks us to be open to receiving the guidance meant for us.

I reflect on my moment in the women's circle. It was wonderfully cathartic. I feel profoundly nurtured in a way that I haven't felt in a very long time. These women acknowledged me as a full-fledged person instead of a disease statistic. My words, thoughts, and life experiences have the power to touch people; my life matters. The realization is both humbling and deeply satisfying.

One by one, people around me begin to gather up their belongings. Some women form small conversational groups, while others stand up and slowly file out of the conference room. Reluctantly, I release my thoughts and lean down beside my chair to unzip my backpack. But, before I can even start packing up my notes, I notice several pairs of shoes step into my peripheral vision. When I look up, I'm surrounded by the faces of several smiling women from the circle.

"Thank you for sharing your story," a plump, motherly woman says. "It was so powerful. It really rocked my world. You've shown me that it is possible to create something extraordinary from the seemingly impossible."

I'm touched and smile back about to thank her.

And then another woman chimes in. "I agree—how far you've come is a miracle. I think that you should share your story with more people, perhaps you might consider writing a book about it." There is a murmuring of assent from several others in the little assemblage now crowded around me.

Several more women join the circle, and one of the newcomers touches my arm. "I heard what Tina just said. Yes, a book is a great idea! I'm totally motivated to clean up my diet and work on myself. You taught me it's never too late to start. Thank you for sharing."

I'm more than a little overwhelmed with all the attention and compliments, but I also feel terrific. As I'm thanking the women around me for their encouragement and advice, I toy with the idea of a book. It might be an excellent way to reach out to other people with a chronic illness. So many are ready for positive change but don't even realize that it's possible—or even where to begin. I remember what that felt like and I know my experience can benefit others. But what the hell do I know about *writing*? I've never published anything before—why would anyone choose to pick up my book? But if sharing my story was the spark that ignited a candle in the dark for even one person, it would all be worth it. Despite my self-doubts, I resolve to explore the idea further.

The next day, I'm approached by women seeking my advice during every break. The first one is a woman with blazing red hair who introduces herself as Alice.

"I loved hearing your story. I was wondering if I could get some suggestions from you about chronic fatigue. My cousin has had it for so long, and I'd love to help her. I know she's ready to try a new approach. Nothing has helped."

I'm flattered to be sought out; this is exactly what I want to do. My mind immediately takes off, formulating a list of things that would help Alice's cousin. "I'd be happy to help, Alice. If you like, I can create a list of dos and don'ts that would get her on the right track. But you need to realize that it is *work*. You need to want it."

Alice's enthusiasm remains unaffected by my cautionary tone. "I can't tell you how much I'd appreciate that, and I know she's ready and willing." She beams back at me gratefully.

At another break, while I'm walking to the restroom, Susan, a tall, willowy blonde falls into step beside me. "Holly, I loved hearing your story. Thank you," she says and touches my arm. "I was wondering if you would share some of your ideas about healing fibromyalgia. Both of my sisters have it, and they suffer so much, all the time. I've felt useless, and I don't know how to help them."

I open my mouth, but before I can respond, I hear, "Holly, sorry to butt in, I hope you don't mind." It's another woman who has walked up to my other side. "I'm Laura, and I heard what Susan just asked. I'd love to hear what you recommend. My best friend has had fibromyalgia for years."

I'm startled and, for a moment, I look back and forth between the two women as if I'm at a Ping-Pong tournament. But then I'm caught up in all the thoughts flowing into my mind on a healing plan to help them. I dive in and enthusiastically share my ideas. I haven't felt this alive in years. Then it suddenly dawns on me, and I wonder why it took so long for me to see it. *This* is my purpose: to be a part of restoring hope, suggesting possibilities, and teaching techniques to create health and wellness. I can use everything that has shaped who I am. I can use all of it to help others: my knowledge of martial arts, my skills as an acupuncturist and qigong practitioner, my metaphysical tools, even my experiences as a person with chronic illness, and much more. This is what I'm *meant* to do. *This* is my path.

By the time the workshop ends for the day, I feel the need to escape for a bit. I'm experiencing a kind of surreal state of shock. I want to be alone with all the thoughts that are buzzing crazily around in my head. I make a beeline for a trail alongside the hotel, which leads down to the ocean. Once I've reached the beach, I gratefully plop myself down on the warm sand and stare out at the ocean.

A few small waves are breaking close to shore, but behind them, the ocean is completely flat. It sparkles like a polished, many-faceted crystal. The water closest to me is a stunning shade of aquamarine, which gradually darkens the farther out I look. Far from shore, there is a line of demarcation where the color darkens until it's almost black. It signals an area where the ocean floor drops off down into the depths from which even light cannot escape: the cold, still, pitch blackness of the abyss. I have an intimate familiarity with that place. For several long, solitary years, it was my entire world.

Laughter jolts me back to the present moment. I turn my head toward the sound and see two petite, middle-aged women strolling at the water's edge. They are carrying their shoes and have their pants rolled up so that they can play in the water with their bare feet. They closely resemble each other, and I realize they must be sisters. Every time the water touches them, they giggle delightedly, like two little girls. Their mood is contagious.

A crooked grin sneaks across my face, and an errant chuckle escapes my lips. I dig my fingers into the warm sand and observe my marvels of dexterity. A warm breeze caresses my skin, and I breathe in the clean, fresh air—the smell of freedom. I smile unabashedly. When I glance up again, the women are gone, but their image has been replaced by the wondrous spectacle of countless tiny rainbows dancing on the reflective surface of the ocean. I hug my knees and simply let myself experience the flood of joy rushing into me.

I feel like a kid again on one of our family vacations at the Jersey Shore. I want so much to share this moment with Mom. I close my eyes and visualize my feelings as a bright pink cloud being absorbed into an enormous red rose. I mentally detach the stem from the ground and watch it float into the heavens straight to her. That gesture feels good, but I'm so excited that I still need to tell someone here on earth. If it can't be Mom, I know the next best person. My hand shakes as I fish my cell phone out of my backpack. It seems to ring forever before it's finally answered. Then I hear a familiar voice, warm and maternal, and all is well.

"Hi Aunt Dot. It's Holly. You'll never guess what's happened!" I blurt out in a rush. "It's all so amazing! Do you have a minute?"

"Of course, dear! You sound excited. It's *so* good to hear that in your voice."

Telling Aunt Dot about all the amazing experiences I've had at Doreen's workshop is like I'm also telling Mom. I can feel her presence right beside me. And when Aunt Dot congratulates me and offers encouragement for writing a book about my experiences, I can sense Mom adding her support as well. It's just enough to tip the scales. I make the decision to write my story.

Often, when major life events happen, their full significance and impact aren't revealed until a later time. Doreen's ATP workshop turns out to be one such event for me. Not only does it illuminate a path for me to take, it also prepares me for the coming events in a way I'd never even dreamed of.

CHAPTER FORTY SEVEN

ANOTHER TRANSITION

To be present at the transition is a great gift from Spirit.
What you do not understand now, you will ... you will.
—Alison Stormwolf

It's only been two weeks since I attended the ATP workshop, and Thanksgiving is quickly approaching. Dad has phoned to find out what my holiday plans are and to catch up on my progress. It's not until the end of the conversation that he casually mentions he's come down with a case of walking pneumonia.

"Dad, are you okay. Do you need me to come out there?" I ask as the cold tendrils of fear snake through my chest.

"No, you don't need to do that. I'm actually feeling pretty good." He's oddly upbeat. "The doctors are watching me. I just wanted to let you know. I'm fine. I'll call if I need anything," he says, but I'm still feeling shaken.

Jay and I touch base with Dad every day. On Friday, it seems as if the danger has passed and he's much better. Saturday morning is an entirely different story.

"Dad's in the hospital," Jay says, not mincing words. The phone almost slips out of my hand.

"What happened? I was talking to him yesterday, and he was fine." A shiver runs through my body, and I fight the urge to panic.

"I just talked to Dad, and he said he had some difficulty breathing, so they admitted him to the hospital." Jay sighs. "He says he's fine."

I can hear the questioning doubt in his voice. "I need to talk to Dad myself. I'll call you back." I quickly dial the hospital. "Dad, what's going on? Are you okay? We were just talking yesterday, and you were feeling pretty good."

"It's nothing to worry about, honey. I just finished a lovely hospital breakfast, and I'm feeling pretty good." He sounds almost normal. "I had a little trouble breathing last night, but it's much better now. Just relax. I'll keep you posted."

I've got a nagging feeling that is growing by the minute. I want to do something for him. I decide to perform a healing meditation. In my mind's eye, I imagine a rose, the most beautiful pinkish red rose that I've ever seen. Into it, I pour love and healing thoughts until the petals become vibrant with energy. I imagine Dad as the recipient of this rose; when it feels complete, I release it to the universe. I'm feeling peaceful as I watch it waft gently up to be used for my Dad's highest good and healing.

Around ten o'clock, my cell phone rings. I'm apprehensive when I see my brother's number on caller ID. "Jay, what's going on?"

"Hol, things are going wrong." His voice is distraught, and my heart sinks like a stone. "Dad had some kind of collapse. He's in intensive care, and I'm heading out there. The soonest I can get there is tomorrow at the crack of dawn." His voice cracks.

"Shit!" I yell. My throat is closing up, and my stomach twists into a ball. "Okay, I'll call you back with my flight."

"Hurry, Hol!"

Not again—oh please, not again! I'm starting to panic, but then I feel Raphael, the archangel of healing, and Michael in my mind. I've been working a lot with Raphael in my morning healing rituals, and there is an immediate sense of support and calming energy flooding through my body.

You are not alone, and your father is not alone. You are both loved very much. He will wait for you, and we're going to help you. Feel the love of All That Is pouring into you.

I hear them loudly in my mind. I'm almost knocked off balance by the intensity of the love and support I feel surging into me. It helps me get a grip while I make my flight arrangements.

Jay and I meet up in Denver and sit together on the plane to Philadelphia. We quietly draw support from each other as the long minutes of the flight tick slowly by. Aunt Dot and Cousin Bev pick us up at the airport, and we race straight to the hospital. It is a déjà vu of the worst kind as Jay and I hurry up to Dad's hospital room. The moment we step inside, I flash back to Mom—hooked up to all the equipment and the ventilator. Dad is fortunately not on a ventilator, but he has oxygen, numerous monitors, and IV's lined up around his bed. I'm so relieved when he opens his eyes and looks at us; my knees feel about to give way. Dad's smile is weak, and his breathing is labored, but he lifts a hand to reach out for us. As one, Jay and I move to stand on either side of the bed and take a hand.

"Hol and I are here. We're not going anywhere. We love you, and you're going to be fine."

I sense a familiar presence in my mind that I've come to associate with Raphael. *Please know what is happening is about your father and his journey. I hear the message clearly. This is his time—just be here for him and send him your love and support. Use our strength to help you.*

My heart is pounding, and I can't speak, but Raphael's presence keeps me focused in the present. I want to be here for Dad in a way that I wasn't able to be for Mom. I squeeze Dad's hand and send him my love. After a time, Jay and I step away and let Aunt Dot and Bev stay with him while we find the physician.

Dr. Benton tells us that Dad's pneumonia took a turn for the worse, but the big problem is his lung capacity. It's already so low that his body isn't strong enough to fight off the pneumonia.

"I've known your father for a long time, and he is quite a lovable character. I'm so sorry," Dr. Benton says. I'm touched to see him wipe a tear from his eye.

It's hard to do this again, so soon. My consciousness is fading, and the world around me is shrinking. Raphael is still with me. *Now is the time you must remain present. We're here with you. Open yourself, and feel our love and support.* He reminds me, and again it helps me ground and remain present.

I'm filled with an odd sense of wonderment. There is a soft cushion of love that is gently supporting my heart. When Jay and I return to Dad's room, he's weaker and his eyes appear unfocused. His breathing is more labored. I'm relieved when a nurse administers morphine, and his awful gasping for air begins to subside. Cousin Bev is also an energy healer. We both take up positions on either side of Dad and hold his hands. We send him healing energy to be used for his highest good.

After a few days of maintaining a vigil for Dad, it's a struggle not to sink into despair. It's like watching Mom in her last days. If not for the comfort of so many—Jay, Bev, Aunt Dot, Raphael, and Michael, my constant companions—I couldn't have held it together. Many friends and relatives stop by to see him and share their love.

On Thanksgiving, Jay, Beverly, and I are with Dad. I'm grateful that Bev is with us to support Dad. She's strong and loving like Aunt Dot, her mother. We have grown closer over our mutual interest in spiritual growth and healing.

I'm sure the universe has orchestrated a parting gift to Dad and me when I turn on the TV to the Thanksgiving football games. Watching football games together had always been a treasured ritual for us. Growing up in Pennsylvania, we've always been diehard Eagles fans. Since the Cowboys are the archrivals of the Eagles, we always cheered for whoever was playing against Dallas. Today, it's the Broncos, our second-favorite team, playing against the Cowboys.

Dad isn't visibly conscious, but when I tell him the football game is on and who's playing, I'm positive he hears me. I feel blessed to receive the gift of one last game with him. I sit next to his head in order to give him a running commentary. My voice grows animated as I describe the plays and throw in exclamations about particular plays or players. It's a cliffhanger when the game goes into overtime with the score tied at 21–21.

My head is close to Dad's, and I'm convinced that on some level he's receiving this game. "Okay, Dad, this is it. It's overtime, and the Broncos have the ball. We can do this!"

My heart is racing, and I imagine us back on the couch at home in the TV room, shouting at our team to get the lead out. "Yes! We've moved into field goal range and the Broncos are going for it." I tear my eyes off the screen to glance quickly at Dad. I know he's hearing me, but I also know there isn't much time left. The roar of the crowd pulls my attention back to the screen. The kick is in the air.

"All right!" I slap my knee and touch Dad's shoulder. "They did it, Dad! We won! We beat the Cowboys!" My voice catches as I fight the tears that are trickling down my face.

As the game ends, I sense Dad's energy is receding. I'm positive he lingered just long enough to share the game with me. I walk over to Beverly for a moment to gather myself. After only a few minutes, I'm suddenly aware of more than the presence of Michael and Raphael—much more. It's seems as if the room is filling to capacity with many angels and spirits.

Michael and Raphael speak as one: *Your father is ready. Let's ease his transition.*

Leaning toward Beverly, I whisper, "Bev, let's gather around Dad. My guides are telling me it's time."

The energy coalescing in the room is intensifying. Even Jay picks up on it. He looks over at Bev and me and then joins us at Dad's side. Jay and

I stand on opposite sides near the head of the bed, while Bev is next to me. Dad's breathing has slowed to almost nothing, and I feel the angels and guides adding to our combined outpouring of love to him. Then something incredible happens. It's almost as if a veil is lifted, and I can see countless shapes of white light hovering all around Dad. I'm actually seeing the angels and spirit-guides that have come to help.

With Dad's last breath—which somehow I seem to know is his last—the light from all the angels and spirits becomes so bright that it's almost blinding. Then, gradually, I see a beautiful white sparkle of light slowly detach itself and leave Dad's body. It's hard to keep from falling to my knees. My head tilts up as I watch this beautiful energy ascend. Dad's spirit hovers for a moment, and I say my final good-bye.

"I love you. Thank you for being my Dad," I whisper.

In the next moment, he is gone along with the host of spirits who came to help, and the room darkens considerably. The veil has dropped back into place. When I look back down at his body, there is no life force there at all. It's just an empty shell.

We are all awestruck by the experience, and for several long minutes no one speaks. I glance sideways at Beverly, and we exchange looks of stunned amazement.

"Did you guys feel that?" Jay finally blurts into the silence. "Something just happened, and it was intense."

The spell is broken. Bev and I both murmur in agreement. Bev puts her arms around me and Jay, unfolding us into a close, nurturing group hug. It's time to lay aside the mantles of caregiver and healer. Our grief draws us together, and we mourn—with the pure hearts of children—the passing of our beloved father and friend.

CHAPTER FORTY EIGHT
FULL CIRCLE

It's the circle of life, and it moves us all, through
despair and hope, through faith and love,
'till we find our place, on the path unwinding.
–Elton John

Dad's passing affects me very differently than Mom's did. With Dad, I had a chance to say good-bye. I was supported by my guides and afforded the opportunity of what I believe to be—a glimpse behind the veil.

I miss him terribly, but I know he's safe and happy with Mom. Gradually, I've learned to accept that I wasn't around to help my parents in the way that I imagined I would be. I can't go back and change history, but I'm still here and fully intend to honor my parents by paying it forward. Six months later, while I still have much work to do in my own recovery, a chance encounter brings me full circle.

Part of my ongoing wellness strategy includes regular body work. Today, I'm going to the grand opening of a new spa in Walnut Creek. They're offering big discounts on all their massage packages. I'm greeted by the pleasant aroma of lavender incense as soon as I walk through the door. The soothing ambient music is gently accented by the exotic twang of an Indian sitar.

At the moment, there's no one at the front desk, so I make myself comfortable on one of the two plush leather sofas along a wall in the reception area. I close my eyes for a moment and relax. It feels good to simply breathe and absorb the relaxing sounds. I imagine all the stress and tension in my body is draining deep into the earth. I continue to visualize that what I let go of is transformed into healing energy, which flows back into me as a sparkling purple light. When I open my eyes again, a young woman has appeared behind the reception desk. She's smiling at me with

322

a look of friendly curiosity. I walk over to check in, noticing several things as I get closer.

She appears to be in her late twenties, but her eyes reflect hardship and struggles that have aged her beyond her actual physical years. I know that look well—it's the same one that I'm used to seeing in the mirror every morning. She's thin, almost to the point of emaciation, and is wearing a fuzzy blue cardigan for warmth, even though the room temperature feels like it's hovering in the mid-seventies. Just as I reach the counter, she shivers and wraps it more tightly around her painfully thin frame. In my mind, her aura registers as dull gray and wispy. It's clear something is wrong.

"Hi, I'm Sarah. Are you Holly?" she asks with a smile. Her voice betrays a bone-deep exhaustion.

"Yes. I'm here for my appointment." My heart reaches out to her. I want to know what's going on with her, but I'm unsure of how to make a connection. While I'm mulling it over, a deeply tanned woman with flaming red hair pokes her head through the door at the back of the waiting area. "Hey Sarah. I'm ready for my 2:30."

"Great! Thanks, Sal. Holly, this is Sally. She's going to be working with you today. Enjoy."

I smile at Sarah and turn to follow Sally through the door to my treatment room. I'm determined to make a connection somehow. I only hope that she's still at the front counter when I'm finished.

As luck would have it, there's no one else in the waiting area when I emerge after my massage session. I'm still looking for a way to break the ice as I hand Sarah my credit card. I notice that she has Band-Aids on her first three fingers. On her other hand, her first three fingers are wrapped in tissue. I understand all too well. She has ulcers on the tips of her fingers. They commonly accompany Raynaud's syndrome. It was partly due to fear of developing those very same ulcers that I kept my hands and feet buried underneath the heating pad at Brenda's house. Noticing the direction of my gaze, Sarah self-consciously slips her hands under the counter.

I sense my moment to speak is now. "Is it Raynaud's—along with maybe some chronic fatigue?" I prompt gently.

Sarah's mouth falls open in astonishment, and nothing comes out for a beat. "Yes, actually. How'd you know?" she replies a bit warily.

"Well, because I had them too—and quite a bit more."

"Really?" Her expression changes from shock to excitement. "You look great. You got finger ulcers too? Oh my god, you look like you have so much energy!" She heaves herself out of her chair to study me even more closely. "Did you really have chronic fatigue? I'm only twenty-eight, and I feel like I'm eighty." She plops back down, defeated. "And I feel like my life is almost over. How did you get well again?"

The questions pour out of her mouth in a fast jumble. She has a pleading expression on her face, and I know she desperately needs to hear something positive that will fan the spark of hope.

I take a deep breath and launch into my story. I tell her everything, including what I did to become well again. She listens with rapt attention; when I'm finished, her eyes are glowing.

"Your story is so amazing! You've gone through so much. It's overwhelming." Sarah nervously touches her fingertips. "Can you tell me what you think helped you with the Raynaud's and chronic fatigue the most?"

I rub my chin thoughtfully. I get the sense that right now she can probably only handle change in smaller doses. What two things could I recommend that would bring her the greatest benefit? I'm already relaxed and grounded from my massage, and so, when I float the question around in my mind, the answer arrives almost instantaneously.

"I think, for you, the two most helpful things that you can do for the Raynaud's and chronic fatigue are juicing and deep breathing," I reply with confidence.

"Okay, the juicing I get, but what do you mean by deep breathing?" she asks, looking slightly perplexed.

This is so right up my alley. "There's a deep breathing technique, which I can teach you, that will help your tissues become super-oxygenated. The lack of oxygen from poor circulation is one of the biggest reasons that the ulcers won't heal."

I'm thrilled at the thought of being able to share a powerful deep breathing technique, which I had learned many years ago from a Qigong master. I had reintroduced it shortly after I started juicing to further bolster my growing reserves of qi. Within a month, I noticed that the sore spots on the tips of my fingers had disappeared—and the circulation in my hands and feet had improved dramatically.

"Oh my god!" Sarah glances at her fingers, and then back at me. "Please would you teach me how to do this breathing thing? I would give anything to have my fingers healed. And can you tell me how to get started juicing?"

"I'd love to. Do you have some paper for me to write on?"

She hurriedly grabs some paper from the printer behind her, and I start writing. By the time I'm finished, I've written up a detailed juicing plan and instructions on how to do the breathing technique. Then we practice the breathing together until I'm satisfied that she has it down. She gives me a tight hug before I go.

When I reach the exit, I glance back at her. She's returned to her chair behind the desk and has immediately resumed the breathing exercise. When she catches me staring, a crooked grin lights up her face. She mouths a silent "thank you" to me.

I step out onto the sidewalk and smile; I'm feeling pretty darn good. As I was telling Sarah my story, I witnessed her expression change from one of defeat to one of hope. It may not last much beyond our interaction today; she may go home and not change a thing. Or perhaps, she'll start juicing and continue the breathing technique for a time but then lose steam and let her determination peter out. Big change requires dogged persistence and hard work. But she met me and witnessed someone, with her own eyes, who has recovered from a place far worse than where she is right now. That's something I know she won't ever forget. And then, when she's truly ready to heal, maybe our chance encounter could serve to reignite her spark of hope. When that time comes, perhaps she'll contact me. Regardless of the path she takes to wellness, I send out a prayer to the universe that she will draw to her whatever she needs to keep her hope alive and heal herself.

I know how critical it was for me to have hope. All we need is a glimmer—the tiniest of sparks—like the one that first winked into existence when my spirit-guides taught me how to energetically heal the pain in my body. From that moment on, things began to change for me. I noticed small miracles of healing that occurred almost daily. And angels, in the guise of ordinary people, appeared in my life at the most opportune moments to lend a helping hand.

Some of my "angels" came from obvious places, such as my brother who had materialized the instant I needed him. Jay had pointed me toward Dr. Mercola, the first Western medical practitioner to express his conviction in my ability to be well. And Dr. Mercola helped me to set up my juicing and nutrition plan. It was like following the links in a chain. Then there was Gregg, the Rolfing practitioner, who broke through my hardened fascia and freed me from my suit of armor. After that, came Dr. Nguyen with his herbal recommendations, and he was followed by Sifu Doug who helped me to reconnect with my qi. And when my physical body was healing nicely, but my spiritual self was in need, in walked Doreen Virtue. Her words had a profound effect on restoring my sense of self-worth, and she helped me to find my life purpose.

But there had been other "angels" who came to my aid in the form of complete strangers. They're easy to miss because they surface in the "less glamorous" guises of cab drivers, grocery clerks, and airport attendants. Sometimes, we find our angels in the unlikeliest of situations. So unlikely, in fact, that we can easily be blinded by our assumptions and our fear. That's how I nearly missed one of my angels.

I was on my way home from an appointment with my rheumatologist. His office was near a run-down area of Oakland named "Pill Hill", so named because of its proximity to a nursing school and hospital. It was shortly after I had gone cold turkey from my Western medications. My symptoms had begun a meteoric rise in intensity, and I could barely drive. It had taken me forever just to get to the appointment, on top of which, I had been kept waiting an entire hour before I was finally called in to see my doctor. As a result, I was running on fumes and feeling dangerously faint. But, worst of all, my mouth was parched, and it was a hot day. I decided I couldn't make it home unless I drank some water.

I pulled my Pathfinder into a mini-mart parking lot and began the long trek into the store. How I managed to pick up a bottle of water, pay for it, and shuffle back to my car still remains a mystery. The real problem only became painfully clear after I reached my car. There was no way I could possibly open the bottle. My hands were too inflamed and too weak to twist off that wretched plastic top! I felt so desperately exhausted that my legs were about to buckle any second.

I looked up from my epic battle with the bottle cap to find myself being scrutinized by a young black man leaning against his shiny, midnight-blue muscle car. He wasn't that tall, but he was massively ripped with tattoos covering both arms and one hell of a lot of gold "bling" dangling around his neck. He casually crossed his mighty meat hooks and glared back at me. The cocky gleam in his eyes suggested that he frequently chewed nails for breakfast and washed them down with a refreshing mug of turpentine. Only the distance of a single empty parking space separated us. I glanced down at the bottle of life-giving water and felt the dryness of my parched mouth screaming for relief.

I made a desperate decision. When I picked my head up again, the young man's expression, which had been wary before, was bordering on hostility. A tiny image of a danger sign flashed momentarily across my mind, and I recognized my situation as being rather tactically dangerous. But what choice did I have?

I swallowed hard, in an attempt to draw forth any remaining moisture in my body, so I could speak. "Excuse me, sir?" I finally squeaked. His expression registered shock at my having spoken, but I dared to press on. "I'm terribly thirsty, but I have a problem with my hands. Would you be so kind as to help me get this open?"

I held the water bottle toward him, and waited—my heart pounding in fear. I knew that I was in no position to defend myself. However, my simple request had a profound effect on him.

His look of hostility faded and was replaced with one of uncertainty. "Uh yeah, okay." He straightened up, uncrossing those huge tattooed meat hooks, and lumbered toward me. I fought the urge to shrink away as he approached.

He took the bottle carefully from my hand, deftly opened it with one quick twist, and handed it back. "Here you go. I hope this helps." His smile was awkward and a little lopsided, as if his facial muscles were extremely rusty and unaccustomed to that configuration.

I was so close to keeling over that I immediately took a big, long gulp of water before responding. "Thank you so much. You're wonderful!" I could've hugged him on the spot, but I didn't want to scare him. Instead, I simply returned his smile and watched his stunned expression as I hoisted myself back into my car. I waved good-bye; he returned it automatically and then caught himself. When I looked back at him in my rearview mirror, he was shaking his head as if snapping himself out of a dream.

As I stroll down the sidewalk along Main Street near Broadway Plaza in Walnut Creek, I feel awakened to new possibilities. It's as if I've entered a new world. I'm curious about the life stories of the people walking by. I sit on an empty bench next to the Barnes and Noble bookstore and continue my people-watching. In the faces of the passersby, I look for more Sarahs and more Hollys, wondering just how many of us are out there. I feel a great need to reach out to them all.

What if my illness had never happened? Who would I be now? Even if I had managed to resurrect my acupuncture practice, I would not have been the same. Without my experience of the abyss, I wouldn't have had the slightest clue about the difficulties encountered with a chronic illness. If a patient had described a situation to me, I believe I could have understood it on an intellectual level. But would I have ever truly comprehended the sheer humiliation, absolute frustration, and intense despair that comes with say—getting stuck putting on a shirt or being unable to open a bottle of water? Absolutely not—there's no possible way. MCTD taught me the true meaning of compassion.

I've learned the hard way what can happen when we don't heed the call of our higher self and fail to follow the direction of our heart. Every time I strayed, I suffered the consequences. Before I became ill, I had diverged from my true path, and it was damaging me. I believe it was the final straw that pushed me over the edge and spiraling into the abyss. I learned that we can create illness in our bodies by not pursuing our true selves; as a result, I prepared myself to be a ripe target for disease.

Ironically, in one sense, MTCD saved my life. If not for my chronic illness, I would probably be an extremely miserable police officer or an ex-cop by now and quite likely, still not following my heart. By working toward what truly makes us happy, we join the flow of life and stop fighting it. To follow our heart is to take the path of least resistance in life—and it benefits everyone.

Everyone can make positive changes for their health and well-being. Everyone can create miracles. We each have the power within ourselves to restore our own health and create a meaningful, happy life. Doctors are not deities or infallible, and we aren't helpless victims. Healing isn't something that someone else gives to us; healing starts from within. The first step in the process of transformation from being a victim of an illness to a victor is to start taking responsibility for where we are right now. The moment we acknowledge that we had a hand in our present situation, we can adjust our sails and choose another direction.

Our potential for healing is *unlimited*, but it's up to us. I shudder to think where I'd be, what nursing home I'd be living in, or what plot of ground I'd be buried in if I had listened to the continuous Western medical dogma. We are our own best advocates, and we must take control of our own wellness program. Our lives are a gift that we have the ability to do anything with. So why not take the reins? It's a choice and a commitment we make to our own well-being. Make no mistake—it is also *work*.

It is precisely during times of hardship and struggle that we best learn to reach inside to connect to the divine part of ourselves—however we define it—to rise above and beyond who we were in order to reach the next level in our life journey. There are no limits except the ones that we *choose* to impose upon ourselves. What would happen if we shook off our chains? What would we do if we lived by following our hearts? Who might we become?

What if Mother Teresa had never sought to become the person she felt herself called to be? What if Mohandas Gandhi had accepted the notion that one person cannot make a difference? His use of non-violent protest to help alleviate poverty, liberate women, and put an end to caste discrimination forever changed the lives of millions. Martin Luther King Jr. was inspired by Gandhi's methods and adopted them to use in the United States to end segregation and promote civil rights. What if Helen Keller had not aspired to the impossible? At the age of twenty-four, she became the first deaf-blind person to earn a Bachelor of Arts degree. She went on to become an advocate for people with disabilities, a suffragist fighting for women's right to vote, a cofounder of the American Civil Liberties Union, and so much more.

We have accepted and internalized so many false beliefs and misconceptions. We have been taught to settle for less than who we are, to ignore our hearts, and to abandon our dreams. And tragically, we've been led to disbelieve our very own body's innate ability to heal.

The truth is that we are much more powerful than we imagine. Once we realize this, we can finally end the nightmare of chronic disease. *And as the butterfly flaps its fragile wings, the breeze is felt around the world.* It begins with one person. It can start with you. As one person steps toward wellness and reaches out to help another, the circle will expand. By "paying it forward," together we can change the world.

I may not have gone where I intended to go, but I
think I have ended up where I intended to be.
–Douglas Adams

AFTERWORD
A CALL TO ACTION

*Truly I say to you, if you have faith the size of a mustard
seed, you will say to this mountain, 'Move from here to
there,' and it will move; nothing will be impossible to you.*
–Matthew 17:20

It is a myth that chronic disease cannot be cured, a myth propagated by a system that has no incentive to find cures. The truth is that there is an abundance of healing choices readily available to us. We must dispel the fog of half-truths and outright deceptions that obscure our perception of things. The crisis of health care—the rising costs of insurance coupled with the rampant and seemingly inexorable spread of chronic disease—is deeply concerning. To make matters worse, some of the very agencies that we have entrusted to safeguard our health are proving to be alarmingly corruptible.

Through aggressive and predatory corporate marketing, we have become a nation of pharmaceutical drug consumers and involuntary guinea pigs for unsafe, inadequately tested medications. We can no longer afford to remain complacent; the stakes have become too high. However, there *is* a *light* at the end of the tunnel. We can take back control of our bodies and our health. The solutions to these issues are simple, cost-effective, safe, and available to us all—right now. Although the system is broken, I promise you that we have the means to fix it, if we so choose. But first, we must have the courage to take a long, hard look at the current state of health care in America. In the United States alone, chronic illness has reached epidemic proportions as evidenced by an increasing mountain of statistical data. By most accounts, chronic diseases—such as heart disease, cancer, and diabetes—are the leading causes of death and disability in the United States.[1] More than half of all Americans have at least one chronic illness.[2] In 2010, approximately twenty-six million people were diagnosed with diabetes, but—even worse—one out of every five Americans can be

331

classified as pre-diabetic.[3] Autoimmune disease, the second highest cause of chronic disease, has become the leading cause of disease in women in the United States, emerging as a public health crisis at levels comparable to heart disease and cancer.[4]

With the prevalence, type, and severity of chronic disease on the rise, the costs of chronic illness are skyrocketing to staggering proportions. On average, people with chronic illness cost three and a half times more to serve than all others. Therefore, the cost of chronic illness actually comprises 75 percent of our total health care spending—a mind-numbing $1.98 trillion! And by the year 2020, it is projected to rise to almost $4.5 trillion, bringing the costs of chronic illness to $3.37 trillion.[5]

It is also extremely important to note that the cost of drugs is the fastest-growing part of our health care bill.[6] Patients are being prescribed more drugs and spending more money on them than ever before. In 2010, that price tag hit $307 billion.[7] This is largely due to the pharmaceutical companies' aggressive and often misleading marketing campaigns combined with huge monetary incentives paid to doctors to prescribe their products. It seems to be working. Drug company revenues climbed more than $200 billion between 1995 and 2010.[8] In the pursuit of those profits, the average American has been turned into a lab rat for corporate greed.

The dangerous and often deadly side effects of unsafe drugs are too often ignored by the FDA and deliberately hidden by drug companies. Many cases are coming to light, more than ever before, and are finally being prosecuted. Recently, the most notable is the Justice Department's case against the drug giant, GlaxoSmithKline, in which it pled guilty and agreed to pay $3 billion to resolve fraud allegations and failure to report safety data. The resolution is the largest health care fraud settlement in American history and the largest payment ever by a drug company.[9]

On November 18, 2004, Dr. David Graham MD, MPH, the Associate Director of the Food and Drug Administration's Office of Drug Safety, gave testimony before the US Senate, regarding the FDA's flawed drug approval process. In his testimony, Dr. Graham asserted his personal belief that the policies within the US Food and Drug Administration were insufficient to protect the public from drugs that carry unacceptable risks.[10] In a 2005 interview with Manette Loudin, he stated the following: "When they look at efficacy, they assume that the drug doesn't work and the company has to prove that the drug does work. When they look at safety it's entirely the opposite. The FDA assumes the drug is safe and now it's up to the company to prove that the drug isn't safe." [11]

The vast majority of prescription and non-prescription medicines are designed to alleviate symptoms—not cure conditions. For every dollar pharmaceutical companies spend on "basic research," $19 goes toward promotion and marketing.[12] Pharmaceutical companies, as profit-based corporations, are inherently motivated more by profit and greed than by the altruistic search for cures to illness and disease. Why shouldn't they be? All the incentives are there to keep the American population sick and on prescriptions with *their* drugs—drugs that aren't safe and with side effects that often cause more problems than the original symptom they were purportedly designed to treat.

Having a chronic illness is bad enough, but what if the *medical system* established to treat disease was actually responsible for more deaths than the disease itself? Sadly, it's true. The horrifying result of the greed and corruption of the pharmaceutical industry and their control of the FDA is that Western medicine is possibly the largest contributor to our worsening health care woes. This is clearly illustrated in an eye-opening book *Death by Medicine*, released in 2011. Written by Gary Null, MD, along with Martin Feldman, MD, Debora Rasio, MD, and Carolyn Dean, MD, ND, it meticulously reviews and analyzes the combined statistical evidence of all of the published literature dealing with injuries and deaths caused by conventional medicine. Their results found that the CDC is mistaken when it claims heart disease is the number one cause of death in America. According to the report, the cumulative number of deaths caused by conventional medicine is estimated to be a mind-blowing 783,936 per year, more than cancer or even heart disease, making **Western medicine the leading cause of death in America**. This fully referenced and verifiable report shows the number of people having in-hospital, adverse reactions to prescribed drugs or unnecessary medical and surgical procedures to be 8.7 million per year. Furthermore, it cites the number of people exposed to unnecessary hospitalization to be 8.9 million annually. The report (among many other things) went on to estimate the ten-year total of iatrogenic (medically related) deaths to be 7.8 million, which is more than all the casualties from all the wars fought by the United States throughout its entire history.[13]

It is long past time for us to act. The system designed to care for us when we are sick or injured is failing us badly. The good news is, however, that in the case of chronic illness, these rampant, life-threatening health issues are almost always preventable, and depending upon the desire and efforts of the patient, they are often curable. The healing protocols used are simple time-tested methods: food-healing, meditation or other form of stress relief, an exercise program including body work, acupuncture, herbs, and various other natural holistic modalities. Even the Center for Disease Control agrees: "Chronic diseases—such as heart disease, stroke, cancer, diabetes, and arthritis—are among the most common, costly, and preventable of all health problems in the United States. Four modifiable health risk behaviors—lack of physical activity, poor nutrition, tobacco use, and excessive alcohol consumption—are responsible for much of the illness, suffering, and early death related to chronic diseases."[14]

Why can't our modern Western medical system act to slow and reverse our blatant health care disaster? Well, the unfortunate truth is that Western medicine is ill-equipped to handle chronic illness. In our current system, there is no plan, method, or program for helping the chronically ill to become well again. Instead, patients are typically managed haphazardly with drugs to alleviate symptoms without ever addressing the cause. And when those drugs cause undesirable side effects, patients are prescribed even more drugs to ameliorate those side effects until the illness for which they sought treatment is no longer their main concern.

In our current health care model, health is a brand name product to be purchased. The ideal consumer is a passive one. The pill-makers rely upon our passive compliance and unquestioning faith in their industry in order to boost their bottom line. But real wellness is a verb, not a noun. When we surrender ownership of our health to for-profit companies with "silver bullet" pills, we set ourselves up to be victimized and become yet another statistic of a broken, dysfunctional system.

True wellness and healing require that we become active advocates of our own health. The more vigilant we become about educating ourselves, the less we can be blinded by slick marketing gimmicks that promise easy fixes with no effort on our part. True wellness and healing require discipline and commitment to change along with the desire and motivation to be well. It is a choice, and the choice is ours to make. Do we make it? Or do we continue to let the fox into the henhouse and then wonder why all the chickens are dead?

Acid-Reflux

Pharmaceutical companies do not create drugs to cure, only to manage certain symptoms. Consider the example of acid-reflux or heartburn medications, such as Prilosec, Nexium, Prevacid, or Zantac, to name a few. These drugs rake in tens of billions of dollars and are among the most often prescribed medications on the market. Their only function is to reduce the acid level in the stomach, which does nothing to solve the problem. Acid reflux commonly occurs when the lower esophageal sphincter (LES) does not work properly and allows acid to seep up from the stomach to the esophagus. One of many reasons for this can be that the pressures in the stomach rises higher than the LES can withstand.[15] This is often the case when large, heavy meals are eaten, meals are eaten at night, or a person reclines directly after eating. In all of these situations, acid-reflux can be eliminated through dietary modifications and chewing habits. By choosing to take acid-reflux medications, the cause is never addressed and the patient is condemned to remain on them for the rest of his or her life.

Moreover, long-term use of the proton-pump inhibitor medications, such as Aciphex, Nexium, Prevacid, Prilosec, and Protonix bring unwanted and dangerous side effects. Stomach acid helps the body absorb calcium, which is needed for healthy bones. Now a new study shows that, when taken long term, the drugs may have a surprising side effect: hip fracture. People over fifty who take the drugs for more than one year have a 44 percent increased risk of breaking a hip, according to University of Pennsylvania researchers Yu-Xiao Yang, MD, and colleagues. Taking proton-pump inhibitors at higher doses—and for longer periods—dramatically increases the risk. Long-term, high-dose use of the drugs ups the risk of hip fracture as much as 245 percent.[16]

In most cases, the drugs that are prescribed for this common ailment are completely unnecessary and could be replaced by the proper food healing choices, which are simple, safe, cheap, effective and easily available to anyone. Furthermore, time-tested, simple herbal remedies, such as mastic gum, slippery elm powder, or even cabbage juice can heal ulcers and repair the stomach lining. When combined with simple dietary changes, a patient can eliminate heartburn or acid-reflux nightmares entirely.

Acid-Reflux Protocol

The acid-reflux protocol is a combination of qigong, herbs, and dietary modifications. There are excellent qigong exercises that can be performed to reduce acid-reflux and strengthen the digestive system. These can easily be taught to the patient in one session. When suffering from acid-reflux, it's imperative to make dietary changes; they are absolutely critical. The patient must eliminate processed foods of any kind, sweets, wheat, dairy, pasta, caffeine, chocolate, alcohol, red meat, turkey, and ham. It is best to eat three-to-five small meals per day. Soups and easily digestible cooked meals with mostly vegetables and small meat portions are best. It is necessary for the patient to learn to chew food thoroughly before swallowing. This practice relieves a huge digestive burden from the stomach and reduces acid-reflux. Meat should not be eaten after 2:00 p.m., and no food after 6:00 p.m. If the patient is starving, they may have a piece of fruit—apple, pear, melon, or papayas are all excellent choices—but they must be chewed thoroughly and into oblivion before swallowing. Additionally, the patient should take a probiotic once a day to improve digestion in the gut.

The big gun of this healing protocol is mastic gum, the resin from mastic trees, which has been used for thousands of years to heal gastrointestinal ailments. It even kills the h. pylori bacteria, which can cause ulcers. It will repair damage to the stomach lining and esophagus caused by the acid-reflux. Patients experience relief within days of beginning this protocol. It is also often helpful to take natural digestive enzymes following a meal. One tablespoon of slippery elm powder, mixed with warm water so that it forms a paste, can be taken once a day to further protect and heal the digestive tract.

Food as Medicine: Phytonutrients

Organic, plant-based food is our alternative medicine of choice: natural, simple, safe, and effective. What is it about vegetables, fruits, legumes, and whole grains that make them such powerful little healers? All plants contain molecular compounds called phytonutrients—"phyto" comes from the Greek word "phuton" meaning "plants." Unlike vitamins, phytonutrients aren't necessary for our survival, and they do not cause any diseases resulting from any deficiency. Their role in plants is to protect them from disease, injuries, insects, drought, excessive heat, ultraviolet rays, and poisons or pollutants in the air or soil. They form part of the plant's immune system. When we eat plants, we receive the benefit of their fabulous phytonutrients and all the protective, disease-preventing properties that go along with them.

Phytonutrients are associated with the prevention and/or treatment of at least four of the leading causes of death in Western countries—cancer, diabetes, cardiovascular disease, and hypertension. They are involved in many processes, including ones that help prevent cell damage, prevent cancer cell replication, and decrease cholesterol levels.[17]

They may serve as anti-oxidants in a bodily system when required; for example, the phytochemical beta-carotene can metabolize to create vitamin A, a powerful anti-oxidant. Additionally, phytochemicals may enhance immune response and cell-to-cell communication, allowing the body's built-in defenses to work more efficiently. Phytochemicals may even alter estrogen metabolism, cause cancer cells to die (apoptosis), repair DNA damage caused by smoking and other toxic exposure, and detoxify carcinogens by working with bodily enzymes.[18]

There are tens of thousands of phytonutrients, and we are just beginning to scratch the surface of what they can do. Phytonutrients are most often found concentrated in the skin and fibrous portions of plants, which highlights the importance of chewing food thoroughly before swallowing. It helps to release the "medicine" in your food.

The education that Western medical practitioners receive on proper nutrition is almost non-existent, and what they do get is often wrong or outdated. Physicians are *not* taught to consider that food could be used to heal their patient, and nutrition is seldom discussed.

During one appointment with a rheumatologist when I was still recovering from MCTD, the physician looked me straight in the eye and said, "What you eat and nutrition have nothing to do with your illness. Nothing you do with it will matter."

It left me flabbergasted. Unfortunately this response is far too common for many patients of chronic disease. Most conventional medicine practitioners are quick to dismiss and discredit any health modality that doesn't involve prescription drugs or surgery. Quite often, these are the same drugs that are being heavily peddled by their pharmaceutical representatives.

Diabetes

There are distinct advantages to tackling a major health concern, such as diabetes, using holistic medicine. One-tenth of our healthcare spending goes toward the treatment of diabetes and its complications. Using 2011 figures for total health care spending, diabetes and its complications cost Americans more than $250 billion. Spending on just the drugs to control diabetes alone is close to $20 billion and is supposed to double by the year 2020. [19]

What is the standard Western medical treatment for diabetes? People diagnosed with type 2 diabetes do not produce or respond normally to insulin, a hormone that regulates the amount of glucose in the blood. Over time, high blood glucose levels can increase the risk for serious complications, including heart disease, blindness, and nerve and kidney damage.[20] Medications for type 2 diabetes are designed to increase the insulin output by the pancreas, decrease the amount of glucose released from the liver, increase the sensitivity (response) of cells to insulin, decrease the absorption of carbohydrates from the intestine, and slow emptying of the stomach to delay the presentation of carbohydrates for digestion and absorption in the small intestine.[21] Unfortunately, these drugs carry a vast array of horrible and unacceptable side effects: cancer, heart failure, fractures, eye and liver problems,[22] and even death.[23] The Western medical protocol for diabetes doesn't involve any attempt to cure it—only to manage it.

Diabetes Protocol

The diabetes protocol that I would recommend involves no drugs. Everything that prescription drugs do, nature can do better—and without side effects. The protocol is designed not only to regulate blood glucose levels, but in many cases it can also reverse diabetes itself, something that Chinese medicine has been doing for hundreds of years. The protocol involves working with the patient on developing an effective exercise regimen, acupuncture, herbs, and a diet plan.

Exercise is particularly important for a diabetic since it activates the enzyme AMPK, a protein well known for regulating fuel metabolism and enabling glucose uptake. Qigong is my recommended exercise, since at the same time it's helping control diabetes, it can be designed to address other medical concerns like back pain, weak knees, asthma, indigestion, poor circulation, energy levels, heart conditions, liver problems, and more.

If the patient is overweight, weight loss is also an important goal, which helps in the reversal of diabetes. Acupuncture and herbs can help with weight loss along with increasing the body's ability to produce and release insulin. Diabetic patients are recommended to bring along a glucose tablet to their session since the blood insulin level can jump after a treatment.

Once again, the most critical part of the protocol is the dietary component. The patient must eliminate processed foods of any kind, sweets, wheat, dairy, pasta, coffee, red meat, turkey, and ham. For the first six months of the program, no fruit. What does the patient eat? Twice a day, the patient needs to eat a quarter of a bitter melon, raw or cooked, and there are many recipes that are available for this vegetable. Bitter melon is the key component in the diet to reverse diabetes. It has been shown to not only act like insulin and increase glucose uptake, but it has also been shown to regenerate the pancreas function, even to the point of helping type 1 diabetes. This is the mainstay of the Chinese protocol to battle diabetes and has been used for hundreds of years.

The biggest problem in type 2 diabetes is not the lack of insulin but rather a diminished response to insulin. The meals eaten are designed not to spike blood sugar, and with a return to a natural diet, the insulin resistance is reversible. Two other critical foods, one of which should be present at every meal, are green beans and Brussels sprouts. They also function as natural insulin in the blood, so that blood sugar doesn't spike after a meal. A juicing combination of Brussels sprouts, green beans, carrots, and dark green lettuce helps strengthen and even regenerate the insulin-generating ability of the pancreas. When eating a snack, the patient is recommended to eat a handful of green beans along with it.

Swiss chard is another valuable vegetable for reversing diabetes. It inhibits an enzyme, alpha-glucosidase, so that fewer carbohydrates are broken down into sugars with the result that blood sugar remains steady. The skin of cucumbers contains phytonutrients that improve the functioning of insulin in the body, and eating one a day is recommended

Cinnamon helps improve the body's response to insulin, and a cup of "cinnamon tea" is recommended every morning by boiling two sticks of cinnamon for thirty minutes. The patient can also add cinnamon powder to a hot cup of water. A cup of cinnamon tea after every meal will stimulate insulin receptors and increase cells' ability to use glucose.

Diabetics also tend to suffer from high cholesterol and high blood pressure. To tackle these accompanying conditions, instead of a vast array of horribly harmful drugs, a few more dietary recommendations are added to the protocol. In the case of high blood pressure, the patient simply eats six stalks of celery a day, no more high blood pressure—another well-established Chinese protocol that's been used for hundreds of years.

To address the high cholesterol, an additional herbal tea is recommended. It's made overnight and then drunk each morning on an empty stomach. It consists of goji berries, dried black fungus mushrooms, and half of an eggplant. The tea actually tastes good. Also, adding eggplant and okra to meals is recommended, as they are the dynamic duo of artery-scrubbers and actually pull fat from arteries. Say good-bye to statin drugs and their side effects—muscle problems, nerve damage in the hands and feet, degenerative muscle condition, cataracts, memory loss, cancer, liver disease, immune depression, acidosis, memory loss, elevated blood glucose, and *diabetes*.[24] It's ironic that one of the potential side effects of cholesterol drugs commonly prescribed for diabetics is, in fact, diabetes.

Toxic Chemicals and Heavy Metal Exposure

Our environment is another key factor that is integral to our health, yet it is often downplayed or completely overlooked by conventional Western medicine. A toxic environment makes us ill. A clean environment promotes our health and well-being. Modern industrial waste practices and manufacturing processes—along with the burning of fossil fuels—have released increasing amounts of toxic chemicals and heavy metals such as mercury, cadmium, lead, arsenic[25], and aluminum into our world. These toxins are present in the pesticides sprayed on our food crops, and they contaminate our drinking water. They can be found in some of the fish and the meat we consume from our toxic laden ecosystems. Many of them, such as aluminum, are incorporated as a common ingredient in a number of consumer body products like deodorant.

Heavy metal poisoning is a major health concern. Dr. Rashid Buttar, Chairman of the American Board of Clinical Metal Toxicology says, "Although acute heavy metal toxicity is recognized by the traditional medical hierarchy, the prevalence, incidence and ubiquitous nature of chronic heavy metal toxicity may be the greatest undiagnosed medical condition and the most unrecognized contributory cause of chronic disease and death in the industrialized world."[26]

As a matter of course for health maintenance, I believe that everyone, especially the chronically ill, should be tested periodically for toxic levels. A simple hair analysis by a reputable laboratory will suffice to assess a patient's heavy metal toxicity levels.

Fortunately, there are a large variety of treatments available to help in the removal or chelation of heavy metals from the body. The simplest, most effective method is one that anyone can do—juicing. Juicing is a natural chelation method, which gently detoxes the body at a pace our biological system can tolerate. I often prescribe juicing as a protocol for my chronically ill patients for this very reason, in addition to the outstanding nutritional benefits.

Chronic Fatigue Syndrome

The CDC defines Chronic Fatigue Syndrome, or CFS, as a debilitating and complex disorder characterized by profound fatigue that is not improved by bed rest and that may be worsened by physical or mental activity. Symptoms affect several bodily systems and may include weakness, muscle pain, impaired memory and/or mental concentration, and insomnia, which can result in reduced participation in daily activities.

CFS is a common symptom from overexposure to heavy metals like lead, mercury, iron, and cadmium and/or toxic chemical exposure—and the patient should be tested for toxicity.[27] Other factors contributing to CFS are insufficient nutrition from poor diet, insufficient sleep, and unabated high levels of stress cumulated over a period of many years. Eventually, the body wears out its reserves and essentially shuts down. The fatigue can be so overwhelming that it's a supreme act of will to move at all. It's a condition of severe depletion on all levels: body, mind, and spirit.

Western medicine fails utterly when it comes to the treatment of chronic fatigue. It is the prevailing notion that there is no cure and the standard practice, once again, is to manage the patient's symptoms with a battery of prescription medications. Antidepressants and sleep medications are typically prescribed, while little to no attention is given to address the severely depleted condition of the patient. Fibromyalgia is often present along with CFS, and in such cases, anti-inflammatories and pain medications will also be prescribed.

Chronic Fatigue Syndrome Protocol

In order to recover, the patient needs to be nourished on all levels—body, mind, and spirit. The patient is treated with a combination of qigong exercises, meditations, visualizations, juicing, acupuncture, herbs, and dietary modifications. Due to the weakened condition, CFS patients may be unable to perform some of the tasks required to restore their health. Family, friends, and community can play a key role in helping the chronic fatigue patient recover.

Massive amounts of nutrition and phytonutrients are required, and therefore juicing is the big gun of this protocol. A quart a day of the "juice of life," which contains twenty-two different vegetables and a few fruits, is recommended. It is juiced using a twin-gear juicer that extracts almost all of the vitamins and minerals from the juiced food items. The patient will quickly notice improvements in energy, cognitive abilities, sleep, and more. The juice is naturally chelating and will cleanse any heavy metals out of the patient over time.

If heavy metals are present, the patient can also add cilantro to the diet, which is another "super-chelating" food. It will even pull heavy metals out of the brain. I would recommend the patient replace all of their body products, cosmetics, and cleaning supplies with natural or organic substitutes in order to reduce continuing exposure to heavy metal contamination. Likewise, it would be highly beneficial to obtain a quality filter for drinking water.

The patient should eliminate processed foods of any kind, sweets, wheat, dairy, pasta, caffeine, chocolate, alcohol, red meat, turkey, and ham from the diet. It is best to eat small meals, three times a day. This helps to relieve the energy burden of digesting a large meal all at once, since energy is a commodity in very short supply with CFS. Soups and easily digestible cooked meals with mostly vegetables and small meat portions are best. Goji berries (½ ounce–1 ounce) are added to the diet per day, as they significantly increase energy, boost the immune system, and promote well-being.

Acupuncture can prove very beneficial to restoring balance to a patient's organ systems, reduce stress, promote relaxation, increase energy, and improve sleep. Herbal formulas are selected to strengthen the patient's immune system and nourish, along with helping to treat specific symptoms. The patient is taught qigong exercises that can be performed in any position, from lying down to standing up, depending upon their current energy level. The qigong exercises are designed to gently strengthen and support the entire body, promote relaxation, and reduce stress. Meditation and visualizations are taught to help reduce stress and promote relaxation.

Healing miracles can be accomplished using simple methods that work far better in the long run and achieve true, lasting results. Western medicine has its applications. It excels in acute, life-threatening conditions, structural deficiencies, some illnesses, and physical trauma. I believe it can best be used to help stabilize a person while they begin their holistic health program. If Western medical practitioners considered using time-tested nutritional and herbal remedies as well as other alternative modalities as the first line of defense and stayed in the periphery (or worked closely with the alternative practitioner) when it comes to chronic illness and a host of other issues, America would be a far healthier nation.

This merged system already exists and functions quite effectively in China. In their health care system, Western medical physicians often work side by side with TCM-trained doctors. The patient is treated with the modality or combination that will best help him or her regain a healthy balance.

I'm living proof that your state of health is in your hands. If I had remained on my downward spiral, taking drugs and then requiring more drugs for each new disaster that happened to me, I would be in a nursing home right now (that is provided I didn't end it myself). I would be an annual taxpayer liability of anywhere from $500,000 to $2 million, depending on what specific procedures or treatments were imposed on my debilitated body. As it turns out, I took responsibility for my own health using nutrition, meditation, massage, physical therapy, herbs, acupuncture, and other alternative modalities. The glorious results are that I have my health back. I feel great. I was on full disability, and now I'm not. The day I stopped it was one of the proudest moments of my life. Once again, I'm a contributing, taxpaying member of society.

It's up to us, as individuals, to change ourselves first and the system second—and we can. When we start making different choices, including saying no to drugs and yes to organic, healing foods then the medical industry will be forced to change along with us! We can lead the way.

My story is not unique. I am one of many who have created wellness for themselves. You and your desire to be well are all you need to get started. It begins with the basics: diet and nutrition, stress reduction, reducing exposure to environmental toxins, and exercise. These lifestyle changes can be incorporated gradually, one small step at a time. Unless you're in a situation similar to mine wherein I needed changes fast, then you change fast. Reclaim your health now! You *can* do it!

BIBLIOGRAPHY

1. HC Kung; DL Hoyert; JQ Xu; and SL Murphy; "Deaths: final data for 2005," *National Vital Statistics Reports* 2008; 56(10). Available from: http://www.cdc.gov/nchs/data/nvsr/nvsr56/nvsr56_10.pdf
2. SY Wu, A. Green, "Projection of chronic illness prevalence and cost inflation," Santa Monica, CA: *RAND Health*; 2005.
3. Centers for Disease Control and Prevention, "National diabetes fact sheet: national estimates and general information on diabetes and pre-diabetes in the United States 2011," Atlanta, GA: US Department of Health and Human Services, Centers for Disease Control and Prevention, 2011.
4. American Autoimmune Related Diseases Association (AARDA), National Coalition of Autoimmune Patient Groups (NCAPG), "The Cost Burden of Autoimmune Disease: The Latest Front in the War on Healthcare Spending," *AARDA Report*, released 3/22/2011
5. California Healthcare Foundation, "US Health Care Spending: A supplement to California HealthCare Foundation's Health Care Costs 101, *California Healthcare Almanac,* 2012 edition available at www.chcf. org.
6. Marcia Angell, M.D., *The Truth About the Drug Companies: How They Deceive Us and What to Do About It,* Random House, 1st edition, August 24, 2004.
7. Kaye Stringer, "US spent $307 billion on prescription drugs in 2010," *Natural News,* 4/27/2011. http://www.naturalnews.com/032200_prescription_drugs_billions.html
8. Alexander Eichler, "Pharmaceutical Companies Spent 19 Times More On Self-Promotion Than Basic Research: Report," *The Huffington Post,* 8/9/2012
9. Department of Justice: Office of Public Affairs, "GlaxoSmithKline to Plead Guilty and Pay $3 Billion to Resolve Fraud Allegations and Failure to Report Safety Data," July 2012, Accessed online at: http://www.justice.gov/opa/pr/2012/July/12-civ-842.html

10. Manette Loudon, "The FDA Exposed: An Interview with Dr. David Graham, the Vioxx Whistleblower," *Natural News*, 8/30/2005. http://www.naturalnews.com/011401_Dr_David_Graham_the_FDA.html

11. Ibid.

12. Alexander Eichler, "Pharmaceutical Companies Spent 19 Times More On Self-Promotion Than Basic Research: Report," *The Huffington Post,* 8/9/2012

13. Gary Null, M.D.; Martin Feldman, M.D.; Debora Rasio, M.D.; and Carolyn Dean, M.D., N.D.; *Death by Medicine*, Mount Jackson, VA: Praktikos Books and Axios Press, 2011

14. Center for Disease Control, CDC, "Chronic Diseases and Health Promotion," http://www.cdc.gov/chronicdisease/overview/index.htm

15. Christian Nordqvist, "What is Acid Reflux? What Causes Acid Reflux?", *Medical News Today*, April 2009, Accessed online at: http://www.medicalnewstoday.com/articles/146619.php

16. Daniel J. Denoon, "Acid Reflux Drugs May Up Fractures: Proton-pump inhibitors—the popular drugs that fight stomach acid—increase the risk of hip fractures, a US study shows", *WebMD*, 2006

17. Jeff Primack, "Conquering Any Disease," Press On Qi Productions, 2008.

18. Ibid.

19. Zhou, Xiauhui, Ping Zhang, Edward W. Gregg, Lawrence Barker, Thomas J. Hoerger, Tony Pearson-Clarke, and Ann Albright. "A Nationwide Community-Based Lifestyle Program Could Delay or Prevent Type 2 Diabetes Cases and Save $5.7 Billion In 25 Years," *Health Affairs*. Vol. 31, No. 1, pp. 50–60.

20. Mayo Clinic Staff, "Type 2 Diabetes: Complications," Mayo Clinic, Accessed online at: http://www.mayoclinic.com/health/type-2-diabetes/DS00585/DSECTION=complications

21. Ibid.

22. January W. Payne, "5 Risks Linked to Diabetes Medications," *US News & World Report,* July 7, 2009

23. The Endocrine Society. "Common diabetes drugs associated with increased risk of death." *ScienceDaily*, 24 Jun. 2012. Web. 9 Sep. 2012.

24. Matthew Herper, "FDA Cautions on Memory, Diabetes Side Effects in Cholesterol-Lowering Drugs", *Forbes*, 2/28/2012, Accessed online

at: http://www.forbes.com/sites/matthewherper/2012/02/28/fda-cautions-on-memory-diabetes-in-statin-drugs/

25. OSHA. *Heavy Metals.* Occupational Safety and Health Administration. Accessed online at http://www.osha-slc.gov/SLTC/metalsheavy/index.html.

26. Dr. Rashid Buttar, M.D., "Chronic Heavy Metal Toxicity," *Know Your Options: The Medical Series*, Dolphin DVD Series, 2007.

27. EIR, "Heavy Metal Toxicity," *Environmental Illness Resource*, Accessed online at: http://www.ei-resource.org/illness-information/related-conditions/heavy-metal-toxicity/

ABOUT THE AUTHOR

HOLLY REESE is a California board-licensed acupuncturist and herbalist. In addition, she also holds certifications in Medical Qigong, Acupressure, Hypnotherapy, and Past Life Regression. Also, as a certified personal trainer and martial arts instructor, Holly has rigorously studied kinesiology, qi, energy work, and meditation for more than thirty years. She holds two black belts, one in Tae Kwon Do and the other in Choy Lay Fut Kung Fu.

Having graduated from MIT with a Bachelor of Science in electrical engineering, she worked as a highly successful computer programmer for ten years before giving it all up to attend acupuncture school. This is her first book.

Holly lives in her beloved San Francisco Bay Area where she is currently working to open a food-healing café and launch a six-month to a yearlong pilot program called "Return to Wellness." It is intended to take a group of 12–24 persons with chronic illnesses and help restore their health by implementing a variety of alternative modalities tailored specifically to the individual and his or her condition. More information about this and her other latest projects can be found on her website at www.hollyreeselac.com.

CPSIA information can be obtained at www.ICGtesting.com
Printed in the USA
BVOW071858171212

308470BV00002B/2/P